THE CHOCTAW FREEDMEN

Dear Friend:—I have enjoyed the privilege of sending for your ~~Sunday School or Public Library~~, a copy of the new volume, entitled, "The Choctaw Freedmen and the Bible in the Public Schools;" indulging the hope that at least its chapters, 3, 7, 47, and 48, relating to the use of the Bible in all the public schools of our land, will be read with interest and great profit by many of the young people—especially those who are preparing to teach, either in the Sunday or Public Schools. The story of the events narrated in these chapters radiates a very illuminating light, that is greatly needed at this time. Very truly,

Rockwell City, Iowa. R. E. Flickinger.

AN OAK TREE

On the southeastern slope, near the Academy,
   A pretty Oak,
      That strong and stalwart grows,
      With every changing wind that blows,
is a beautiful emblem of the strength, beauty and eminent usefulness of an intelligent and noble man.

    "He shall grow like a Cedar in Lebanon; like a tree planted by the rivers of water, that bringeth forth his fruit in his season."

ALICE LEE ELLIOTT
1846-1906

THE CHOCTAW FREEDMEN

AND
THE STORY OF
OAK HILL INDUSTRIAL ACADEMY
VALIANT, MCCURTAIN COUNTY
OKLAHOMA

NOW CALLED THE
ALICE LEE ELLIOTT MEMORIAL

Including the Early History of the Five Civilized Tribes of Indian Territory,
the Presbytery of Kiamichi, Synod of Canadian, and the Bible
in the Free Schools of the American Colonies, but
Suppressed in France, Previous to the
American and French Revolutions

By
Robert Elliott Flickinger
A Recent Superintendent of the Academy and
Pastor of the Oak Hill Church

ILLUSTRATED BY 100 ENGRAVINGS

HERITAGE BOOKS
2008

HERITAGE BOOKS
AN IMPRINT OF HERITAGE BOOKS, INC.

Books, CDs, and more—Worldwide

For our listing of thousands of titles see our website
at
www.HeritageBooks.com

A Facsimile Reprint
Published 2008 by
HERITAGE BOOKS, INC.
Publishing Division
100 Railroad Ave. #104
Westminster, Maryland 21157

Copyright © 1914 Robert Elliott Flickinger

Copyright © 2002 Angela Walton-Raji

Copyright © 2002 Heritage Books, Inc.

Originally published
Under the Auspices of the
Presbyterian Board of Missions for Freemen
Pittsburgh, Pa.

— Publisher's Notice —
In reprints such as this, it is often not possible to remove blemishes from the original. We feel the contents of this book warrant its reissue despite these blemishes and hope you will agree and read it with pleasure.

International Standard Book Number: 978-0-7884-2222-5

TABLE OF CONTENTS

I. GENERAL FACTS
Introduction—List of Portraits

I	Indian Territory	7
II	Indian Schools and Churches	15
III	The Bible, An Important Factor in Civilization	31
IV	The American Negro	39
V	Problem of the Freedman	46
VI	Voices From the Black Belt	59
VII	Uplifting Influences	65
VIII	The Presbyterian Church	84
IX	The Freedmen's Board	90
X	Special Benefactors	96

II OAK HILL INDUSTRIAL ACADEMY

XI	Native Oak Hill School and Church	101
XII	Era of Eliza Hartford	107
XIII	Early Reminiscences	114
XIV	Early Times at Forest	124
XV	Era of Supt. James F. McBride	131
XVI	Era of Rev. Edward G. Haymaker	134
XVII	Buds of Promise	146
XVIII	Closed in 1904	154
XIX	Re-Opening and Organization	155
XX	Prospectus in 1912	162
XXI	Obligation and Pledges	169
XXII	Bible Study and Memory Work	173
XXIII	Decision Days	183
XXIV	The Self-Help Department	185
XXV	Industrial Education	196
XXVI	Permanent Improvements	202
XXVII	Elliott Hall	210

CONTENTS

XXVIII	Unfavorable Circumstances	216
XXIX	Building the Temple	227
XXX	Success Maxims and Good Suggestions	241
XXXI	Rules and Wall Mottoes	259
XXXII	Savings and Investments	272
XXXIII	Normals and Chautauquas	275
XXXIV	Graces and Prayers	279
XXXV	Presbyterial Meetings and Picnics	282
XXXVI	Farmer's Institutes	287
XXXVII	The Apiary, Health Hints	294
XXXVIII	Oak Hill Aid Society	300
XXXIX	Tributes to Workers	308
XL	Closing Day, 1912	325

III THE PRESBYTERY AND SYNOD

XLI	Presbytery of Kiamichi	335
XLII	Histories of Churches	345
XLIII	Parson Stewart	351
XLIV	Wiley Homer	360
XLV	Other Ministers and Elders	370
XLVI	Synod of Canadian	382

IV THE BIBLE IN THE PUBLIC SCHOOL

XLVII	The Public School	391
XLVIII	A Half Century of Bible Suppression in France	418

OAK HILL CHAPEL

ELLIOTT HALL—1910

LIST OF ILLUSTRATIONS

Alice Lee Elliott
Elliott Hall II
Choctaw Church and Court House 14
Alexander Reid, John Edwards 15
Biddle and Lincoln Universities 70
Rev. E. P. Cowan, Rev. John Gaston, Mrs. V. P. Boggs.. 91
Eliza Hartford, Anna Campbell, Rev. E. G. and Priscilla G. Haymaker 108
Girls Hall, Old Log House 109
Carrie and Mrs. M. E. Crowe, Anna and Mattie Hunter..116
James McGuire and others 117
Wiley Homer, William Butler, Stewart, Jones 148
Buds of Promise 149
Rev. and Mrs. R. E. Flickinger, Claypool, Ahrens, Eaton 160
Reopening, 1915, Flower Gatherers 192
Mary I. Weimer, Lou K. Early, Jo Lu Wolcott 193
Rev. and Mrs. Carroll, Hall, Buchanan, Folsom 224
Closing Day, 1912; Dr. Baird 225
Approved Fruits 256
Planting Sweet Potatoes and Arch 257
Orchestra, Sweepers, Going to School 274
Miss Weimer, Celestine, Coming Home 275
The Apiary; Feeding the Calves 294
Log House Burning, Pulling Stumps 298
Oak Hill in 1902, 1903 299
The Hen House, Pigpen 295
The Presbytery, Grant Chapel 352
Bridges, Bethel, Starks, Meadows, Colbert, Crabtree....353
Crittenden, Folsom, Butler, Stewart, Perkins, Arnold, Shoals, Johnson 378
Teachers in 1899, Harris, Brown 379
Representative Homes of the Choctaw Freedmen 406
The Sweet Potato Field 407

INTRODUCTION
To the 2002 Edition

While on a research trip in 1995 to Oklahoma, I became interested in locating a book mentioned in a bibliography I had seen. The book told the story of a little-known and long-forgotten school for the children of former Choctaw Nation slaves, and I was anxious to see it. I learned that a copy existed at the Oklahoma Historical Society Archives. Unlike other books of the period, it was kept in the vault of the library where the rare books were stored. I requested the book. When it was brought to me, I saw immediately how frail the book was and realized, also, how wonderful it was.

The Choctaw Freedmen and The Story of Oak Hill Industrial Academy provides a seldom-seen glimpse into a story yet to be fully told - that of the Freedmen of the Choctaw Nation and what life was like for these former slaves in Indian Territory. On one level it is the story of a small boarding school. On another level, it reveals a piece of the history of the Five Civilized Tribes and of the Presbytery of Kiamichi. And, on a final level, it gives a sense of the place where black Oklahomans, from the southeastern vicinity of the new state, were sending their young men and women for education and training.

Plans for the establishment of Oak Hill did not arise from the tribal council or the leaders of the Choctaw Nation but from the efforts of Henry Crittendon, one of the more dynamic leaders in the southeast Oklahoma community. Though not a Freedman himself, he was a leader in the Freedman community and his influence throughout southeastern Oklahoma was to last for several decades.

Sponsored by the Presbyterian Church, this co-ed private boarding school represented one of the church's many missionary efforts. It was a rare center of learning for these children of the former black slaves of the Choctaw. The school was complete with chapel, boys' and girls' dormitories, farm, and facilities for classes. The school sought not only to provide an education for the students but to also provide its own provisions for the campus with the school farm, which included a smokehouse, a hothouse, and livestock.

Like the well-known Piney Woods School in Mississippi, Oak Hill Academy taught vocational skills as well as academic subjects. Many of the graduates went on to teach in other schools for black children. The academy also sent many of its graduates to various colleges nationwide, and many from Oak Hill were among the faculty in various black institutions throughout the south.

The book is filled with dozens of photographs of the Freedmen and, more significantly, at least thirty of the images are portrait-style photos with names identifying them. The faces of the students clearly reflect their African ancestry and some also reflect their Choctaw ancestry. Many of the students were bilingual in Choctaw and English, and, as children of former slaves from the Choctaw Nation, many were also bi-cultural. Of those students who are identified, the researcher can follow up on their lives and those of their parents through research in the Dawes interviews.

In addition to the portraits of the students, there are equally beautiful photographs of the school. The beauty and elegance of Oak Hill Industrial Academy was in sharp contrast to the earlier schools built for the Choctaw Freedmen, which were meager at best. They were called "colored neighborhood schools", and most were simple log structures where the basics of reading were taught but oftentimes only sporadically. Oak Hill was known for its well-manicured lawns, boys' and girls' residences, and a spacious campus offering both academic training as well as vocational training. The school would also benefit from the funds of Julius Rosenwald and the services of the Anna T. Jeannes, teachers whose philanthropic efforts would provide even greater services to the students.

The Oak Hill would eventually be absorbed by the segregated school system of southeastern Oklahoma. Much knowledge about the Freedmen as a distinct people faded as Oklahoma took on the personality of a southern state, with its attitudes and policies of separation of ethnic groups.

Today there are no remnants of the glories of the once beautiful Oak Hill. The manicured lawns have turned brown and the Victorian-style student residences no longer stand. In the 1980s, only a parking lot for industrial vehicles stood on the school grounds. Nothing speaks of the splendor of the academy's beauty or of its successes and the hope given to the Freedmen children of the Choctaw Nation.

The republication of Robert Flickinger's book is well timed and is enthusiastically received. The legacy of this long-forgotten institution will reveal an important segment of Choctaw Freedmen history, of Choctaw Nation history, and of Oklahoma history. The status of the Freedmen was often debated by the officials of the nation beginning with the end of slavery in 1865, through the adoption of the Freedmen in 1885, and continuing until the end of the Dawes Commission enrollment period.

Although neighborhood schools came and went in the Choctaw Nation, such as the short-lived Tushka Luska, the establishment of the imposing Oak Hill campus was a significant statement that the thirst for knowledge truly existed in the Indian Territory. The academy's story reflects the legacy of a people once erased from the pages of history. The reprinting of this long-forgotten book will retell a small chapter of a greater story still waiting to be told - that of the Choctaw Freedmen in the Indian Territory.

Angela Walton-Raji
Catonsville, Maryland
October 2002

INTRODUCTION

"The pleasant books, that silently among
Our household treasures take familiar places,
Are to us, as if a living tongue
Spake from the printed leaves, or pictured faces!"

THE aim of the Author in preparing this volume has been to put in a form, convenient for preservation and future reference, a brief historical sketch of the work and workers connected with the founding and development of Oak Hill Industrial Academy, established for the benefit of the Freedmen of the Choctaw Nation, Indian Territory, by the Presbyterian church, U. S. A., in 1886, when Miss Eliza Hartford became the first white teacher, to the erection of Elliott Hall in 1910, and its dedication in 1912; when the name of the institution was changed to "The Alice Lee Elliott Memorial."

Some who rendered service at Oak Hill Academy, bestowed upon it their best work, while superintendent, James F. McBride and Matron, Adelia M. Eaton, brought to it a faithful service, that proved to be the crowning work of their lives.

The occasion of receiving a new name in 1912, is one that suggests the eminent propriety of a volume, that will commemorate the labors of those, whose self-denying pioneer work was associated with the former name of the institution.

INTRODUCTION

Another aim has been, to place as much as possible of the character building work of the institution, in an attractive form for profitable perusal by the youth, in the homes of the pupils and patrons of the Academy. As an aid in effecting this result, the volume has been profusely illustrated with engravings of all the good photographs of groups of the students that have come to the hand of the author; and also of all the teachers of whom they could be obtained at this time. The portraits of the ministers and older elders of the neighboring churches have been added to these, to increase its general interest and value.

In as much as Oak Hill Industrial Academy was intended to supply the special educational needs of the young people in the circuit of churches ministered to by Parson Charles W. Stewart, the pioneer preacher of the Choctaw Freedmen, and faithful founder of most of the churches in the Presbytery of Kiamichi, a memorial sketch of this worthy soldier of the cross has been added, that the young people of the present and future generations may catch the inspiration of his heroic missionary spirit.

> "All who labor wield a mighty power;
> The glorious privilege to do
> Is man's most noble dower."

The ministers of the neighboring churches, in recent years, have been so helpfully identified with the work of the Academy, as special lecturers and assistants on decision days, and on the first and last days of the school terms, they seem to have been members of the Oak Hill Family. The story of the Academy would not be complete, without a recognition of them and their good work. This recognition has been very gratefully accorded in a brief history of the Presbytery of Kiamichi and of the Synod of Canadian.

AIM OF AUTHOR

The period of service rendered by the author, as superintendent of the Academy from the beginning of 1905 to the end of 1912, eight years, was one of important transitions in the material development of Indian Territory.

The allotment of lands in severalty to the Indians and Freedmen was completed in 1905, and the Territorial government was transformed into one of statehood on Jan. 1, 1908. The progress of their civilization, that made it possible for the Indians in the Territory to become owners and occupants of their own homes, supporters of their own schools and churches and to be invested with all the powers and duties of citizenship, is briefly reviewed in the introductory chapters.

The author has endeavored to make this volume one easily read and understood by the Choctaw Freedmen, in whose homes it is expected to find a place, and be read with interest and profit many years.

He has done what he could to enable as many of you as possible to leave the impress of your personality on the world, when your feet no longer move, your hands no longer build and your lips no longer utter your sentiments.

The hope is indulged that every pupil of the Academy, whose portrait has been given an historic setting in this volume, will regard that courteous recognition, as a special call to make the Bible your guide in life and perform each daily duty nobly and faithfully, as though it were your last.

> A life on service bent,
> A life for love laid down,
> A life for others spent,
> The Lord will surely crown.

Whilst other denominations have rendered conspicuous and highly commendable service in the effort to educate and evangelize the Indians and Freedmen, in this volume mention is made only of the work of the Presbyterian church. This is due to the fact the Presbyterian church, having begun missionary work among the Choctaws at a very early date, it was left to pursue it without a rival, in the particular section of country and early period of time included in the scope of this volume.

Such as it is, this volume is commended to him, whose blessing alone can make it useful, and make it to fulfil its mission of comfort and encouragement, to the children and youth of the Freedmen who are sincerely endeavoring to solve the problem of their present and future destiny.

Fonda, Iowa, March 15, 1914.   R. E. F.

PART I
GENERAL FACTS

RELATING TO THE INDIANS OF INDIAN TERRITORY, THE CHOCTAW FREEDMEN AND PRESBYTERIAN BOARD OF MISSIONS FOR FREEDMEN.

"In history we meet the great personalities, who have crystalized in their own lives, the hopes and fears of nations and races. We meet the living God, as an actor, and discover in passing events, a consistent purpose, guiding the changing world to an unchanging end."—W. A. Brown.

"Four things a man must learn to do,
If he would make his record true;
To think without confusion, clearly;
To act from honest motives purely;
To love his fellowmen sincerely;
To trust in God and heaven securely."
—Vandyke.

"The study of history, as a means of cultivating the mind and for its immediate practical benefit, ever since the days of Moses, who wrote the pioneer history of Israel, and Herodotus, the father of profane history, has formed a necessary part of a liberal and thorough education."—History of Pocahontas County, Iowa.

I
INDIAN TERRITORY

EARLY HISTORY OF THE FIVE CIVILIZED TRIBES—OPENING OF INDIAN TERRITORY — OKLAHOMA — CLEAR CREEK, OAK HILL, VALLIANT.

"Let us develop the resources of our land, call forth its powers, build up its institutions, promote all its great interests and see whether we, also, in our day and generation may not perform something worthy to be remembered."— Daniel Webster.

INDIAN Territory, now Oklahoma, was a part of the public domain, that was reserved for several tribes of Indians whose native hunting grounds were principally in the Southern states. While they remained in their native valleys they proved a menace to the safety of the frontier settlers, and in times of war were sure to take sides against them. Thomas Jefferson in his day advised that they be located together on some general reservation. This was gradually effected during the earlier years of the last century.

The official act of congress constituting it an Indian Reservation did not occur until 1834, but a considerable number of the Choctaws, Chickasaws and of some other tribes were induced to migrate westward and locate there previous to that date. Other leading tribes that were transferred to special reservations in Indian Territory were the Cherokees, Creeks and Seminoles.

THE FIVE CIVILIZED TRIBES
The Choctaw Indians recently occupied lands in the

states bordering on the Gulf of Mexico. In 1820 a considerable part of them, ceding their lands in Georgia, were located on a reservation in the Red River valley west of Arkansas. In 1830 they ceded the remainder of their lands in Alabama and Mississippi and all, together with their slaves, were then transferred to their new reservation in the southeastern part of Indian Territory.

The Chickasaws, who originally occupied the country on the east side of the Mississippi river, as early as 1800 began to migrate up the valley of the Arkansas. In 1805, 1816 and in 1818 they ceded more of their lands and more of them migrated westward, many of them going to the country allotted to the Choctaws. In 1834, when the last of their lands in the Gulf states were ceded, they were located on a reservation south of the Canadian river, west of the Choctaws. These two tribes lived under one tribal government until 1855, when they were granted a political separation.

The Cherokees, previous to 1830, occupied the upper valley of the Tennessee river, extending through the northern parts of Georgia and Alabama. In 1790 a part of the tribe migrated to Louisiana and they rendered important services in the army of Gen. Jackson at New Orleans in the war of 1812.

In 1817 they ceded a part of their native lands for others and the next year 3,000 of them were located in the northwestern part of Arkansas in the valleys of the Arkansas and White rivers. In 1835 the remainder of them were located just west of the first migration in the northeast part of Indian Territory.

The Creek Indians originally lived in the valleys of the Flint, Chattahoochee, Coosa and Alabama rivers and in the peninsula of Florida. About the year 1875, a part of them moved to Louisiana and later to Texas. In 1836 the remainder of the tribe was transferred to a reservation north of the Canadian river in Indian Territory.

The Seminoles were a nation of Florida Indians, that was composed chiefly of Creeks and the remnants of some other tribes. After the acquisition of Florida from Spain in 1819 many slaves in that section fled from their masters to the Seminoles. The government endeavored to recover them and to force the Seminoles to remove westward. These efforts were not immediately successful, Osceola, their wily and intrepid chief, defeating and capturing four of the generals sent against them, namely, Clinch, Gaines, Call and Winfield Scott. He was finally captured by his captors violating a flag of truce. In 1845 they were induced to move west of the Mississippi and in 1856, they were assigned lands west of the Creeks in the central part of Indian Territory.

These five tribes, the Choctaws, Chickasaws, Cherokees, Creeks and Seminoles, were the most powerful in numbers. After their settlement in Indian Territory, they made considerable progress in elementary education and agriculture, their farm work being principally done by their slaves previous to the time they were accorded their freedom in 1865. As a result of their progress in the arts of life, during the last half of the last century, these were often called "The Five Civilized Tribes, or Nations."

In 1900 when the last census was taken of them in their tribal form their numbers were as follows: Choctaw nation, 99,681; Chickasaw, 139,260; Cherokee, 101,754; Creek, 40,674; Seminole, 3,786.

The Osage Indians were early driven to the valley of the Arkansas river. They were conveyed to their reservation west of that river, in the north part of Indian Territory, in 1870. The supplies of oil and other minerals found upon their reservation have caused some of the members of this nation to be reputed as quite wealthy.

Other tribes that were located on small reservations in the northeast part of the Territory were the Modocs, Ottawas, Peorias, Quapaws, Senecas, Shawnees and Wyandottes.

During this early period the Union Indian agency established its headquarters at Muskogee, and it became and continued to be their principal city, during the period of their tribal government.

OPENING OF INDIAN TERRITORY

On April 22, 1889, 2,000,000 acres of the Creek and Seminole lands were opened to white settlers, and there occurred an ever memorable rush for lands and a race for homes. An area as large as the state of Maryland was settled in a day. On that first day the city of Guthrie was founded with a population of 8,000, a newspaper was issued and in a tent a bank was organized with a capital of $50,000. Oklahoma and other cities sprang up as if in a night.

On June 6, 1890, the west half of Indian Territory was created a new territory, called Oklahoma, with its capital at Guthrie, and with later additions it soon included 24,000,000 acres.

On June 16, 1906, President Roosevelt signed the enabling act, that admitted Oklahoma, including Oklahoma and Indian Territories, as a state, one year from that date. On November 6, 1906, occurred the election of members to the constitutional convention, that met at Guthrie January 1, 1907. The first legislature met there January 1, 1908. Two years later the capital was moved to Oklahoma City.

INDIAN TERRITORY

The growth, progress and advancement of the territory of Oklahoma during the sixteen years preceding statehood in 1907 has never been equaled in the history of the world, and in all probability will never be eclipsed. This was due to the mild and healthful climate of this region, and a previous knowledge of its great, but undeveloped agricultural and mineral resources. So great has been the flow of oil near Tulsa, in the north central part of the state, it has been necessary to store it there in an artificial lake or reservoir.

OKLAHOMA

The surface of Oklahoma consists of a gently undulating plain, that gradually ascends from an altitude of 511 feet at Valliant in the southeast to 1197 feet at Oklahoma City, and 1893 at Woodward, the county seat of Woodward county, in the northwest. The principal mountains are the Kiamichi in the southern part of Laflore county, and the Wichita, a forest reserve in Comanche and Swanson counties.

Previous to statehood Indian Territory was divided into 31 recording districts for court purposes. In 1902 when Garvin was founded it became the residence of the judge of the southeastern judicial or recording district, and a small court house was built there for the transaction of the public business. In 1907, when McCurtain county was established, Idabel was chosen as the county seat. The location of Oak Hill Academy proved to be one and a half miles east of the west line of McCurtain county. In 1910 the population of McCurtain county was 20,681, of Oklahoma City 64,205; and of the state of Oklahoma, 1,657,155.

CLEAR CREEK

During the period immediately preceding the incoming of the Hope and Ardmore Railroad in 1902, the most important news and trading center, between Fort Towson and Wheelock, was called "Clear Creek." Clear Creek is a rustling, sparkling little stream of clear water that flows southward in a section of the country where most of the streams are sluggish and of a reddish hue. The Clear Creek post office was located in a little store building a short distance east of this stream and about three miles north of Red river.

A little log court house, for the administration of tribal justice among the Choctaws of that vicinity, a blacksmith shop and a Choctaw church were also located at this place. These varied interests gave to Clear Creek the importance of a miniature county seat until Valliant and Swink were founded.

OAK HILL

During this early period the oak covered ridge, extending several miles east of Clear Creek, was known as Oak Hill and the settlement in its vicinity was called by the same name.

When the first church (1869) and school (1876) were established among the Freedmen in this settlement, the same name was naturally given to both of them. It has adhered to them, amid all the changes that have occurred, since the first meetings were held at the home of Henry Crittenden in 1868.

VALLIANT

Valliant was founded in 1902, and was so named in honor of one of the surveyors of the Hope and Ardmore, a branch of the Frisco railway. It is located in the west end of McCurtain county eight miles north of Red river. It has now a population of 1,000 and a branch railroad running northward.

The country adjacent to the town consists of beautiful valleys and forests heavily set with timber, principally oak, walnut, ash and hickory, and with pine and cedar along the streams. The soil is a rich sandy loam, that is easily cultivated and gives promise of great agricultural and horticultural possibilities. It is in the center of the cotton belt and this staple is proving a very profitable one. The climate is healthful and the locality is unusually free from the prevalence of high winds.

II
INDIAN SCHOOLS AND CHURCHES

BEFORE THE CIVIL WAR.—EFFECTS OF THE CIVIL WAR.—TRANSFER OF THE FREEDMEN'S WORK.—THE INDIANS MAKE PROGRESS TOWARD CIVILIZATION.—WHEELOCK ACADEMY.—SPENCER ACADEMY.—DOAKSVILLE AND FORT TOWSON.

"God, who hath made of one blood all nations of men and determined the bounds of their habitation, commandeth all men everywhere to repent."—Paul.

WHEN Columbus landed on the shores of America, the Indians were the only people he found occupying this great continent. During the long period that has intervened, the Indian has furnished proof, that he possesses all the attributes which God has bestowed upon other members of the human family. He has shown that he has an intellect capable of development, that he is willing to receive instruction and that he is capable of performing any duty required of an American citizen.

Considerable patience however has had to be exercised both by the church in its effort to bring him under the saving influence of the gospel, and by the government in its effort to elevate him to the full standard of citizenship. Results are achieved slowly. His struggles have been many and difficult. He has needed counsel and encouragement at every advancing step.

In the former days, when the Indian supported his family by hunting, trapping and fishing, he moved about from place to place. This was finally checked in Indian Territory by the individual allotment of lands in 1904. He has thus been compelled by the force of circumstances, to change his mode of life. He has gradually discovered he can settle down on his own farm, improve it by the erection of good buildings, and either buy or make the implements he needs for cultivating the soil.

The great commission to the church to "go into all the world and preach the gospel to every creature," will not be completed until the American Indian and the Freedmen, who were his former slaves, have been brought under its uplifting influence.

The Presbyterian church throughout all its history has been the friend and patron of learning and inasmuch as the evangelistic work among the Indians and Freedmen, has been largely dependent on school work for permanent results, it began to establish schools among the Indians at a very early date. The work among the five civilized tribes was begun many years before they were transported from the southern states to Indian Territory. Some of these missionaries migrated with them and continued both their school and church work in the Territory. Rev. Alfred Wright, who organized the Presbyterian church at Wheelock in December, 1832, and died there in 1853, after receiving 570 members into it, began his work as a missionary to the Choctaws in 1820.

The aim of the government in its educational work among the Indians, as elsewhere in the public schools of the country, has been mainly to make them intelligent citizens. The aim of the church, by making the Bible a daily textbook, is to make them happy and hopeful Christians, as well as citizens. In the early days there was great need for this

INDIAN SCHOOLS AND CHURCHES 17

educational work, and in the Presbyterian church it was carried forward by its foreign mission board, with wisdom, energy and success.

In 1861 the Presbyterian church had established and was maintaining six boarding schools with 800 pupils and six day schools among the Indians in the Territory. Two of these schools, Spencer and Wheelock Academies, were located in the southern part of the Choctaw Nation.

In 1840 the Presbytery of Indian was organized and in 1848 the Presbytery of the Creek Nation. In 1861 these included an enrollment of 16 churches with a communicant membership of 1,772.

EFFECTS OF THE CIVIL WAR

At the outbreak of the civil war in 1861, all of these schools and churches were closed, and the next year the Presbyterian church became divided by the organization of the Southern Presbyterian church, under the corporate name, "The Presbyterian Church in the United States."

At the close of the war it was left to the Southern branch of the church to re-establish this school and church work in the Territory. It undertook to do this and carried parts of it alone for a number of years. The task however proved to be too great; the men and means were not available to re-open the boarding schools, and to supply the churches with ministers. The arrangement was accordingly made for the foreign mission board of the Presbyterian church, to resume its former work as fast as workers could be obtained.

In 1879, four ministers returned and opened six churches among the Choctaws, Creeks and Cherokees.

In 1882 Spencer Academy was re-opened at Nelson, by Rev. Oliver P. Starks, a native of Goshen, New York, who, for seventeen years previous to the Civil War, had been a missionary to the Choctaws, having his home at Goodland.

The Indian Mission school at Muskogee was also re-opened that year by Miss Rose Steed.

In the fall of 1883 the Presbytery of Indian Territory was re-established with a membership of 16 ministers, 11 churches, 385 communicants and 676 Sunday school scholars.

In 1884 Wheelock Academy was re-opened by Rev. John Edwards, who for a couple of years previous, had been located at Atoka. This was a return of Edwards to the educational work among the Choctaws. From 1851 to 1853 he served at Spencer Academy, north of Doaksville, and then from 1853 to 1861 had charge of Wheelock Academy, as the successor of Rev. Alfred Wright, its early founder.

In 1883 two teachers were sent, who opened a school among the Creek Freedmen at Muskogee, known as the "Pittsburgh Mission." A teacher was also sent to the Freedmen among the Seminoles.

After a few years the Pittsburgh Mission was transferred from Muskogee to Atoka, where it supplied a real want for a few years longer. In 1904 when adequate provision was first made for the Freedmen in the public schools of that town this mission was discontinued.

TRANSFER OF THE FREEDMEN'S WORK

During this same year, 1884, the Presbyterian Board of Missions for Freedmen, Pittsburgh, Pa., received the voluntary transfer from the Southern church of all the work it had developed at that date among the Choctaw Freedmen. This transfer was made in good spirit. The motive that prompted it was the conviction and belief the Presbyterian

INDIAN SCHOOLS AND CHURCHES 19

church could carry it forward more conveniently, aggressively and successfully.

The work that was transferred at this date consisted of Rev. Charles W. Stewart, Doaksville, and the following churches then under his pastoral care, namely: Oak Hill, Beaver Dam, Hebron, New Hope and St. Paul (Eagletown). Parson Stewart had been licensed about 1867 and ordained a few years later. With a true missionary spirit he had gone into these various settlements and effected the organization of these churches among his people. During the next two years he added to his circuit two more churches, Mount Gilead at Lukfata and Forest, south of Wheelock, and occasionally visited one or two other places.

INDIANS MAKE PROGRESS TOWARDS CIVILIZATION

About the year 1880 the social and moral condition of the Indians in Indian Territory was described as follows:

"About thirty different languages are spoken by the Indians now in the territory. The population of the territory, though principally Indians, includes a lot of white men and negroes, amongst whom intermarriages are frequent. The society ranges from an untutored Indian, with a blanket for his dress and paganism for his religion, to men of collegiate education, who are manifesting their christian culture and training by their earnest advocacy of the christian faith.

"The Cherokees were the first to be brought under direct christian influence and they were probably in the lead of all the Indians on the continent in civilization, or practice of the useful arts and enjoyment of the common comforts of life."

"In 1890, the year following the opening of the first land in the territory to white settlers, the mission work in the territory was described as "very interesting and unique." The Indian population represented every grade of civilization. One might see the several stages of progress from the ignorant and superstitious blanketed Indian on the western reservations to the representatives of our advanced American culture among the five civilized nations. Our missionaries have labored long and successfully and the education, degree of civilization and prosperity enjoyed by the Indians are due principally, if not solely, to the efforts of consecrated men and women, who devoted their lives to this special work. Although their names may not be familiarly known among the churches, none have deserved more honorable mention than these faithful servants of the Master, who selected this particular field of effort for their life work.

"Events are moving rapidly in Indian Territory. Many new lines of railroad have been surveyed, and when they have been built, every part of the Territory will be easily accessible.

"A new judicial system with a complete code of laws has recently been provided, and with liberal provision for Indian citizenship and settlement of the land question it is safe to predict a speedy end to tribal government.

"This means the opening of a vast region to settlement, the establishment of churches and the thorough organization of every form of christian work. For this we must prepare and there is no time to lose. Our churches and schools must be multiplied and our brethren of the ministry must be fully reinforced by competent educated men trained for christian work. What the future has in store for the whole Territory was illustrated by the marvelous rush into and settlement of Oklahoma Territory during the last year.

"A wonderful transformation has taken place. The unbroken prairie of one year ago has been changed to cultivated fields. The tents of boomers have given place to well built homes and substantial blocks of brick and stone. Unorganized communities have now become members of a legally constituted commonwealth. Here are found all the elements of great progress and general prosperity and the future of Oklahoma Territory is full of great promise.

"Here the Presbyterian church has shown itself capable of wrestling with critical social problems and stands today as the leading denomination in missionary enterprise. Every county has its minister and many churches have been organized. Others are underway. With more ministers and liberal aid for the erection of churches the Presbyterian church will do for Oklahoma what it has done for Kansas and the Dakotas."

In 1886 the mission school work among the Indians was transferred from the care of the foreign to the home

INDIAN SCHOOLS AND CHURCHES

mission board. Those in charge of the school work of Spencer Academy at Nelson resigned that work and the school was closed.

In 1895 the Mission school work at Wheelock Academy was undertaken and continued thereafter by the Indian Agency, as a school for orphan children of the Indians.

WHEELOCK ACADEMY

Wheelock Academy for nearly four-score years was the most attractive social, educational and religious center in the southeast part of the Choctaw nation. It was located on the main trails running east and west and north and south. But when the Frisco railway came in 1902, it passed two miles south of it, and a half dozen flourishing towns were founded along its line.

There remain to mark this place of early historic interest the two mission school buildings, a strongly built stone church 30 by 50 feet, a two story parsonage and cemetery. The church is of the Gothic style of architecture, tastefully decorated inside and furnished with good pews and pulpit furniture.

REV. ALFRED WRIGHT

Among the many old inscriptions on the grave stones in the Wheelock cemetery, there may be seen the following beautiful record of the work of one, whose long and eminently useful life was devoted to the welfare of the Choctaw people:

SACRED
to the memory of the
REV. ALFRED WRIGHT
who entered into his heavenly rest
March 31, 1853, age 65 years.
Born in Columbia, Connecticut, March 1, 1788.
Appointed Missionary to the Choctaws 1820.
Removed to this land October, 1832.
Organized Wheelock Church December, 1832.
Received to its fellowship 570 members.
AS A MAN
he was intelligent, firm in principle,
prudent in counsel, gentle in spirit,
kindness and gravity,
and conscientious in the discharge of every
relative and social duty.
AS A CHRISTIAN
he was uniform, constant, strong in faith,
and in doctrine, constant and fervent in prayer,
holy in life, filled with the spirit of Christ
and peaceful in death.
AS A PHYSICIAN
he was skillful, attentive, ever ready to relieve
and comfort the afflicted.
AS A TRANSLATOR
he was patient, investigating and diligent,
giving to the Choctaws in their own tongue the
New and part of the Old Testament,
and various other books.
AS A MINISTER
his preaching was scriptural, earnest, practical,
and rich in the full exhibition of Gospel truth.
He was laborious, faithful and successful.
Communion with God, faith in the Lord Jesus,
and reliance upon the aid of the Holy Spirit,
made all his labor sweet to his own soul
and a blessing to others.
In testimony of his worth, and their affection,
his mourning friends erect this
Tablet to his Memory.
"There remaineth therefore a rest to the people
of God."

REV. JOHN EDWARDS

Rev. John Edwards, the successor of Rev. Alfred Wright, was a native of Bath, New York. He graduated from the college at Princeton, New Jersey, in 1848, and from the theological seminary there in 1851. He was ordained by the Presbytery of Indian Territory December 11, 1853.

THE CHOCTAW CHURCH, CLEAR CREEK.

THE CHOCTAW COURT HOUSE, CLEAR CREEK.
Both buildings ceased to be used about 1899.

REV. JOHN EDWARDS.
Wheelock Academy, 1853-61; 1882-95.

REV. ALEXANDER REID.
Spencer Academy, 1849-1861.

INDIAN SCHOOLS AND CHURCHES

He became a teacher at Spencer Academy, north of Fort Towson, in 1851, and continued until 1853, when he became the successor of Rev. Alfred Wright as the stated supply of the Choctaw church and superintendent of the academy at Wheelock. At the outbreak of the Civil War in 1861 he passed to California and after teaching two years in San Francisco, served as stated supply of various churches during the next twenty years, having his residence during the latter part of that period at Oakland.

In 1882 he returned and resumed work among the Choctaws, locating first at Atoka. In 1884 he re-opened the academy at Wheelock, and continued to serve as its superintendent until 1895, when it became a government school. He remained the next year in charge of the church. He then returned to California and died at San Jose, at 75, December 18, 1903.

In 1897, Rev. Evan B. Evans, supplied the Choctaw church at Wheelock one year. As its membership of 60 consisted principally of students living at a distance, and they were absent most of the year, the services were then discontinued. A few years later the services were resumed at the town of Garvin, where another stone church was built in 1910, during the efficient ministry of Rev. W. J. Willis.

SPENCER ACADEMY

Rev. Alexander Reid, principal of Spencer Academy, was a native of Scotland, and came to this country in his boyhood. He graduated from the college at Princeton, N. J., in 1845, and the theological seminary there, three years later. He was ordained by the Presbytery of New York in 1849 and accepting a commission to serve as a missionary to the Indians of the Choctaw Nation in Indian Territory, was immediately appointed superintendent of Spencer Academy, ten miles north of Fort Towson.

He was accompanied by Rev. Alexander J. Graham, a native of Newark, New Jersey, who served as a teacher in the academy. The latter was a roommate of Reid's at Princeton seminary, and his sister became Reid's wife. At the end of his first year of service he returned to Lebanon Springs, New York, for the recovery of his health, and died there July 23, 1850. Rev. John Edwards immediately became his successor as a teacher.

Alexander Reid while pursuing his studies, learned the tailor's trade at West Point and this proved a favorable introduction to his work among the Choctaws. They were surprised and greatly pleased on seeing that he had already learned the art of sitting on the ground "tailor fashion" according to their own custom.

The academy under Reid enjoyed a prosperous career of twelve years. In 1861, when the excitement of war absorbed the attention of everybody, the school work was abandoned. Reid, however, continued to serve as a gospel missionary among the Indians until 1869, when he took his family to Princeton, New Jersey, to provide for the education of his children.

While ministering to the spiritual needs of the Indians his sympathies and interest were awakened by the destitute and helpless condition of their former slaves. In 1878 he resumed work as a missionary to the Choctaws making his headquarters at or near Atoka and in 1882 he was appointed by the Foreign Mission Board, superintendent of mission work among the Freedmen in Indian Territory. In this capacity he aided in establishing neighborhood schools wherever teachers could be found. In order that a number

INDIAN SCHOOLS AND CHURCHES

of them might be fitted for teaching, he obtained permission of their parents to take a number of bright looking and promising young people to boarding schools, maintained by our Freedmen's Board in Texas, Mississippi and North Carolina. He thus became instrumental in preparing the way, and advised the development of the native Oak Hill School into an industrial and normal boarding school.

In 1884, owing to failing health, he went to the home of his son, Rev. John G. Reid (born at Spencer Academy in 1854), at Greeley, Colorado, and died at 72 at Cambridgeport, near Boston, July 30, 1890.

"He was a friend to truth, of soul sincere, of manners unaffected and of mind enlarged, he wished the good of all mankind."

UNCLE WALLACE AND AUNT MINERVA

Uncle Wallace and Aunt Minerva were two of the colored workers that were employed at Spencer Academy, before the war. They lived together in a little cabin near it. In the summer evenings they would often sit at the door of the cabin and sing their favorite plantation songs, learned in Mississippi in their early youth.

In 1871, when the Jubilee singers first visited Newark, New Jersey, Rev. Alexander Reid happened to be there and heard them. The work of the Jubilee singers was new in the North and attracted considerable and very favorable attention. But when Prof. White, who had charge of them, announced several concerts to be given in different churches of the city he added,

"We will have to repeat the Jubilee songs as we have no other."

When Mr. Reid was asked how he liked them he remarked,

"Very well, but I have heard better ones."

When he had committed to writing a half dozen of the plantation songs he had heard "Wallace and Minerva" sing with so much delight at old Spencer Academy, he met Mr. White and his company in Brooklyn, New York, and spent an entire day rehearsing them. These new songs included,

"Steal away to Jesus."
"The Angels are Coming,"
"I'm a Rolling," and "Swing Low."

"Steal Away to Jesus" became very popular and was sung before Queen Victoria.

The Hutchinson family later used several of them in their concerts, rendering "I'm a Rolling," with a trumpet accompaniment to the words:

"The trumpet sounds in my soul,
I haint got long to stay here."

These songs have now been sung around the world.

When one thinks of the two old slaves singing happily together at the door of their humble cabin, amid the dreary solitudes of Indian Territory, and the widely extended results that followed, he cannot help perceiving in these incidents a practical illustration of the way in which our Heavenly Father uses "things that are weak," for the accomplishment of his gracious purposes. They also serve to show how little we know of the future use God will make of the lowly service any of us may now be rendering.

These two slaves giving expression to their devotional feelings in simple native songs, unconsciously exerted a happy influence, that was felt even in distant lands; an influence that served to attract attention and financial support to an important institution, established for the education of the Freedmen.

INDIAN SCHOOLS AND CHURCHES

NEW SPENCER ACADEMY

In the fall of 1881 the Presbyterian Board of Foreign Missions re-established Spencer Academy in a new location where the postoffice was called, Nelson, ten miles southwest of Antlers and twenty miles west of old Spencer, now called Spencerville.

Rev. Oliver P. Stark, the first superintendent of this institution, died there at the age of 61, March 2, 1884. He was a native of Goshen, New York, and a graduate of the college and Theological Seminary at Princeton, N. J. In 1851, he was ordained by the Presbytery of Indian which, as early as 1840, had been organized to include the missions of the American Board.

As early as 1849, while he was yet a licentiate, he was commissioned as a missionary to the Choctaws, and, locating at Goodland, remained in charge of the work in that section until 1866, a period of seventeen years. During the next thirteen years he served as principal of the Lamar Female Seminary at Paris, Texas. His next and last work was the development of the mission school for the Choctaws at Nelson, which had formed a part of his early and long pastorate.

Rev. Harvey R. Schermerhorn, became the immediate successor of Mr. Stark as superintendent of the new Spencer Academy and continued to serve in that capacity until 1890, when the mission work among the Indians was transferred from the Foreign to the care of the Home Mission Board. The school was then discontinued and he became pastor of the Presbyterian church at Macalester. After a long and very useful career he is now living in retirement at Hartshorne.

These incidents, relating to the work of the Presbyterian church among the Indians, especially the Choctaws, have been narrated, because the men who had charge of these two educational institutions at Wheelock and Spencer Academies, were very helpful in effecting the organization of Presbyterian churches, the establishment of Oak Hill Academy and a number of neighborhood schools among the Freedmen in the south part of the Choctaw Nation.

DOAKSVILLE AND FORT TOWSON

Rev. Cyrus Kingsbury, an early Presbyterian missionary to the Choctaws, was located at Doaksville near old Fort Towson. He secured the erection of an ample church building and rendered many years of faithful service. He died and was buried in the cemetery at that place in 1870.

Doaksville, though no longer entitled to a place on the map, is the name of an important pioneer Indian village. Here the once proud and powerful Choctaws established themselves during the later twenties, and were regarded as happy and prosperous before the Civil War.

Fort Towson was built by the government to protect them from incursions on the part of the wild Kiowas and Comanches, who still roamed over the plains of Texas. The name of Ulyses S. Grant was associated with it just before the Mexican war. The generous hospitality of Col. Garland, who died there after a long period of service, is still gratefully remembered.

During its most prosperous days, which were long before the Civil War, a considerable number of aristocratic Choctaws, claiming large plantations in the neighboring valleys, dwelt there near each other. Some were men of culture and university education, while others were ignorant and superstitious. Some had previously enjoyed the acquaintance and friendship of Andrew Jackson and Zachary Taylor, and greatly appreciated the privilege of manifesting their chivalrous spirit. Berthlett's store, now used as a stable, was a noted trading establishment and place of social resort. Its owner was a native of Canada, who had come to live among the Choctaws.

While living in this beautiful country, where they were paternally protected from poverty at home and the encroachments of enemies abroad it has been said they were so addicted to private quarrels and fatal combats, that there was scarcely a Choctaw family that did not have its tragedy of blood. These fatal tribal feuds, however, seldom occurred except on gala days, and the preparations therefor included a supply of "fire-water."

The old Doaksville cemetery occupies the slope of a hillside near a little stream skirted with timber. Some of the leading pioneers of the Choctaw nation were buried here. The marble tablets that mark their graves were brought by steam boat from New Orleans, up the Mississippi and Red rivers to a landing four miles south. Some of the graves are walled and covered with a marble slab, while others are marked by the erection over them of oddly shaped little houses. In the early days, the full-bloods were in the habit of burying with the body some favorite trinket or article of personal adornment. Many of the grave stones attest the fact that the deceased while living enjoyed a good hope of a blessed immortality through our Lord Jesus Christ.

III

THE BIBLE AN IMPORTANT FACTOR IN CIVILIZATION AND EDUCATION

THE BIBLE A POWER IN THE FORMATION OF CHARACTER. —THE ARCHITECT GREATER THAN THE CATHEDRAL.— THE BIBLE THE BASIS OF THE AMERICAN PUBLIC SCHOOL SYSTEM.—VALLEY OF DIAMONDS.—IMPORTANCE OF CHRISTIAN TEACHERS.

"From a child thou hast known the HOLY SCRIPTURES, which are able to make thee Wise unto Salvation."
"All scripture is given by inspiration of God, and is profitable for instruction; That the man of God may be perfect thoroughly furnished unto all good works."—Paul

WHILST our religious educational institutions where unsectarian instruction in the Bible is fundamental, have been producing good results of the highest order, those educational institutions where only secular instruction is given, have been contributing a very small proportion of the world's consecrated moral leaders. Of 1,600 home missionaries, 1,503 received their training in Christion educational institutions. Of 600 foreign missionaries, 551 received their training in Christian educational institutions.

It is not correct to say that one standard of education is as good as another. Fourteen American colleges, recently established in China by the Christian Missionaries, though only meagerly equipped, but manned by those of unquestioned Christian character, and teaching the plain saving truths of the Bible, have become educational centers, from which have gone out the leaders in a peaceful revolution that occurred there in 1912, that have brought the boon of civil and religious liberty to one-fourth of the population of the world. Under the beneficent influence of a few Christian leaders this ancient empire has been lifted off its hinges and a new life and spirit of progress have been infused into a civilization, hoary with centuries of stagnant heathenism. In this wonderful transformation, effected by trained Christian teachers, the church and the world have seen the fulfillment of the Bible prediction, "A nation shall be born in a day."

Training for a noble Christian life is many times better than training merely to make a living. The demand for good and true men, to serve as leaders in church and state was never greater than at present. The aim of the church is to supply the world with capable leaders that are "Christ-led and Bible-fed."

A right education knows no limit of breadth. It includes a knowledge of the Infinite as well as the finite. It recognizes the fact that finite things can not be rightly understood without knowing their relation to the Infinite. Our Lord Jesus, who came into the world to make known the will of the Father, "holds in his girdle the key to all the secrets of the universe, and no education can be thorough without the knowledge of Him."

Christian schools are established for the culture of souls. Their aim is to develop men and women as persons to the full extent of their powers for the sake of their contribution to the personal welfare and progress of society.

THE BIBLE A POWER IN THE FORMATION OF CHARACTER

All things being equal the thorough Christian makes a better mechanic, a better farmer, a better housekeeper, teacher, doctor, lawyer or business man, than one who is not a Christian. It is the work of a Bible school of instruction to equip its graduates with the very best elements of character and progress, and send them forth tempered and polished for the conquest of the world.

The young have characters to be molded, ideals to be formed, capacities to be enlarged, an efficiency that may be increased, an energy to be centralized, and a hope and faith to be strengthened. The Bible, in the hands of the tactful and faithful Christian teacher accomplishes all of these results, by its precepts and interesting biographies.

The Bible, furnishes the young correct ideals of a noble and useful manhood. The common greed for money, position and outward appearance is weighed in the balance and found wanting.

The Bible is the fountain of all true character, and furnishes the means for the betterment of one's self. It furnished the principles and ideals that enabled Washington, Lincoln, Frances Willard, Queen Victoria, Gladstone and others, to achieve greatness as statesmen, rulers or national leaders; and enabled Cary, Judson, Moffat, Livingstone and others to invade dark, dangerous continents that they might become heralds of gospel light and liberty where they were most needed. "Buy the truth, sell it not, and the truth shall make you free," was the ringing message they proclaimed to men, women and children.

THE ARCHITECT GREATER THAN THE CATHEDRAL

A tourist, visiting the famous cathedral at Milan, expressed his great surprise at the wonderful vision and perfect ideal of the man, who designed it. A guide remarked, that the mind of the architect, who wrought out the hundred striking features of the design, was greater than the magnificent cathedral. This led another to remark, "Only a mind inspired by Christ could have designed this wonderful building." How true! The love of Christ constrains his people to bring to his service and worship their noblest powers of mind and body.

When the tourist viewed the works of art, which included some of the world's most famous statuary and paintings, he found the master pieces of Michael Angelo, the sculptor, were Moses and David, both of them characters from the Bible; and the most wonderful paintings were those of the person of our Lord Jesus, the only Redeemer of the world.

Hayden and Handel, two of the world's most famous musical composers, were inspired to write their great choral masterpieces, the "Creation" and the "Messiah" as a result of their careful study of the sacred scriptures..

The best the world has produced in law, literature, poetry, music, art and architecture has been the embodiment of ideals, that have received their inspiration from reading God's Holy Word, and experiencing saving knowledge of the redeeming work of His blessed Son.

Abraham continues to be the "father of the faithful;" Moses, author of the Pentateuch, continues to be the world's greatest lawgiver and leader of men; Joshua effecting the conquest of Canaan on the principle, "Divide and Conquer," continues to be the inspirer of successful military strateg-

THE BIBLE AN IMPORTANT FACTOR 35

ists; David author of Psalms, continues to be the world's greatest poet; Joseph, Daniel and Isaiah, continue to be the best ideals for rulers and their counselors; Nehemiah, the best representative of a progressive and successful man of affairs; Peter and John, the most noted examples of loyalty to truth; Paul, the most zealous advocate of a great cause; and our Lord Jesus continues to be the ideal of the world's greatest teachers and benefactors.

THE BASIS OF THE AMERICAN PUBLIC SCHOOL SYSTEM

"The Bible, the basis of moral instruction in the public school," was the interesting theme of an address it was the privilege of the author to deliver at a teachers' institute forty years ago, when engaged in teaching in central Pennsylvania. The conviction then became indellibly impressed, that the Bible is really the basis of the American public school system. The fact is now noted with a good deal of interest, that the legislature of Pennsylvania in 1913, enacted a law, distinctly recognizing this fact, and providing that at least ten verses from the Bible shall be read every school day, in the presence of the scholars in every public school within the bounds of the state. Every teacher refusing to comply with this law is subject to dismissal..

Every state in the Union should have a law of this kind. The Bible is not merely the book of books, it is the only one that has correct ideals for young people. It awakens the desire for more knowledge and inspires the courage to do right.

THE VALLEY OF DIAMONDS

Ruskin, in "The Ethics of Dust", referring to the valley of diamonds, remarks that "many people go to real places and never see them; and many people pass through this valley of diamonds and never see it."

One great object to be attained in the education of the mind is to awaken an earnest desire for truth. All real life, whether it be in the school, shop or field, consists in using aright the true principles of life, that are found in the Word of God. Every human heart, that has been illuminated by this Word of Truth, finds that along the pathway that leads to God, there are hidden the gems and jewels of eternal truth, that prevail in every department of life. These gems are hidden only from the careless and indifferent. Those that make a diligent search are sure to find them. This longing desire for truth is not only the mark of a good student, but the assurance also that such a one, if circumstances are favorable will continue to make progress after school days have ended.

Many pupils, during their youthful school days, fail to perceive the real mission of their education. They do not then fully appreciate the real gold of truth, that cultivates in them "those general charities of heart, sincerities of thought, and graces of habit, which are likely to lead them, throughout life to prefer frankness to affectation, reality to shadows, and beauty to corruption." This enlightenment is pretty sure to come to them later, if the Bible has been their daily text book.

THE CHRISTIAN TEACHER

The acceptance of the Bible as the Word of God should be regarded as essential, on the part of all teachers of children and youth.

If the Bible is the great fountain of saving truth and the highest authority on human conduct, and it is to be used as a daily text book, then, it naturally follows, the

THE BIBLE AN IMPORTANT FACTOR

teacher should be "a workman approved unto God, apt to teach and rightly dividing the word of truth." Persons who do not believe in the Bible do not care to teach it, and when they are required to do so, they are pretty sure to vaunt their unbelief. The influence of such teachers tends to establish unbelief instead of awakening a longing desire for more truth.

Emerson in one of his essays, after pressing the fact that the soul is the receiver and revealer of truth, states an undeniable fact, when he says:

"That which we are, we shall teach, not voluntarily but involuntarily. Thoughts go out of our minds through avenues, which we never voluntarily opened. Character teaches over our head. The infallible index of true progress is found in the tone the man takes. Neither his age, nor his breeding, nor his company, nor books, nor actions, nor talents, nor all together can hinder him from being deferential to a higher spirit than his own. If he has not found his home in God, his manners, his form of speech, the turn of his sentences, the build, shall I say of all his opinions, will involuntarily confess it, let him brave it out how he will."

The longings of the human heart are unsatisfied, until the soul finds its home in God, its creator and preserver. Teachers that ignore this fact, lack one thing that is vitally important. Our Lord Jesus, the great teacher, expressed its relative importance when he said: "Seek ye first the Kingdom of God, and his righteousness; and all these things will be added unto you."

A RAILROAD PRESIDENT

James J. Hill, a prominent railroad president recently made this important statement:

"We are making a mistake to train our young people in various lines of knowledge for undertaking the big tasks of life, without making sure also that those fundamental principles of right and wrong as taught in the Bible, have become a part of their equipment. There is a control of forces and motives, that is essential to the management of the vast affairs of our nation, which comes only through an educated conscience; and to fail to equip young men, who are to manage the great affairs of the future, with this control and direction, is a serious mistake of the age and bears with it a certain menace for the future."

In a recent issue of the Asembly Herald there appeared the following very pertinent paragraphs on this subject, credited to the Synod of Tennessee:

"In common with all good citizens, we rejoice in the progress of the cause of popular education in our land. The intelligence of our citizenship is a bulwark to the country. But unless the education of the future citizen is complete and symmetrical, the body politic becomes a body partly of iron and partly of potter's clay. The education of the head and the hand without the heart is not enough.

"The popular education has no place for the heart in all of its splendid equipment. This is not a reflection on the fine system. It is merely the statement of a melancholy fact. The average state school, high or low, is absolutely colorless as to religion. Even the morality that is taught is not the morality of the Christian religion, but of philosophical ethics that differ but little from the ethics of the pagan.

"Our state schools have no place for the God of the Bible, nor for the Bible of the only living and true God. The poetry of Homer and Horace are sufficiently honored, but the finer poetry of Moses, Job and David are unknown in the courses of study of our schools, except now and then as specimens of Oriental song. The wise sayings of Plato and Socrates are reckoned worthy of profound study, while the vastly greater sayings of our Lord Jesus and Paul are unknown. Cicero and Demosthenes are commended as great models of public address, while Isaiah and Ezekiel are seldom mentioned in the four years of college life, or in the longer years of the secondary schools.

"That education is incomplete and inadequate for life's best, which does not include the whole man, and put first things first. If the heart be not educated and the conscience be not enlightened, the best trained hand may strike in a wrong manner, and the best trained mind pronounce wrong judgments. . Our citizenship must be Christian if it is to promote a Christian civilization."

IV

THE AMERICAN NEGRO

RELIGIOUS INSTINCT. — LOYAL AND PATRIOTIC. — THE FREEDMAN. — HOMELESS AND ILLITERATE WHEN EMANCIPATED. — FIRST SCHOOLS DURING THE CIVIL WAR. — FREE NEGROES AND COLLEGE GRADUATES. — 50th ANNIVERSARY.

"All nations whom thou hast made shall come and worship before thee and glorify thy name." David.

RELIGIOUS INSTINCT

IN commendation of woman's loyalty and sense of obligation to our Lord Jesus, it has been said of her, "She was last at his cross and first at his grave, she staid longest there and was soonest here." In recognition of this fact when he rose from the dead he appeared first to one of them, Mary Magdalene.

To the credit of men of African descent, it may be said, that one of them performed the last act of kindness to our Lord Jesus, and the first individual conversion, of which we have an account in the book of Acts, relates to another one.

Simon, who assisted Jesus to bear his cross to the place of crucifixion, was a native of Cyrene in North Africa. The eastern church canonized him as Simon, the Black one, because his was the high and holy honor of bearing for the weary Christ, his cross of shame and pain. Our Lord Jesus was not long in the black man's debt. A few hours later, he paid it back by bearing for him all his weary burdens, on the very cross the African had borne for him. That was a good start for the Black man.

Philip, directed by an angel of the Lord to go south and join himself to the chariot occupied by the Eunuch, a man of great authority under the Queen of Ethiopia, found him reading the prophet Isaiah. Explaining the scriptures to him the eunuch confessed his faith in Jesus, was baptized with water found at the roadside and resumed his journey, homeward from Jerusalem, rejoicing. The record of this Black man's conversion is the first one of an individual in the book of Acts.

The religious trait of the American Negro has often been the subject of favorable comment. He has never, in all his history, been swayed by the false teachings of infidels, atheists or anarchists.

Dan Crawford, a Scotch missionary, the successor of Livingstone in the central part of the dark continent, recently stated he had discovered the fact, that the most ignorant and degraded natives of central Africa, have a religious instinct, that includes a belief in one God and the immortality of the soul.

Penetrating the jungles of the interior beyond the reach of a previous explorer, he found a tribe of nearly nude cannibals. He saw one of them eating human flesh. Meeting Ka la ma ta, their chief, the next day in the presence of several hundred of his tribe, he made special inquiry in regard to their knowledge of God. The result was an astounding surprise.

Kalamata, gave their name of God as Vi de Mu ku lu the Great King. When further questioned he said:

"We know there is a God for the same reason we know where the goats went on a wet night, when we see their deep foot-prints in the mud. We see the sun and the sun sees us. We see the wonderful mountains and the flowing streams, and both tell us there is a God. He is the one who sends the rain. No rain, nothing to eat; no God, no anything."

Concerning a future life he expressed the thought, the body is the cottage of the soul. The dead do not really die. When one dies they do not say, "he departed", but "he has arrived."

The American Negro, like his native ancestor, has always manifested this religious instinct.

Under the influence of a natural instinct the bee invariably builds its cell in the same form for the next brood and the storage of honey for it; the butterfly prepares the cradle and food for offspring it never sees, and the migratory birds follow the sun northward in the spring and southward on the approach of winter. All this is natural instinct.

Religious instinct is something very different from the natural instinct of any creature. It is a natural power possessed by man alone, and has its sphere in the human conscience. Paul, writing to the Romans in regard to the barbarians of his day, observed, "God is manifest in them, for the invisible things of God, even his eternal power and Godhead, are clearly seen by the things that are made."

LOYAL AND PATRIOTIC

The Negro in America has always been loyal and patriotic. He has rendered a voluntary service in the army and navy of the United States that is worthy of special commendation. The records of the war department show that the number of colored soldiers, participating in the several wars of this country was as follows:

Revolutionary War, 1775-1781   3,000
War of 1812   2,500
Civil War, 1861-1865   178,975

In the war with Spain in Cuba in 1898 the first troops that were sent to the front were four regiments of colored soldiers, and the service they rendered was distinguished by bravery and courage.

THE FREEDMAN, HOMELESS AND ILLITERATE

In 1860 the number of Negroes that were in a state of slavery was 3,930,760. In 1910 their number in the southern states had increased to 9,000,000; and in the northern states to 1,078,000.

The Emancipation Proclamation of President Lincoln was issued January 1, 1863, but it was preceded by a preliminary one on September 22, 1862, that gave the public a notice of 100 days of the coming event.

The Act of Emancipation that severed the relation binding them to their masters, left them in a very forlorn and deplorable condition. They were homeless and penniless in a country, that had been rendered more or less desolate, by the ravages of war and bloodshed. No provision had ever been made for the spread of intelligence among them. It has been estimated that only about five per cent of them at that time could read and write. Their homeless and illiterate condition rendered them comparatively helpless and dependent.

In 1885 the number of voters enrolled among the Freedmen was 1,420,000 and of these as many as 1,065,000 were then unable to read and write. These illiterate voters then represented the balance of power in eight southern states and one sixth of the national electoral vote. This was a matter of vital importance to the nation as well as the states.

In 1900 the per centage of the Freedmen that could

read and write had been increased to 55.5 per cent. and in 1910 to 69.3 per cent.

At this latter date however only 56.3 per cent of their children, of a school age, were enrolled as attending school, which left more than one million yet to be provided for.

FIRST PUBLIC SCHOOL

The first day school among the Freedmen was established at Fortress Monroe, Virginia, by the American Missionary Association on September 17, 1861. This school became the foundation of Hampton Institute, to which the ragged urchin wended his way on foot and slept the first night under a wooden pavement, that has since been known as Booker T. Washington.

In 1862 similar schools were established at Portsmouth, Norfolk, and Newport News, Virginia; Newbern and Roanoke Island, North Carolina, and Port Royal, South Carolina. In December of that year Gen. Grant assigned Col. John Eaton the supervision of the Freedmen in Arkansas, with instruction to establish schools where practical.

After the Emancipation Proclamation of January 1, 1863, schools for the Negroes began to be established in those parts of the south occupied by the Federal armies, General Banks establishing the first ones in Louisiana.

In 1865 the Freedman's Bureau was established, and it made the maintenance of schools one of its objects until 1870, when it was discontinued. The work has since been left to the supervision of the several states, aided by the generosity of the friends of Christian education through the missionary agencies of their respective churches.

It is estimated that since 1870 the Freedmen, who constitute nearly one half the population of the southern states have received for the support of their schools, only one eighth of the public funds appropriated for the maintenance of common schools. In the rural districts teachers only are furnished, and these are supplied on the condition the Freedmen in the district build, furnish and maintain the school building, the same as they do their church buildings.

The number of free Negroes in the United States in 1860 was 487,970. The states having the greatest number of them were Pennsylvania, New York, Ohio, Maryland, Virginia and North Carolina.

A few of these had become graduates of colleges before the war and were thus fitted for intelligent leadership. The beginning and increase in number of these colored college graduates has been as follows; In 1829, 1; in 1849, 7; in 1859, 12; in 1869, 44; in 1879, 313; in 1899, 1,126; and in 1909, 1,613. About 700 of them have graduated from our northern colleges the largest number having attended Oberlin college at Oberlin, Ohio, and Lincoln University at Oxford, Pennsylvania. In 1910 the whole number that had graduated was 3,856.

50th ANNIVERSARY

The 50th anniversary of the Emancipation Proclamation was observed by a number of the states in September, 1913. In Pennsylvania it consisted of an exposition at the city of Philadelphia, that lasted one month. The exhibit, showing the progress of the negroes from their infantile condition of 50 years ago, was characterized as "wonderful", and the occasion, one for devout thanksgiving and encouragement on the part of those, who have labored patiently and faithfully for their civil, social, moral or religious development.

The Presbyterian was the only one of the white churches that attempted an exhibit of its work at this exposition. Its exhibit consisted of photographs of churches and schools, and accounts of the results of the work. It included specimens of industrial work done in the schools by the sewers, cabinet workers and other artisans. It was under the direction of Rev. John M. Gaston, field secretary of the Presbyterian Board of Missions for Freedmen.

V

THE PROBLEM OF THE FREEDMAN

DIFFERENT STANDPOINTS.—REPRESENTATION IN CONGRESS.—13th, 14th AND 15th AMENDMENTS.—NEGRO SENATORS AND REPRESENTATIVES.—DISFRANCHISEMENTS.—RESULTS CONTRARY TO EXPECTATION.—PROVIDENTIAL LEADING OF JOSEPH, ISRAEL, NEHEMIAH AND DANIEL SUGGESTIVE.—A DIVINE MISSION.—THE FREEDMAN'S FRIENDS.—FRIENDLY COUNSELS.—THE GOLDEN RULE.

"Justice and judgment are the habitation of thy throne; mercy and truth shall go before thy face."
"Righteousness exalteth a nation but sin is a reproach to any people."

THE "Problem of the Negro" is an old and familiar phrase. It relates to the fact, that, however many and great have been the benefits derived from his labor and loyalty, the best management of him has been a troublesome problem to the statesmen of this country, ever since the declaration of independence, and especially the Freedman, since his emancipation.

Like a prism or cube, this problem has several sides, but unlike these symbols, its various sides are unlike each other. The solution of it has always appeared to be different when viewed from different angles of vision. Observers in one part of our country unite in saying, "this is the best way to solve this problem," while others in another section insist, they know a better way. The statesman

THE PROBLEM OF THE FREEDMAN   47

views it from one point of view, the labor leader from another and the Christian philanthropist from still another standpoint.

The first part of this problem, the one relating to the fact of his freedom, has already been solved. The solution of this introductory part of the problem caused preliminary struggles in Kansas and other places, including the Civil War. It served to bring out that which was noblest and best in Harriet Beecher Stowe, William Lloyd Garrison, Frederic Douglass, Henry Ward Beecher, Horace Greeley, Charles Summer, Abraham Lincoln and others.

The parts that remain to be solved relate to his uplift from ignorance, poverty and degradation, to the attainment of the ability to support himself, by a fair chance in the labor market, and the enjoyment of approved educational, religious and political privileges.

He has been accorded the right to own property, and is enjoying that right to the full extent of his ability to acquire and hold it.

He has been accorded limited educational and religious privileges, and has made a very commendable progress along both of these lines.

It is at this point we reach the difficult and unsolved part of the problem.

The intelligent and prosperous portion of them in the South, though native and loyal Americans, are discriminated against, and denied rights and recognitions, that are accorded other nationalities, though illiterate. The popular reason assigned, for locally withholding from all of them certain privileges of citizenship, is the fact that a great number of them continue to be illiterate.

In several of the states the Freedman is denied the privilege of enjoying the instruction of competent white teachers in their state and public schools, and in all of them he is prohibited from attending white schools, as in Pennsylvania and other northern states. The discriminations against them are so general, that it is almost impossible for any of them to acquire skill as workmen, or become fitted to serve their own people in the professions, except from those of their own number, or institutions of learning provided specially for them.

REPRESENTATION IN CONGRESS

During the last forty years, the Freedmen have been counted as a part of the population, in apportioning the districts for the election of Representatives in the Congress of the United States. This inclusion of their number, in the arrangement of the districts, has enabled the states to which they belong, to have a considerable number of additional congressmen, that they would not have had, if the districts had been arranged according to the white population, which alone has been permitted to vote.

Since 1910 the additional number of Congressmen, representing the suppressed vote of the Freedmen, has been 32 in a total of 82 members. These additional representatives, based on the population representing the suppressed vote of the Freedmen, have come from the different states as follows: Alabama, 5; Arkansas, 2; Florida, 1; Georgia, 6; Louisiana, 4; Mississippi, 5; North Carolina, 4; South Carolina, 4; Texas, 1. Total, 32.

This is an unexpected and a rather anomalous condition. It places the Freedmen in this country on a plane somewhat similar to that accorded the Philippines and Porto

THE PROBLEM OF THE FREEDMAN 49

Ricans, as regards the matter of government and participation therein.

It also, however, suggests the goal towards which education, religion and consequent material prosperity are gradually uplifting the race. This goal is clearly expressed in the following amendments to the Constitution of the United States.

AMENDMENTS TO THE CONSTITUTION

Article XIII. Section I. Neither slavery nor involuntary servitude, except as a punishment for crime, whereof the party shall have been duly convicted, shall exist within the United States, or any place subject to their jurisdiction. —(Ratified Dec. 18, 1865.)

Article XIV. Section I. All persons born or naturalized in the United States and subject to the jurisdiction thereof, are citizens of the United States, and of the state wherein they reside. No state shall make or enforce any law, which shall abridge the privileges or immunities of citizens of the United States; nor shall any state deprive any person of life, liberty or property, without due process of law, nor deny to any person within its jurisdiction the equal protection of the laws.

Section 2. Representatives shall be apportioned among the several states according to their respective numbers, counting the whole number of persons in each state, excluding Indians not taxed. But when the right to vote at any election for the choice of electors for president and vice-president of the United States, representatives in congress, the executive and judicial officers of a state, or the members of the legislature thereof, is denied to any of the male inhabitants of such state, being twenty-one years of age, and citizens of the United States, or in any way abridged, except for participation in rebellion or other crime, the basis of representation therein shall be reduced in the proportion, which the number of such male citizens shall bear to the whole number of male citizens twenty-one years of age in such state.—(Ratified July 28, 1868.)

Article XV. Section 1. The right of citizens of the United States to vote shall not be denied or abridged by the United States or by any state on account of race, color, or previous condition of servitude.

Section 2. The congress shall have power to enforce this article (or these articles) by appropriate legislation.—(Ratified March 30, 1870.)

NEGRO SENATORS AND REPRESENTATIVES

As a result of these amendments two negroes, one free born, the other a Freedman were elected to the United States senate, namely, Hiram R. Revels, 1870-1871; and Blanche K. Bruce, 1875-1881, both from Mississippi.

Twenty others have enjoyed the privilege of serving as representatives in congress, during the thirty-two years intervening between 1869 and 1901. The first of these was Jefferson Long of Georgia, who served alone in 1869 and 1870. During the next four years 1871 to 1874, there were four representatives, representing Alabama, Florida, Mississippi and South Carolina, the last having two colored representatives during this entire period. Their number was then reduced to two representatives, and finally to none since 1901, save that there were three during the terms commencing 1877, 1881 and 1883. Their last representatives were George W. Murray of South Carolina, 1893 to 1897; and George H. White of North Carolina, 1897 to 1901.

Five of these twenty representatives were re-elected and served terms of four years; three served six years, and Joseph H. Rainey of South Carolina enjoyed the unusual privilege of serving ten years, 1875 to 1885. Eight of them were from South Carolina, four from North Carolina, three from Alabama and one from Florida, Georgia, Louisiana, Mississippi and Virginia.

DISFRANCHISEMENTS

During the seventies and eighties the Freedmen were to a considerable extent disfranchised by means of "election devices, practices and intimidations."

THE PROBLEM OF THE FREEDMAN 51

Since 1890, when Mississippi took the lead, a number of the states have passed laws restricting the right of suffrage on their part to such tests as the payment of their annual taxes, previous to a certain date; ownership of a certain amount of land or personal property, the ability to read and write the constitution of the state or of the United States, and the "Grandfather Clause" which permits one unable to meet the educational or property tests to continue to vote, if he enjoyed that privilege, or is a lineal descendant of one that did so, previous to the date mentioned therein, usually 1867.

The following states have enacted laws containing the "Grandfather Clause:" South Carolina, Louisiana, Alabama, Virginia, North Carolina, Georgia and in 1910, Oklahoma. This part of the Oklahoma statute reads as follows:

"But no person who was on January 1, 1866, or at any time prior thereto, entitled to vote under any form of government, or who at that time resided in some foreign nation, and no lineal descendant of such person shall be denied the right to register and vote because of his inability to so read and write such Constitution."

RESULT CONTRARY TO EXPECTATION

This historic record, of representation in the highest legislative council of the nation, is very suggestive. That the Freedmen should have been accorded the largest number of representatives just after the dawn of freedom, when their general condition has always been described as extremely deplorable, that this number should have been gradually diminished with the spread of intelligence among them; and that finally they should have no representative during the last thirteen years, when their progress in education and material prosperity has been, at their fiftieth anniversary, declared to be "wonderful," certainly does not seem to be in accordance with what one intuitively would expect to be the natural order of things.

It is quite natural the present order of things should awaken and develop a feeling of protest on the part of the Freedmen, for they appreciate rights and privileges as well as other races and nations.

Their segregation, enforced on all alike in cities, public places and conveyances results also in many disappointing and humiliating experiences to those who are leaders among them.

The existing order is, however, an expression of local public sentiment and of the wisest statesmanship of those, who claim to be the best friends of the Freedman, because they live nearest to him and know better than others how to provide for his needs, including rights and privileges.

He enjoys the privileges of public protection to life, property and the pursuit of happiness, but to a considerable extent is denied the privilege of representation in making laws and exercising the power of government.

These historic facts relating to the gradual curtailment of the privilege of representation in legislation and government have been noted, not merely because they form an important part in a full statement of the negro problem, but as a prelude to the following facts, and suggestions to the Freedmen.

PROVIDENTIAL LEADING

The history of the negro in America has been one of providential leading and apparently to enable him to work out his own destiny. From the time the Dutch slave ship in 1619 landed the first importation, consisting of 20 slaves, at Jamestown, Virginia, to the present time, every important event or change in his condition has come to him from

THE PROBLEM OF THE FREEDMAN 53

others, who without aid or suggestion from him have been moved to act for him.

The experience of Joseph, in passing through the pit and the prison, on the way to his real mission, the experience of Israel in Egypt from the death of Joseph until the time of their deliverance at the Red Sea, and the experience of Nehemiah and Daniel, captives at Babylon, who were there providentially led and prepared for the most signal services of their lives, seem like historic parallels flashing from inspired Bible story, their comforting and prophetic light on the servile and dark experiences of the negro in America.

In all of these instances the persons were subject to the control of others, the way seemed dark, trying and utterly disappointing, and the opportunities, that prepared the way for important transitions, came unsought and in ways wholly unexpected. The things that proved of greatest importance in every instance were the intelligence, integrity, patience and piety of the individual.

The Godfearing integrity of Joseph was expressed when he resisted a great temptation by saying, "How can I do this great wickedness and sin against God?"

Israel in Egypt submissively and obediently undertook to make the full tale of brick when unsympathetic taskmasters withheld the usual and necessary amount of straw.

Nehemiah, a captive cupbearer of a heathen prince, won his confidence and when honorably permitted to return and rebuild the wall of Jerusalem, nobly answered his idle opposers, "I am doing a great work I cannot come down to you."

Daniel, when a captive youth, "purposed in his heart not to defile himself with the King's meat or the wine which he drank," or be swerved from his fidelity to the living and true God by threats of the lion's den. When the lives of the wise men of Babylon were in danger of being suddenly taken by royal command, he is introduced to King Nebuchadnezzar with the significant words, "I have found a MAN of the captives of Judah that will make known to the King the interpretation." He was a man whose power of vision enabled him to forecast the future correctly and possessed the courage to act prudently. Though a captive and denied many privileges, he proved himself an intelligent and trustworthy man and, serving as a special counsellor of five successive heathen kings, achieved for himself the worthy reputation of being the greatest statesman of his age.

All of these men discovered, that their imprisonment or captivity was a part of the divine plan, that providentially led and prepared them for their real mission, which in each instance proved to be one of prominent usefulness.

All of them were true patriots, but none of them were "office seekers" or "corrupt politicians." They loved more than any other their own native land, because of its sacred literature and religious institutions, but they were loyal and true to those who ruled over them in a foreign land. If any of them had manifested a political ambition, the divine plan, in regard to their promotion and usefulness, would have been immediately frustrated, and the memory of their names would have perished with their generation.

A DIVINE MISSION

May we not believe that God had a plan and purpose, in bringing the negro to the christian colonies, that established our government on the fundamental principles of

THE PROBLEM OF THE FREEDMAN

civil and religious liberty. His condition during the period of servitude, which lasted 246 years, was perhaps in many places but little worse than that of most of his kinsmen in Africa, during this same period; while now, at the end of the first fifty years of freedom, the condition and prospects of the intelligent and prosperous ones among them, are declared to be better than those enjoyed by their kinsmen, any where on earth.

THE FREEDMAN'S FRIENDS

The Freedman has hosts of friends, who are interested in his welfare. He has interested neighbors, amongst whom he lives, and also friends at a distance. Both are trying to solve the problem of his true relation to American institutions and privileges. While both have been co-operating together to a considerable extent and in a very commendable manner for the betterment of his condition, it remains to note however that if one is considered by the other as moving too slowly, or too rapidly, one acts as a gentle spur or check to the other.

This is the harmonizing process that is now going on among the friends of the Freedman. He is scarcely regarded as a participating factor in this harmonizing process. There are times when to him every new event seems to be one moving him in the wrong direction. His natural impulse, on experiencing these apparently adverse movements, is to raise the voice of bitter complaint against one set of his friends. When this is done in a personal or partisan way it is offensive and always does more harm than good. This method of procedure should therefore never be approved or adopted.

FRIENDLY COUNSELS

A respectful protest against a wrong and an appeal to have it removed, addressed to the person or body having the power to remove it, is an inherent right and a proper method of procedure whenever deemed advisable.

"Love thy neighbor as thyself" should be regarded as a fundamental principle by every Freedman. When the herdmen of Abraham and Lot had a little trouble over cattle and pastures, Abraham, who had received all the land by promise and Lot was really a troublesome intruder, discovered the greatness of his soul and settled the difficulty by saying to Lot,

"Let there be no strife, I pray thee, between me and thee, and between my herdmen and thy herdmen, for we be brethren.
"Is not the whole land before thee? Separate thyself from me, if thou wilt take the left hand, then I will go to the right, or if thou depart to the right hand, then I will go to the left."

Do not become impatient. Your friends at a distance, especially those in the churches, are generously endeavoring to help you to climb the ladder of progress, until a larger proportion of the race has been uplifted to the plane of an enlightened christian civilization.

That the Freedman, notwithstanding his wonderful progress during the last fifty years, is still in an infantile condition, is freely confessed. It was eighty years from the time the helpless babe was uplifted from the river, before Moses was called to be the leader and deliverer of Israel. The uplift from the river and training in his case came from the gentle hands of others. This fact is quite significant.

THE PROBLEM OF THE FREEDMAN 57

The Freedman who, avoiding the worthless and corrupt politician and over zealous office seeker, makes a good success of his farm and co-operates cordially with his friends and neighbors in effecting the educational and moral uplift of his race, will be happiest while he lives and do most to hasten the day, when political privileges, now temporarily withheld, will be restored to those who are found capable and worthy of their enjoyment.

If you happen to live in a state where your neighbor does not wish you to be a politician and hold office, do not worry. There are thousands of citizens every year and in all parts of our land, who do not vote and merely because they do not care to do so.

The voice of protest, against the useless and corrupt politician, is now heard in all parts of our land. In many of our cities, he has already been relegated to the junk heap, by the adoption of the commission form of government. Two of the states, Kansas and Oklahoma, are now vieing with each other, to see which shall be first to adopt the same system in the management of the public affairs of the state, and thus dispense with a lot of unnecessary public officials.

"A public office is a public trust" and affords an opportunity to render a useful and honorable service, but holding public office is not essential to the happiness and prosperity of any of us. An over eager desire to hold public office often suggests nothing more, than an effort to find employment for the idle. The better way, as in the cases of Saul and David, kings of Israel, and of Washington and Grant, commanders-in-chief of our armies, is to let the office seek the man.

THE GOLDEN RULE

"As ye would that men should do to you, do ye also to them."

The application of the Golden Rule to this part of this problem, suggests that every man is entitled to recognition according to his worth.

"Our country can fulfil its high mission among the nations of the earth, conferring lasting benefits on ourselves and all mankind, only by guaranteeing to its humblest citizen his just right to life, liberty, protection from injustice, the enjoyment of the fruits of his own labor and the pursuit of happiness in his own way, as long as he walks in the path of rectitude and duty and does not trespass upon the rights of others," declares ex-President Roosevelt.

"Morality, and not expediency, is the thing that must guide us," is the emphatic declaration of President Woodrow Wilson. The false assumption that "the end justifies the means has come from self-centered men, who see in their own interests the interests of the country, and do not have vision enough to read it in wider terms, the universal terms of equity and justice."

VI

VOICES FROM THE BLACK BELT

"If any man hear my voice and open the door."

IN a discussion of the Negro problem it is eminently appropriate the Freedman and his neighbor be accorded the privilege of expressing their respective views. The thoughts expressed in this chapter have been gleaned principally from the columns of the Afro-American, a colored weekly, published by the faculty of Biddle University, Charlotte, North Carolina.

The problem of the negro relates to his capacity for improvement and self-support. Is the American negro, after centuries of slavery, that kept the race in an infantile condition, capable of development and self support?

Over this question the people of our country have expressed differing opinions, many insisting that the servant condition is the better one for the American negro. The Presbyterian Standard, published at Charlotte, N. C., a section of country in which the latter sentiment still prevails, recently bore this testimony to their progress.

"While it is true of them as a mass that they are an infantile race, it is not true of them in many individual cases. There are thousands of them, who have advanced wonderfully during the last fifty years. They have made progress in every line. They are owning more farms every year, and in our cities they are buying homes, which sometimes would do credit to a more enlightened people. Their churches are not only built in better taste, but their preachers are becoming better educated, and are exerting a stronger moral influence than ever before."

This frank statement fairly represents the sentiment of the thoughtful christian people of the south. Some who have thought otherwise have been led to admit that, "while great advance has been made by a race only fifty years old, it is still in its infancy and therefore in the servant condition." Nor is it any exception in this respect.

Through adversity and hard treatment, the Irish people who first came to this country were largely in a servant condition. They accepted it. They became our domestics and built our railroads. But "Pat" is not on the railroad now. He is found occupying the seat of the chief justice, or serving as private secretary of the president and filling many other positions of honor and influence throughout the country.

What is thus true of the Irishman, is also true of other Europeans, who came to this country. It is an honor to them, that they truly appreciated their condition, accepted it and, through an honest and valiant struggle, rose above that condition to something better.

The American negro is now making it evident, that he is no exception to this general law of progress, under favorable conditions. It is neither necessary nor prudent to blind their eyes in regard to their real condition and status. Their best friends are those who encourage them to accept the situation in which they have been placed by an over ruling providence, and, through a noble endeavor, worthy of divine favor, rise to something better.

Their friends assist them best by aiding and encouraging them to make this noble endeavor, without which they cannot rise. The mass of the people must have native teachers and preachers to serve as leaders. This suggests the need of two kinds of educational facilities. A common industrial education, that will enable the mass of the people to achieve success in their daily avocations; and some special educational facilities of a higher grade, to prepare the needed supply of teachers, preachers and other leaders.

The mass of the people need an education, the scope of which will reach their physical, mental and spiritual natures. Their greatest need is instruction in the Bible, that it may exert its saving power on their early lives and animate them with noble aspirations.

THE CRY OF THE BLACK BELT

"They shall cry unto the Lord because of the oppressors and he shall send them a Saviour and a great one and he shall deliver them."—Isaiah.

The following appeal in behalf of the Freedmen, by Rev. A. W. Verner, D. D., president of Scotia Seminary, Concord, North Carolina, one of the five normal schools of the Presbyterian board, especially intended for girls, is so well and forcibly expressed, we are sure it will be appreciated by every reader.

"The urgent call from the black belt is the cry of souls in distress, the cry of humanity. Fifty years of unprecedented progress, in every line of industrial and intellectual pursuits and religious development, on the part of a considerable number of the colored people, show clearly, that the negro is capable of receiving and using to good advantage the education and training of the christian school.

"Industrial education, that lacks genuine christian culture, does not provide leaders of the right character to redeem the race, and many of our friends in the south do not care to open to the negro the doors of opportunity, to develop and manifest the best that is in him. It is therefore to the christian church of the north and to individuals, who have come to recognize the bond of human brotherhood, to whom this infant race still makes its appeal.

"The sad and degraded condition of great masses of the race in many localities of the south, ought to be an appeal, silent indeed but sufficiently strong, to awaken the sympathy of every one, capable of being touched by the cry of needy humanity. As a representative of the great Presbyterian church, that has called me into a very important and necessary field of her work, I earnestly appeal to our people to do more for the establishment and fostering of christian schools among the great masses of the black belt.

The christian church and the christian school have something to give, that can be gotten nowhere else. The public school where established and industrial training where available are good and necessary. But the christian school is still needed and very greatly, to give moral and spiritual ballast to the individual. The leaven of gospel power and purity is needed, to give moral strength to the character and the highest degree of usefulness in life.

CHRISTIAN EDUCATION

"Christian education is not narrow, it takes in every phase of training that is essential to produce a well developed and useful life. It touches and tints industrial training with a brighter and richer glow. It quickens the faculties of the mind, adds keenness to the power of perception, forms permanent habits of industry and strengthens the will or purpose to do right.

"Christian education emphasizes the fact that it is not merely book learning—storing the mind with knowledge of facts or training the hands to work, but includes moral elevation, as well as intellectual development. It includes everything that tends to make the life purer, better and more useful. It begets and fosters a spirit of hopefulness. It develops that patience and perseverance that is needed for the best performance of every day's duties.

"Christian education emphasizes personal purity, purity of the family life and the sacredness of the marriage relation. Its whole trend and effect is upward. Its genius is moral, spiritual, industrial, domestic, social and individual elevation. It creates a hunger and thirst for higher and better things. It is the mountain summit from whose height one gets a broader vision, a clearer view of the possibilities and demands of life and a truer conception of all human relations.

This is the provision that must be made for our black brother. Nothing less will meet his needs. A great responsibility rests with negro leaders who have attained a good degree of intelligence and refinement, but a greater responsibility still rests upon the people of richer blessing and greater power.

"If the spirit of true democracy, which declares, 'opportunity for every one, according to his capacity and merit,' and the spirit of christianity, whose principle is, 'Help for the weaker as the stronger is able to give it,' be exercised toward the negro, many of the difficulties will vanish, better conditions will prevail and more desirable results will be secured."

This cry of humanity from the black belt of our land is very touching and suggestive. It suggests the negro's greatest and most urgent needs, the Bible, the Bible school and the christian teacher.

It is the silent appeal of Joseph while passing through the pit and the prison in the land of Israel's enslavement. Beyond these dark and unpleasant experiences there awaited for Joseph a career of great usefulness in the land of his previous imprisonment.

Let us recognize the fact that God has a great use for the Freedman in this our native land, because he has providentially brought him here and increased his number so greatly.

A spirit of true patriotism, as well as the tie of christian brotherhood, prompts the lending of a helping hand and an encouraging word, while he solves the problem of his own destiny of great usefulness in the home, the school, the church, in the shop, on the farm and in the fields of professional opportunity and business activity.

It may be truly said of the Freedmen that they represent the poor of this world, of whom the Lord Jesus said, "Ye have the poor always with you, Me ye have not always. Inasmuch as ye have done it unto one of the least of these, my brethren, ye have done it unto Me."

VII
UPLIFTING INFLUENCES

FROM DARKNESS TO LIGHT.—AN HISTORIC COMPARISON.

"Look unto the rock whence ye were hewn, and to the hole of the pit whence ye were digged."—Isaiah 51:1.

FROM DARKNESS TO LIGHT

THE historic incidents, having an uplifting influence that occurred among the Choctaw Freedmen of Indian Territory, from the time of their first instruction in the Bible to the establishment and present development of Oak Hill Industrial Academy, when briefly summarized, seem like a reproduction on a miniature scale of those greater events that occurred among the Christian nations of Europe and America preceding the adoption of their systems of public instruction.

I. THE CHOCTAW FREEDMEN

Rev. Cyrus Kingsbury, a generous hearted missionary to the Indians, having charge of a church building at Doaksville, encourages the slaves in the vicinity to meet in it occasionally on Sabbath afternoons, for the purpose of receiving instruction in the Bible and shorter catechism.

This Bible instruction does not result in the organization of a church at that place, but opportunity is given for the manifestation and development of the religious instinct of a number of persons, amongst whom there are two young men, who were destined later to become influential leaders among the enslaved people whom they represented.

After their emancipation, one locates on the west bank of the Kiamichi river and later becomes known as Parson Stewart, the organizer and circuit rider of a sufficient number of churches, at the time of his decease in 1896, to form the Presbytery of Ki a mich i.

The other, accompanied by several personal friends, migrates fifteen miles eastward and founds a home in the Oak Hill neighborhood. In the course of a short time he is visited by the parson and his home becomes a house of worship, where a church is organized and Henry Crittenden is ordained as its ruling elder.

A Sunday school for Bible instruction follows the establishment of public worship, and two years later it is followed by the establishment of a week-day school, for the benefit of all the children and youth in the neighborhood. Eight years later, when the trained missionary teacher arrives, the inspiration of a new life is infused into the church and Sunday school, and the week-day school becomes an important industrial academy, where the Bible is the basis of the moral and religious instruction. In 1905 they receive an allotment of lands that they may become independent owners of their own homes. In 1908 statehood brings the rural public school and in 1912, an intelligent Freedman is entrusted with the management of the Industrial Academy, church and farm.

This sequence of events includes the dark period of slavery and illiteracy followed by instruction in the Bible, the light of the world; the development of the native preacher of the gospel as a leader, the organization of the church, followed by the Sunday school, the week-day school, the

UPLIFTING INFLUENCES

academy, normal, public school and finally a native superintendent of the academy and independent ownership of land.

II. THE EUROPEANS AND AMERICANS

THE DARK AGES

The period from the 8th to the 12th centuries of the christian era has been classed by historians as the "Dark Ages" of the world, because of the general prevalence in Europe of ignorance, superstition and barbarism. Some of the leading events that occurred during this gloomy period, immediately following the decline and fall of the Roman Empire, tended almost wholly to check the spread of intelligence and the prosperity of the people, rather than to promote their welfare. The Scrptures were neglected and the clergy as well as the people became worldly, ignorant, selfish and superstitious.

THE SARACENS AND NORMANS

These unfavorable events included, at the beginning of this period, the invasion of Palestine and southern Europe including Spain, its most western state, by the Mohammedans of Arabia, often called Saracens and Infidels, who were fanatically inflamed with a passion to destroy with the sword all the people of the world, who would not obey Mohammed, their prophet. During the next century Germany, Britain, Holland and France, then called Gaul, were ruthlessly invaded by conquering hordes of the adventurous and barbarous Normans, who came from Norway, Sweden and Denmark, countries north of the Baltic Sea.

THE CRUSADERS OR CROSS-BEARERS

These invasions were followed by the period of the Crusaders, 1096 to 1271, when as many as seven great armies or multitudes of people were assembled at the call of the popes, and wearing crosses on their shoulders, marched through the intervening countries to Palestine. Their object was to rescue the city of Jerusalem and the holy sepulchre from the infidels. The first crusade was organized in France, and it enlisted an army of 800,000. Godfrey, duke of Lorraine, was placed in command, and the multitude was arranged for the march in three divisions. Peter, the hermit, a wrong-headed monk, was appointed leader of the first division and experienced an inglorious and irreparable defeat on the way. Godfrey, after the siege and conquest of Jerusalem in 1099, was chosen King to rule over Palestine and the holy city, as his kingdom. At the time of his coronation he made the noble remark, that,

"He could not bear the thought of wearing a crown of gold in that city, where the King of Kings had been crowned with thorns."

The brave soldier and manly man, who gave expression to this noble sentiment, died the next year.

Under weak and unskilful chiefs the crusaders while on the way wandered about like undisciplined bands of robbers, plundering cities, committing the most abominable enormities, and spreading misery and desolation wherever they passed. There was no kind of insolence, injustice and barbarity of which they were not guilty. The seven successive crusades drained the wealth of the fairest provinces and caused the loss of a prodigious number of people.

Those of the first crusade, that remained in Palestine, were divided by sordid ambition and avarice, and in 1187 Saladin, sultan of Egypt and Syria, the most valiant chief of the Mohammedan warriors, recaptured Jerusalem and subsequent crusaders were not able to regain it.

UPLIFTING INFLUENCES

FIRST RAYS OF LIGHT

The first rays of light, that serve to dispel the darkness of prevailing night, may be briefly summarized in the following leading events.

In 901 **Alfred the Great**, king of England, founds a seminary at Oxford to promote the study of sacred literature. Later it becomes a university, the first one in Europe, and it is still distinguished as one of the greatest institutions in the world for publishing the Scriptures in a form suited for the use of preachers and christian teachers. Two centuries later the second university is founded at Cambridge, England.

About 1170 **Peter Waldo** of Lyons, France, committing to memory such portions of the Scriptures as he could obtain, and taking for his favorite saying, the command of our Lord to the rich youth, "If thou wilt be perfect, go and sell that thou hast, and give to the poor, and thou shalt have treasure in heaven, and come, follow me," commences to preach the gospel, as the Apostles had done, in the homes of the people and in their market places. As he attracts followers, who also commit portions of the Scriptures, he sends them out like the seventy, two and two, to preach the Word of God. They are called Waldenses, after the name of their leader, and oppose corrupt doctrines and practices with the plain truths of the Word of God. They oppose the crusades, as fanatical expeditions on the part of those who were not Jews, and therefore were unjust and unlawful. They insist the church consists not merely of the clergy or priests, but includes the whole family of believers.

The advocacy of these principles and by laymen, causes them to be excommunicated, then anathematized and finally to be condemned by a council at Rome in 1179. Peter

Waldo, their leader, flees from land to land, preaching as he goes and dies in Bohemia in 1197.

In 1215, King John of England, yielding to the insistent demand of the barons, issued the Magna Charta, (Great Charter) the first grant of English constitutional liberty, pledging the right of trial by jury and protection of life, liberty and property from unlawful deprivation. It is immediately denounced by the pope, Innocent III, who absolves the king from all obligation to keep the pledges therein expressed and solemnized by the royal oath.

In 1366 **John Wiclif,** a graduate of Oxford and member of the English Parliament, presents to that body indisputable reasons, why, without the approval of the Parliament, not even the king of England could make their lands subject to a tax claimed by a foreign sovereign, representing the papacy. As a religious leader, he instructs his followers, called "poor priests," to pass from village to village and city to city, and to preach, admonish and instruct the people in "God's Law." He accomplishes the translation of the Latin Vulgate into the English of his day, that his countrymen might have the Scriptures in their own language.

Charles V, king of France, has the scriptures translated into the French language, for the enlightenment of his people.

During this 14th century seventeen universities are founded and they include the one at Geneva in Switzerland, Heidelberg in Germany and Prague in Bohemia.

THE MORNING STAR

In 1401 John Huss of Bohemia, the Morning Star or John Baptist of the Reformation, appears as "the voice of one crying in the wilderness." His mother, left a widow in early life, gave him to the service of the Lord as he lay in

BIDDLE UNIVERSITY, CHARLOTTE, N. C.

BETHESDA MISSION, WYNNEWOOD, OKLA.

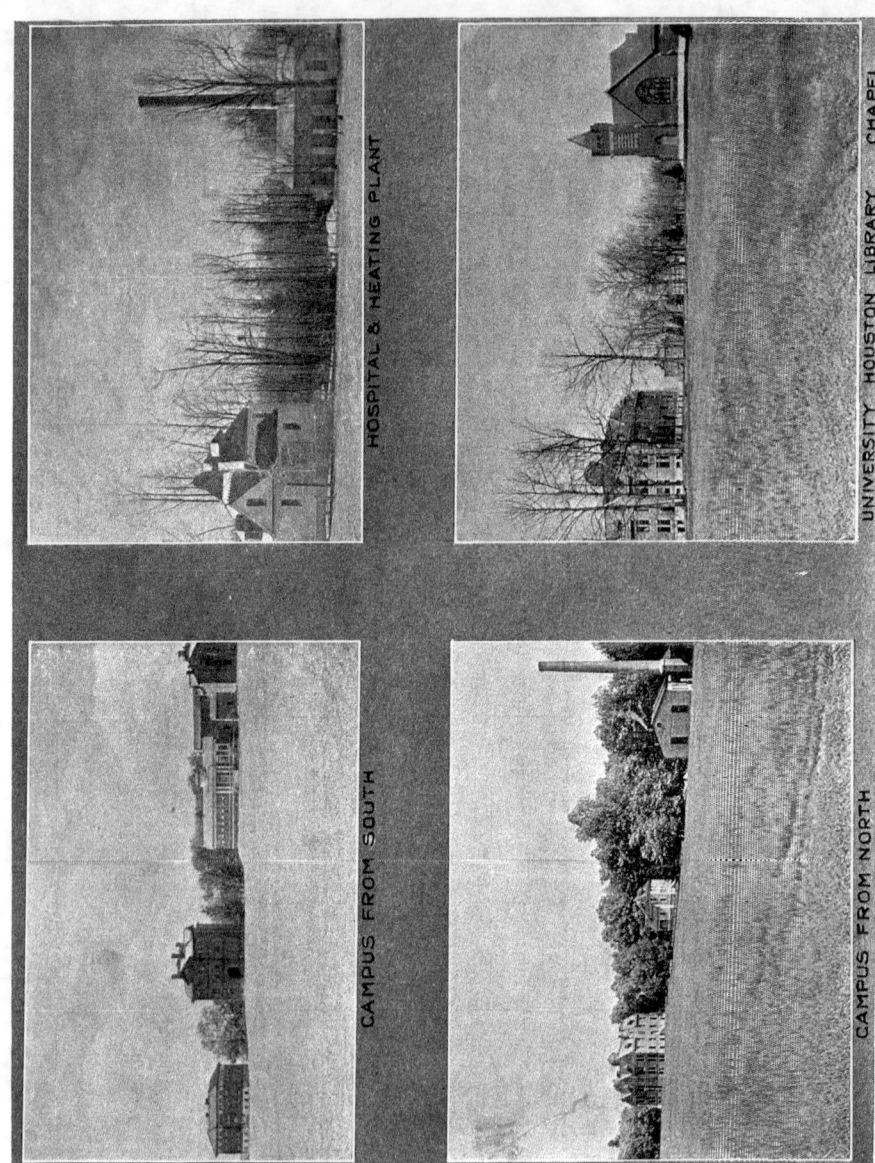

UPLIFTING INFLUENCES.

the cradle, and later, like Hannah of old, took him to the school at Prague.

When he became a preacher he found the Lord's vineyard a desert, the ministers of religion, the priests, ignorant, worldly and dissolute, and the popes of that period no better than the priests. The people, designedly chained to the basest superstitions and following the example of their leaders, have cast aside the restraints of chastity and morality. His heart touched with pity at the sight of the religious destitution of the people, his anger, like that of Moses "waxed hot" against those, who should have given them the gospel of their salvation. Encouraged by the example of Wiclif to make known the truth, he affirms the supreme authority of the scriptures, proclaims against the abuse of the clergy and endeavors to regenerate the religious life of both priests and people. His glowing zeal for the honor of God and the church move the people in a way until then unknown; but the priests, unwilling to reform or longer endure his piercing protests, falsely accuse him of heresy. In 1416, after fifteen years of selfdenying and heroic service, he is condemned at Constance and suffers martyrdom at the stake. A century later Luther, who imbibed his heroic spirit, said of him, "The gospel we now have was born out of the blood of John Huss."

THE FIRST PRINTED BIBLE

The art of printing is invented and the Vulgate, a Latin Bible, is the first book printed. It is issued in 1450 and is printed on a hand press at Mentz, Germany. Previous to this event and date all books were in the form of costly manuscripts and their number could be increased, only one copy at a time, by penmen called copyists.

The mariners compass is invented and in 1492 Columbus discovers America, and thirty years later Magellan sails around the world.

During this 15th century the universities of Glasgow and St. Andrews are founded in Scotland, Mentz and eighteen others, on the continent.

III. THE REFORMATION
MARTIN LUTHER
"Arise, shine, for thy Light is Come."

In 1517, Martin Luther, the apostle of the German nation, a man of learning and undaunted courage, whose equal had not been known since the days of Paul, appears as the valiant and steadfast leader of the Reformation in Germany. In 1530 he becomes the founder of the Evangelical Lutheran church, and aided by Melancthon, succeeds in translating and giving to the German people the Bible in their own language, and in preparing the Augsburg confession that has since served as a standard of faith and bond of union for the Lutheran churches in Europe and America.

Emotion and imaginative piety have become the handmaids of superstition; and patriotism, lacking courage, has covered its face. He writes hymns and patriotic songs, that inspire the German heart with loyalty to the truth and devotion to their Fatherland.

JOHN CALVIN

In 1527, John Calvin, a man of great learning and glowing eloquence with burning zeal for the honor of his Master, appears as the leader of the Reformation in France, but nine years later, joins Farrel, the successor of the zealous but fallen Zwingli, in Switzerland, and becomes head of the

UPLIFTING INFLUENCES 73

university at Geneva. He secures the adoption of a constitution, that gave and also limited the authority of the church to spiritual, and of the state to temporal matters; and thus prepares the way for the separation anew of church and state, and the enjoyment of civil and religious liberty.

Educated for the priesthood, he is assigned a parish and there obtained a copy of the Scriptures. When he discovered the erroneous teaching and practices of the church of Rome, he resigns his charge and completes a course in law and another in theology in the University of Paris. He becomes a man void of fear and is borne onward on the wings of a living faith. Following the example of Paul in his letters to the churches, and of Augustine, bishop of Hippo (391-446) in North Africa, he undertakes to state in a systematic form the great facts and doctrines of the Bible, as one of the best means of opposing and overcoming prevailing errors and corrupt practices in church and state.

He feels the Spirit of God moving him to blazon triumphantly, the thought of God's sovereignty and man's utter dependency, in order to dash in pieces the prevalent selfrighteousness. His writings, by emphasizing the supreme authority of the Divine Word, have tended to raise the moral standard of individuals and communities, and by emphasizing the moral law, to lessen the distinction between the "sins" of the Bible and "crimes" of the civil law. Their tendency has been to make the moral law the rule for states as well as persons.

Presbyterianism, or government of the church by ruling elders and presbyters as in the apostolic period, and Republicanism, government by representatives, are advocated with transcendent ability, and success. After the death of Luther in 1546, Calvin exerts a great influence over the thinking men of that notable period in Switzerland, France, Germany, Holland, Italy, England and Scotland. The young preachers, sent out from the university at Geneva, establish 2,150 reformed congregations in these countries, and in 1564, the last year of his life, the confession of the reformed churches in France is officially recognized by the state.

An ardent and effective friend of civil liberty, he makes the city of his adoption the nursery of a pure, noble civilization; and the little republic of Geneva becomes the sun of the European world. Animated by his example and principles, William, prince of Orange, in 1580, establishes the Dutch Republic in Holland, and it becomes "the first free nation to put a girdle of empire around the world."

Bancroft, the historian, in summarizing the influences that contributed to American Independence makes this creditable reference to Calvinism.

"We are proud of the free states that fringe the Atlantic. The Pilgrims of Plymouth were Calvinists, the best influences in South Carolina came from the Calvinists of France. William Penn was a disciple of the Huguenots; the ships from Holland, that in 1614 brought the first colonists to Manhattan (New York), were filled with Calvinists. He that will not honor the memory and respect the influence of Calvin, knows but little of the origin of American Liberty."

WILLIAM TYNDALE

In 1530 Henry VIII aided by William Tyndale, the new translator of the New Testament and Pentateuch, and in 1547 Edward VI, his successor, promote the establishment of the Reformation in England. A change of rulers in 1553 leads to the martyrdom of Archbishop Cranmer, bishops,

Latimer and Ridley, and of John Rogers, the zealous reformer—four of the noblest men England ever produced.

It was the noble-hearted, youthful Tyndale who, when he came to perceive that the Word of God was the gift of God to all mankind and all had a right to read it, that declared to one of the clergy opposing him, "If God spares my life, ere many years, I will cause a boy that driveth the plow to know more of the Scriptures than you do."

JOHN KNOX

In 1560, John Knox, a pupil of Calvin, establishes the Reformation in Scotland and under his leadership the church of Scotland from the first adopts the system of doctrines and the forms of worship and of government established at Geneva.

HUGUENOTS OF FRANCE

In 1557, Admiral Coligny, taken prisoner at the battle of St. Quentin, is confined at Gaud in Spain. Securing a copy of the Scriptures he reads it, and, after his release, becomes the enthusiastic leader of the Hu gue nots of France. They represent the most moral, industrious and intelligent of the French people, but those who love the "Mass", which involves no moral obligation, hate them on account of their chaste and devout lives. In 1572, when a bloody persecution arises against them, they begin to emigrate to England, Germany, Netherlands, Switzerland and the Colonies of North America.

It was Fenelon, one of the preachers of the Huguenots in France under the feudal system, about the year 1710, that gave utterance to the patriotic sentiment, emphasized in this country since the rise of the great trusts, "That governments exist and have a right to exist, only for the good of the people, and that the many are not made for the use and enjoyment of one."

THE BIBLE

In 1559 the Puritans protest against the act of uniformity passed by the English Parliament, imposing uniformity in religious worship.

The Bible has now come to be regarded as of so much importance to the clergy and people, that as many as fifty-five learned men during this 16th century devote their time and attention to its exposition and illustration; and twenty-seven new universities are established.

The Reformation is an insurrection or revolution against ecclesiastical monarchy and absolute power in the church, or spiritual matters. It establishes freedom of inquiry and liberty of mind in Europe. The Bible and theology occupy the attention of the greatest minds, and every question, whether philosophical, political or historical is considered from the religious point of view.

THE INQUISITION

In 1235, Pope Gregory IX, establishes the Inquisition, a cruel court of inquiry for the suppression of those who question the authority of the papacy to rule over them in the church. It becomes very active in Italy, France, Spain, Portugal and Ireland. It is not suppressed in France until 1834, after a period of six centuries.

In 1540, Ignatius Loy o la, an illiterate Spanish soldier and priest, with papal authority, organizes the society of the Jesuits, to require christians to renounce whatever opinions may separate them, and, accepting the doctrines and worship of the Roman Catholic church to acknowledge the pope as Christ's sole vicegerent on earth.

UPLIFTING INFLUENCES 77

The Inquisition had previously proved a bloody court but this order is intended to make it more effective in suppressing freedom of thought and action in matters relating to education and religion.

The events that occur during the period of the Inquisition are harrowing to relate. The historians of that period have recorded, among others, the following executions and massacres.

The duke of Alva, a Spanish general and persecutor who died in 1582, condemned 36,000 of his countrymen to be executed.

On the night of August 24, 1572, the anniversary of St. Bartholomew, Charles IX, of France, by offering his sister in marriage to the prince of Navarre, a Huguenot, assembles at the nuptials in Paris five hundred of the most prominent of the Huguenots, including Admiral Coligny, their venerable leader, and, at a given signal an unparalleled scene of horror ensues. Before the break of day, these noble leaders and 10,000 of their faithful followers, in Paris that night, are ruthlessly slaughtered. The horrid carnage, against these defenceless friends of truth and right, is extended to Lyons, Orleans, Rouen and other cities until 50,000 are massacred at this particular time. The total loss of France by the Inquisition has been estimated at 100,000 persons.

It is estimated that, during a period of seven years Pope Julius II effected the massacre of 200,000 persons. The Irish massacre at Ulster in 1641 cost Ireland the loss of more than 100,000 of her best citizenship. It is estimated that during a period of thirty years as many as 900,000 persons suffered martyrdom for the truth at the hands of the secret order of Jesuits. During the entire period of persecution by the papacy, a vast multitude, numbering many millions in addition to these, were proscribed, banished, starved, suffocated, drowned, imprisoned for life, buried alive, burned at the stake or assassinated.*

These dark historic events illustrate the price that had to be paid for letting the light shine when darkness prevailed in the high places of the world. Every martyr for the truth was a torch bearer, whose light was extinguished. The countries that suffered the greatest loss of their best citizenship received a check of more than a century's growth. The hand on the dial of progress was turned backward wherever the blighting inquisition was felt. Its blighting effects may yet be seen in Italy, Spain, Portugal, Ireland and other countries where the papacy exerts a controlling influence. Men, whose deeds are evil and they are unwilling to repent, hate the light and endeavor to suppress it, by killing the torch bearer, "lest their deeds should be reproved."

A knowledge of these conditions that prevailed at the time is necessary to enable one to appreciate the importance and greatness of the work of the Reformers and their faithful followers during the 16th century in giving the Bible to the people at the risk of their lives.

INDEPENDENT OWNERSHIP OF LAND

In 1620 the Pilgrim Fathers, bringing with them the Bible as a precious treasure, establish a colony at Plymouth Rock, Massachusetts, where they hope to enjoy civil and religious liberty to a fuller extent than they were able to do elsewhere. Other colonies are established along the Atlantic coast, from New England to Georgia, but no one of them exerts a moral influence, quite so potent as this one,

---

*See Cottage Bible on Revelation XVII 6.

UPLIFTING INFLUENCES 79

in the events and councils that precede the laying of the foundations for this great government.

They now enjoy individual or independent ownership of lands, a privilege they did not enjoy under the feudal system that had its rise in the 10th century and was continued until the French Revolution in 1799. Under the feudal system the land was owned by dukes, earls and barons, who, as members of the House of Lords, alone participated in the government.

The orators of the pulpit, commonly called preachers of the gospel, aside from the academies, colleges and universities, are the principal teachers of the people, and for the purpose of instruction, they use but one book—the Bible.

In 1635 other colonies of Puritans, under Roger Williams and Thomas Hooker settle Rhode Island and Connecticut, respectively; and religious liberty is accorded Rhode Island by its charter in 1663.

WESTMINSTER ASSEMBLY

In 1648, the Westminster Assembly, convened by the Long Parliament five years previous, and composed of 10 Lords, 20 Commoners and 121 Clergymen, representing the churches in England, Scotland and Ireland, to prepare a statement of the doctrines of the Bible, that might form the basis of religious liberty and a bond of union of the Protestant churches, completes its work, by publishing a Confession of Faith, Form of Government, Larger and Shorter Catechisms. This confession does not give rise to any new denominations nor result in any union; but it is received and adopted as the standard of faith by all the branches of the Presbyterian church in England, Scotland,

Ireland and America. This confession is a natural sequence of the authorized King James Version of the Bible in 1611.

In 1704, the newspaper is established in America; and the first postoffice, in 1710.

RISE OF METHODISM

In 1738 John and Charles Wesley, young preachers of the Church of England, having spent three years as missionaries among the Moravians in Georgia, return to London, where, preaching the gospel as a proclamation of free forgiveness to sinners, and with it, repentance and faith in Christ, they soon find the pulpits of that city closed against them. Supported by Lady Huntington and aided at the first by George Whitefield, the most gifted of their early associates and the first Methodist to preach in the open air, they lay the foundations that soon develop into the Methodist church, by establishing new congregations and organizing them into classes, each under a local leader, who by means of weekly testimonies, exhortations and corrections was to look after the moral conduct and promote the spiritual life of the members.

SUNDAY SCHOOLS AND MISSIONARY SOCIETIES

In 1782 when there are a sufficient number of printed Bibles available for use, Robert Raikes of London makes the suggestion and Sunday schools are established, that the people in every worshipping congregation may co-operate with their preachers in instructing the young and rising generation in the great truths contained in the Bible.

From 1792 to 1800, the three great modern missionary societies of England are organized, and during the next ten years the first two are organized in this country.

In 1804, the British and Foreign Bible Society, and in

1816, the American Bible Society, are established in London and New York, to promote the multiplication and circulation of the Bible.

CIVIL AND RELIGIOUS LIBERTY

In 1776 the Declaration of Independence and American Revolution develop brave and patriotic leaders like George Washington, Thomas Jefferson, Samuel Adams, John Adams, Benjamin Franklin, Patrick Henry, John Witherspoon and others, who fight the battles and solve the problems of civil and religious liberty in America. Liberty and independence become familiar watchwords.

In 1787 when the Constitution of the United States is adopted, civil and religious liberty is assured. Protection is to be given to religion but there shall be no taxation for its support in church or school, and public education is left to the several states.

Those, who framed this remarkable Constitution and thus prepared the way for America to become the land of "Liberty Enlightening the World," expressed their sentiments in regard to the urgent need of general instruction in the Bible, in the ordinance for the government of the Northwest—the country north of the Ohio, as follows: "Religion, morality and knowledge, being necessary to good government and the happiness of mankind, schools and the means of education shall forever be encouraged."

In 1841 Congress makes provision for grants of unoccupied lands in the states for the better support of the public schools and the establishment of state universities.

In 1862 Congress makes provision by further grants of unoccupied lands for the establishment of State Agricultural Colleges. About this same period Normal Schools are established in the states and they gradually take the place of many of the Academies previously established by Christian people.

In 1863 Abraham Lincoln in order to maintain the Union "one and inseparable," becomes the emancipator of 4,000,000 slaves; and America becomes "the land of the free" as well as "the home of the brave."

The Boston News Letter, the first American newspaper is established in 1704, and the New England Courant, the second one in 1720. The first Colonial post office is established in 1710. In 1765, when the Stamp Act was passed, there are forty newspapers published in America; and one of the most influential of these is the Philadelphia Gazette, by Benjamin Franklin, the man who "wrested the lightning from heaven and scepters from tyrants."

The religious papers of the Presbyterian church are established a half century later, and as follows: The Herald and Presbyter, at Cincinnati in 1830; the Presbyterian at Philadelphia in 1831; and the Interior, now Continent, at Chicago in 1870. As a civilizing agency the press not only rivals but increases many fold the power of the pulpit.

The public press, especially the religious newspaper, noting the progress of events relating to the extension of the Redeemer's Kingdom becomes a very potent factor in promoting an enlightened Christian civilization.

UPLIFTING INVENTIONS

During the 19th century civilization receives a general and wonderful uplift as a result of many important inventions, that, to a greater or less extent, are enjoyed by all the people. They include the steam engine, steamer, railway, telegraph, telephone, phonograph, cylinder printing press and folder, electric light and motor, gasoline and kerosene engines, cotton gin, spinning jenny, sewing machine, mower, reaper, steam thresher and separator, mammoth corn sheller, tractor, gang plow, typewriter, automobile, bicycle, aeroplane, vaccine, serum and wireless telegraph.

THE COMPARISON.

The intelligent American citizen of the present time is the product of all these forces, to the extent he has come under their uplifting influences. He is the product of centuries of enlightened struggle and successful effort. If the early Roman was proud of his history and privileges as a citizen much more profoundly thankful may be the American of this twentieth century.

The forces that have given him the uplift from the Dark Ages include the Bible in his own language, the faithful preacher of the Gospel, the Evangelical Reformer, the brave Military Leader, the God-fearing Statesman, the Church, Sunday school, the public, high and Normal school, the Academy, Christian College, Agricultural College, University, ownership of land, civil and religious liberty.

What these institutions have done for the intelligent American citizen they are now beginning to do for the Freedman, as he is brought under their uplifting influence. They suggest both to him and his friends, the greatest or most important needs of the Freedmen.

VIII

THE PRESBYTERIAN CHURCH.

IT EMPHASIZES THE BIBLE AS FUNDAMENTAL IN EDUCATION.—A ZEALOUS MISSIONARY ORGANIZATION.—AS CATHOLIC IN SPIRIT AS THE GOSPEL.

"Walk about Zion, tell the towers thereof; mark ye well her bulwarks, that ye may tell it to the generation following."—David.

THE Presbyterian Church has always stood for Religion and Education—Religion as the basis of true education, and Education as the promoter of positive practical religion.

CHRISTIAN LEADERS.

The Presbyterian Church wishes to see the young people of every generation provided with the best means for their intellectual and spiritual progress. It wishes to see them prepared, not merely for active and successful participation in the onward work of the world, but also in full and hearty sympathy with the great work of Christ and his people, for the spiritual salvation of the nations. It knows there is no good reason, why a stirring leader of men should not be a Christian; nor why a Christian should not be eminently successful, in taking his place among men as a forceful factor in the life of the world.

The Presbyterian Church believes in the system of state schools from the primary, public and high schools, to the University. These schools provide for general education. Millions of children would never be in school, were it not for these state provisions and for compulsory public education. These schools are however not all perfect, since they do not provide for moral and religious training, the great underlying principles of reverence and righteousness, that must enter into every life in order to fit it for the performance of christian and patriotic duty.

The Presbyterian church takes a patriotic interest in our whole public school system, and believes that all the children should be trained in those that are under public direction, so that all the children and youth of the nation shall be a united, intelligent and patriotic body, fitted for good citizenship.

At the same time it believes in special church institutions of higher learning, that shall be adapted to train our young people for intelligent leadership in the church, and enable them to become doubly useful in the home, social circle and in public life. Our christian academies and colleges are valuable institutions. These furnish to the church and the world the greatest number of ministers, missionaries, college presidents and christian statesmen. Parents everywhere, find these christian institutions furnish the best advantages, and that they are the safest and most economical. No institutions furnish higher or more profitable culture. They combine all that is best in real culture and education of the intelligent faculties, with a true religious conception of life; so that all who yield to their best influences go forth from them pure-hearted, stronger and better prepared to engage in life's duties successfully; for they take with them the personal assurance of the gracious presence and abiding blessing of our Father in Heaven.

In a christian educational institution, the spirit of the instructor is one that regards the student, as of more value than the subject taught. Its aim including the christian college, is not research, the work of a university, but to make men. The ordinary branches that are taught are regarded as instrumentalities, for making a well trained man of the student.

The key to success in the battle of life, is found in the struggle, which insures control of one's self. This is the secret of a good education. In an important sense, all education must be self-education. Professor Huxley gave good emphasis to this thought when he wrote: "Perhaps the most valuable result of all education, is the ability to make yourself do the thing you have to do, when it ought to be done, whether you like it or not; it is the first lesson which ought to be learned, and, however early a man's training begins, it is probably the last lesson he learns thoroughly." An eminent educator used to say to his class: "He, who will become a scholar, must learn to command his faculties."

The Presbyterian church honors God and exalts him to the throne of absolute supremacy over all his creatures. It honors Him by using the instrumentalities he has appointed. It receives the Bible, as the very word of God, and adopts it as the only rule of faith and practice.

The Presbyterian church from the beginning has been a zealous missionary organization. At the meeting of the First General Assembly arrangements were made to send the gospel to "the regions beyond,"—the frontiers and the various tribes of American Indians. The agencies, then organized as committees, have become the great Boards of Home and Foreign Missions, that now receive and distribute, each, more than a million dollars annually.

THE PRESBYTERIAN CHURCH

A ZEALOUS MISSIONARY ORGANIZATION.

It is gratifying to know that the colored people, although emotional and demonstrative, have nevertheless an intelligent appreciation of the views and methods of the Presbyterian church.

A prominent minister of a southern church is quoted as having said: "The Presbyterian church can do for the colored people of the south what no other church can do."

FABLE OF PERSIAN TENT.

There is a Persian fable that tells of a young prince who brought to his father a nutshell, which, when opened with a spring, contained a little tent of such ingenious construction, that when spread in the nursery the children could play under its folds,; when opened in the council chamber the King and his counsellors could sit beneath its canopy; when placed in the court yard the family and all the servants could gather under its shade; when pitched upon the plain, where the soldiers were encamped, the entire army could gather within its enclosure. It possessed the qualities of boundless adaptability and expansiveness.

This little tent is a good symbol of our Presbyterian system. It is all contained within the nutshell of the Gospel. Open it in the nursery, and beneath its folds parents and children sit with delight; spread it in the court yard, and beneath its shadow the whole household assembles for morning and evening worship; open it in the village and it becomes a church, under whose canopy the whole town may worship. Open it upon the plain, and a great sacramental army gathers under it. Send it to the heathen world, and it becomes a great pavilion, that fills and covers the earth.

The Presbyterian church is as Catholic as the Gospel in its spirit of brotherly love, and readiness to co-operate with all who love our Lord Jesus Christ. It recognizes the ordination of the Episcopalian and the baptism of the Baptist. It joins cordially with those who would place the crown upon the brow of Jesus by singing only the Psalms of David, and responds with an approving echo to the hearty "Amen" of the Methodists. It is capable of an expansion, that will include all shades of our common humanity, and is working valiantly to usher in the day, when the prayer of our Lord Jesus shall be fulfilled: "That they may be one; as Thou, Father art in me, and I in Thee, that they also may be one in us; that the world may believe that Thou hast sent me."

"The Presbyterian church stands," says Rev. W. H. Roberts, D. D., "as it has stood during its entire history, for the unconditional sovereignty of God, for the Bible as the only infallible rule of faith and life, for simplicity of worship, representative government, a high standard of christian living, liberty of conscience, popular education, missionary activity and true Christian Catholicity."

President Benjamin Harrison said of it: "The Presbyterian church has been steadfast for liberty, and it has kept steadfast for education. It has stood as stiff as a steel beam for the faith delivered to our fathers, and it still stands with steadfastness for that essential doctrine—the inspired Word. It is not an illiberal church. There is no body of Christians in the world, that opens its arms wider to all who love the Master. Though it has made no boast or shout, it has yet been an aggressive missionary church from the beginning."

LINCOLN UNIVERSITY.

Lincoln University in Chester county, Pennsylvania, was established in 1854 under the leadership of Rev. John M. Dickey, D. D., pastor of the Presbyterian church of Oxford, for the classical and theological education of negroes.

The extent and thoroughness of the courses of instruction at this institution have been amply justified by the success of its graduates; many in the ministry, and others, in founding similar institutions of a high grade in the south, as at Columbia, S. C., Salisbury, N. C., Holly Springs, Miss., and a number of other places. Its aim is to furnish trained professional leaders, and it is accomplishing this object in splendid form. Established before the Freedmen's Board, it has continued to be maintained without its aid.

IX

THE PRESBYTERIAN BOARD OF MISSIONS FOR FREEDMEN.

ORGANIZED IN 1865.—WOMEN ENLISTED IN 1884.—BOARDING SCHOOLS.—TRAINS CHRISTIAN LEADERS.—WORTHY OF GENEROUS SUPPORT AND ENDOWMENT.

"The Spirit of the Lord is upon me, because he hath appointed me to preach the Gospel to the poor; he hath sent me to heal the broken-hearted and preach deliverance to the captives."—Luke.

THE emancipation of 4,000,000 slaves, at the close of the Civil War, was the sudden opening of a new and a vast field of opportunity and duty, before the Christian churches of this land.

The education and moral elevation of the Freedmen became in both church and state, a very serious and vital question. Ever since the foundation of the government, the church, through the voluntary establishment of academies and colleges, has been co-operating with the civil government, in the effort to develop in all parts of our land an intelligent christian citizenship.

The Presbyterian Board of Missions for Freedmen was organized as a committee in 1865, the last year of the Civil War. In 1882 this committee was made and incorporated as a Board. Its work then assumed a more permanent form and the contributions to its work began to be greatly increased. The contributions received that year were $68,-

THE LATE MRS. V. P. BOGGS
Secretary Women's Department, Freedmen's Board

REV. E. P. COWAN, D. D.
Secretary and Treasurer

REV. JOHN GASTON
Associate Secretary

Presbyterian Board of Missions for Freedmen

268.08. In 1913 the amount received to be applied to this work was $323,899.29. The amount of property held by it and used for educational and church purposes is $1,831,610.09. The office of the board is at Pittsburgh, Pennsylvania.

WOMEN ENLISTED IN 1884

In 1884 the interest of the women of the Presbyterian church was enlisted in behalf of the women and girls among the Freedmen. The progress of the work of the Women's Missionary societies, in establishing and maintaining educational institutions, is worthy of special mention.

During their first year they contributed $3,010; the second, $7,966; the third, $17,075; and in 1913, $85,236.09.

In raising this last amount 675 Sunday schools and 1082 Young People's societies co-operated with 3591 Women's societies.

To the women, almost entirely, is due the establishment and maintenance of most of the boarding schools now supported by the board. The names of some of the most consecrated workers and liberal contributors have been commemorated in the names of most of these institutions. That this fact may be noted and as a matter of general information, the following list of twenty-four of them is given.

LIST OF BOARDING SCHOOLS

I. FOR MALES ONLY

Biddle University, Charlotte, North Carolina.
Harbison Agricultural College, Irmo, South Carolina.

II. SEMINARIES FOR GIRLS ONLY

Scotia, Concord N. C.
Mary Allen, Crockett, Texas.
Ingleside, Burkeville, Va.
Mary Holmes, West Point, Miss.
Barber Memorial, Anniston, Ala.

III. CO-EDUCATIONAL

Allendale Academy, Allendale, S. C.
Albion Academy, Franklinton, N. C.
Alice Lee Elliott Memorial, Valliant, Okla.
Arkadelphia Academy, Arkadelphia, Ark.
Boggs Academy, Keyesville, Ga.
Brainard Institute, Chester, S. C.
Emerson Industrial Institute, Blackville, S. C.
Fee Memorial Institute, Nelson, Ky.
Gillespie Normal, Cordele, Ga.
Haines Industrial, Augusta, Ga.
Kendall Institute, Sumpter, S. C.
Mary Potter Memorial, Oxford, N. C.
Monticello Academy, Monticello, Ark.
Cotton Plant Academy, Cotton Plant, Ark.
Coulter Memorial Academy, Cheraw, N. C.
Redstone Academy, Lumberton, N. C.
Swift Memorial College, Rogersville, Tenn.

In addition to those in these boarding schools, 112 teachers are employed in the maintenance of this same number of day schools.

In his last annual report, April 1, 1913, Rev. E. P. Cowan, D. D., secretary of the Board submitted the following interesting summary of its work.

"The Freedmen's Board has ever kept in mind the one great fact that its work is, first, last and all the time, missionary work. We have aimed from the very beginning to follow a course that would commend itself to every man's conscience in the sight of God. We have always sought the counsel and advice of good men on the field, at times nearer our work than ourselves, and better able to judge of its condition. We have endeavored to exert such an influence over the people among whom we have labored, so that no one could object to it except he were a heathen or an infidel. As a consequence, all the opposition we have met with in all these years has been as nothing, compared with the sympathy and encouragement we have received from good men.

"We have this year issued our forty-eighth annual report. This annual report shows that we have now in connection with our church, four colored Synods, composed of sixteen colored Presbyteries, in which there are four hundred and four church organizations, with twenty-six thousand, one hundred and thirty-two communicants, two hundred and eighty-nine ordained ministers of the Gospel, and thirteen hundred and seventeen ruling elders.

"Within these Presbyteries, there are one hundred and thirty-six schools, and in these schools there are 16,427 pupils, taught by 448 teachers, all of whom are professing christians, and by a rule of the Board, members of the Presbyterian church.

"In all these schools, the Word of God and the Shorter Catechism are regularly and daily taught. On the mind and heart of every living soul that passes in and out of our schools, there is impressed the fundamental and far-reaching truth, that the chief end of man is to glorify God and to enjoy Him forever, and that the Word of God, which is contained in the Scriptures of the Old and New Testaments, is the only rule to direct us how we may glorify and enjoy Him.

"These churches and schools, and ministers and teachers—588 workers in all—are housed in 470 buildings, of which 300 are church buildings, 70 are manses, and 100 are school buildings. The value of these buildings is estimated at $1,561,000. The cry comes up to us without ceasing for either more room, or better accommodations. Should we answer these cries promptly, and without regard to the question as to where the money is to come from, we should be hopelessly overwhelmed with debt within one year."

TRAINS CHRISTIAN LEADERS

The Freedmen are naturally religious and hitherto their churches have been their principal social centers. Under uneducated leadership, the only kind possible at first, their church life was characterized by a loose moral standard, poor business methods and boisterous worship. In many places it still lacks a realization of the real needs of the race.

"The true standard bearers of better things have been the relatively few ministers and churches that have been noted for their educated ministry, restraint in worship, rigid morals and careful supervision."

The wisdom of the policy of training capable christian leaders, was emphasized at the last General Assembly at Atlanta, by Rev. H. A. Johnson, D. D., in the following pertinent paragraph:

"The vital need of the negro people is a trained christian leadership. Their problem can never be solved by elementary education for the masses, or industrial training for those who enter the trades and till the farm. They must have thoroughly trained christian teachers and ministers of the Gospel and should also have the other professions represented among their leaders. The men, who are conspicuous leaders among the negroes in industrial training are publicly saying that they expect such organizations as the Presbyterian church to furnish the ministers and teachers for their people, while they furnish the farmers, the carpenters and other tradesmen. The task of furnishing this trained leadership is being bravely attempted by our Board within the limitations of their available resources. Every intelligent student of the problem must realize how supremely important is this phase of the work."

WORTHY OF GENEROUS SUPPORT AND ENDOWMENT

The Board of Missions for Freedmen of the Presbyterian church merits the intelligent sympathy and cordial co-operation not only of our whole church but of all the friends who favor christian education among the dependent colored people in the south part of our land.

It educates ministers and teachers, and supports them in their work. It builds academies, seminaries and colleges, and aids in the erection of churches and manses. Its 24 boarding schools, having normal and industrial departments, are distributed so that there is one or more in every southern state.

It now owns and controls school, church and manse properties that represent a value of one and a half million dollars.

Its permanent investments, that bring an annual income for the promotion of its work however, are yet only $200,202.50. In these days of big business, the evidence of unusual prosperity, it ought to have an endowment of one million dollars.

Education is the most costly of all philanthropic enterprises. The following reason recently expressed for a large endowment of the College Board applies with equal force to the Freedmen's Board.

"A million dollar corporation is now considerably more than twice as efficient, as an instrument to accomplish results than one of a half million. In this day of large things the men who are interested in education, prefer to employ as their agent, an organization whose resources are large enough to place its permanent and financial stability beyond question. A bank with a million dollars of capital has considerable advantage over one having only a quarter of a million. The law, 'To him that hath shall be given,' still prevails among the children of men."

The members of the Freedmen's Board have been selected, because of their manifest interest in the educational and spiritual welfare of the colored people; and they are conscientiously striving, to the best of their ability, to promote the interests of the Freedmen, in behalf of the great body of generous hearted christian people whom they represent.

The work of the Freedmen's Board has hitherto by its charter been limited to the Freedmen in southern states. At the next General Assembly, an effort will be made to extend its work, so as to include the negroes in the northern states.

X

SPECIAL BENEFACTORS.

GEORGE PEABODY.—JOHN F. SLATER.—DANIEL HAND.—EMILINE CUSHING.—ANNA T. JEANES.—CAROLINE PHELPS STOKES.—JOHN D. ROCKEFELLER.—NEGRO PHILANTHROPISTS.

"He loveth our nation and hath built us a synagogue."

THE educational needs of the Freedman have called forth several large benefactions from individual contributors. George Peabody of Danvers, Massachusetts, in 1867 and 1869, established a fund of $3,500,000 for the promotion of general education in the South. One half of this amount happened to prove unavailable. A large part of the remainder was used in the establishment and endowment of the Peabody teachers college for whites at Nashville, Tennessee, leaving only a small part of it for use among the Freedmen.

In 1882, John F. Slater of Norwich, Connecticut, created a trust fund of $1,000,000, for the purpose of uplifting the emancipated population of the southern states and their posterity. The income of this fund, now increased to $1,500,000, is used to promote normal and industrial education.

In 1888 Daniel Hand of Guilford, Connecticut, gave the American Missionary Association of the Congregational church $1,000,000, and a residuary estate of $500,000 to aid in the education of the Negro.

SPECIAL BENEFACTORS

In 1895 Miss Emiline Cushing of Boston left $23,000 for the same object.

In 1907 Miss Anna T. Jeanes of Philadelphia, Pa., left an endowment fund of $1,000,000 to aid in maintaining elementary schools among the Freedmen. Booker T. Washington was named as one of two trustees of this fund. Its distribution contemplates a three fold plan. First, something additional is to be secured from the school authorities. Second, the co-operative efforts of the people are essential. Third, the effectiveness of the school is improved and its neighborhood influence widened by the introduction of industrial features. In 1911, the income from this fund was so widely distributed as to reach the work in as many as 111 counties in 12 different states; and summer schools were aided in six of them.

In 1909 Miss Caroline Phelps Stokes created a fund of $300,000 for the erection of tenement houses in New York City; and the education of negroes and Indians, through industrial schools.

From 1902 to 1909, John D. Rockefeller gave $53,000,000 to establish a fund for the promotion of general education in the United States. The schools of the Freedmen have received from this fund $532.015.

NEGRO PHILANTHROPISTS

The Freedmen have fallen heir to the estates of some free negroes, that became wealthy. It is interesting to note the following ones.

Tommy Lafon of New Orleans, a dealer in dry goods and real estate, in 1893, left for charitable purposes among his people, an estate appraised at $413,000.

Mary E. Shaw of New York City, left Tuskeegee Colored Institute $38,000.

Col. John McKee of Philadelphia, at his death in 1902, left about $1,000,000 worth of property for education, including a provision for the establishment of a college to bear his name.

Anna Marie Fisher, of Brooklyn, N. Y., in 1911, having an estate of $65,000 left $26,000 for educational institutions.

The successful achievement of these four free Negroes and their generous regard for the welfare of their kin-folks, suggest the possibilities of which they are capable, as financiers and philanthropists, when circumstances are favorable.

PART II
OAK HILL INDUSTRIAL ACADEMY

"It is said that the Athenians erected a statue to Æsop, (564 B. C.), who was born a slave; or as Phaedrus phrases it:
"They placed the slave upon an eternal pedestal,"
"Sir, for what the enfranchised slaves did for the cause of constitutional liberty in this country, the American people should imitate the Athenians and, by training the slave for usefulness, place him upon an eternal pedestal. Their conduct has been beyond all praise.

"They have been patient and docile; they have been loyal to their masters, to the country, and to those with whom they are associated; but, as I said before, no other people ever endured patiently such injustice and wrong. Despotism makes nihilists; tyranny makes socialists and communists; and injustice is the great manufacturer of dynamite. The thief robs himself; the adulterer pollutes himself; and the murderer inflicts a deeper wound upon himself than that which slays his victim.

"If my voice can reach this proscribed and unfortunate class, I appeal to them to continue, as they have begun, to endure to the end; and thus to commend themselves to the favorable judgment of mankind; and to rely for their safety upon the ultimate appeal to the conscience of the human race."—John J. Ingalls, U. S. Senate, 1890.

THE NATIVE OAK HILL SCHOOL
1876-1886

CHURCH ORGANIZED JUNE 29, 1869.—SUNDAY SCHOOL IN 1876.—SCHOOL HOUSE, 1878.—OLD LOG HOUSE, 1884.—APPEAL FOR ACADEMY.

"The vineyard which thy right hand hath planted."
"Who hath despised the day of small things?"

S the preaching of the gospel and the organization of a church preceded the establishment of the school, the following facts in regard to the church are first noted.

THE OAK HILL PRESBYTERIAN CHURCH

The Oak Hill Presbyterian church was organized about June 29, 1869, with six members, namely, Henry Crittenden, who was ordained an elder, Teena Crittenden, his wife, J. Ross Shoals and his wife Hettie Shoals, Emily Harris and Reindeer Clark.

The services at first were held in the home and later in an arbor at the home of Henry Crittenden, one mile east of the present town of Valliant, and now known as the home of James and Johnson Shoals. After a few years the place of meeting was transferred to an arbor about two miles southwest of Crittenden's, and two years later, 1878, to the Oak Hill schoolhouse, a frame building erected that year on the main east and west road north of Red river. It was located on the southwest quarter of section 27, near the site on which Valliant was located in 1902. It is reported, that Henry Crittenden was the principal contributor towards the erection of this building. His cash income though meager was greater than others and he gave freely in order that a suitable place might be provided both for public worship and a day school for the neighborhood.

Parson Charles W. Stewart of Doaksville, a representative of the last generation of those who were slaves to the Indians, was the minister in charge from the time of organization until the spring of 1893, when he retired from the ministry. He was succeeded at Oak Hill by Rev. Edward G. Haymaker, the superintendent of the academy, who continued a period of eleven years. He was succeeded by **Rev. R. E. Flickinger**, whose pastorate of nearly eight years was eventfully ended at the dedication of the new colored **Presbyterian** church at Garvin, on October 3, 1912. Rev. William H. Carroll, relinquishing his work on that same day as the first resident pastor of the Garvin church became the immediate successor at Oak Hill.

Those who served as elders of the Oak Hill church and are now dead were Henry Crittenden, J. Ross Shoals, Robert Hall, Jack A. Thomas and Samuel A. Folsom. The elders in 1912 are James R. Crabtree, Matt Brown and Solomon H. Buchanan.

In 1912 a site for a new chapel, intended only for the uses of the local congregation, was purchased in a suburb on the west side of Valliant. The trustees chosen at this time were Mitchell S. Stewart, formerly an elder, Matt Brown and James R. Crabtree. They were duly authorized to incorporate and manage the erection of the new church building.

THE NATIVE OAK HILL SCHOOL

The Negroes who were slaves of the Indians, about the year 1880 were enrolled and adopted as citizens, by the tribes to which they respectively belonged, and they then became entitled to a small part of their public school funds. The amount accorded the Choctaw Freedmen was about one dollar a year for a pupil that was enrolled as attending school. This made possible the employment of a teacher for a short term of three months in the vicinity of a few villages, where a large enrollment could be secured, but left unsupplied the greater number living in the sparsely settled neighborhoods.

Our Board of Missions for Freedmen, ever since its organization, has made it the duty of every negro minister commissioned by it, to maintain a school in their respective chapels several months each year, in order that the children of the community might have an opportunity to learn to read the Bible.

The first native teacher in the Oak Hill congregation was J. Ross Shoals, one of the elders of the church, who had a large family and principally of boys. His work was that of a Bible reader or Sunday School teacher. About the year 1876 he began to hold meetings in the south arbor on Sabbath afternoons for the purpose of teaching both old and young to read the Bible with him. Nathan Mattison succeeded him the next year at the same place as a Sabbath school teacher.

In 1878, George M. Dallas, a carpenter, was employed to build a small frame school house on the southwest quarter of section 27, and after its completion he taught that year the first term of week day school among the colored people of that section. Others that succeeded Dallas, as teachers in this frame school house, were Mary Rounds, Henry Williams and Lee Bibbs.

OLD LOG HOUSE

In 1884, Henry Williams transferred the day school to the "old log house" on the northeast quarter of section 29, a mile and a half northwest of the school house. The motive for this change was the fact there was no supply of good water near the school house, while at the new location there was a good well and a large vacant building available for use.

Robin Clark, its owner and last occupant was an active member of the Oak Hill church.

After occupying this building one or two years he moved to another one near Red river and generously tendered the free use of this one for the Oak Hill school. In 1885 Henry Friarson, another native teacher, taught the school in this same "old log house."

All of these native teachers did the best they could, but deeply felt their insufficiency for the task laid on them, by the pressure of an urgent necessity. All had personal knowledge of the existence and unusual privileges afforded the children and youth of the Choctaws at Wheelock and Spencer Academies. It was also easy for them to see that as farmers they succeeded as well in securing good results from the cultivation of the soil as many of their Choctaw neighbors, and this fact tended to increase their desire to have a "fair chance" and equal share in the matter of educational privileges for their children.

The Oak Hill church and school happened to be near the center of the widely scattered group of a half dozen churches that formed the monthly circuit of Parson

THE NATIVE OAK HILL SCHOOL 105

Charles W. Stewart. All who were interested in securing a good mission school approved this location as the most convenient for all of them, and, heartily uniting in an appeal for one, pledged their united support of it, when it should be established.

APPEAL FOR OAK HILL

The appeal of the Choctaw Freedmen was presented to the Presbyterian Board of Missions for Freedmen by Rev. Alexander Reid and Rev. John Edwards, the missionaries in charge of the Indian work at Spencer and Wheelock Academies, respectively.

In the early days many of the old Negroes were located near these educational institutions and they were sometimes sent by their masters to work for the missionaries. These men living in their midst had opportunity to witness their extreme poverty, utter ignorance and general degradation. They also heard their personal appeals for the light of knowledge and Bible truth. Their sympathetic interest was awakened and began to manifest itself towards them.

They were occasionally accorded the privilege of attending religious services, and at Doaksville, during the ministry of Rev. Cyrus Kingsbury, were permitted to hold occasional Sabbath afternoon meetings in the Choctaw church. Primers, catechisms and testaments were sometimes presented to them, and in this way a few of them learned to read the Bible. The kindly interest of these missionaries won their esteem and confidence and awakened in many of them an abiding love and affection for the Presbyterian church.

It is related that when one of them was asked to unite with another church because it was "more free" he replied, "You are too free for me, I need a stricter church. I believe in staying by the old missionaries. They were our friends when we were slaves. They treated us well and did us good, and I mean to stay by their church as long as I live."

SLAVERY AMONG INDIANS

The state of religion among all of the people, both Indians and Negroes, was low, "very low". One of the missionaries described that of the Negroes as being like that of the Samaritans. "They fear the Lord and serve their own gods. As their fathers did, so do they. Their condition is bad, morally and religiously."

It could not easily have been otherwise. The tendency of slavery, under the most favorable conditions has always been in the direction of a low standard of morals and life. Slavery to untutored Indians, in a sparsely settled timber country, suggests the most deplorable condition imaginable. Such a slave lacking the example of intelligence and uprightness, often common among white masters, was subjected to generations of training in every phase of depravity and had no incentive whatever to live a better life.

When, however, these slaves of the Indians were accorded their freedom and became entitled to a part of the public school fund of the Choctaws, they manifested an earnest desire to have ministers and teachers sent them, that they might have churches and schools of their own.

Their great need was a boarding school where the boys and girls especially those in the remote and neglected rural districts, could be taken from their homes and trained under the personal supervision of christian teachers, to a higher standard of living, and, some at least, become fitted to serve as teachers of their own people.

XII
ERA OF ELIZA HARTFORD
1886-1888.

THE HEROIC PIONEER.—FEBRUARY 14, 1886.—BOARDING SCHOOL, APRIL 15th, 1886.—PRISCILLA G. HAYMAKER.— NEW SCHOOL BUILDING IN 1887.—ANNA E. CAMPBELL.

"I'll go where you want me to go."

THE story of Oak Hill as an Industrial Academy, begins with the work of Miss Eliza Hartford of Steubenville, Ohio, the first white teacher in the "Old Log house". She was commissioned by the Freedmen's Board in January, 1886, and was sent in response to the appeal of the colored people of the Choctaw Nation.

The missionaries, Reid and Edwards, had commended as the most favorable location for such an educational institution the rural neighborhood occupied by the Oak Hill church, two miles east of Clear Creek in the valley of Red river.

They referred to this as a "pivotal location" for such a school, and wrote, "Here we want to see a good school established that shall grow into a normal academy. The location is central and healthful. If in charge of white teachers, such a school will attract scholars from all the other settlements."

HEROIC PIONEER

Oak Hill, like other schools of its kind, had its early period of heroic effort and self-sacrificing toil, before the usual comforts and conveniences of civilized life could be enjoyed. This was true of the entire period of service on the part of Miss Hartford, February 1886 to August 1888.

When she arrived at Wheelock, where she met a friend, Miss Elder, engaged in teaching the Indians, Rev. John Edwards served as an aid, in making a tour of inspection over the field, of which she was to be the missionary teacher and physician. This journey was made on horseback, which was the most speedy and comfortable mode of travel, over the rough and winding trails through the timber at that time.

As a result of this survey and a call at the home of Henry Crittenden, an elder of the Oak Hill church and a "local trustee of the neighborhood, under the Choctaw law," it was decided that the "old log house" was the best place to establish the school; and the best place for her to live was at the home of the colored elder, Henry Crittenden, three miles east. She was expected to make her daily journeys on horseback; and, in connection with the work of the school, to visit the people at their homes, furnish medicines for the sick and give instruction in regard to their care.

In her description of the old log house Miss Hartford states, "The windows are without sash or glass and the roof full of holes. The chimneys are of hewn stone, strong and massive. The house is of hewed logs, two stories in height and stands high in the midst of a fine locust grove. The well of water near it seems as famous as Jacob's well."

At the request of Mr. Edwards the colored people in the vicinity, after repairing the roof and windows, clean-

ELIZA HARTFORD.

ANNA E. CAMPBELL.

PRISCILLA G. HAYMAKER.

REV. EDWARD G. HAYMAKER

THE GIRLS' HALL, 1889-1910.

THE OLD FARM HOUSE.
The Pioneer Home of a Choctaw Chief, Leflore, and of the Oak Hill School.

ed, scrubbed and whitewashed the inside of this old log house, and thus prepared it for its new and noble era of usefulness.

FEBRUARY 14, 1886

On Sabbath, February 14,1886, one week after the arrival of Miss Hartford, her first meeting was held and a Sunday school was organized under her leadership. At its close a prayermeeting was held in which she read the scriptures, the hymns and a sermon.

On Tuesday, February 16, 1886, the school was opened with seven pupils. The opening exercises consisted in the reading of a chapter by the new teacher, the singing of a hymn and prayer by elder Henry Crittenden. The latter was profoundly impressed with the fact that, in the auspicious opening of the school that morning, the colored people of that section were realizing the answer to their oft repeated prayers, the fulfilment of their long delayed hopes.

The new teacher had never heard such a prayer in any school she ever attended. He thanked Our Heavenly Father, "That the prayers of his people were answered. In their bondage they had cried unto Him and He had heard their cry. In their ignorance and darkness they had asked for light and the light had come." He prayed for the teacher that "God would give her wisdom and enable her to be faithful." He prayed for the children and their parents that, "they might be able to see and appreciate what God had done for them," and for the school, "that it might abide with them and become an uplifting power to them and their children."

On the following Monday the number of the pupils had increased to fourteen. The chills were prevalent and frequently half the pupils would be seen huddling around the log fire in the chimney fireplace, and making a chattering noise with their teeth.

A BOARDING SCHOOL

On April 15, 1886, Miss Hartford began to live at the school building and some of the pupils brought their cornmeal so they might live "wid de teacher," and Oak Hill became a boarding school with an enrollment of 24 pupils.

At a prayer meeting of the women held soon after this event, it was decided to build a kitchen at the west end of the log house so "de chillen might have a place to bake and eat their corn bread." While they were building this kitchen a man who saw them said to Miss Hartford, "It makes the men feel mighty mean to see the women doing that work." She repeated to him the following words from the third verse of the fourth chapter of Paul's epistle to the Philippians: "I entreat thee also, true yokefellow, help those women which labor with me in the gospel, whose names are in the book of life." The result was very gratifying. He got his team, hauled the rest of the materials and then helped them to complete it. This improvement increased the facilities and also the general interest in the school.

In September 1886 pupils began to arrive from distant places and whilst some of them were retained in the building others were located among the friends in the neighborhood. In February following, all the available room in the log house was occupied and the work of the school proving too great for one teacher, another one was requested. The institution had now acquired the name, "Oak Hill Industrial School."

PRISCILLA G. HAYMAKER

In April 1887, Miss Priscilla G. Haymaker, of Newlonsburg, Westmoreland county, Pa., arrived to aid in the management of the school, and this event was the occasion for another thanksgiving on the part of the people. At a meeting then held they decided to build a house that could be used for a school house and chapel, using the materials in the Oak Hill school building of 1878. The men agreed to donate all the work they could, and, with ox teams, delivered the lumber in the old building. The Board gave $50.00 and Rev. John Edwards $25.00 towards the purchase of new lumber. It fell to the lot of Miss Hartford and Elder Henry Crittenden to pay some of the balances due on this building, and their contributions were remarkably large ones for those early days.

Miss Hartford, at the time this building was undertaken, was given special permission to solicit money to furnish the new school building, to fit up the "old log house" for a boarding house, and scholarships of $15.00 each. She went east and returning in August found the new building ready for the desks.

Miss Haymaker solicited and received the promise of a large bell that had been used by her father on the old farm at Newlonsburg, Pa., that the people might rejoice over the possession not merely of a chapel and school building, but one "wid a bell."

The time appointed for opening the fall term was now near at hand and yet the old log house was not ready for the boarders, that were expected soon to fill it, owing to the fact no workmen could be found to do the work. Miss Hartford and Miss Haymaker, with the help of a boy, made the bedsteads and tables with their own hands, the latter manifesting considerable skill in the use of the saw and hammer. On September 1st the boarders began to arrive and on the 15th, 60 pupils were enrolled of whom 36 were boarders. Every boarder was expected to bring 12 bushels of corn, and with scholarships of $15.00 each, there was no danger of starving. The girls were required to do the housework and the boys to provide the wood. Miss Haymaker was not used to roughing it and before the close of November she was compelled to return to her home, broken in health.

ANNA E. CAMPBELL

Miss Anna E. Campbell of Midway, Pa., who had previously been sent for, arrived at Oak Hill two days after the departure of Miss Haymaker, and with her the long expected bell, from the old home of the latter. The following Sabbath, the first one on which they were called together for worship by the clarion tones of the new bell, was another glad day for the people, and they extended to Miss Campbell a very cordial welcome, as the new assistant of Miss Hartford. She remained until the end of the term, June 15th, 1888.

Miss Campbell held temperance meetings every Saturday and some objected to them, because "dey was teachin de risin generashun dat it was wrong to drink whiskey or use tobacco, while de Bible said it was good for de stomik." During this second term six of the pupils, repeated the Catechism and nine united with the church.

During the summer of 1888 Miss Hartford remained alone to take care of the homeless children, and maintain the Sunday school and prayer meeting. Other parents began to call and plead for room for their children. Believing the time had come when another and a larger building was

ERA OF ELIZA HARTFORD

necessary in order to receive them, she rode a long distance to confer with a carpenter, in regard to the erection and cost of a frame building for boarders. He arranged to call and make an estimate, but while she waited for him, her health began to fail. The exposures, burdens and privations proved too great for her, single handed and alone, and she felt constrained to return to her home. She was unable to return to Oak Hill and died at Richmond, Ohio, July 9, 1901. Miss Campbell was also unable to return and the school was left without a teacher.

XIII
EARLY REMINISCENCES

ELIZA HARTFORD. — PRISCILLA G. HAYMAKER. — ANNA E. CAMPBELL.—THE NIGHT SCHOOL.—HARDSHIPS AT OAK HILL.

"Books are keys to wisdom's treasures;
Books are gates to lands of pleasure;
Books are paths that upward lead;
Books are friends. Come let us read."

THE following reminiscences, gleaned from letters written by these three heroic young lady teachers, will be read with interest. They discover in their own language, their feelings of hopefulness and loyalty while coping with unexpected embarrassments and unusual privations. Single handed and alone they penetrated the wilds of Indian Territory to a secluded spot, where they were a half day's ride from their nearest white friends, and thirty-five miles from the railway.

Holding aloft the Bible, the true standard of the cross, they rallied the ignorant and uncivilized natives appreciatingly around it, more worthily and long before our famous explorers decorated the North Pole with the American flag.

The mail was carried once a week from Clarksville to Wheelock, ten miles east, the nearest post office.

TEACHING ELIZABETH WASHING

At the end of her first year, March 19, 1887, when she was still working alone, having school, Sunday school, preaching and boarding house all in the old log house, Miss Hartford wrote to a friend, as follows:

"This ought to be a resting day for me, but I am always tired on Saturday. This has been my wash day and I will give you my experience with a girl of fifteen, who is very ignorant about the simplest things relating to work. It is useless to tell Elizabeth how to do any work, unless one goes with her and shows her every change. Today I had her wash her own clothes by my side, while I washed mine, to show her how, and how speedily she ought to do her own work. The only way to succeed in having them work is to work with them.

'These poor Freedmen have a just claim on the church. They are far below their white brothers and sisters, but they are not to be blamed for it. Slavery has made them so, and we must do something to lift them up. This however, will not be done by sending them to expensive schools, to make ladies and gentlemen of them, but where they will learn to work thoughtfully and be taught the pure religion of the Bible. The worst ones among them are very religious in their way.

A "FEELIN' MEETIN' "

"On last Sabbath we had an example of the way they like to do things. Their old black preacher always preaches on the Sunday school lesson. He comes early to hear what I say and then 'enlarges on de subjec in de afternoon.' I cannot tell you how hard it is sometimes to sit still and listen to the old man's explanations. Last Sabbath he dwelt a long time 'on de fact Rebecca was a shameful deceiver an dat Jacob was another one.'

"In the afternoon, after two hours of preaching services he concluded, 'as it was still early in de day' they would sing a hymn and any who wished to jine de church could come 'for'ud and give us der hand.'

"As soon as they started to sing, a woman fell in some sort of spell. She was sitting near me on the same bench. Instantly it occurred to me they were getting up one of their 'feelin' meetin's', as they call them, and I was frightened half out of my wits. Fearing they would get to shouting and pounding each other, I ran out as fast as I could. There were about fifty of them packed in one little room sixteen feet square and I was up in front. It was one of the friendly tribe that shouted, and had I been wise, I would have known what was coming. My flight spoiled the meeting, but if you would appreciate my feelings just imagine you are alone in a small room with fifty darkies and fifteen or twenty of them commence shouting and breaking benches. I had a severe headache and have not felt well all week.

"After I ran out the people laughed and the poor woman recovered quite suddenly. By the time I was safe in my own room the meeting was dismissed. I was nervous and discouraged. I called the old preacher to my room and gave him a lecture. He said he did not believe in shouting and had no idea of any one doing so. I am afraid some of the shouting ones will be offended but I could not help it. It was the first time I have felt afraid since I came here.

"The school children think it was the 'best meetin' they were ever at.' They say 'Miss Hartford did look so funny when she got scared.' I tell them they may laugh at me but not at the poor woman who shouted. I tell them that shouting and falling in fits is not religion, that the poor woman was probably a good christian, but her shouting and spells do not make her one.

" 'Mamma says,' said one of them, 'that she first took religion wid one of them spells and dey allus' come when she gits happy.' "

"Poor things! I tell you this to show you in what a sad state they are. They have had enough preaching to make them think they are religious, but have had no real Bible teaching, and there are ten thousand of them in this nation. The Board has concluded to send Miss Haymaker here and I am glad.

BOTHERSOME "BREDDERIN"

The Board talks about sending a new preacher here, I hope they will send a strong healthy consecrated white man. A sickly man has no business here. Common sense and grit are needed more than learning. It will be no easy task for a white preacher to manage these black Presbyterians. I suspect it will require more tact and will power to manage this set, than one of our city churches.

A half dozen old fellows claiming to be elders tried to run 'de Sunday School and de teacher' until I read to them a letter from Dr. Allen, secretary of the Board. Not one of them can read, but they take great pride in being elders.

Mrs. M. E. Crowe.

Carrie E. Crowe

Anna T. Hunter.

Martha Hunter.

James McGuire and Others, 1901.

EARLY REMINISCENCES

Some were appointed elders in other churches and they think that makes them elders here. It will be a sad day to them when they learn they are not elders here, and I fear they will not then be willing to remain as members.

I have written you a long letter and it is all about the darkies; but no doubt you are expecting that.

HARD WORK AND MISERABLE LIVING

"I am not so strong, in fact feel ten years older than one year ago. I fear I cannot stand the heat this summer. I said 'heat' but do not mean that exactly. This climate is rather pleasant, if we could only provide comforts. It is the constant hard work and miserable way of living that makes it so bad.

"No white person could eat what these women prepare, —bread, always of corn, and fat pork, swimming in grease. Give them flour, they stir in a lot of soda and serve you biscuit as green as grass. They have no idea of better cooking and will not take the pains to do better. We are going to teach them to cook, scrub and wash clothes.

"Write soon and tell me whether you called on mother, when you were in Steubenville.
Your Friend,
Eliza Hartford."

Six months later when she returned from a short visit to her mother she writes:

"The weeds were so high I could scarcely see the house. I had to pay forty dollars from my own earnings on lumber hauled for the new school building, but which Elder Crittenden says, was taken by thieves. I paid it to save our credit and am glad I had it to give.

"We have now nineteen boarders. I am almost worked to death and it takes all my patience to stand it."

BETSY BOBBET

A letter dated January 6, 1888, bears the stamp, "Oak Hill Industrial Academy." A change in her assistants had taken place in November previous and she writes:

"Miss Haymaker before leaving had miserable health and I have had a hard time since my return. I think Miss Campbell will do well. The attendance now ranges from 45 to 60 and I am not able to do anything except the school work. Four of the children have had chills and fever, and I have had to rise at night to care for them. I have been trying to do the work of three people and not complain. Still I'd like to grumble a little, if I could find the right one to talk to. I am beginning to feel a little like Josiah Allen's wife, when she said, 'Betsy Bobbet, you're a fool, or else me.'

"Still I had rather be regarded foolish, by working hard for the good of others, than take advantage of another.

Pray for me for I need your prayers.

Eliza Hartford."

MISS HAYMAKER'S EVENTFUL JOURNEY.

Miss Priscilla G. Haymaker made her first journey to Oak Hill about the first of April, 1887. She passed by way of St. Louis to Texarkana, Arkansas, 50 miles east of Clarksville, over the Iron Mountain railway. This part of the journey was made during the night, and most of the time she was the only lady in the car. The crowd on the train was one of ruffians, who spent the time playing cards, drinking whiskey and showing their revolvers.

The conductor said to her, "Lady you have a rough crowd to ride with to night, but I will not leave you long." He was as good as his word. He sat in the seat with her when in the car and returned promptly when required to be absent.

At Clarksville she found the driver from Wheelock awaiting her arrival at the hotel. As early as four o'clock the next morning everything was in readiness for making the trip to Wheelock in a covered wagon. It soon began to rain and continued raining all day. It was 8 o'clock at night when the team arrived at Wheelock.

The cordial welcome extended by Rev. John Edwards, Superintendent, and his wife and the teachers at Wheelock Academy, was one not soon to be forgotten. It was greatly appreciated and enabled her to feel she had gotten back again to a place of civilization.

Miss Haymaker, the first assistant of Miss Hartford, April to November 1887, was a native of Newlonsburg, Pa., daughter of George R. and Priscilla Haymaker.

On October 1, 1890, she returned to Oak Hill and served as the principal teacher in the Academy the next six years. In the fall of 1892 she was joined by her brother Rev. E. G. Haymaker, who then became superintendent. On October 13, 1896, she became the wife of John Blair of Chambersburg, Pa., and they still reside there.

MISS CAMPBELL'S TRIP FROM CLARKSVILLE.

Miss Anna E. Campbell, the successor of Miss Haymaker arrived at Clarksville, the same day the latter passed through that place on her way home in November, 1887.

The proprietor of the hotel called her very early the next morning and informed her he had secured a mule team driven by a negro to take her to Oak Hill. When she was leaving the hotel he solicitously inquired,

"Do you carry a gun?"

"No I haven't any weapon except a little pocket knife," she answered. He then said, "In going into Indian Territory you ought to have a gun, you may need it."

Mr. Moore, the railway agent, a man from Ohio, noticing by the check of her trunk, that she came from Pennsylvania, was very courteous and gave his name. He charged the driver to protect the lady at the risk of his own life; all of which he solemnly promised to do, by promptly answering, "Yes sah, dat I will."

The bell and two barrels of clothing for Oak Hill were put on the wagon and they made the load a pretty good one for the team. After driving northward all day it began to grow dark and they had not yet reached the ferry across Red River. The crossing was made however without accident.

When the landing had been completed the driver remarked:

"I don't reckon we will get dar, 'coz I doesn't know de way now."

Fortunately there were several houses not very far away on the bluff along the river, and after a few inquiries, a white family was found that very kindly gave Miss Campbell shelter for the night.

The woman at once offered her a sniff of snuff as a token of good will. When the snuff was very politely declined, she laconically remarked:

"Well, some folks don't."

Miss Campbell arrived at Oak Hill, ten miles distant from the ferry, the next day, after experiencing a "stuck fast" in the mud on the way.

Miss Campbell was a native of Midway, Washington county, Pa. She became the assistant of Miss Hartford in November, 1887, two days after the departure of Miss Haymaker and remained until June 15, 1888. At that time she expected to return about the first of October following. But when her trunk had been packed for that purpose circumstances arose at home that made it necessary for her to remain and take care of her parents, both of whom were aged and infirm. On March 7, 1905, she became the wife of James H. McClusky and now lives on a well cultivated productive farm near Monongahela, Pa.

EARLY REMINISCENCES

MISS HARTFORD'S NIGHT SCHOOL.

On requesting Alexander M. Reid, D. D., of Steubenville, Ohio, the early home of Eliza Hartford to obtain and send a photo of her, he reported her death at Richmond, Ohio, July 9, 1901; and stating that a photo could not be found among her relatives, sent instead the following beautiful incident, growing out of her work as a teacher of night school in that place before she came to Oak Hill.

MATTHEW FINDING HIS OPPORTUNITY

Rev. Charles C. Beatty, D. D., a former Moderator of the General Assembly who had become almost totally blind, at the close of a prayer meeting held in the Second Presbyterian church, said to Miss Hartford, "Could you not name one of your boys here to lead me home?"

She replied, "Yes, here is Matthew Rutherford; he will lead you home."

On the way home Dr. Beatty asked Matthew, what he was doing: He replied, "I dig coal in the day time and go to the school of Miss Hartford at night."

When near home Dr. Beatty inquired, "Matthew, how would you like to go to school and get an education?" He said, "I would like it very much."

Dr. Beatty then said, "Matthew, you may quit digging coal and go through the school and High School. Then if you have a good standing, I will send you to college. If the Lord should then seem to be calling you to be a minister, I will enable you to pursue your studies at Allegheny Seminary.

Matthew, who was a native of England and exceedingly grateful for this recognition and counsel, quit the mines and entered school. He graduated from Washington and

Jefferson college in 1884, and from the theological Seminary, three years later. Since 1896 he has been the highly esteemed pastor of the third Presbyterian church, Washington, Pa., and Bible instructor in the college since 1900. He received the degree of Doctor of Divinity in 1909.

This incident serves to illustrate the readiness of the friends of Christian Education to aid young people of limited means, who are trying to educate themselves; and the care they also take to know they are worthy. It also shows the importance of young people industriously and economically doing what they can to help themselves. That is their best recommendation.

If young Rutherford, while working in the mines, had indulged in spending his evenings at places merely of amusement or entertainment as many do, he would have missed the golden opportunity of his life. The unexpected and gracious offer came to him, while he was attending night school and the weekly prayer meeting. It was while he was taking advantage of these opportunities for intellectual and moral improvement, within his reach, that he found the true and faithful friend, whose assistance he most needed.

HARDSHIPS AT OAK HILL.

Miss Hartford, before coming to Oak Hill, spent several years as a teacher among the Mormons at Silver City, Utah. This was a period when missionary work was difficult and dangerous. She resigned that work on account of the failing health of her aged mother.

She patiently and hopefully endured many privations and hardships in faithfully and energetically carrying forward the work entrusted to her. These were greatest at Oak Hill than elsewhere.

At Oak Hill she was unable to relieve the natural conditions that produce malarial troubles. She felt very deeply the loneliness of dwelling in the wilderness, where there was no white person in the neighborhood to render assistance in time of special need, or sympathetic friend to express a word of comfort and encouragement. Then she could not avoid the incessant strain of continuous work and worry under surroundings and limitations, that could not be removed and tended to produce that nervous exhaustion, which results in complete prostration. This nervous strain was increased by every advancing step in the progress of the work. Relief from this malady is not found in the use of medicines, but in a complete change of scenes, diet and employment. She and her two faithful helpers were compelled to seek this form of relief.

XIV
EARLY TIMES AT FOREST.

FOREST CHAPEL.—LIFTING THE COLLECTION.—PRIMITIVE MID-WEEK MEETINGS.

"I have considered the days of old, the years of ancient times."

THE following reminiscences of early times at Forest church are narrated for their intrinsic as well as historic interest. The first one reveals an order of service, that is very general in the colored churches. It is one that affords the deacon, if he be a man so disposed, to spontaneously introduce considerable native wit and humor into the part of the service entrusted to him; and if he does, it very naturally prepares the way for unexpected shouts of joy and gladness on the part of those who are emotional or subject to the sudden impulse of ecstatic delight.

FOREST CHAPEL.

Forest Chapel, as is suggested by its name, was located in the large and dense oak forest along Red river eight miles south of Wheelock. Its post office has been successively, Wheelock, Fowlerville, Parsons and since 1906 Millerton. The Forest church was organized by Parson Stewart about 1886, and was served by him once a month the next seven years. In 1898 it became a remote part of the field of Rev. William Butler of Eagletown, who also endeavored to visit it once a month.

The chapel was a lonely, dingy and dilapidated building, inside as well as outside. It was about 20 by 30 feet and was built entirely of rough lumber. The side walls consisted of one thickness of wide inch boards, nailed at the top and bottom, and having a thin strip over the cracks on the outside. The roof was covered with long, split, oak clapboards, that invariably look black and rough at the end of a year. The pulpit consisted of a box-like arrangement that stood on a small platform at the center of one end. The seats consisted of a half dozen rough benches without backs, that could be arranged around the stove in cold weather, or in three fold groups for a picnic dinner, the middle one being used for a table on such occasions and the other two for seats around it. No paint or even white wash ever found a place on this building. It was the largest and best building in the neighborhood, and the popular resort for all of their social gatherings.

The leading men of the congregation consisted of two elders, both venerable and devout survivors of the slavery period, neither of whom could read, and a deacon, who was one of the only two of the older people who could read a little.

LIFTING THE COLLECTION

It was regarded as the duty of the deacon to "lift the collection" at the Sabbath services. This gave him a very prominent part in the services, for the collection is not lifted by passing the hat or basket, but each contributor, after the general call brings their offering and lays it either on the pulpit or a little stand near it. However novel this arrangement may at first appear to those unaccustomed to it, it must be remembered that a method somewhat similar to this was in use in the Temple in Jerusalem, when our Lord

Jesus, taking his seat opposite the treasury, saw the poor widow cast in her two mites and commended her very highly.

It was not unusual for the deacon to announce before hand the amount needed and then, as the offerings are presented, to state the amount received from time to time, until finally the whole amount is obtained. This part of the service was always enlivened by singing some soul-stirring songs, that everybody could sing. Occasionally it would take the form of a good natured rivalry, as to which could appear the most happy and joyous, the deacon, vociferously announcing from time to time as their offerings came in, the latest result of the collection, or, the people, whose merry singing would occasionally develop into a shout of ecstatic enjoyment, on the part of one or more of their number.

PRIMITIVE MID-WEEK MEETINGS

The early preachers, having monthly appointments, were always very faithful in exhorting and encouraging the elders of their distant congregations to maintain regular Sabbath services, for the study of the Bible and Catechism, and a mid-week meeting for praise and prayer. The people were encouraged to attend all these meetings and cordially cooperate with the elders in making them interesting and instructive.

The older generation at Forest was one that had a foretaste of slavery in their early days, but not a day of school privileges, except as the Bible was read or taught at their meetings on the Sabbath. The lack of school privileges in the neighborhood and its remote seclusion from the outside world, had the effect of leaving these colored people to continue their primitive ways and methods of doing things, to

EARLY TIMES AT FOREST 127

a later date than in many other more highly favored communities.

The following narrative contains an account of the mid-week meetings held at Forest about the year 1897 when Miss Bertha L. Ahrens, a white missionary teacher of our Freedmen's Board opened a mission school in the chapel. It shows how the people, that lived in the gross darkness of utter ignorance, groped for the light and earnestly endeavored to extend it, when the gospel was first presented to them.

The mid-week meetings are held regularly when not prevented by rain or cold weather. The people live in little shanties scattered through the timber near springs of water and are poorly clad. In good weather they "begin to gather" about 8:30 p. m. and continue to "gather" until 9:30, when Elder "B." taking his place at the left of the pulpit, "reckons that they's all here that's going to com." Elder F. sits down beside him and neither of them can read. Deacon L. who serves as chorister, occupies a shortseat in front of the pulpit. The wives of the elders, the lady missionary and other leading sisters occupy seats—a bench—at the right of the pulpit.

The meetings are opened by the deacon, who reads two lines of a hymn and, winding out a tune, the people unite in singing them. Two more lines continue to be read and sung until the hymn has been completed.

When the deacon is not present Elder "B." says: "Will some of you select something to sing?" If no brother is present, who can read, a sister or the missionary, or perhaps one of her school boys, may "line out" a hymn and may even "raise it" but the tune must be one "the old folks can sing." If the one who "raises the tune" breaks down with it, any one may pick it up and go on with it to the end of the two lines that have been "lined out."

The missionary's organ is in position ready for use, but it must be silent in the prayer meeting, and also at the preaching service. It is a new and troublesome innovation. It takes the prominence in the singing, that belongs to the officers of the church. The missionary cannot wind and slur the tunes on it, the way the old folks have learned to sing them, and it robs the singing of its old-time sweetness and power. The organ therefore remains silent.

After the first hymn, Elder "B." who never allows any one else, not even the preacher, to lead the prayer meeting, now calls on some one to "read us a lesson from the Bible." This was an innovation introduced into the prayer meeting after the arrival of the lady missionary. It is at first merely tolerated, comments and explanations are strictly forbidden. These restrictions in regard to the Bible in the meeting were due to the influence exerted by the wife of Elder "B." who had been the first real leader of the church and was still regarded as a "mother in Israel, whose opinions should be respected." She felt that God had taught her by visions and dreams, and believed he would teach others the same way. Elder "F." however, is not satisfied till he and others have heard the "Word of God" and permission to read it is given.

"Down to pray," is the next request of the leader, and the voice of every one present is expected to be heard in this part of the meeting. A sister, whose seat is near a window, begs the Lord to "come this-a-way, just a little while, to lay his head in the window and hear his servant pray." A brother near the front door responds approvingly, "Yes sir," and bids him, "Walk in, and take a front seat."

EARLY TIMES AT FOREST

The prayer of a devout sister after one or two petitions, becomes an earnest exhortation to all the sinners to repent and be saved.

Some seemed to believe their prayers have to travel long journeys and are better long than short. Some prayers are chanted with a pleasing variety of the voice, while others are agonized by using many repetitions. All are witnessed to by "amen" and similar words of attestation; for these are "live christians", and have no use for "dead meetings."

Elder "F." who sits beside the leader, sometimes insists on "making some remarks." If the leader whispers to him "make it short," and he does not give good heed, the starting of a familiar hymn is the method adopted to "bring him down."

At a meeting held on the forenoon of Christmas, Elder "F." was feeling too happy and grateful to restrain himself. His theme was "Our Wonderful Saviour," and he began to exhort sinners to open their hearts to him. He became so absorbed in the greatness and importance of his theme as not to heed the usual whisper of the leader or even the starting of the familiar hymn. The situation is one of embarrassment to the leader. The one that proves equal to it is Elder "B.'s" wife. She walks over to him, grabs him by both arms and pushes him down on his seat, saying, "Bud, you talks too much, sit down now and keep still." She laughs as she says this, the elder smiles as he sits down, and the meeting proceeds in good form.

The usual way of closing the mid-week meeting was about as follows: Elder "B." says, "Well we's done about all we can do. Let us sing something and go home." If elder "F."

does not call for the new hymn, they have recently learned from the organ,

"Lord dismiss us with thy blessing," they stand and sing a familiar one. Elder "B." then says: "Amen!" and dismisses the congregation with a wave of his hand.

In the Sunday school the attitude of the people toward the Bible, the organ and the lady missionary was altogether different. Here she is the recognized leader, both in the singing and Bible instruction. As they profit by her instruction, and listen a few times to some of their familiar hymns on the organ, the younger people manifest pleasure and delight and the early prejudices of the older ones are gradually forgotten.

The first elders of Forest church were Simon Folsom, Charles Bibbs and Lee Bibbs. Charles Bashears was soon afterward added to their number and died in 1912. His wife exerted a leading influence in the earlier years of this church.

The allotment of lands in 1905 made it necessary to move Forest church to another location; and in 1909, it was moved about two miles east in the valley of Red river.

XV
ERA OF JAMES F. McBRIDE
1888-1892

GIRL'S HALL IN 1889.—ADDITIONAL SCHOOL ROOM.—McBRIDE DIES JAN. 29, 1892.—MRS. McBRIDE.

"Seest thou a man diligent in his business, he shall stand before kings, he shall not stand before mean men."

ERA OF SUPT. McBRIDE

ABOUT October 1, 1888 Mr. and Mrs. James F. McBride arrived to take charge of the work as superintendent and matron. Their arrival was the occasion of another joyful meeting on the part of the colored people who came to see the "suptender, and express their great joy over the new start that was to be given the school."

Mrs. McBride at a later date, referring to the appearance of things on the day of their arrival at this, their new home, wrote:

"I can still see how the old log house looked as we drove up; so dilapidated. A broken down porch ran along the front of it, and we had to climb over an old rail fence to get to it. Our first meal was corn bread made with water—without salt—and stewed dried peaches."

When the school opened they were assisted by Miss Carrie Peck, Celestine Hodges and Mary Grundy.

A new era was now inaugurated in the management of the school. Ownership as yet extended only to the farm buildings, which consisted of the old log house, and barn, purchased from Robin Clark, and the new school building. The first effort was now made to utilize two small fields of cleared land and the neighboring timber to raise stock and crops for the local support of the school.

GIRLS' HALL

In 1889 a commodious Girls' Hall was built having ample facilities for carrying and boarding a considerable number of students. The enjoyment of anything like ordinary home comforts on the part of the teachers began with the occupancy of this building. It became the home of the family of the superintendent, teachers and the girls; and the old log house was fitted up for occupancy by the boys. An additional room was also added to the school building.

As the patronage of the school increased Mr. McBride felt there was need for a suitable Boys' Hall. He made the plans for it and, enlisting the interest of the women of Indiana, they provided the money for it. On January 29, 1892, after three and one half years of faithful service and before his hopes could be realized by merely starting the work on the new building, his death occurred and the progress of the improvement work was again arrested.

Mr. McBride was educated at Hanover, Indiana, and had previously taught in several other schools. He was an active christian worker and had been ordained a ruling elder in the Presbyterian church. He anticipated the future needs of the school by planting fruit trees, that, during these later years, have borne bountiful crops of fruit.

The other assistants of Mr. McBride were Mary Coffland, principal in 1889 and assistant principal 1890 to 1892; Miss Priscilla G. Haymaker, who returned to serve as principal in 1890 and continued until 1896. Other assistants were Anna McBride, Bettie Stewart, colored, and Rilla Fields who served from the fall of 1891 to the spring of 1895.

MRS. J. F. McBRIDE

During the next eight months the management of the institution devolved upon Mrs. McBride; and she continued to serve as matron until the spring of 1899, a period of eleven years. She gave to this institution many of her best years for service, and the best work of her life. She became specially interested in a number of young people at Oak Hill and aided them to attend other schools of our Board. She is now living at Coalgate, Okla.

XVI

ERA OF REV. EDWARD G. HAYMAKER
1892-1904

A TERM ANNOUNCEMENT.—BOYS' HALL 1893.—LAUNDRY AND SMOKEHOUSE, 1895.—MR. AND MRS. HAYMAKER.—MRS. McBRIDE.—OTHER HELPERS.—ANNA AND MATTIE HUNTER.—MRS. M. E. CROWE.—PRAYING FOR WATER.—APPEAL FOR HOSPITAL.—CARRIE E. CROWE.

> "Learning is wealth to the poor,
> An honor to the rich,
> An aid to the young,
> A support and comfort to the aged."

ERA, 1892-1904.

ON October 1, 1892, Rev. Edward Graham Haymaker became superintendent and continued to serve in that capacity until the spring of 1904.

The following extracts, from a circular announcement, sent out in script form, for one of the early years of this period, are full of historic interest.

"Oak Hill Industrial school for colored children is situated 5 miles north of Red river and 25 miles east of Goodland, the nearest R. R. station. School opens Oct. 2nd. and will continue for a term of six months. It is important that all who attend be on hand at the opening. The sum of $10.00 for citizens and $12.00 for non-citizens will be charged which must be paid in advance, or assurance given for its payment. The price of tuition has been raised by the Board as the Choctaw fund seems to be cut off. It only amounts to 1 cent a meal or 3 cents a day for board and 1½ cents for lodging. Cheap enough. The Board pays the large part of the bill.

"Shoes must in all cases be provided by parents and guardians. Girls will be provided with other articles of

ERA OF REV. EDWARD G. HAYMAKER

clothing as far as possible, but no such provision can be made for boys. Books for all will be provided free, and all will be required to work certain hours each day. Boys will not be allowed to use tobacco.

"A course of study has been arranged and pupils completing the course will be given a diploma, which will admit to any of the higher schools under the Board.

E. G. Haymaker, superintendent."

BOYS' HALL

During this period a Boys' Hall was erected in 1893, a laundry and smokehouse in 1895. In 1902 the school building was moved from the oak grove at the railway to its present position on the campus and the height of it increased.

Most of the pupils were boarders and most of them were girls. The girls were encouraged to learn to sew that at Christmas they might be the wearers of a new calico dress made with their own hands.

All were required to read the Bible and encouraged to commit the shorter catechism, the World's briefest and best commentary on the Bible.

MR. AND MRS. HAYMAKER

Rev. E. G. Haymaker was a native of Newlonsburg, Westmoreland County, Pa. He graduated from Washington and Jefferson College in 1885 and from the Western Theological Seminary at Pittsburg, in 1890. In 1887 he was licensed by the Presbytery of Blairsville, and in 1890 was ordained by the Presbytery of Kittanning. After serving Midway and Union churches, Cowansville, Pa., two years, on Oct. 1, 1892, he became superintendent of Oak Hill and continued until the spring of 1904, eleven and a half years.

Mrs. Haymaker, who became matron of the Boys Hall in 1894, was a native of Pennsylvania and was educated in the public schools and Wilson Female College at Chambersburg. She was a teacher at Wheelock Academy at the time of her marriage in 1894.

During the period of service on the part of these and all previous helpers the necessaries of life had to be hauled long distances. The daily supply of water had to be hauled one and a half miles. The nearest post office most of the time was at Wheelock, ten miles east. Previous to 1902, when Valliant was founded the nearest trading stations were Paris and Clarksville, Texas, and from 1889 to 1903 Goodland, twenty-eight miles west. All the surfaced lumber in the Girls' and Boys' Halls, built in 1889 and 1894 had to be hauled from Paris.

Travel over the rough crooked trails and unbridged streams in the timber, whilst not unhealthful in good weather, was always a slow, tedious experience, rather than a source of pleasure. To live at Oak Hill meant to enjoy a quiet secluded home, so far removed from the currents of the world's activity, as to be almost unaffected by them.

Mrs. McBride continued to serve as matron until 1899, a period of ten years. The school had then a history of 13 years. On reviewing the signs of improvement and progress among the colored people that might be attributed to the good influence of the Oak Hill school, she wrote as follows:

"The community has greatly changed since this school was established. When Mr. McBride and I went to the field murders were common in the neighborhood of Oak Hill, but they are rare now. The people are now improving their places, cultivating more land, planting orchards and building board houses, having several rooms. They have more stock than formerly and their outlook seems hopeful; but alas! their religious life is sadly neglected. One half the pupils are from Presbyterian families, and those who come from other denominations learn to love our church, its doctrines and form of worship."

ERA OF REV. EDWARD G. HAYMAKER 137

Parson Stewart of Doaksville, who had been the faithful pastor of the Oak Hill church from the time it was founded in 1869, continued to serve it once a month until the spring of 1893, a period of 24 years. He was then at the age of 70 honorably retired from the active ministry, and the superintendent of the academy, became his successor in the pastorate of the Oak Hill church.

OTHER HELPERS.

The other assistants, during the period Mr. Haymaker was superintendent were as follows:

Principals: Anna T. Hunter, 1895 to 1901; Sadie Shaw, 1898-9; Carrie E. Crowe, 1901 to 1903; Verne Gossard, 1903 to 1904.

Assistant Teachers: Mattie Hunter, 1895 to 1901; Mrs. Mary Scott, 1901-1903; Jessie Fisher, 1903 to 1904; Rilla Fields, 1892 to 1895; Howard McBride, 1892-93.

Assistants in the Cooking Department: Mary Gordon, 1894-5; Fannie Green (Col.), Josephine McAfee (Col.), Sadie Shaw, 1897, Lou K. Early, Josie Jones, Lilly E. Lee, Mrs. Martha Folsom (Col.), 1902-3, and Mrs. Emma Burrows, 1903-4.

Matrons: Mrs. M. E. Crowe, 1899-1903; Carrie Craig, 1903-04.

ANNA F. and MATTIE HUNTER

of Huntsville, Ohio, were educated, Mattie in Indianapolis and State Normal at Terra Haute, Indiana, and Anna in similar schools in Ohio.

Anna taught at Wheelock, I. T., from 1885 to 1890, under the Home Mission Board, and then three years under the Freedmen's Board at Atoka. In 1895 she became a teacher at Oak Hill and, serving one year as an assistant, served four years as principal 1896 to 1901, being absent in 1898.

Mattie was an assistant at Oak Hill from 1896 to 1901, having previously taught at Wheelock two years, 1889 to 1891.

The work of these sisters at Oak Hill was greatly appreciated. A number of the views of the early days, that appear in this volume are due to their thoughtfulness, and skill in the use of a Kodak.

MRS. M. E. CROWE.

Mrs. M. E. (Rev. James B.) Crowe in 1899 became the successor of Mrs. McBride as matron of the Girls' Hall and continued until the spring of 1903. It seemed to her like the dawning of a new era in the life of a Choctaw Negro girl, when she entered a Christian training school like Oak Hill. After an opportunity for observation she wrote as follows:

"It gives us no small satisfaction to see the rapid improvement during the first year on the part of those who come to our school. It is very gratifying to witness the surprise of their parents, when they return after the lapse of a few months. This work may seem small when compared with the great South; but these Choctaw Negroes are ours now to mould as we will. The time is near when this country will be thrown open to white settlers; the hordes,—both white and black—will then pour into this section and our opportunity will be gone if we do not seize it now. We have had this year the clearest evidence of God's approval of this work. Oak Hill needs much in the way of facilities. We are thankful for every word of sympathy and the help received this year from societies and friends. I would like to speak of individual pupils; of the transformation we see going on in their characters, and also of their efforts to profit by the instruction given."

Rev. James B. Crowe, in 1887 had charge of the Presbyterian church of Remington, Indiana. In 1890 he was appointed by the Freedmen's Board to serve the colored people at Caddo and Atoka. Anna and Mattie Hunter were then teaching at Atoka, and Mrs. Crowe became a teacher at Caddo. In 1893 her health failed and, returning to the North he died soon afterward. Later Mrs. Crowe became matron at Oak Hill. She is now living at Hartford, South Dakota.

PRAYING FOR WATER

"The Lord is my Shepherd, I shall not want."

When Oak Hill became a boarding school and a heavy draft was made on the old well, that at the first had attracted the school there, it "went dry." After this unexpected occurrence it never furnished an adequate supply of water for the school and stock. During all of the 90's great inconvenience was experienced in securing and keeping on hand an adequate supply during term time. When the supply was exhausted the work in the laundry and kitchen had to stop, until a new supply was obtained.

The nearest sources of supply, during this "lack of water" period, were Clear Creek and a large spring near it, both one and a half miles distant. At first two barrels were used to haul water and the team had to make daily trips during term time. Later a long water tank, that held a wagon load, was substituted for the barrels. Hauling water in barrels kept two boys out of school a considerable part of their time. They did not seem to care, yet the feeling prevailed that it was not right.

In the fall of 1899 when Mrs. M. E. Crowe became matron, the lack of water was so distressing it was made the subject of prayer. Mrs. F. D. Palmer, a secretary of the Board visited the school at this period and after an address, the question was asked, "How many will join in prayer for water to be given Oak Hill?" Quite a number responded and, at the ringing of the retiring bell, a circle of prayer would form in the girls' sitting room and sentence prayers were offered for that one object.

About three weeks later, Mrs. Palmer met the women of the First Presbyterian church, Wilkinsburg, Pa., and, among other needs of the schools visited, referred to the urgent need for water and a cook stove with a large oven at Oak Hill. At the close of her address an elderly lady, Mrs. Rebecca S. Campbell, arose in the back part of the room and said, "My sister-in-law, Anna E. Campbell, taught in that school some years ago; and I will give one hundred dollars for a good well and wind wheel for it, that it may be a useful and worthy memorial of a dear son, Frank Campbell, who died at thirty in 1900, and of Annie's work in 1888."

The Endeavor society added fifty dollars for a large cook stove that would serve as an oven.

In this reminiscence, the faithful teacher, the circle of prayer, the visit of the secretary, the address, and the presence at the meeting of a woman with a responsive heart and offering, seemed links in a chain of providential circumstances, that made those who were interested feel sure the school at Oak Hill was "precious in the sight of the Lord." Their prayer for water had been heard and the answer was assured.

In 1903 this difficulty was overcome by placing an aermoter over the well, sunk the previous year, to do the pumping for the stock. The stock then enjoyed the free range of the timber and consisted of considerable herds of cattle and hogs.

ERA OF REV. EDWARD G. HAYMAKER

APPEAL FOR HOSPITAL

"Ask and it shall be given you."

In the early spring of 1903, writes Mrs. M. E. Crowe, matron, one of the girls became ill and feared she was going to die. A special bed was made for her in my own sitting room.

After her recovery Mrs. Crowe wrote Mrs. Mary O. Becker, Mexico, N. Y., a personal stranger but previous contributor to the school, soliciting her aid to provide a hospital or separate room for the care of sick girls.

A favorable response was received. A partition was removed to make a long room and provide for a stove. Soon afterwards there was received from the Women's Missionary Society represented by Mrs. Becker, three single beds, bedding, gowns, slippers, sponges, water-bottles and all the other articles necessary for the complete equipment of a sick room, including three changes of clothing for the sick.

The promptness of this response and the generosity of the donation, awakened feelings of heartfelt gratitude, on the part of the recipients.

A few years afterwards Mrs. Crowe related this incident to a group of ladies at Mitchell, South Dakota, standing in the recess of a bay window.

The pastor of the church, now an evangelist, was busy in an adjoining room, separated only by a curtain. The reference to Mrs. Becker attracted his attention. At the close of her remarks he entered the room and stepping to the window, pointed to some pictures and said:

"These pictures at your side are of Mrs. Becker's home and son. She helped me to get an education. That may not have meant much to others but it meant a great deal to me. It was a fulfilment of the promise.

"I will guide thee with mine eye."

Mrs. Crowe further states, "Many that were under my care became christians and I know that many of them are now doing great good.

"One, when leaving for home at the close of the term, remarked, "All things are going to be different with me at home, but I'm goin' to try to live a christian."

"They need to be taught how to live as well as to die; So many have died. They are not careful of their feet.

"They are unable to get good books at reasonble prices, and the shoddy stuff they do read only tends to make them dreamy and careless."

CARRIE E. CROWE.

Carrie E. Crowe, principal teacher at Oak Hill 1901 to 1903, and again in 1905, is one to be remembered as having devoted her best years and noblest gifts to the educational work among the Freedmen. It was during the early 80's and through the influence of her cousin Mrs. R. H. Allen, D. D., whose husband was then in the beginning of his work as secretary of the Presbyterian Board of Missions for Freedmen, she was led to consecrate herself to this greatly needed work.

Her first commission was as leading teacher in Scotia Seminary, Concord, North Carolina. During one of the vacations while here, she and Miss D. J. Barber developed a new school at Hendersonville, North Carolina that was continued a number of years under the care of our Freedmen's Board and the personal direction of Sadia L. Carson.

During another vacation she devoloped a school at Nebo, Marion county, N. C. This school came to be known as the Boston Mission. While she was caring for it, her father, who was a Colporteur of the American Tract Society, and her mother came and made their home with her. The maintenance of this school was not pleasing to all the people of that community; and when a total abstinence organization was effected and some regarded it as a menace to the local illicit manufacture of intoxicating liquors, the ill feeling was manifested by the complete destruction and loss of their home. Her parents were so distressed over this destructive work of the "white caps" and the seriousness of the loss sustained that both died a few months later at Durham, N. C.

After the experience of these great trials that came in quick succession, she was requested to open a day and Sunday school and visiting Mission, among the operatives of the Pearl Cotton Mills at Durham. When failing health made it necessary to relinquish this work, it was extended to the other mills at that place and continued by the women of the Southern Presbyterian church, at whose request this work had been originally undertaken.

On resuming work under our Freedmen's Board the first year was spent at Nottoway, near Burkeville, Nottoway county, Virginia.

The next year, 1897, the Mary Holmes Seminary, destroyed by fire at Jackson Jan. 1, 1895, was rebuilt and reopened at West Point, Miss., by Rev. Henry N. Payne, D. D. and she became the principal teacher in that institution. On March 6, 1899, their principal building was again destroyed by fire. After three years of faithful service and another sad experience that tended to impair her health, she became in 1901 principal at Oak Hill Academy, Indian Territory, but after two years, by special request, returned and resumed her former position as leading teacher at West Point, taking with her two pupils from Oak Hill, Lizzie Watt and Iserina Folsom.

In the fall of 1905 she returned to Oak Hill Academy and remained until the month of February following, when she was called to the bedside of the late Mary Holmes at Rockford, Illinois.

Her work since that date has been limited to more healthful localities, namely Gunnison, Utah, and the Spanish Mission in Los Angeles, California. At both of these places she served under commissions issued by our Board of Home Missions.

She is now enjoying the rest of a quiet and frugal life in retirement at Escanto, California, within easy distance of a brother and wife, whose kindness is constant, and having as a companion, a friend, who is as a sister in their modest home.

Her last teaching among the Freedmen was at Oak Hill Academy and she seemed to have a special interest in the young people of that section. This interest was awakened by the fact that during her first term of service at West Point several girls were sent there from the vicinity of Oak Hill, which was then represented as a new country, without previous educational and good church privileges.

She had the earnest desire to follow these girls when they returned to their home communities to see to what extent their christian training at West Point would tend to elevate and ennoble their own lives and through them the lives of others.

This is the desire of every friend of Christian education. It cannot be given too great emphasis. Pupils that give assurance they will "make good" find that there are friends somewhere, when their need is known, ready to "help them to help themselves." It ought to be a source of constant and life-long encouragement to every pupil, specially aided by friends in any of our christian educational institutions, to know that the personal interest of their teachers and friends follows them through life to see and know, that they have profited by their youthful christian training. They are expected to be teachers and leaders in thought and action in their respective communities.

XVII
BUDS OF PROMISE
1884 to 1904.
FAVORED YOUTHFUL CHOCTAW FREEDMEN.

"And Hannah took Samuel to the Temple of the Lord and said to Eli, the priest; I have lent him to the Lord as long as he liveth."

THE object of this chapter is to note the names and careers of a number of the young people that during the early days, were sent or encouraged to attend other educational institutions. As early as 1884, two years before Miss Hartford came to Oak Hill, Rev. Alexander Reid, of Atoka took the lead in arranging for two young men to go to Biddle University, Charlotte, North Carolina, and five young ladies to Scotia Seminary, at Concord, North Carolina. Later the teachers at Oak Hill aided and encouraged others to attend these and other christian institutions of learning established elsewhere by our Freedmen's Board. The present is an opportune time for noting the results, in the way of increased happiness and added usefulness to these young people by one or more years of special training in youth.

In 1884 Richard D. Colbert of the Beaver Dam church was sent to the preparatory school at Biddle University and remained till June 1887. After his return he taught school eleven years. He was then licensed by the Presbytery, and has been preaching the gospel ever since that time.

In 1884 Henry Williams of Doaksville, (Fort Towson) was sent to Biddle University and remained three years. On his return he became a teacher of public school and in 1892 married Annie Ball.

In 1884 Celestine Hodges a daughter of Samuel and Charlotte Hodges, Wheelock, was sent to Scotia Seminary and remained four years. On her return in 1888, she became a teacher and has been teaching most of the time since, serving the first two years as an assistant at Oak Hill.

She became custodian of the buildings, after the departure of Miss Hartford, and was teaching the Oak Hill school, when Mr. McBride arrived a month or so after its opening. Two years later she founded a school and Sunday school along Sandy Branch, that a few years later developed into the church, that bears that name. She is now located upon and improving her own farm southwest of Antlers.

In 1884 Susan Homer, daughter of Wiley Homer, Grant, was sent to Scotia Seminary and remained two years. On her return she served as a teacher until she married Albert Brown. She is now a widow, occupying and improving her own farm, near Grant.

In 1884 Marie Jones and her sister Fannie Jones, daughters of the late Caroline Prince (1911), and Virginia Shoals, daughter of J. Ross and Harriet Shoals, all from the Oak Hill church, were sent to Scotia Seminary.

Marie Jones ofter spending some time at school engaged in teaching and later became the wife of Mr. Sands, a Methodist minister, now located at Kingston, New York.

Fannie Jones remained at Concord, going to school and working in the city until 1898, when she located at St. Louis, where she became the wife of Mr. McNair, and taught school a number of years. She is now occupying the old home near Oak Hill.

Virginia Shoals, now Mrs. Perry, returned in 1901, She has taught school several years and is now living on her own allotment of land near Red River, where she has founded and is endeavoring to maintain a christian home.

Mary Homer (B. 1873) a daughter of Wiley Homer, Grant, after completing a course at Oak Hill attended a Choctaw government school, 1890 to 1894. She engaged in teaching until her marriage to Martin Shoals. She is now improving her own farm and educating her children at Oak Hill.

Hattie Homer (B. 1876), a sister of Mary, after attending a Choctaw government school at Grant 1890 to 1894 and completing a course at Oak Hill, taught school until she became the wife of Nick Colbert, an elder of the Beaver Dam church, after his decease she married Bud Lewis and is now occupying and improving her own farm.

Harriet Stewart (B.1873), and Fidelia Perkins, daughter and step-daughter of Parson Stewart, in 1892 were taken by Mrs. Emma F. McBride, matron, to the Mary Allen Seminary at Crockett, Texas. They remained until Harriet was promoted to the senior and Fidelia to the junior class. Both of them engaged in teaching.

Harriet Stewart after teaching a few years in 1898 became the wife of Rev. Pugh A. Edwards, a minister of the A. M. E. church and is now occupying and improving her farm near Hugo.

Fidelia in 1900 married Thomas H. Murchison, and located at Garvin, where she and her husband have taken a very active part in promoting the work of the Presbyterian church. She served as one of the first superintendents of the

REV. WILEY HOMER.

REV. WILLIAM BUTLER.

REV. AND HARRIET STEWART EDWARDS.

REV. AND MARIA JONES SANDS.

FAVORED YOUNG CHOCTAW FREEDMEN.

Sunday school and he as an elder. She is now serving her sixth year as teacher of the public school at Millerton. She is a good penman, an acceptable teacher and is making a record of commendable usefulness.

Martha Jones, a daughter of Caroline Prince, and Nannie Harris a daughter of Charles B. Harris, in 1893, were sent to Crockett, Texas.

Nannie Harris contracted consumption and died the next year after returning from the school, and Martha Jones going with one of her teachers, located at Frankfort, Kentucky.

Johnson Shoals, son of J. Ross and Hattie, was an early pupil at Oak Hill, and an assistant teacher at that institution during the last term, 1912-1913. He has enjoyed a four years' course of study at Tuskeegee, and four years at the Iowa State Agricultural college, Ames, Iowa. During the last four years he has been working on the old home farm during the summer and teaching school during the winter, which is an ideal plan for the average young man to pursue in early life.

Malinda A. Hall in 1900, after completing the grammar course at Oak Hill Academy, was sent by Mrs. Edward G. Haymaker to Ingleside Seminary at Burkeville, Virginia, where she graduated in 1904. She has taught public school one or more years. Commencing in February 1905 she rendered five years of faithful and efficient service as teacher of domestic science and superintendent of the christian Endeavor society at Oak Hill Academy. In 1911 she became the wife of William Stewart and they are now improving their own new farm home south of Valliant.

Edward D. Jones, a class mate of Malinda Hall and native of Bluff, Okla., after completing the grammar course in 1900, graduated from Jackson college, Jackson, Miss., five years later, and in 1909 from the Medical school at Raleigh, N. C. He has since been engaged in the practice of medicine in his native state and is now located at Nowata, where he has acquired an extensive and lucrative patronage.

In 1903 when Carrie E. Crowe returned to Mary Holmes Seminary at West Point, Miss., she was instrumental in having Lizzie Watt and Iserina Folsom, both Oak Hill pupils, follow her to that institution.

Lizzie Watt was from Arkansas. Going with her mistress to spend some time at Winona Lake, Ind., she there met Mrs. M. E. Crowe, matron at Oak Hill. So great was the interest awakened she became a pupil at Oak Hill that fall, and remained until she was encouraged to go to the Mary Holmes Seminary. When last heard from, through the head of that institution, she was teaching and doing well.

Iserina Folsom, daughter of Moses and Martha Folsom, after her return from West Point in 1905, married Amos Ward, a farmer, and lives at Grant.

Samuel A. Folsom of the Forest church, and early pupil at Oak Hill, in 1903-5 spent two years at Biddle University. On his return he taught one year at Oak Hill Academy, aided in the erection of the temporary Boys' Hall after the fire of Nov. 8. 1908; and, serving as foreman of the carpenters, made it possible for the superintendent to erect Elliott Hall in 1910, by employing only the labor of students and patrons of the academy. On becoming a member and elder of the Oak Hill church, be enjoyed the privilege of representing the Presbytery in the General Assembly at Denver in May, 1909. Returning later in search of health he died there at 29, Jan. 11, 1912.

George Shoals, in 1903-05, spent two years at Biddle University. Since his return he married Redonia Grier and they are now improving their own farm near Grant.

George Stewart, 1903-5 spent two years at Tuskegee. In 1910 he married Ara Brown, an Oak Hill student, and they are now industriously and successfully improving their own farm near the academy at Valliant.

In 1904, when the Pittsburg Mission at Atoka was closed, Mrs. O. D. Spade, one of the teachers, took Lucretia C. Brown, a pupil of eight years, to her home at Bellefontaine, Ohio, and enabled her to graduate from the Grammar and High schools of that city in 1910. In 1912, after rendering one year of earnest and faithful service as assistant matron at Oak Hill Academy, she became the wife of Everett Richards, one of the older students at Oak Hill that year; and they are now improving and enjoying their own farm home near Lukfata. When their home was gladdened by the birth of their first born on Christmas night, 1913, they named it, Lucian Elliott, in honor of Mrs. Spade, her youthful benefactress.

Samuel S. Bibbs and Henry D. Prince in 1904 went to Biddle University and remained one year. Henry, after supporting his venerable mother until her decease in 1911, is now industriously engaged in improving his own farm near the academy. S. S. Bibbs in 1912 married Fannie McElvene, and is now located at Broken Bow, where he is making a good record in a new section of the country.

On March 4, 1906, James Stewart and Mary Garland, two previously promising Oak Hill students, were married at the academy. They are now industriously and earnestly developing a comfortable home on their own farm.

These incidents relating to the special education of the first young people among the Choctaw Freedmen are quite suggestive and interesting.

These young people may be said to represent buds of promise found in the wilderness, where the wild flowers bloom that are cared for only by a Heavenly Father's eye. They are transplanted for a time, where they may receive Bible instruction, industrial training and a foretaste of the privileges of an enlightened christian civilization. They are then returned to the wilderness with the Bible in hand, like the Huguenots and Pilgrim Fathers, when they first came to America, to become the standard bearers of truth, purity and industry, founders of prosperous christian homes, and intelligent promoters of the best interests of their people.

Their education and training was the first intelligent effort to provide a supply of competent native teachers and preachers for the colored people in the south part of the Choctaw Nation. However humble their station and limited their attainment, they represent the first generation of native teachers.

It was also an effort to introduce into the homes of the people on their return, correct ideals of an intelligent christian civilization. It was the day of small things and of humble beginnings.

It is encouraging to note that in all instances where they remained long enough in school to make sufficient progress, they became teachers and Sunday school superintendents on their return to their own neighborhoods. Some of them are still teaching and one after teaching eleven years has made a good record as a faithful minister of the gospel.

BUDS OF PROMISE 153

Those that have married have in most instances become the founders of prosperous christian homes, and the most influential leaders in their several communities. By their industry, frugality and piety, they are proving themselves, in a very commendable way, to be "the salt of the earth and the light of the world," among their own people.

Several of them died soon after their return from school. This is a disappointment that is more deeply felt in Mission work than elsewhere. The proportion of short lives in this list is perhaps no greater than would be found in similar lists taken from other sections of the country. Good health and the disposition to take good care of it are very important assets, on the part of those who are encouraged to take special courses of training in missionary educational institutions.

These incidents were not without their influence on the mind of Alexander Reid in leading him to approve the plan of establishing a boarding school for the Freedmen in Indian Territory and Oak Hill as the most needy and favorable location for it. The Board was maintaining missions at Muskogee and Atoka, but those locations were not then attractive. One of his last acts in 1885, his last year, was the purchase of the Old Log House from Robin Clark for the use of the school.

The fact this emigration to distant schools continued, after the establishment of Oak Hill as a boarding school, awakens a little surprise. Only a very limited number of them in later years, remained at Oak Hill to complete the Grammar course. The good old rule of local prosperity "Patronize Home Industries," or institutions, seemed to have been forgotten. The sentiment began to prevail that any school abroad was better than one at home. The general prevalence of this sentiment tended to put a slight check upon the successful development of the work at Oak Hill. It was bereft of the presence and co-operation of its older and best trained pupils, just when their example of self-control and habits of study were beginning to exert a good influence over the new ones.

XVIII
CLOSED IN 1904

In the spring of 1904, as there was no one available to manage it, the school was closed, and a student was entrusted with the care of the buildings, stock and crops.

As this was the year the land in Indian Territory was allotted to the Indians and their former slaves, individually, Mr. Haymaker remained until he secured the allotment of two tracts of forty acres each, on which the buildings of the academy were located, one to a graduate student and the other to a friendly full blood Choctaw woman; with the understanding that, when the restrictions should be removed, the allottees or owners would sell them to the Board of Missions for Freedmen, to be held and used as a permanent site for the institution.

In August Miss Bertha L. Ahrens of Grant, a missionary teacher of the Board, became the custodian of the buildings and other property belonging to the institution.

A few days later, Soloman Buchanan, a former student from Texas, returned and making his home there, began to take care of the stock and crops. His general efficiency, manifest interest and good staying quality enabled him to become ever since a very valuable helper, during term time.

XIX
REOPENING AND ORGANIZATION
1905.

TWO-FOLD ORGANIZATION OF THE WORKERS.—NEW FEATURES.—CHARACTER BUILDING.—VISIT OF MRS. V. P. BOGGS.

>"Do all the good you can,
> By all the means you can,
> In all the ways you can,
> In all the places you can,
> At all the times you can,
> To all the people you can,
> As long as ever you can."—Wesley.

AFTER two weeks of voluntary service in the vicinity of the Academy, visiting churches, schools, institutes and towns, making the trips through the timber with a team of faithful but superannuated mules, and delivering addresses in as many as eight different places, during the month preceding, the academy was reopened for a three months term in February, 1905, under the management of Rev. and Mrs. R. E. Flickinger of Fonda, Iowa. They had for their assistants, Miss Adelia M. Eaton, Fonda, Iowa, matron, Miss Bertha L. Ahrens, principal, Miss Malinda A. Hall and Henry C. Shoals, assistants in the cooking and farming departments, and Solomon Buchanan, a volunteer student accompanist and general helper.

TWO FOLD ORGANIZATION OF THE WORKERS

The moral and religious instruction was organized after the following manner. The Bible was supplied and read by all as a daily text book in the school. The lady principal served as superintendent of the Sunday school, and as organist and chorister at all the other meetings. The assistant superintendent took charge of the primary department of the Sunday school, the matron, the Bible class; the assistant matron, the intermediate class, and the general management of the work among the Christian Endeavorers, selecting and aiding the leaders in their preparation for and conduct of their meetings on Sabbath evenings, in which all the students were required to participate. Mr. Buchanan served as organist for the Sunday school and accompanist on the piano at the other meetings.

The superintendent, in addition to attending and participating in the Sabbath school and Endeavor meetings, which were held on Sabbath mornings and evenings, conducted the preaching service on Sabbath morning, the Bible memory meetings at 2:30 on Sabbath afternoons and the mid-week service, which was held on Friday evenings.

VOICE CULTURE.

The training and development of their youthful voices, for efficient participation by song or story in religious meetings on their return home, was made a distinct aim and object at the Friday evening meetings.

This special vocal training was based on the fact, that in all the recorded instances of the manifestation of divine or spiritual power, it has been communicated through the use or instrumentality of the human voice. The annual results, of this training of their voices for a sacred use, were a very gratifying surprise to all the patrons of the school.

The superintendent also conducted the family worship at which all of the students and teachers were present. It consisted in the daily reading of the Scriptures and prayer immediately at the close of the morning and evening meals. Twice a week the young people united in repeating a Psalm or other appropriate selection and the Lord's Prayer.

He also invariably attended and participated by a word of encouragement in the Sunday school and Endeavor meetings.

CHARACTER BUILDING

It was the constant endeavor of the superintendent to make the hours spent together on Sabbath afternoons and Friday evenings, not only the most instructive and profitable of all the week to the students, in the matter of their character building, but also the most joyous and happy to all of them. All cares and troubles were forgotten, while repeating responsively and cheerily together many of the most thrilling and comforting passages of the Bible, or singing merrily the beautiful hymns, plantation melodies, sacred anthems and patriotic glees, that enlisted mutual attention and interest. The joyous blending of their many happy, youthful voices, sometimes soft and low, then rising and swelling with all possible animation into full chorus, while singing together the "Beautiful Story" that "Never Grows Old" and "Must be Told," "Break Forth into Joy," "Before Jehovah's Throne," "Hail to the Flag," "Freedom's Banner" and similar familiar selections, are sweet and blessed treasures of the memory, that are invariably recalled with pleasure and delight.

NEW FEATURES

In addition to the branches that had been previously taught, arrangements were now made for special instruction in voice culture and vocal music, one hour a week for all the pupils; and the young men in agriculture, horticulture, house-painting, carpentry and masonry.

The aim of these new departments was to awaken an intelligent interest and make every one familiar with the principles that would enable them to make
    The Farm,
        The Garden,
            The Orchard,
                The Dairy,
                    The Cattle,
                        The pigs and Poultry,
all a source of greatest profit to them as owners.

An earnest effort was also made to check the stream of migration to distant schools, by bringing the work at Oak Hill to such a degree of efficiency as to meet the real needs of every young person in its vicinity.

This was successfully accomplished by a voluntary and gratuitous establishment, on the part of the superintendent and principal, of Normal and Theological departments, that were maintained as long as there was any real need for them; the former until the fall of 1907, the last year under territorial rule preceding the establishment of county normal institutes; and the latter in 1910, when the last licentiate was ordained to the full work of the gospel ministry.

VISIT OF MRS. V. P. BOGGS, SECRETARY

The late Mrs. V. P. Boggs, secretary of the Women's Department of the Freedmen's Board was a welcome visitor in the fall of 1907. Her observations were afterwards summarized in a printed report as follows:

"Since the re-opening of Oak Hill Academy in February 1905 it has had an era of prosperity that promises permanency. Many improvements have been made, new buildings for farm purposes have been erected, much of the land has been refenced and is gradually being brought under a high-

REOPENING AND ORGANIZATION 159

er state of cultivation, and there is a general improvement in the appearance of the entire premises, that reflects credit on the management, as well as upon the boys who do the work. The literary work progresses under well trained teachers, and a normal department has been added that teachers may be better fitted to supply the schools, which it is hoped will be maintained in the south part of the Territory. The home department is managed, to the comfort and happiness of all by the wife of the superintendent, who 'looketh well to the ways of her household.' The matron's duties, which include the general management of all matters relating to the work in the Girls' Hall, including the sewing, laundry and kitchen departments, are performed with conscientiousness and enthusiasm. A former graduate student is rendering very efficient service in the cooking department."

"The property of the Board, farm and buildings, is the most attractive and prosperous in appearance in that region. The location is beautiful, the buildings good for that section are well painted, the ground well fenced and in good order. Some good farm buildings have been erected by the students and they have painted other large buildings in a very workmanlike manner. Considerable land has been redeemed from a state of wildness. Thrift and order are apparent everywhere indoors and out."—V. P. Boggs, Secretary Woman's Department.

SUCCESSION OF HELPERS.

The succession of helpers during the eight years, 1905 to 1912, inclusive, when Rev. R. E. Flickinger was Superintendent, was as follows:

Assistant Superintendent: Mrs. Mary A. Flickinger, Feb. 1, 1905, to Aug. 1, 1909.

Principals: Miss Bertha L. Ahrens, Feb. 1, 1905,- Feb. 1, 1911, having been previously custodian of the premises from Aug. 1, 1904; Mrs. W. H. Carroll, Feb. 1, to May 27, 1911; Rev. W. H. Carroll, Oct. 1, 1911, to June 13, 1912.

Matrons: Adelia M. Eaton, Feb. 1, 1905, to June 5, 1908; Mrs. John Claypool, 1908-09; Mary I. Weimer, 1909-1911; Jo Lu Wolcott, Feb. 27 to June 13, 1912.

Assistant Teachers: Carrie E. Crowe, Oct. 1, 1905 to Jan. 31, 1906; Mrs. Sarah L. Wallace, Feb. 1 to Mar. 31, 1906; Mary A. Donaldson, April 1 to May 31, 1906; Rev. W. H. Carroll, Oct. 28, 1907, to May 28, 1908, and Oct. 25, 1909, to Apr. 28, 1910; Samuel A. Folsom, Oct. 26, 1908, to May 28, 1909; Solomon H. Buchanan, Nov. 15, 1910, to 1911; Mrs. W. H. Carroll, Oct. 16, 1911, to June 13, 1912.

Assistants in the Cooking Department and Sewing Room: Malinda A. Hall, Feb. 1, 1905, to June 30, 1909, and Nov. 15, 1910, to June 15, 1911; Mrs. Virginia Wofford, 1909; Ruby Moore and Ruby Peete, 1909 to 1910; Lucretia C. Brown, 1911 to 1912; Ora Perry, 1912.

Pianist and Librarian: Solomon H. Buchanan, 1905-1912, except 1909.

Foremen, Carpenters: Samuel A. Folsom and Edward Hollingsworth in 1910.

Whilst the great need of the colored people in the South is the opportunity for intellectual, manual, moral and religious training, to all of which they are readily responsive and make encouraging improvement, it remains a fact, that the material development of the southern states depends in a great measure upon the general education and intelligence of the colored people; and that a manifestation of prejudice against their general education through public or mission schools is sinful, impolitic and unpatriotic.

It is only a few years since the report was made that in Florida 64.5 per cent, in South Carolina, 69.5, and in Louisiana, 76.4 per cent of the children of school age were unprovided for with school privileges.

Under favorable conditions it is a delightful work to supply a need for which there is so great and urgent a de-

MRS. MARY A. FLICKINGER.

MRS. JOHN CLAYPOOL.

BERTHA L. AHRENS.

ADELIA M. EATON.

ROBERT ELLIOTT FLICKINGER.

mand, and such manifest appreciation, and, that means so much in promoting the intelligence and thereby increasing the happiness and prosperity of so many of the common people, whose general education tends to make our nation greater.

XX
THE PROSPECTUS IN 1912

SCHOOL AND WORK PERIODS.—FARM WORK.—IMPROVEMENT WORK.—SAWING WOOD A PICNIC.

"Art and science soon would fade
And commerce dead would fall,
If the farmer ceased to reap and sow
For the farmer feeds them all."

IN 1912 the prospectus of the academy included the following announcements:

Free tuition and books are accorded neighborhood pupils under thirteen, that attend regularly after the time of their enrollment. Those over fourteen are expected to pay fifty cents a month. The hope is expressed that every one living near the Academy will see the propriety of making the same noble endeavor to enjoy its valuable privileges for improvement that is made by the many patrons who live at a distance.

An opportunity will be afforded a limited number of both boys and girls over fourteen years to work out their term expenditures, with the exception of $5.00 which must be paid at the time of enrollment. This opportunity to work one's own way through school is given to two boys and two girls during the term at one time and to others during the vacation period.

After spending six and one-half or seven hours at study in the class room, three hours, in the latter part of the after-

THE PROSPECTUS IN 1912   163

noon of each day, are devoted to industrial training and work on the farm, in the shop, kitchen, laundry or sewing room. All work during this period is required to be done by the rule, which is first stated at the time of assignment, and afterwards illustrated during the hours of work; and the student is required to work as silently, thoughtfully and earnestly as during the hours previously devoted to study.

Parents are requested to note that girls are not allowed to wear white waists, skirts or dresses, except at the time of commencement and that each student must supply their own toilet soap, combs and shoe polish.

The Bible is a required text book and every student is expected to commit an average of one verse and read one chapter each day during the term. The passages committed to memory are recited in concert to the superintendent at the Bible Memory Service held every Sabbath afternoon.

The actual cost of carrying a boarding student through the term is about $50.00. Every student that pays $28.00 or does extra work to that amount enjoys a scholarship of equal amount contributed by the many friends who are supporting the institution. Under this arrangement the student that does most to help himself receives most from the friends who are ready to co-operate with him. The doors of the Academy are thus open to the penniless and homeless boy or girl, if they have a desire to be useful and are willing to work; but young people who lack funds and at the same time are unwilling to do extra work to cover the first half of their expenses, are not regarded as either promising or desirable.

Since one half the cost of carrying boarding students at the Academy has to be provided for by the generous offerings of friends, who are interested in their temporal, moral and spiritual welfare, every student is expected to show his appreciation of this fact, by being always thoughtful and earnest, during all the hours set apart each day for study and work. Only those who learn quickly how to be silent, thoughtful and earnest workers, make that improvement in study and work which forms the chief element in the reward of teachers and friends.

The student that makes the most encouraging progress is the one that enters at the beginning of the term and continues to attend and work faithfully until the end of it.

The annual report of the superintendent of Indian Territory for the year 1907 shows that at the Indian Orphan School at Wheelock, eight miles east of Oak Hill, the cost of carrying each pupil a term of nine months was $155.17, or an average of $17.05 a month. A comparison of these figures with the cost at that time at Oak Hill, $25.00 a term of seven months, or $3.60 a month, it is easy to see that the economy practiced in a mission school is much greater than in one under government control.

SCHOOL AND WORK PERIODS

Provision is made for eight hours of school work on the part of the teachers, the first five days of every week of the term, and one hour on Saturday evening. These are daily enjoyed by all the smaller pupils. But all over fourteen years, after enjoying $6\frac{1}{2}$ hours in the school room, are expected to work three hours each day in the latter part of the afternoon, and on Saturdays until 2:30 p. m.

The two leading objects that are attained by this arrangement are, the opportunity to give and receive practical instruction in the rules, or best methods of doing every part of the work in the home or on an improved farm; and enable those for whose benefit the institution has been established, to perform the work that is necessary to be done for the daily comfort of the students during term time, and the successful and economical management of the farm which now contains 270 acres, of which 140 acres are enclosed and 100 are under cultivation.

THE WOOD SUPPLY

The sawing and splitting of the wood at the two woodpiles, to meet the daily demands of the many and large stoves, that have to be kept constantly running, is the regular morning and evening chore of those of the boys, that are not otherwise employed at that time about the buildings or stock. The preparation of the fuel in the timber and again at the woodpiles is, to say the least, a long and rather monotonous employment. Boys who do not manifest an interest in this part of their early training, by reason of its necessity and general healthfulness, are prone to regard it as a very wearisome employment, until they acquire skill in the matter of position and movement, and then their delight is manifested in efforts to outdo one another.

THE FARM WORK

In order that friends at a distance may know something of the regular methods of work during the three-hour work periods of each day and during the period of the term the following notes are added:

During the first four or more weeks of the term, all the available student help is busily employed gathering in the crops of cowpeas, potatoes, corn and cotton. In order that their undivided attention may be given to this important work at this time, all the wood needed for fuel during this period has to be brought from the timber, before the end of the previous term.

As soon as the crops have been gathered the long campaign for the year's supply of wood in the timber,—about 25 cords,—has to be undertaken and continued from week to week, especially on Saturdays until the end of the term.

If the necessary materials are on hand, this is the golden time to start the older and best trained boys on the permanent improvement work outlined for the year, such as fence building, sprouting, clearing of new lands, the construction of conveniences for the school, home or farm, the repair of old the erection and painting of new buildings and finally, the preparation of the ground and planting of the crops for the next year.

The boys, however, are never taken to the timber or fields when the ground is damp or the weather is cold and unfavorable. When from these causes they cannot work to advantage, they continue their studies in the class room, all the day.

The two winter months of January and February have been ordinarily unfavorable for student work in the timber or fields. The work is then, to a considerable extent, limited to the carpenter shop, cellar, or indoor work on new buildings.

IMPROVEMENT WORK

In order that the work performed by the students during the industrial hours of each week, may serve to promote the welfare of the institution as well as for training the individual, it devolves upon the superintendent and matron to have ready suitable work, and all the tools and materials necessary to execute it, when the students are ready for assignment.

This work includes the chores morning and evening, the preparation of the fuel—about twenty-five cords an-

THE PROSPECTUS IN 1912

nually, first in the timber and then at the woodpile—the cultivation of the farm and garden, the harvesting of the crops and the care of the stock, all of which may be termed necessary routine work.

In addition thereto there may be permanent improvement work, such as the clearing of new lands for cultivation and enclosing them with good fences, the repair of old and the erection of new buildings and the manufacture of articles of furniture or comfort, for the better equipment of the many rooms in the buildings.

A plain statement of these two kinds of work will indicate to nearly every one the prime importance of endeavoring to accomplish as much improvement work as possible each term. There is now more of this improvement work pressing for immediate attention than possibly may be done during the next three years, but it needs now to be contemplated, intelligently provided for, and then executed as speedily as possible.

SAWING WOOD, A PICNIC

Saturday forenoon has come to be recognized as the special fuel or timber day of each week. It is a busy and bustling day for all. For this day's work two dozen boys are organized and equipped with axes, a splitting outfit, four cross-cut saws and the mule team. The axe men are divided into two squads, the axe men or stumpers who cut down trees, and the trimmers who trim the trunks and large branches. Three boys are assigned to each crosscut, two of whom are expected to keep the saw running steadily, while the third one, who is supposed to be resting, carries a light lever and, with the weight of his body raises the log under the crosscut, so it will not bind the saw as it goes through it. By taking turns at the saw and lever, the hardness of this work is greatly relieved, and it sometimes is surprising to see the amount of work, done by the small boys, when they have "a mind to work." If the logs are large or the saw runs hard, it is not unusual for them to couple together and merrily make the running of the saw a four-handed affair. The superintendent, or one of the older boys acting as a foreman, goes before the saws and with an axe marks out the work for them, so they can work speedily, and so that every piece that may serve for posts, long or short, or for fence props or rails, is cut the proper length.

The boys have worked faithfully and industriously in the timber on Saturday forenoons. A rest of fifteen minutes has always been given, about the middle of the forenoon. When the signal is given, they assemble at some convenient place, where there are several logs suited for seats; for all are required to be seated as the best way to rest their weary limbs, during this period.

A pail of fresh water and a paper sack filled with soda crackers is always provided for their enjoyment at this time. A smile of pleasure and delight is sure to light up the countenance of every boy, when, taking his turn, he thrusts his hand into the paper sack and draws therefrom his appointed number of crackers.

At these periods of rest and lunch all usually seem as happy as if they were enjoying a regular social picnic dinner. Amid the merriment and pleasantry of the occasion they seem to forget all consciousness of weariness, or thought that their work is hard, and resume it again with pleasure and delight.

XXI
OBLIGATION AND PLEDGES ..

OBLIGATION.—ENDEAVOR. — SELP-HELP STUDENTS. — TEMPERANCE.—THE INTOXICATING CUP.—PRESIDENT LINCOLN.—PRESIDENT HARRISON.

"Thy vows are upon me O God. I will pay my vows unto the Lord, in the presence of all his people."—David.

I. THE STUDENT'S OBLIGATION

ON being received as a student of this institution, I do solemnly promise, God helping me, that I will be obedient to the rules of this institution and endeavor to prove myself an earnest student and thoughtful, faithful worker; that I will be prompt in responding to every call, pay the cost of repair to any furniture or glass broken, as a result of thoughtlessness or carelessness on my part; and that I will refrain from the use of profane or angry words to man or beast; and also from the use of tobacco, cigarettes, snuff, dice, gamblers cards, and intoxicating liquors as a beverage, while I enjoy the privileges of the academy.

II. CHRISTIAN ENDEAVOR PLEDGE

Trusting in the Lord Jesus Christ for strength, I promise him that I will strive to do whatever he would like to have me do; that I will pray to Him and read the Bible every day, and that, so far as I know how, throughout my whole life, I will endeavor to lead a christian life.

III. PLEDGE OF SELF-HELP STUDENTS

As long as I am accorded and enjoy the privilege of a home and of a student at Oak Hill Academy, recognizing the fact that my time during the periods of work does not belong to me, but to the institution;

I solemnly pledge my word and honor, God helping me, that I will refrain from making any engagement elsewhere, that might interfere with the faithful and constant performance of the duties devolving on me at Oak Hill; that I will conscientiously keep my word as to the time of my return, when absent from my home at the academy; that I will yield a prompt and cordial obedience to all the rules and regulations relating to the conduct of students at the academy, and that I will constantly endeavor to show myself worthy the confidence and esteem of the superintendent and his helpers; and not leave the institution until I have honorably met all of my obligations.

IV. TOTAL-ABSTINENCE PLEDGE

"Abstain from all appearance of evil."—Paul.

"With malice toward none and charity for all, I the undersigned do pledge my word and honor,

GOD HELPING ME

To abstain from all Intoxicating Liquors as a beverage and that I will, by all honorable means, encourage others to abstain.

OBLIGATION AND PLEDGES 171

An acre of government land costs $1.25, and a bottle of whiskey about $2.00. How strange that so many people prefer the whiskey.

THE INTOXICATING CUP

Within this glass destruction rides,
And in its depths does ruin swim;
Around its foam perdition glides,
And death is dancing on its brim.

WHAT THEY THINK ABOUT IT

A curse.—Queen Victoria.

A scandal and a shame.—Gladstone.

It stupefies and besots.—Bismark.

The devil in solution.—Sir Wilfred Lawson.

The mother of want and the nurse of crime.—Lord Brougham.

Saloons are traps for workingmen.—Earl Cairnes.

ABRAHAM LINCOLN

The following is the pledge of Abraham Lincoln, the great emancipator.

"Whereas, the use of alcoholic liquors as a beverage is productive of pauperism, degradation and crime, and believing it is our duty to discourage that which produces more evil than good; we, therefore pledge ourselves to abstain from the use of intoxicating liquors as a beverage."

When Lincoln signed the pledge he was a tall awkward youth, and the only one that went forward at the meeting in the log school house to sign it that night. When he was president, "Old Uncle John," who induced him to sign it, called on him at the White House and Lincoln said:

"I owe more to you than to almost any one of whom I can think. If I had not signed the pledge in the days of my youthful temptation, I should probably have gone the way of a majority of my early companions, who lived drunkard's lives and are now filling drunkard's graves."

After reconstruction, the next great question is the overthrow of the liquor traffic.—Abraham Lincoln.

WILLIAM HENRY HARRISON

"Gentlemen I have now twice refused your request to partake of the wine cup. That should be sufficient. I made a resolve when I started in life, that I would avoid strong drink: I have never broken that pledge. I am one of a class of seventeen young men who graduated; the other sixteen fill drunkard's graves, all due to the pernicious habit of wine drinking. I owe my health, happiness and prosperity to the fact I have never broken my pledge of total abstinence. I trust you will not again urge me to do so."

This noble answer was given to friends who were dining with him at the old Washington House in Chester, Pa., when he was a candidate for president.

XXII
BIBLE STUDY AND MEMORY WORK

AIMS IN BIBLE STUDY.—SELF-CONTROL.—TRAINING THE MEMORY AND VOICE.—DIVINE TRUTH THE NEED OF ALL.—ONE BOOK IN THE HOME.—COMMITTED TO MEMORY.—THE BIBLE ONLY IN SUNDAY SCHOOL.—A LIFE-LONG GOLDEN TREASURE.—A FOUNTAIN OF BLESSING.—UPLIFTING POWER IN NEW HEBRIDES.

"Hold fast the form of sound words; * * * that ye may be able to give to every one that asketh, a reason of the hope that is in you."—Paul.

THE development of the Bible-memory work, that, during the later years of this period, moved forward very rapidly, was one of small beginnings and slow progress at first. The meetings were held at half past two o'clock on Sabbath afternoons.

The girls were formed into one class and their meeting was held in the sitting room of the Girls' Hall. The boys met immediately afterwards in the office of the superintendent in the Boys' Hall.

The weekly lesson consisted in committing to memory five to seven verses in the more important chapters of the New Testament and Psalms, commencing with the ten commandments in Exodus XX, 1-17. The passages assigned were read and studied every week in the school under the direction of the principal, in order that all the younger pupils, as well as the older ones, might be able to repeat them on Sabbath.

At the meetings, which were conducted by the superintendent, the lesson assigned would have to be read over several times in concert before their voices would acquire the right movement and expression. The effort to train the memory, by committing scripture verses, was one from which many of them shrank as being too irksome, and the weekly lesson of one verse a day would have to be repeated a number of times, before most of them could continue to be heard to the end of the lesson. The previous lessons were then reviewed, to fasten them more firmly on the memory. The advance lesson was then read together that all might surely know its place and extent.

AIMS IN BIBLE STUDY

"Accurate Bible Knowledge" and "Character building" were the keynotes of the instruction given at these meetings. A third object, that was constantly kept in view, was the training and development of their youthful voices for public address in religious meetings. This was accomplished by making a large use of the concert drill, both in reading and repeating the classic and beautiful passages of the Bible.

The tendency of the new pupils to speak and act badly from sudden impulse, was freely admitted at these meetings. As a means of enabling them to put a check on their impulsive dispositions and acquire the art of self-control, the following questions were prepared and asked of each, at the opening of the lesson hour.

1. During the week that has passed, have you refrained entirely from the use of profane or quarrelsome words and actions?

2. Have you been uniformly respectful and obedient to all of your teachers?

3. Are you using your spare moments each day for some good purpose, that will promote your best interests?

BIBLE STUDY AND MEMORY WORK 175

The cordial and helpful cooperation of Miss Adelia Eaton, our first matron, in connection with this Bible memory work at the period when it was most difficult to awaken interest and enthusiasm in it, was very greatly appreciated. Although her presence was not required, she voluntarily arranged to be present at every meeting. She seldom if ever participated in the meetings, but she invariably arranged the room in the most convenient form for the meeting and continued to patiently aid and encourage those of the girls, to whom this memory work was the hardest, until the last moment before the meeting. The increased attendance of later years, made it advisable to hold these Bible meetings in the chapel, and there both classes met together.

TRAINING THE MEMORY

The memory, the natural power of retaining and recalling what has been learned, is the basis of all progress in study. It is the faculty that enriches the mind by preserving the treasures of labor and industry. The beauty and perfection of all the other mental faculties are dependent on it. Without its aid there can be no advancement in knowledge, arts and sciences; and no improvement in virtue, morals and religion.

Those who cannot read acquire knowledge by hearing, and their vision is occupied principally with large rather than small objects. It was soon a matter of observation that the children of illiterate parents in whose homes there are no books, find it very difficult to learn to read, after they have passed fourteen years of age. That which is natural and easy in childhood, becomes more difficult the longer it is delayed. They form the habit and find it much easier to acquire knowledge like their parents by the ear, or "by air" as it is sometimes called, than by poring over the letters and words of a printed line in a book. Many that are over fourteen before they are sent to school shrink from the mental discipline and labor of learning things so small as letters and words, and seek relief by looking elsewhere than on the printed page.

By the aid of a memory that has been trained for service in childhood, one is able to learn easily and rapidly; and also to express their treasures of knowledge in such a way as to give life and animation to every word that is uttered.

The memory is very responsive to training in childhood and youth. Its retentive power may then be very greatly increased by judicious exercise and labor, which have that distinct end in view, just as the limbs gradually grow stronger by daily exercise. If it is accustomed to retain a moderate quantity of knowledge in childhood, it is strengthened and fitted for more rapid development in youth. That is the golden period to learn the "form of sound words," that shall exert a moulding influence upon the entire life.

Repeated acts form a habit, and habits of thought may be aided by a methodical system in the arrangement of intellectual possessions. Frequent review, repetition, conscious delight in the things to be learned and association of the new with the known, are important aids to the memory, that may be profitably observed throughout the entire life.

DIVINE TRUTH THE NEED OF ALL

Truth is the natural food for the mind and does for it what bread and meat do for the body. The mental faculties include the intellect, the power of thought; the memory, the conscience, the power that enables one to distinguish be-

BIBLE STUDY AND MEMORY WORK 177

tween right and wrong; and the judgment, the power of decision. There are no truths so well adapted for the best training and development of all these faculties, as the great and important ones that God has so attractively and plainly revealed in His holy word. The poetic parts of the Old Testament and the words of Jesus in the New, are adapted alike for the comfort and instruction of childhood, manhood and old age. "Man shall not live by bread alone, but by every word that proceedeth out of the mouth of God." "I am the living bread which came down from heaven; if any man eat of this bread he shall live forever."

ONE BOOK IN THE HOME

One aim of the requirement to commit one verse a day in the Bible presented to each pupil was, of course, to make even those, whose terms in school were the shortest, familiar with some of the most important parts of the one book, they were expected to take to their homes; but another distinct aim was to develop the memory of every pupil so as to make the mastery of other books easier and their progress in them more rapid.

Every pupil was encouraged to train their memory to be their ready and faithful servant, so that it would recall a line, a verse or a rule, when it had been carefully traced the third time, by the eye.

The definitions and rules form the most important parts of most of the necessary text-books above the primary department. The future value of these studies, as well as the pupils advance in them while in school, depends on his ability to understand, apply and easily remember the rules. The thorough teacher will discard the use of those superficial authors, whose books lack these important parts, tersely and plainly stated. The sooner that a pupil learns to follow, obey and never to violate a rule, the sooner does he begin to advance rapidly and profitably in his studies.

COMMITTED TO MEMORY

The memory work of a term, according to the rule, one verse a day, would usually carry the student through the following passages:

The Oak Hill Endeavor Benediction, Numbers 6, 24-26 and Rev. 1, 5-6; The Ten Commandments Exodus 20, 1-17; Words of Comfort, Confession and Devotion, Psalms 1st, 8th, 19th, 23d, 27th, 50th, 51st, 90th, 103d, part of the 119th, 122d and 150th; Wise Counsels, Proverbs 3d and 4th; A new heart promised, Ezekiel 36,25-32; John Baptist's Message, Matthew 3d; The Beatitudes and Sermon on the Mount, Matthew 5th; The Divinity of Christ, John 1st; His Farewell Address, John 14th; The Bible inspired, 2 Timothy 3, 14-17. Also the first half of the Westminster Shorter Catechism, with its ever memorable beginning, "Man's Chief end is to glorify God and enjoy Him forever."

Every new pupil is encouraged to read the Bible in course, an average of one chapter a day or seven each week, making report of progress at the Bible hour each Sabbath afternoon. By this plan many of them read, during their first term, the books of Matthew, Mark, Luke, John, Acts and Romans.

THE BIBLE ONLY IN THE SUNDAY SCHOOL

The Inter-National lessons are always prepared for the Sunday school hour, but always and only from the Bible in the hand of each scholar. The teachers only are supplied with other helps, and even these are used only during the period of preparation. The Bible, black board, map and charts only are used by the teacher and students during the

BIBLE STUDY AND MEMORY WORK

Sunday school session. This use of the Bible only in the Sunday school, served to create a demand for it on the part of every scholar and attendant, and to increase the familiarity of each with their own copy of it. It is a good plan for any teacher or Sunday school, that wishes to promote reading and circulation of the Scriptures in the homes of the people.

A LIFE-LONG GOLDEN TREASURE

He has a rich treasure whose memory is well stored with words from the Holy Scriptures. Such a treasure is "more to be desired than gold, yea, than much fine gold." It is a life-long treasure to those who secure it in youth. It cannot be taken away, but it may be imparted to others. Whoever shares this treasure with others, sows the good seed of the Kingdom of God and realizes in his own soul, that he "who sows bountifully shall also reap bountifully."

Committing the scriptures to memory was a delightful employment to the Psalmist, who said: "Thy word have I hid in my heart," and again, "Let my heart be sound in thy statutes." "Thy statutes have been my songs in the house of my pilgrimage." "I will never forget thy precepts; for with them thou hast quickened me and caused me to hate every false way." "Thy word is a lamp unto my feet, and a light unto my path." "Order my steps in thy word; for the entrance of thy words giveth light."

A BEAUTIFUL TRIBUTE

The following beautiful tribute to the Bible, printed by Soper and Son, Detroit, was pasted on the inside of the front lid of every Bible presented to the students.

This Book contains the mind of God, the state of man, the way of salvation, the doom of sinners, and the happiness of believers. Its doctrines are holy, its precepts are binding, its histories are true, and its decisions are immutable.

Read it to be wise, believe it to be safe, and practise it to be holy. It contains light to direct you, food to support you, and comfort to cheer you. It is the traveler's map, the pilgrim's staff, the pilot's compass, the soldier's sword, and the Christian's charter. Here Paradise is restored, heaven opened, and the gates of hell disclosed, Christ is its grand subject, our good its design, and the glory of God its end. It should fill the memory, rule the heart, and guide the feet. Read it slowly, frequently, prayerfully. It is a mine of wealth, a paradise of glory, and a river of pleasure. It is given you in life, will be opened in judgment, and be remembered forever. It involves the highest responsibility, rewards the greatest labor, and condemns all who trifle with its sacred contents.

A FOUNTAIN OF BLESSINGS

The Bible is an infallible revelation from God in regard to his own character, will and works. One result of a practical faith in it is the development of an heroic missionary spirit. The noblest heroisms that mark the history of the human race have had their inspiration in implicit faith in the Bible. "Men in whom life was fresh and strong, and women, the embodiment of gentleness and delicacy, have met the martyrs death of fire, singing until the red-tongued flames licked up their breath."

It is the fountain from which have come the principles of a pure morality and "all sweet charities." It has been the motive power that has effected the regeneration and reformation of millions of men. "It has comforted the humble, consoled the mourning, sustained the suffering and given trust and triumph to the dying."

Rational minds will ask for no higher proof, that the Bible, as a revelation from God is reliable, than the nature and results of the faith that is based upon it. The results include the noblest phenomena of human experience, the richest fruitage of our christian civilization. The Bible is the one great regenerative and redemptive agency in the world, and this soon becomes apparent, whenever it is read in the homes of the people.

UPLIFTING POWER IN NEW HEBRIDES' ISLANDS

A very interesting illustration of this fact has been narrated by John Inglis a Scottish Missionary to the New Hebrides. On going there about the middle of the last century, he selected for his abode an island occupied by cannibals. Among the things he took with him was a mason's hammer. When he began to dress and square the hard rocks of the neighborhood to build the chimney of his house, the novelty of the operation drew a crowd of the natives around him. They looked on in wonder, and were surprised to see the hammer break in pieces and bring into shape those hard stones, which no one had before attempted to break.

Missionaries, like philosophers sometimes find "sermons in stones," as well as "good in everything." On this occasion, he took the stones and the hammer as his text and gave them a short practical sermon as follows:

"You see these stones and this hammer. You might strike these stones with a block of wood till you were tired and you would not break off a single chip; but when I strike with a hammer you see how easily they are broken, or cut into needful shapes. Now God tells us that our hearts are like stones, and that his Word is like a hammer. Some white men came among you before the arrival of the missionaries, and you continued as much heathen as ever. But when the missionaries came and spoke to you, you gave up your heathenism, began to keep the Sabbath day, to worship God and to live like christians. What caused this difference? The words of the missionaries were not any louder or stronger than those of the other white men. The difference was merely this—the other white men spoke their own words; they spoke the words of men; and that was like striking these stones with a piece of wood. But the missionaries instead of speaking to you their own words read to you the

Words of God; and that was like this hammer striking, breaking and bringing into shape your stony hearts."

This illustration took hold on their imagination; the sermon on the stones and the hammer was not soon forgotten. Many years afterwards, some of the older natives when leading in prayer in the church would offer the petition, "O Lord, thy word is like a hammer, take it and with it break our stony hearts and shape them according to the rule of Thy holy law."

There were 3,500 natives on this island. Through the influence of God's Word, for no other means were employed save the human voice to make it known, all of them were led to abandon heathenism and place themselves under Christian instruction.

These people had no money but they could gather and prepare arrowroot. They were encouraged to bring this to the missionaries, in order to secure a supply of Bibles for the island, with the result that in a few years they sent $2,500 to the British and Foreign Bible society, London, for copies of the New Testament and Psalms; and a few years later $3,500 to pay for the printing of the Old Testament in their own language.

There is no instance on record of a like number of heathen people, so poor, being persuaded to contribute so much money to obtain any other book; and why not? It is because the Bible alone is divine and this divine power has subdued human hearts. "Is not my word like as a fire? saith the Lord; and like a hammer that breaketh the rock in pieces?"—Jer. 23. 29.

The Bible is the Book of the Lord, a "sure word of prophecy, whereunto we do well to take heed, as unto a light that shineth in a dark place." It challenges us to "prove all things and hold fast that which is good."

XXIII
DECISION DAYS

CHRISTMAS.—WASHINGTON'S BIRTHDAY.

"How long halt ye between two opinions? If the Lord be God follow him." —Elijah.

EVERY new student at the time of his enrollment was requested to state whether or not he was a member of church. If a negative response was received, he was kindly informed it would be regarded as a serious disappointment, if he did not become an active Christian worker, during the period he enjoyed the privileges of the Academy. As a means of enabling every one to manifest their decision to live a Christian life, Decision days were held frequently during the term. The first one always occurred at least one week before Christmas; and the others about the Day of Prayer for Colleges, Easter and Memorial Sabbaths. When advantage could not be taken of a voluntary visit on the part of a neighboring pastor the co-operation of one of them was always solicited.

On the first occasion Rev. William Butler was present, Feb. 11, 1906, and took for his theme in the morning, the Good Shepherd, and in the evening, the New Heart, his own heart was gladdened by seeing twenty-three young people come to the front in response to his appeal and pledge themselves to live a Christian life. A month later the pastor's heart was gladdened anew by receiving fourteen of them into the membership of the church and administering baptism to ten of them. Two lears later, as the result of an evangelistic meeting held on the evening of the closing day of the Farmers' institute, January 1, 1908, Mr. Butler, who was one of the speakers at the institute, had the pleasure of seeing twenty-one other students manifest a decision to live a Christian life. Rev. Wiley Homer, T. K. Bridges and Samuel Gladman, assisted and with encouraging results on other decision days.

In 1910, Washington's birthday, Thursday, was observed by a patriotic and evangelistic meeting at which impressive addresses were delivered by Rev. W. J. Willis of Garvin and Rev. A. B. Johnson of McAlester. Among those present were thirteen that had not previously manifested a decision. In response to the appeal of Mr. Willis, every one of these thirteen voluntarily arose, came forward and gave their pledge to live a Christian life. The attainment of a voluntary pledge from every student in attendance at that time made this an eventful occasion. It was also deeply impressive. Every one joined in the joyful congratulatory procession.

As it was the last glad and happy decision day before the loss of the Girls' Hall, which occurred on the second Sabbath following, it has been commemorated by an engraving from a photo, thoughtfully taken before hand by Miss Mary Weimer, in which may be seen David Michael, Livingston Brasco, and William Shoals, who have just returned from the timber with vines and white flowers to decorate the chapel for this meeting.

XXIV

THE SELF-HELP DEPARTMENT

FOOLISH NOTIONS.—A PROMISING GIRL.—THOUGHTLESS BOYS.—THOUGHTFUL YOUNG PEOPLE.—VACATION WORKERS.—JAMESTOWN COLLEGE.—SUPPORT OF SELF-SUPPORTING STUDENTS.—HOW IT WORKS.—ENLARGEMENT AND PERMANENT IMPROVEMENT.—SELF-SUPPORT MEANS INDEPENDENCE.—PARK COLLEGE.

"If any would not work, neither should he eat."—Paul.

THE unexpected disappointments experienced in establishing the self-help department are worthy of a brief mention. They serve to illustrate some foolish notions that prevailed among some of our first patrons, and prepare the way for a good suggestion.

The aim of this department is to enlarge the scope of the training work of the institution by the employment of students, as far as possible, to do the necessary work during vacations as well as the chores during the school-terms; and by this means, reducing the number of hired helpers, afford lucrative employment to the greatest number of students, as a means of self help.

In view of the needy and helpless condition of the people in their new homes, and the urgent prospective demand for more teachers, one would naturally suppose every family would be eager to take advantage of such an opportunity. The scheme however was a new one and it was regarded with suspicion and disfavor. The effort to have leading families, those that seemed to stand in the nearest relation to it by having previously enjoyed its privileges most freely, cooperate in the establishment of this plan, by permitting one of their children to remain at the academy during the vacation period or even do extra work a part of the day during the term, and thereby be able to continue and complete a course of study that would fit them for teaching, proved a complete disappointment. This disappointment was the occasion of two earnest appeals before two different meetings of the Presbytery, but neither of them received more than a respectful hearing, no favorable response.

Some, whose children had been previously carried from year to year gratuitously, no doubt, regarded it as the innovation of a stranger, who was adroitly depriving them of their former rights and privileges; while others seemed to view it as a discovery to their neighbors, that they were not able to pay for the education of their children. Some of the larger girls at the academy, when requested to arrange to do some extra work at the school declined, saying they had homes of their own and did not have to work for others away from home.

A PROMISING GIRL

That this was not the sentiment, however, of all the larger girls appears in the following incident. A very promising girl of sixteen came to the school of her own accord. She was animated with the desire to become a christian teacher. About the middle of the term, a younger brother called with the request from her mother, that she return home. No reason was assigned and she knew of no good one. She sent her mother word that she desired to remain, and resumed her studies. Two weeks later an older brother called with a pre-emptory demand that she return

THE SELF-HELP DEPARTMENT 187

home with him. The reason assigned by her mother for this unexpected and arbitrary request was, "Daughter can get along without school as well as her mother." It seems scarcely necessary to state that this promising and aspiring young lady was not permitted to return.

THOUGHTLESS BOYS

The first to acquiesce in the arrangement to pay a part of their term expense by working at the academy during the vacation were some boys, who had not learned to work; and it seemed impossible for them to conceal the fact that they did not want to work. They were not old enough or did not know enough to appreciate the privileges accorded to them; and as many as three of them ran away, when most needed.

The work deserted by two of these boys was undertaken by a third one, not then a student. He was a willing worker and at the end of the summer found that his job at the academy was his best one during the season. He illustrated the difference between the worthy and the worthless. The worthy achieve success where the worthless make a miserable failure.

THOUGHTFUL YOUNG PEOPLE

It was left for some thoughtful young people living at a distance to come, take advantage of the opportunities thus afforded and make this self-help or industrial department a real, visible and practical success. While deriving a life-long benefit for themselves, they have conferred a lasting benefit to the institution by remaining long enough to reach the higher grades. Their efficient service in various lines of work has served to show that the varied and thorough training given during recent vacations has been very valuable to them.

The vacation period has afforded the best opportunity for instruction and practice on the organ, for reading the many good books in the library and for special training in farming, carpentry and in the various kinds of work, like canning fruit or the manufacture of sorghum, that require attention only during the summer months. It has hitherto seemed to be the golden period of the year when the personal responsibility and general efficiency of the student has been most rapidly developed, a fact no doubt due to the freer daily association with the superintendent and teachers. The full course of training provided at the institution can be fully enjoyed only by those who remain during the summer months.

VACATION WORKERS

The vacation workers have always been regarded as members of the Oak Hill family and every personal want has been promptly supplied. The habit of reading or learning something every day, kept them prepared for doing their best work on the first as well as their last day of the term; while others would take a week or month, perhaps before they could settle down to good work in the school room. They were allowed a reasonable credit for every day they worked during the vacation and were not requested to do any extra work during the term, except in cases of emergency. The self-help students, who rendered extra service during the term, dropped one study, and they also received a reasonable allowance for all the extra work they performed.

JAMESTOWN COLLEGE

Effective christian work by students at home during the summer vacation was admirably illustrated by the young people attending the Presbyterian college at Jamestown, North Dakota, during the summer of 1913. Every student at the close of the term had formed the decision to lead a christian life. Under the inspiration of a resident lawyer, John Knouff, a number of them became members of the mission band that had for its object the ingathering of new scholars into their own Sabbath schools, and the college they were attending.

The result was a very pleasant surprise and a source of great profit to all of them. They reported the organization of a score of new Sunday schools in neglected communities, and an enrollment of 1231 new scholars through their instrumentality. An incidental result was a greatly increased enrollment of new students at the college they had so worthily represented.

SUPPORT OF SELF-SUPPORTING STUDENTS

Where does the money come from that is necessary to meet the monthly allowances placed to the credit of the self-help students? This is a very practical question and a few thoughts on it may be helpful.

When a farmer employs a man to help him on his farm he expects to pay him from the annual cash income, when the products of the farm are sold. This would naturally be true of the boys who do the farm work at Oak Hill if there was a surplus to sell; but hitherto it has not been sufficient to meet the demands of the boarding department and stock.

It would however not be true of the work of the boys who build fence, clear new land or erect and improve buildings. The product of the labor of these students is a permanent improvement, that increases the value of the land to the owner, and it cannot be sold annually for cash, like the products of the farm.

But the superintendent has to pay cash for the groceries consumed by these students the same as for the others; and when their monthly allowance for labor is transferred to the enrollment or other account book, it represents an item for which some one must furnish him the cash. Where will he get his money? Who will furnish it to him? Manifestly he must look to the owner of the property for it, and the owner in this instance is the Board of Missions for Freedmen. By using tools and implements the student has been trained in their use and the results of his work have become a permanent possession of the Board.

In as much as most permanent improvements do not ordinarily bring any direct annual income to the Board, but serve rather to increase the facilities of the school and provide additional opportunities for self-help, the question arises, "Where does the Board get the money for the support of the self-supporting students?"

The answer to this inquiry is, the Board has to solicit and receive it from the friends of christian education.

This is a very important statement and it is often not very clearly understood. When the actual cost of carrying a student through a seven months term is found to be about $50.00 then that is the lowest amount that will enable the superintendent to carry a vacation worker, as a self-supporting student, through the period of an entire year.

HOW IT WORKS

There are some features of this problem that are quite interesting. The student that does the most for the permanent improvement of the institution that has educated him, commonly called his "Alma Mater," or fostering mother, finds at the time of completing his course, that by that

THE SELF-HELP DEPARTMENT 191

means he has done most for himself, by advancing more rapidly than others in the course of training and study. He has also done something in the way of increasing the facilities for the education and uplift of his race.

Whilst his employment was creating a demand for a benevolent gift from some friend of christian education he was unconscious of that fact, and is happy in the consciousness, that he is earning his way through school like a man;—one, who wants to make most of himself. He goes forth to enter upon the duties of active life as a true or "good soldier" prepared to "endure hardness," if necessary, and ready to lend a helping hand to other worthy young people.

ENLARGEMENT AND PERMANENT IMPROVEMENT

The zealous interest of the superintendent in this self-help industrial department appears in the broad foundation he endeavored to lay for it in the purchase of so many acres for the Oak Hill farm.

There were other good motives that prompted the purchase of land, when the opportunity was afforded to do so at its virgin price in 1908, such as provision for future supplies of wood as a cheap fuel, about twenty-five cords a year being needed, and, ample pastures for the herds of cattle and hogs, that are easily and profitably raised and greatly needed, but the most urgent motive was the earnest desire to provide an agricultural base large enough to enable the self-help department of the academy to become in time self-supporting.

"Enlargement" and "permanent improvement" became the watchwords while laying the foundation for this department.

The manifest need of it had been deeply and indellibly impressed. The conviction also prevailed that, when properly organized and developed, so as to meet their most urgent needs, the self-help department in an educational institution works like a live magnet in attracting the patronage of many worthy young people.

Permanent improvement year after year by self-supporting students, seeking training is an arrangement that has in it the germ of expansion, that means enlargement and growth with passing years. This was the ideal towards which we were moving with might and main. We wanted to plant the live magnet, that would make Oak Hill an attractive and pre-eminently useful educational center for all the Choctaw Freedmen.

There are no annual taxes on lands used for public or mission school purposes, and all the annual income tends to lessen to the Board, the local expenses of the teachers and students. The net income from the farm is the surplus that remains after deducting the cost of management from the gross receipts.

Whenever this net income is more than sufficient to cover the local support of the teachers, it goes toward the support of the self-supporting students; whenever it is sufficient to cover all of their monthly allowances, this self-help department is self-supporting; and special remittances from the Board will not then be needed for the worthy, industrious and ambitious young people, in that department. The attainment of this object is worthy of noble and constant endeavor.

It is also worthy of note, that good agricultural lands, purchased at the government price in a new section of the country that is destined to be filled with new settlers, is always a good investment. The land rapidly increases in value

OAK HILL IN 1905.

FLOWER GATHERERS FOR DECISION DAY.
February 22, 1910.

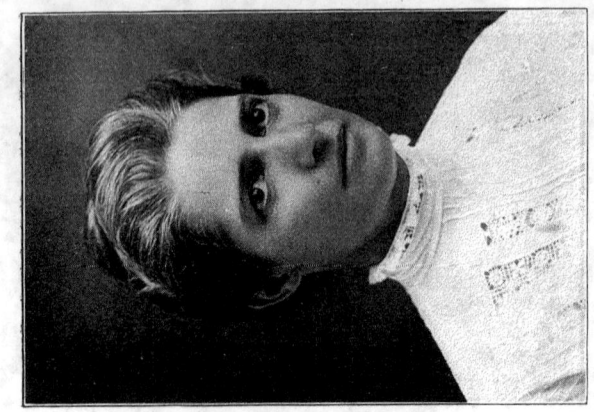

Jo Lu Wolcott.

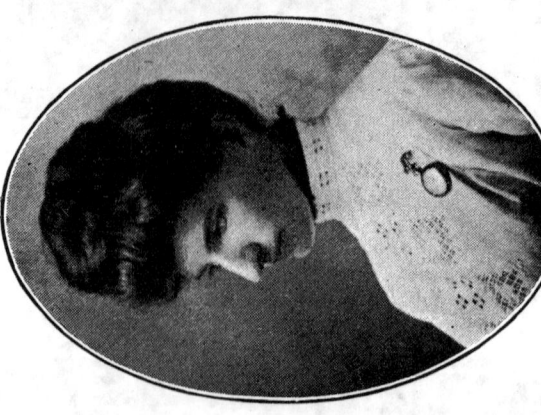

Mary I. Weimer.

Lou K. Early.

THE SELF-HELP DEPARTMENT

where the incoming of new settlers causes a rapid increase in the population.

This annual increase in the value of new land is known as its "unearned increment." This unearned increment is now accruing to the Board on every acre that has been purchased. Those that were purchased first have already doubled in value.

Every acre of land added to the Oak Hill farm at its virgin price means now, by reason of its annual income and gradual increase in value, a live unit added to the permanent endowment of the institution and enlarges the scope of the self-help department.

SELF-SUPPORT MEANS INDEPENDENCE

The negro needs to be taught to be "self-dependent, self-reliant and self-respecting."

Wherever public schools have been established and supplied with good teachers and text-books, they have rendered efficient service in improving the condition of the people. The lack of text-books has caused many of the rural schools to prove very inefficient, one text-book often having to serve as many as three pupils, Then there are yet large sections of some of the southern states in which there are no public schools for the colored people.

In proportion as the colored people attain a general christian education and become progressive, industrial workers, do they rise to their natural inheritance; an inheritance that brings to them what America now holds of freedom, justice, opportunity and benevolence to the oppressed of other lands, that are coming a million a year, to locate in this land of civil and religious freedom.

Among their essential needs to self-support are a fair

industrial opportunity, distribution, education and equal protection of the laws.

Whenever too many unskilled workers, including women and children, crowd into towns and cities, the number that have to live in poverty-stricken hovels is greatly increased. Their general health and good morals are also endangered.

Every youth will do well to adopt the thrilling watchwords of the early American patriots, "Virtue, Liberty, and Independence."

PARK COLLEGE

Rev. John A. McAfee, the eminent founder of Park College, Parkville, near Kansas City, Missouri, realizing the need of hardy and energetic ministers during the pioneer days of Missouri and Kansas, manifested a commendable wisdom and foresight in the planting of that institution, by making special provision for the self-help of those, who were candidates for the ministry and those wishing to be missionary teachers. The self-help department then established has greatly promoted its growth, and increased its usefulness. The visitor now sees a beautiful campus of 20 acres occupied by massive stone buildings erected largely by student labor. They include a fine administration building, chapel, library, observatory, boarding and professors houses, and a half dozen large dormitories. He will also find an attendance of 420 students, and a farm of 500 acres cultivated by them.

Its worthy representatives in the ministry may now be found in nearly every state of the Union and many, as foreign missionaries and teachers, are doing a noble work in other lands. A large proportion of its most worthy representatives owe their present position and usefulness to the opportunity for self-help, provided in the agricultural and

THE SELF-HELP DEPARTMENT 195

mechanical departments, while pursuing their studies at this classical institution.

It was founded in 1875 and was named after Col. George S. Park, the friend and helper of Rev. John A. McAfee. He donated the original college building and one hundred acres of land. At present the college owns 1000 acres, 500 of which are in the college farm. Both of its worthy founders died about the year 1890, but the good work of the institution they planted is going forward with annually increasing usefulness. Though established more recently than many others, it is now very highly prized as one of the most important of our Presbyterian colleges, in maintaining the supply of well trained ministers and christian teachers.

A SUGGESTION TO PARENTS

Having stated the aims and advantages of the self-help department the following suggestion to parents seems appropriate.

If you have a bright son or daughter that can be spared for a time at home, take your child, as Hannah did Samuel, while he is young enough to learn rapidly, to the superintendent of the academy, and, if the way be clear, enter into an agreement as Hannah did, that he shall remain there, if needed, until he has completed the course of study provided at the institution, earning his expenses, as far as possible, by his own industry.

Regard your contract as a matter of honor and refrain from calling him away when his services have begun to be of some value to the institution, merely because you need some one to do a few day's work. Encourage him to be true and faithful, that he may win and hold the esteem and confidence of his instructors.

If a number of parents will pursue this policy, the academy will accomplish its mission and prove a boon and blessing to you as a people, one generation serving another.

XXV
INDUSTRIAL EDUCATION

A TRAINING PERIOD.—INDEPENDENT HOMES.—DOMESTIC TRAINING.—HIGHLAND PARK COLLEGE.—BOOKER T. WASHINGTON.—SAM DALY.

"Six days shalt thou labor and do all thy work." "What thy hand findeth to do, do it with thy might."

PUBLIC education is at present passing through a transition stage. The emphasis in the school courses of previous generations was upon the culture of the mind and the appeal was made for a high classical training, but now that the work on the farms as well as in the shops is largely done by costly machinery, the emphasis of school work is being rapidly transferred to the hand, and the appeal is for manual or vocational training and domestic science.

Its aim is to reach and train for a successful self-supporting career, the great majority of young people who cannot pursue their studies beyond the fifth to the eighth grades.

Our country has made wonderful progress in the arts and sciences including new inventions, during the last half century. The scope of the "Natural Philosophy" and "Familiar Science" of a few years ago has been very greatly enlarged.

The country has been spanned and crossed in every direction by great systems of standard and interurban railways. Automobiles are in popular use on the highways and powerful tractors do the threshing, corn-shelling and plowing on the farm. Oil engines and electric motors are in use on the farms and in the homes of the people. The last of the good agricultural lands have been opened for settlement and are now occupied. Agriculture, animal husbandry, horticulture, dairying and even housekeeping have been reduced to a science, by the statement of essential principles, the same as in architecture and civil-engineering. Success in them depends on a practical knowledge of the art, as well as a theoretical knowledge of the science.

A few years ago the pressing demand was for teachers and normal instructors for their preparation. The demand for teachers in constantly increasing numbers continues, but it is now rivaled by the present demand for young people, who understand the principles of mechanical construction, whose hands have been trained to use costly and delicate machinery aright and properly care for it. Success and self-support on the farm as well as elsewhere now require the trained hand as well as the intelligent mind.

INDEPENDENT HOMES

Self-support is essential to the possession of a permanent and happy home.

No home can be permanent while there is no assured means of support. While the father depends on uncertain day labor and the mother knows little or nothing of economy in the household and even less about the care, training and discipline of children, there can be but little progress made in the home or church life.

Dependent homes mean dependent churches, while prosperous homes mean self-supporting churches. In this fact is found a great motive for the church in her educational missionary work to make suitable provision for teaching the young the useful or necessary arts of life, and some knowledge of the sciences, while offering to them the bread and the water of life, through the establishment of christian educational institutions.

DOMESTIC TRAINING

A recent debate in the House of Congress at Washington developed a unanimous sentiment, that a good cook is more cultured than a pianist, and that girls should not be allowed piano lessons until they learn how to cook good biscuits. We have read of girls "whose heads were stuffed with useless knowledge, but not one in twenty knew the things that would be serviceable to her through life. They could not sew or cook."

At Oak Hill it is different. Every girl at ten begins to take her monthly turn in learning to cook, mend and sew. She is taught the art and the rules of these useful employments the same as those of reading, writing and arthmetic in the school room.

The business of housekeeping is thus early introduced to the mind of the child, to awaken its thoughtfulness and develop efficiency in the future work of managing a home. This connects the teaching of the school with the life of the home. It makes the instruction a real and practical help instead of being merely theoretical. It affords pleasant and profitable employment to the pupils during spare moments that would otherwise be lost in idle loafing or play.

The business of housekeeping is attracting the attention of schools of learning and of legislatures more and more every year. Some states, like Indiana, are making large investments to promote training in domestic science in the schools of the state. The great results achieved in re-

INDUSTRIAL EDUCATION

cent years by health regulations, in checking and suppressing contagious diseases, have greatly increased the scope of this instruction. It now includes in the higher schools, the new applications of the principles of nutrition, the chemistry of cleaning and the laws of hygiene, or health.

HIGHLAND PARK COLLEGE

At Highland Park College, Des Moines, Iowa, having an enrollment of 2,500 young people in the capital city of one of our most highly favored states in the valley of the Mississippi, ninety-five per cent of them never go beyond the seventh and eighth grades and only two percent go to higher institutions of learning. This eminently successful institution attracts young people from all parts of our land and this last year from twelve foreign countries. 500 young men, one fifth of its enrollment are in shops. This institution is the embodiment of the genius and a splendid monument to the memory of its founder, Dr. O. F. Longwell, who for twenty-four years served as its president, having previously secured a remarkable development of the Western Normal college at Shenandoah.

BOOKER T. WASHINGTON

The industrial scheme of Booker T. Washington at Tuskeegee is an intelligent negro's idea of what the illiterate negro needs to help himself. It is undoubtedly the best scheme to enable him to attain self support.

Started as a private enterprise its patronage soon overtaxed its equipment of buildings and attracted public aid from the legislature of Alabama, and later large gifts from many wealthy people in our larger northern cities, some of whom endeavor to visit it once a year to note its annual progress and needs.

The remarkable success of this industrial institution and the immeasurable amount of good it has already done, during the lifetime of its founder, in bettering the temporal welfare of thousands of colored people in the south, have tended to make it the most prominent illustration of practical and successful industrial education among the colored people of this or any other land.

SAM DALY

Sam Daly of Tuscaloosa, an illiterate janitor of the University of Alabama, previous to 1903, and died at Atlanta, while attending the Presbyterian General Assembly in May 1913, is a splendid illustration of what one may do for the good of his race.

At the time of his death he left to be cared for by others a 500 acre farm of his own, fourteen miles from town on which he was voluntarily caring for 270 convicted and vice steeped colored boys from the cities of that state.

He established an industrial school for boys on his own farm, to save convicted and bad boys from prison; received them from the police judges and conveyed them to the farm. They had become a nuisance and burden to the public, but he housed, fed and clothed this large family without receiving a dollar of public funds of Jefferson county; and from the church, only forty dollars, for a sleeping room for them and the salary of a teacher. The rest of their support was obtained from their daily toil on the farm.

At last the number of boys and the cost of keeping them became so great, he was compelled for their sakes to put a mortgage of eighteen hundred dollars on his farm. This impelled him to go to the Assembly (South) to make an appeal for funds. Unfortunately he suddenly became ill and died before he was able to make his appeal. His last words were: "Take care—take good care ob mah little niggahs!"

He had saved, by industrial occupation and farming, for good citizenship in Alabama, three hundred boys convicted of crimes and misdemeanors. It was a sad disappointment to him that he was unable to present to the Assembly an appeal on behalf of those still under his care.

Sam Daly was a good janitor, but when he began to make good men of useless and bad boys, his value to the state of Alabama was increased many fold. This brief record of his generous, energetic and heroic work is made that it may serve as an inspiration to devise other similar ways of being useful and helpful.

XXVI
PERMANENT IMPROVEMENTS.

PAINTING BOYS HALL.—SURFACE DRAINAGE.—ORCHARD IN 1906.—HOG HOUSES.—SHEDS FOR HAY AND THE STOCK HOGS.—OAK BRIDGES.—TEMPORARY BOYS HALL.—ADDITION TO THE ACADEMY.—GOOD FENCES AROUND THE CAMPUS.—GARDEN, STOCK YARD AND CULTIVATED FIELDS.—ELLIOTT HALL.—PULLING STUMPS.

"So built we the wall; for the people had a mind to work." Nehemiah.

THE improvements undertaken and completed by means of the student help began with the removal of old rubbish, the accumulation of years, and the impenetrable briar thickets near the buildings. During the latter part of the first spring term in 1905 the boys applied two good coats of lead and oil in cream and white to the Boys' Hall. The work was well done although it was the first work of the kind any of them had ever attempted. The appearance of the building was greatly improved, and every boy was delighted to find how quickly the painter's art could be learned.

The black picket and crooked worm fences around the buildings were then removed and replaced with good board and wire fences. The extent of good and substantial fences, erected during this period, aggregate about 100 rods of board and picket fences around the campus, garden and stock yards; 12 large farm gates, all hung between tall posts with overhead tie; and 780 rods of web and barb

PERMANENT IMPROVEMENTS 203

wire fence; all set with good Bodark or Locust posts, top down and reenforced with a strong oak stub in every panel, making a valuable permanent improvement.

In March 1906 a young orchard was planted consisting of 50 trees, that include a number of the best varieties of apples and peaches suited for that section. These were supplemented with a similar lot in 1913.

The purchase of lands, begun in 1908, as soon as the restrictions were removed, was continued until 1912 when the aggregate included fifteen different purchases, making 270 acres and costing $2050.00.

Twenty-five acres were cleared of previously ringed and dead trees and thirty more were enclosed and cleared of underbrush and useless trees.

The surface drainage work begun in 1905 and completed in 1912, included outlets to all the little ponds near the buildings, the deepening of the artificial pond north of the buildings, a deep drain with branches through the meadow and another one through a large slough at the northwest corner of the farm.

BUILDINGS

The first building erected was a log house 24x32 feet with a good cistern in 1906, and for the number of its conveniences it is an excellent model. A cut and description of it will be found in the latter part of this volume.

A new shed was also built that year, on the east side of the commons, for the convenient, daily care of the growing herd in the pastures.

In 1907 a belfry and farm bell were put on the comb of the roof of the first girls' hall. An axle was obtained and a wooden wheel and frame were made for the large old bell, and it was then mounted in the tower of the chapel.

The new highway along the railroad to Valliant was cleared of trees and the materials converted into posts and fuel. Two substantial oak bridges, five and ten feet long respectively, were constructed over the streams on this road to make it passable for the loaded Oak Hill team during term time.

A string of hay sheds, 64x16 feet, was constructed on the south side of the feed lot and two portable racks for feeding hay and fodder economically and conveniently from the sheds.

In 1908 the enrollment having reached 115, the seating capacity of the academy was increased by lifting all the seats and adding an additional row of thirteen double seats to their number. The academy was then painted two coats inside and outside and the woodwork of the old desks was brightened and tinted to correspond with the new ones. These improvements made it look more beautiful and attractive than ever before.

The porches on the south and west sides of the girls hall were repaired by the insertion of new joists where needed and the laying of new floors.

TEMPORARY BOYS' HALL

In 1909, the Boys' Hall having been lost a few days after the opening of the term, November 8, 1908, a temporary boys' hall 55x24 feet was hastily constructed, its dedication taking place Feb. 28, 1909, after an address by Rev. Wiley Homer of Grant. This meeting was held on a beautiful Sabbath afternoon and the speakers and singers occupied the wide platform on the west end of the building. This building was erected entirely by the student boys. The materials in it cost $410 and it had apartments for an office, one teacher and twenty-five boys.

PERMANENT IMPROVEMENTS

It was intended as a place for the workmen while erecting a new hall for the boys, the material in it then to be used in lining the new building.

The blistered condition of the front of the girls' hall and academy from the intense heat of the fire were then relieved by a thorough scraping, sandpapering and repainting.

Owing to the limited accommodations for the boys in this building, and for the large number of pupils in the primary department in the academy, an extension of twelve feet, with an upper room for special students, was added that fall to the academy. While this improvement was under construction, other boys built a new wood shed, obtained in the timber and prepared the supplies of fuel, and built 170 rods of new fence. A considerable quantity of sand was also hauled for the foundation of the new hall for the boys.

ELLIOTT HALL

In 1910, the erection of Elliott Hall became a necessity after the disastrous fire which occurred on March 13th. This building is 80x32 feet, with an extension 6x32 feet, in front, and a two story addition 18x16 feet, for kitchen store and bath rooms, at the northwest corner over a large brick-walled cistern.

This building absorbed the attention of all for more than a year, although it was opened for occupancy on November 14th. It was a great undertaking with the few workmen obtainable. The clearing away of the rubbish, the excavation for the cellar 28x75 feet and the construction of the foundation wall, and the same for the large cistern took a good deal more time than was expected, and all of it was heavy and hard work for every one that participated in it. It was the 15th of June when the cement wall around the main part of the foundation was completed by the superintendent, who placed the rock, cement and reinforcing materials in the walls with his own hands as a precaution against defects.

The construction of the frame work was entrusted to Samuel A. Folsom, who, acting as foreman of the carpenters, succeeded in getting the building ready for occupancy at the end of five months, or November 14th. So great, however, was the amount of unfinished work in the halls and rooms upstairs and of cement lining needed for the excavation walls in the cellar that a considerable number of students were employed principally at this work during that and the following term.

Every part of the work on this building was very faithfully performed. It is a creditable monument to the memory of every one that wrought upon it. It is symmetrical and, though plain, is handsome in appearance and very convenient in its uses; as an administration building, girls dormitory and boarding house. The lumber was furnished and delivered by J. R. Bowles of Swink; David Folsom made the window and door frames; Solomon Buchanan served as foreman of the painters, and he and George Stewart built the walls of the cistern and the first story of the chimneys. Edward Hollingsworth, in addition to important work on other parts of the building, served as foreman of the construction of the stairways, belfry and porches. It represents an expenditure of $6,500 in cash and student labor. This does not include the services of the superintendent, who had previously prepared the plans for the building and personally superintended its construction.

LATER IMPROVEMENTS

During 1911 and 1912 while some were putting the finishing touches on Elliott Hall, the last being the insertion of the fixtures in the two bath rooms and the construction of a closed room in the cellar for canned fruit and vegetables, the other boys removed the old oak stumps from the north field, drained a slough covering four acres of land, cleaned twenty acres of land for cultivation and built 160 rods of good fence around it. They also built a pretty and very convenient semi-monitor hen house, with open front and two out-yards.

PULLING STUMPS

During the month of March, when the ground was moist and favorable, a squad of the larger boys would sometimes be equipped and employed in pulling stumps. This was a new employment for all of them, but they soon learned to make a cheering success of it.

The working outfit consisted of two levers, a very large and a smaller one, a log chain, sixty feet of inch rope, and for each of the workmen a shovel and an axe. The method of procedure was to assign them in teams of two each, to remove the earth from around a lot of stumps to the width and depth of about eighteen inches. The larger lever, having the middle fold of rope attached to its smaller end, was placed in a vertical position at the lower side of the stump and firmly fastened to its crown with a log chain, the latter passing over its top from the opposite side. The small lever was placed in position at the side opposite the larger one, for the use of the foreman. When all the boys, in two lines facing each other, had hold of the ends of the rope and the signal was given, "Ready for a pull," something was sure to happen; usually the uprooting of the stump, but sometimes the breaking of the log chain, which was sure to result in making a good natured pile of the boys. The team did the pulling the first half day, but the boys did it afterwards, because they were more available and enjoyed it.

WALL OF ELLIOTT HALL

The concrete wall under Elliott Hall, built by the superintendent and student boys in the spring of 1910, was the first work of that kind in this section of the country. The sand was found and obtained without cost along a stream in the neighboring timber. The filler consisted of rock and broken brick from the chimneys of the three buildings that that had been previously consumed by fire, and they were incorporated in the wall by hand. The iron used for reinforcing the concrete was all obtained from the scrap pile of the burned buildings. The processes, or methods of procedure, were new to all the workmen. As the work advanced it called forth expressions of distrust, rather than confidence and commendation. The mixing of materials had to be strictly forbidden save in the presence of the superintendent, whose hands afterwards placed them in position on the wall.

After the lapse of four years this wall is solid as a rock in every respect. It has now the reputation of being not only the first, but also to this date one of the most perfect and substantial concrete walls in that section.

WORKING ACCORDING TO RULE

An expert carpenter has observed, "It takes the average apprentice about one year to discover, that he does not know how to drive a nail with the skill of an expert;" one who drives it through hard woods without bending and

PERMANENT IMPROVEMENTS 209

brittle, without splitting. This skill is however always more quickly acquired, when a rule like the following is given the apprentice at the beginning of his training. "Gripping the hammer near the end of the handle and setting the nail slightly slanting from the edges toward the solid center, strike the top of it fairly with the center of the hammer, starting and finishing it with gentle taps."

Whenever a new tool or implement was put in the hand of a student, the rules governing its use were fully explained, and a constant effort was made to have the student do all work by rule; whether it was on the farm, in the kitchen, laundry or shop, as well as in the class room. The essential parts of the text books, that were reviewed most frequently, were the definitions and rules. A good position is the first essential in reading, writing, speaking, sawing, planing or plowing; and the second is to grasp and use aright the tool or implement, whether it be the pen, pencil, brush, axe, hammer or saw. The good effect of patiently taking the time to make every one familiar with the rules governing the tools and work, became noticeable very soon on the part of the older students, both in the better quality of the work and the larger amount of it performed. Progress in studies and success in the shop or field depends largely on the ability to follow the rule, and the decision never to violate it.

XXVII

ELLIOTT HALL

THE GIRLS HALL LOST AND REPLACED.—OLD LOG HOUSE
—DAVID ELLIOTT.—ALICE LEE ELLIOTT.

"Be noble! and the nobleness that lies in other men, sleeping but never dead, will rise in majesty to meet thine own."—Lowell.

LOSS OF THE GIRLS HALL

ON Sabbath afternoon, March 13, 1910, as we left the chapel at the close of a very delightful and profitable Bible Memory service, a cloud of black smoke was seen moving rapidly around the buildings across the view before us and suggesting a fire in one of the buildings. It was a sad and sickening surprise. Quickly the word was passed, "The Girls' Hall is on fire." Rushing into this building to locate and if possible to suppress the conflagration, we found it had originated on the third floor, and that a tub of water had already been applied to it by attendants in the building, without any hope of checking it, as the flames were spreading rapidly over the dry roof, fanned by a strong breeze from the west. The roof was inaccessible both from the inside and the outside, and in a very few minutes both sides of it were covered with a fiery sheet of low, devouring flame similar to that occasionally seen, when fire sweeps rapidly over ground covered with dry underbrush.

In a very little while the entire building was consumed, and with it the laundry, smokehouse, old log house, new woodhouse, stock tank, ten rods of the campus fence, fifteen cords of wood, the food supplies on hand and nearly all the furniture and equipment of the Girls' Hall, the home of the institution.

A fair estimate of the loss sustained is as follows: Girls' Hall 36x56, $2550: contents, $1175; other buildings and contents, $250; total $3975.

The girls rooming on the second story, obedient to instruction, hastened to their rooms and secured all their effects, but six that were rooming on the third story lost their trunks and extra clothing.

It is impossible to describe how deeply was felt the loss of everything at this time, coming as it did so soon after the loss of the Boys' Hall in 1908. It had been the comfortable home of the Oak Hill family since 1889. To the superintendent it meant not merely the loss of the property, a kind of loss that is always more or less deeply felt, but a check of several years upon plans outlined for the permanent improvement of the work of the institution.

This loss was a staggering blow to the superintendent until he learned the next day that the matron, Miss Weimer, with the cooperation of Miss Hall, was willing to practice the self denial needed to make a heroic effort to recover from it. When this information was received, twenty of the larger girls were constrained to remain, while the rest were sent home. Some of these were provided for in the second story of an addition to the academy building, then nearly completed, and the school room under it served for a dining room and kitchen. The school work was resumed the next day, under Miss Hall with student assistants. The girls that remained proved helpful in executing the extra work then necessary, and the experience of self denial no doubt proved a profitable one to them.

The old log farm house 46x16 feet, was the last of the four Oak Hill buildings to yield to the flames. It was built by the Choctaw Indians about the year 1840, soon after they were transferred from Mississippi. It was very substantially constructed and by skilled workmen, who no doubt came from Fort Towson. The Girls' Hall stood between it and the well, indicated by the aermotor east of it.

This building was the pioneer home of the academy. The stages of progress in its use were as follows. The native school was transferred to it in 1884. Eliza Hartford began to occupy it in 1886, first as a day school, and three months later as her home with a boarding school. In the fall of 1887, a kitchen was added to the west end of it, and it was then used as a home for the teachers and girls, and the school was transferred to the new school building. Two years later it became a dormitory for the boys. After 1895 it was used for storage, a smith and carpenter shop. The picture showing it on fire is from a photograph taken by Miss Weimer, after the roof had fallen and the Girls' Hall was entirely consumed.

DAVID ELLIOTT

The erection of the fine building known as Elliott Hall, was made possible by the receipt of a gift of $5,000 from Mr. David Elliott, of LaFayette, Indiana, who expressed the desire that a school might be established among the Freedmen that would be a memorial of Alice Lee Elliott, deceased, his previously devoted wife. It was dedicated to her memory on June 13, 1912.

Elliott Hall is now the commodious and comfortable home of the Oak Hill family. It provides a convenient office for the superintendent, library and reception room, places for the boarding and laundry departments, rooms and bath rooms for the girls. It occupies a beautiful and commanding position on the gentle elevation known as Oak Hill. It stands on the very site previously occupied by the old log house, but parallel with the survey lines. It forms a center around which all other needed buildings can be conveniently and permanently located.

Elliott Hall is the largest and finest of the buildings hitherto erected at the academy, and the first of the larger ones to be built by the local Freedmen. This noteworthy achievement, occurring so soon after the reopening in 1905, and the introduction of industrial training in the shop as well as on the farm, is suggestive of the real and substantial progress made by the young men.

It is also an encouragement to every patron of this institution, for it practically illustrates the progress that may be made by every thoughtful and industrious youth. In view of the fact that there are few or no opportunities for the young Freedmen to learn carpentry and painting elsewhere in its vicinity, this achievement becomes one in which every Freedman may justly manifest a laudable pride and express devout thanksgiving.

The memorial offering of Mr. Elliott, that made it possible, is the largest individual donation yet made to this institution. It came at a time of our saddest and greatest need. It is a gift to be very greatly appreciated. Every Freedman in the region of country benefited and blessed by this institution, may well be profoundly thankful for this manifestation of personal interest in your intellectual and material welfare.

ALICE LEE ELLIOTT

Mrs. Alice Lee Elliott, in memory of whom Elliott Hall and the Oak Hill Industrial Academy were named in 1910, was the faithful and devoted wife of David Elliott, an elder of the Spring Grove Presbyterian church near LaFayette, Indiana. She was the daughter of John and Maria Ritchey, who left Ohio soon after their marriage to found a new home of their own on the frontier in Indiana. She was born, January 7, 1846, and was called to her rest in her sixty-first year, June 27, 1906.

She received a good education in her youth and her marriage occurred March 2, 1875. Three years later she became a member of the Dayton Presbyterian church, of which her husband was already a member, and at once became an earnest and zealous christian worker.

When in later years Mr. and Mrs. Elliott transferred their membership to Spring Grove Presbyterian church, because their services were more greatly needed there, she became a very successful teacher in the Sabbath school and an enthusiastic leader in their missionary work.

She was amiable and winsome. Although she lived amid the surroundings of wealth, she was the constant friend and helper of all classes. Her home was always a delightful retreat for the ministers of the gospel and those who represented worthy causes of benovelence and charity. The Bible, the favorite family church paper and the missionary magazine were always on the center table and read regularly.

She was animated with the noble desire to be eminently useful and took advantage of every opportunity to benefit and bless others. Others were captivated and enthused by her happy, hopeful spirit, and have accorded to her this beautiful tribute, "Many daughters have done virtuously, but thou excellest them all."

When her voice became silent and her eyelids closed in

death it seemed to her surviving husband that she was worthy and the world would be made better by the erection of a living or useful, as well as granite memorial. Accordingly when her last earthly resting place was duly marked with an appropriate granite memorial, he made a donation of $5000 to the Presbyterian Board of Missions for Freedmen, for the establishment of an educational institution for the benefit of the colored people of this land, that should bear her name.

After the loss by fire of two of the main buildings at Oak Hill Industrial Academy in 1908 and 1910, this fund was used for the erection of a main building—Elliott Hall—and the school has since been called the Alice Lee Elliott Memorial.

The Bible and shorter catechism are to be regularly and faithfully taught to all pupils, as fundamental in the development of a good moral character. The hope is indulged that the beautiful story of her unselfish and eminently useful life will prove an incentive to constant, noble endeavor on the part of every one that enjoys the privileges of the institution that now bears her honored name.

ENDOWMENT

Other friends who have it in mind to leave a legacy to this greatly needed institution, will do well to consider the propriety, if possible, of sending the funds to the Freedmen's Board while living, as Mr. Elliott did, and receive from the Board, if desired, an endowment bond bearing interest payable annually to the donor, during the continuance of the donor's life. By this arrangement the gift becomes a profitable source of annual support to the donor, and an immediate benefit to the institution, without costs and discounts.

XXVIII
UNFAVORABLE CIRCUMSTANCES

LOSS OF HELPERS AND BUILDINGS.—BOLL WEEVIL.—STATE-HOOD CHANGES.—EFFICIENT SERVICE REQUIRED.—INFERENCES.—BURDENS AND FRIENDS.

"All these things are against me."—Jacob.

THE new era, that had been so auspiciously continued for three years, and gave promise of rapid and substantial material development, was destined soon to be interrupted by the experience of three dark days that occurred, one soon after the other.

On June 5, 1908, one week after the end of the term and after three and one half years of faithful and efficient service as a matron, the death of Miss Adelia M. Eaton occurred at the institution.

On the 7th of November following the Boys' Hall, and most of its contents were consumed by fire.

In the spring of 1909 Mrs. Flickinger experienced a serious injury by falling from the open conveyance while on the way to Valliant, and, going home for treatment during the summer was unable to return in the fall and resume her former duties.

On March 13, 1910, the Girls' Hall, laundry, smokehouse, wood house and Old Log House, together with most of their contents, suddenly disappeared in smoke.

Nothing was then left of this cherished and promising institution, except the chapel, temporary hall for the boys,

UNFAVORABLE CIRCUMSTANCES 217

built the previous year, and a lot of ashes and burned rubbish, the sight of which suggested the loss of comforts and working outfit; hopes and plans indefinitely deferred if not completely blasted, and the expenditure of a vast amount of labor and time to replace and refurnish the buildings destroyed; and the utter impossibility of any immediate recovery from the oft-repeated and fatal checks imposed on the enrollment, ever since the loss of the Boys' Hall in 1908.

BOYS' HALL 1895-1908

Two rays of light relieved the darkness of the gloom that followed the experience of these staggering losses.

(1). All of the lady helpers manifested the real spirit of missionary heroes. Presuming they were greatly needed during the period of reconstruction, instead of running away when there seemed to be no suitable place for them, they discovered a readiness to suggest possible and acceptable arrangements for their comfort. (2) There was also available for assistance, a clever squad of intelligent and trained student boys, one of whom, having served for a term as an assistant teacher, was believed to be capable of serving as a foreman of the carpenters; thus making it possible to erect buildings entirely by the aid of colored workmen and principally by student labor.

THE BOLL WEEVIL

In 1903 the Mexican boll weevil in its northward migration from Brownsville, Texas, crossed Red river and, during the next seven years, continued to deprive the farmers in the country north of that river of all profit on the cotton, their principal money crop; and greatly to injure the corn, their food crop. These long repeated ravages of the weevil came at a time when the colored people were by no means prepared to meet them.

In 1904 and 1905 they had been allotted 40 acres of unimproved timber lands appraised at $3.25 an acre, or $130. The allotment was the occasion of many changes in their location. They were really pioneer settlers, in their own native country and without funds to make needed improvements. They were happy in the possession of a home they could call their own, and entertained great hopes for the future. But this new and destructive pest, year after year for seven years, completely checked the prosperity they had so hopefully anticipated. The years came and went and they had nothing to sell worthy of mention to bring them money.

In April 1905, at the first meeting of the Presbytery after the reopening, many of the colored people voluntarily and enthusiastically united in making pledges for the purchase of the land needed for the buildings and farm at Oak Hill. But of the many generous hearted friends, who united in pledging about $300.00 at this time, only ministers and teachers receiving aid from the board, and a couple of others ever became able to pay these pledges.

Parents bringing their children to school, with only a few or no dollars in hand, would make pledges of payment during the term. The amount proposed was $25.00 for boarding a pupil seven months, about one half the real cost. When they became convinced they had no money to send, some would send for their children during the term, while others would leave them at the end of the term without notice, and even make it necessary for the superintendent to pay their way home.

These disappointing experiences had a two-fold effect on the school. They meant the loss, not merely of some expected income, but almost invariably of the pupil and patron, and the constant change of the student body prevents the development of the higher grades which must be reached by the students, if the school is to accomplish its mission, namely the training and development of christian teachers.

The term reports of the last eight years will show that all the full term students that continued long enough to reach the higher grades, 7th and 8th, were self supporting ones, who were either sent to remain at the academy during the vacation periods until they completed their course, or were accorded the opportunity to work out a part of their expenses at the academy. The full term students whose boarding was entirely paid by their parents did not average a half dozen a term.

Inability to provide for their board, meant the loss of the brightest and most promising pupils of the earlier years, about the time they reached the fifth grade. But a good boarding school can be developed only where the conditions are favorable for the continuance of the pupils from year to year, until they reach the higher grades. The fact that the 7th and 8th grades were reached only during the last two years and then only by the self-supporting young people is quite suggestive, not merely of a past embarrassment, but of that which should be an important feature in the future management of the institution, namely, a constant endeavor to increase the opportunities for young people to support themselves by the employment furnished at the institution.

STATEHOOD CHANGES

Another embarrassment was experienced as a result of the changes incident to the establishment of statehood.

The constitutional convention that met at Guthrie, the old capital, Jan. 1, 1907, changed the map of Indian Territory. From the time the Indians were located in it until that date the civil divisions consisted of the general allotments to the different tribes or nations and Oak Hill was near the center of the southern part of the Choctaw nation. In 1907 when the boundaries of the counties were established Oak Hill was near the west line of McCurtain county. The first election of county officers occurred that fall and they entered upon their duties on Jan. 1, 1908. It was made the duty of the county superintendent to divide the county into school districts so as to meet the needs of the colored people as well as the whites and Indians.

On Sabbath, Jan. 20, 1908, the first superintendent of

UNFORTUNATE CIRCUMSTANCES

McCurtain county called at the academy and left the papers showing the establishment of Oak Hill district No. 73, for the colored people of that neighborhood. The district included the northeast quarter of section 29, on which the academy is located and the southeast quarter of the section adjoining it on the north. The board of education for this Oak Hill district was organized on February 20th following, by the election of Henry Prince, chairman, Rev. R. E. Flickinger, Secretary; and Malinda A. Hall, treasurer. All this was done at a time, when the county superintendent could not think otherwise, than that the teachers and work at the academy were in some way under his jurisdiction. A little later the Oak Hill district was quietly quashed and its honorable board of education went into "inocuous desuetude."

This incident is narrated because it illustrates what was then taking place all over McCurtain county, and all the other counties of the new state. The law provided that a district and a school might be established wherever there were six pupils to attend the school and the people furnished a building for it. In a short time three schools for the colored people were established in the vicinity of the academy, and parents were made to believe that they must send their children to these schools or penalties would be imposed on them. A host of colored teachers from Texas and other localities were attracted to the new state to meet the needs of the public schools, now for the first time established in the rural districts.

The mission schools previously established for many years in the chapels of the churches of the Presbytery of Kiamichi became public schools and the pastors that continued to teach became public school teachers. Parents were also for the first time in their lives, taxed for the support of their local school. Will they be able and willing to pay their annual taxes and additional tuition or board at Oak Hill for the education of their children.

These important changes, occurring both in the immediate neighborhood and also in distant ones that furnished the supply of students for Oak Hill, were destined to exert considerable influence on the work of that institution. What the effect of that influence would be, was a matter of great anxiety and constant watchfulness on the part of the superintendent. The previous missions of our Freedmen's Board at Muskogee, Atoka and Caddo were abandoned as unnecessary as soon as the increasing population of those towns made adequate provision for the public education of their colored children. Shall this be the outcome of the work at Oak Hill, now that the rural districts are supplied with public schools and teachers?

EFFICIENT SERVICE REQUIRED

That these changes would temporarily affect the enrollment of Oak Hill, even under the most favorable circumstances was believed to be inevitable. This problem was all the more difficult to meet, while undergoing the experience of repeated checks, that made it necessary to send pupils home during term time on three different occasions and twice to check their incoming on account of "no room."

The most efficient and faithful service possible, on the part of the superintendent and teachers, was believed to be the best means of meeting this crisis. Parents and young people must also have a little time for observation, that they might see and be convinced of the greater value of the work at the academy.

To visitors at the academy the difference was very

UNFORTUNATE CIRCUMSTANCES 223

quickly perceived. These were some of the things that attracted their special and favorable attention.

The Bible was in the hand of every pupil, and even the youngest were familiar with many of its most beautiful and instructive passages.

Every pupil had all the text books he needed from the day he entered the school.

All that were old enough were required to spend an hour each evening, in quiet study under the helpful and encouraging eye of the principal, in addition to the forenoon and afternoon hours.

All were forming the habit of using their spare moments to advantage, by reading some good books from the library, a church paper, or practicing on some useful musical instrument.

Their voices were being correctly and rapidly developed for intelligent use in song and public address.

In the visible results of their work they witnessed their skill in the necessary arts of life, such as farming, stock raising, carpentry, painting, masonry, cooking, baking and sewing.

And then it was very unusual for any pupil to return home at the end of the term, without having voluntarily become an active christian worker in the endeavor meeting and Sunday school.

During the spring term in 1905 only 34 pupils were enrolled. During the next three years the increase was very encouraging, the enrollment reaching the full capacity of the buildings at 115, May 31, 1908.

The loss of buildings that began with the opening of the next term compelled a reduction in the enrollment. For

1909 and the subsequent years it was 84, 108, 90 and in 1912, 95.

INFERENCES

It would seem from the foregoing facts, that, whatever demand there was for the Oak Hill Mission as a school for local elementary instruction in the earlier years of its history, the conditions of the country, to which its work must now be adjusted, have experienced a very great change. So long as there are families living in sparsely settled districts, that are not provided with ample school privileges; or the interest of parents in the welfare of their children leads them to prefer the select boarding school, under well-known christian influences, to the rural school; elementary instruction will be needed at Oak Hill. But the greater need now is for the higher christian education that will best fit the young people to become intelligent and successful teachers, and for the industrial training that will fit them for the performance of the necessary duties of life.

A comfortable home on a well-tilled farm, that is every year increasing in value, is the ideal and happiest place for ambitious young people. Such a home affords healthful employment, the greatest freedom and is usually a very profitable investment.

The young farmer needs not only a knowledge of soils, their drainage and how to use them to best advantage, but also a practical knowledge of carpentry and painting, to enable him to erect good buildings economically and to take proper care of them afterwards.

The teacher needs this knowledge and training, that he may create a constant demand for his services during the long summer days when he is not teaching.

Rev. W. H. Carroll.   Sudie B. McNiell.   Mrs. W. H. Carroll.

Lucretia C. Brown.   Everett Richard.

Malinda A. Hall.   Solomon H. Buchanan.   Samuel A. Folsom.

Closing Day, 1912. Rev. Dr. Baird at left on the Porch.

UNFORTUNATE CIRCUMSTANCES

The young minister needs this knowledge more than many others, and a great deal more than is generally appreciated, to enable him to give intelligent counsel to his people, when they have need to make repairs or build new churches and parsonages.

As these higher and special lines of industrial instruction are perfected and emphasized, and the facilities for self-help both during term time and vacation are gradually increased, the efficiency and patronage of the academy will continue to increase with the progress of the years.

BURDENS AND FRIENDS

The deficit in the running expenses on June 30, 1911, the last day included in the annual report of that year was $1,693.95. This was the largest deficit at the end of any previous month, and was a big one with which to commence the improvement work of our last year. It was due to the fact that the completion of Elliott Hall with good materials and workmanship, including furniture, cost nearly $1,500 more than was expected, and the appropriation made for it.

We were called upon to experience some serious losses and bear, for considerable periods of time unusually great and heavy burdens. The burden twice became so great, indeed, as to awaken the fear that another straw would break the camel's back. Happily the needed relief came in time to avert that unhappy experience, or check the aggressive onward progress of the improvement work.

When the burden became large and a matter of personal anxiety, it also became the measure of the valuable and loyal co-operation of the new friends who came to our assistance, in addition to our Board of Missions for Freedmen; which is the first and final resort for the resources that are necessary to successfully administer, and gradually develop the work of this institution.

We deem it appropriate to gratefully record the names of those who have most signally aided us in the management of the finances, so as to keep them locally on a cash basis, namely, the Security State bank of Rockwell City, Ia.; 1st National bank of Valliant; and in succession the following dealers in Valliant: O'Bannon & Son; A. J. Whitfield and Planters Trading Co.

Hon. T. P. Gore, United States Senator from Oklahoma, (blind), has favored this institution by sending for its library more than a dozen valuable volumes, among which are 2 Year Books of the Department of Agriculture; 2 Handbooks,—I & II,—of theAmerican Indians; Report of the Commissioner on Education for 1911, in two volumes; Report on Industrial Education; Manual of the United States Senate; Directory of Congress, and several other smaller volumes.

SPECIAL ADDRESSES

During our last term the institution was favored with encouraging and instructive addresses from the following distinguished visitors: Rev. Duncan McRuer of Pauls Valley, Moderator of the Synod of Oklahoma; Rev. E. B. Teis of Anadarko, Pastoral Evangelist for the Presbytery of El Reno; Rev. Phil C. Baird D. D., Pastor of the First Presbyterian church of Oklahoma City; and by Rev. Wiley Homer, Rev. William Butler, Rev. W. J. Starks and Rev. T. K. Bridges, pastors of local churches, and Rev. M. L. Bethel, Oklahoma City.

XXIX
BUILDING THE TEMPLE

AN EXERCISE FOR CHILDREN'S DAY, ILLUSTRATED BY A TEMPLE AND AN ARCH.

"I have no greater joy than to hear that my children walk in the truth."—John

Giving all diligence add to your faith, virtue; and to virtue, knowledge; and to knowledge, temperance; and to temperance, patience; and to patience, godliness; and to godliness, brotherly kindness; and to brotherly kindness, charity. He that lacketh these things is blind."—Peter.

IT was the good fortune of the author to be called to serve as chorister and superintendent of rural Sunday schools, and leader of the choir of the church, in his early youth. At the beginning of his ministry, he discovered the relative importance of this work among the young, by reading the observation of the sainted Samuel Miller to the effect; if he could repeat the period of his ministry, he would give ten times more time and attention to the work among the children. This importance was very acceptably emphasized during the eighties, by the enthusiasm of Rev. James A. Worden, D. D., of our Sunday school Board, and the appointment of a Sabbath in June, to be annually observed as Children's Day.

One of the most prominent features of our ministry has been, a persistently active participation in the work among the children and young people. Other engagements have not been permitted to interfere with attendance at Sunday school and Endeavor meetings, or an appointment to meet the children at any of the regular times of rehearsal of songs and exercises for Easter, Christmas, Children's Day and other anniversaries. All the young people were encouraged to participate in the effort to make these rallying days, occasions of special instruction and delight. A number of pretty, and sometimes elaborate, designs were devised to add their illuminating effect to the exercises. Two of these designs, a temple and an arch, both having for their object, a visible representation of the divinely appointed elements of a good character, according to the apostle Peter, and animating power of the indwelling spirit, manifested by a conscientious observance of the command to remember the Sabbath, have been deemed worthy of an illustration in this volume, that those who participated in them, and others, may be able to reproduce them for the instruction and delight of others.

Exercises, that consist of passages from the Scriptures, are more valuable than others to the children, when committed to memory, and they learn them very readily, when an immediate use is to be made of them at a public service. The passages suggested for use in these exercises include many of the most important ones in the Bible, and as they practice, in the presence of each other, all become more or less familiar with every one of them. The superintendent or leader is expected to arrange the length and number of the exercises, to suit the number and ages of those available to participate in them. A single verse may be best for the child; but a glance over the additional passages may be very helpful to the pastor or other person, delivering a short address at the close of the children's exercises.

A very pleasing feature of these designs is the fact, they are constructed by the children as one after the other, or two together, carry their part to the platform and render their exercise. One or two are appointed to serve as Masterbuilders to receive the stones or tablets, when delivered, and place them in their proper position.

BUILDING THE TEMPLE

A good character is an enduring monument. A good name is rather to be chosen than great riches.

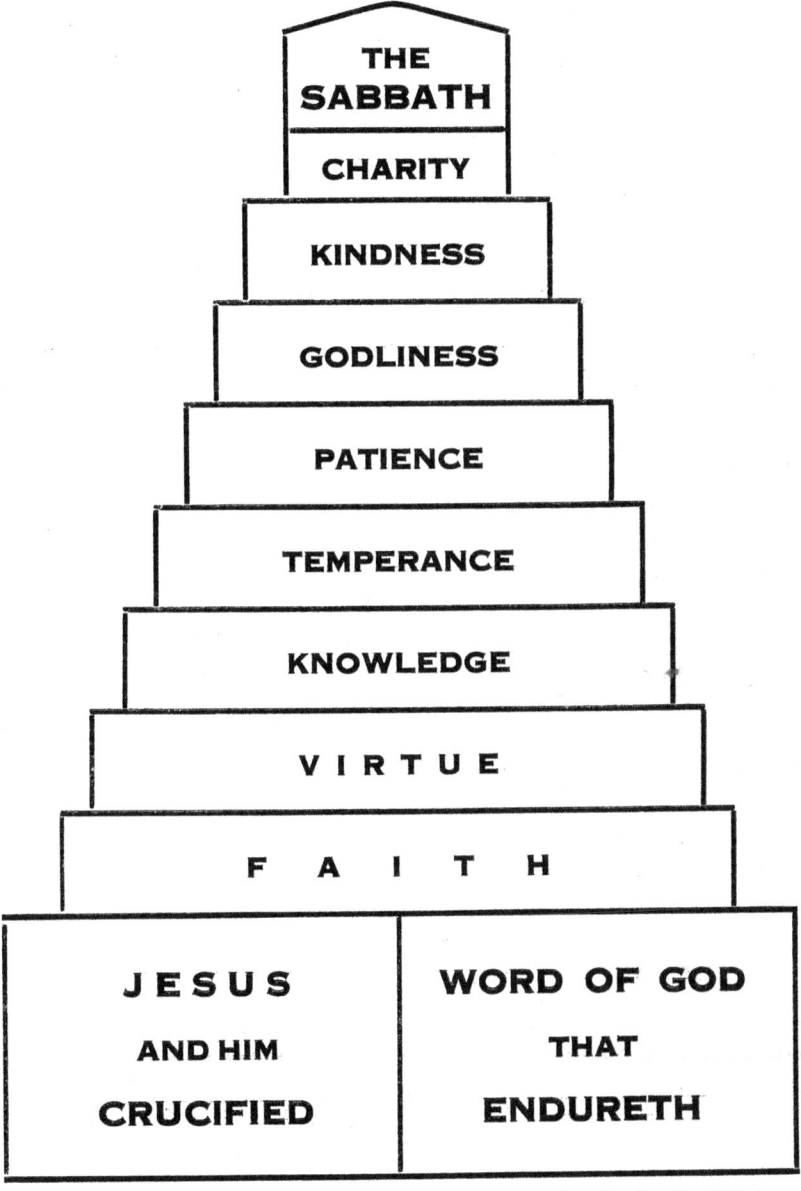

AN ENDURING TEMPLE.—A temple for time and eternity, showing the divinely appointed elements of a good character (2 Peter 1:5-8), their sure foundations; the person and work of our Lord Jesus and the inspired Word of God; and their crowning bond, the Sabbath.

AN EXERCISE FOR CHILDREN'S DAY

(The two master builders standing together)

Master Builder. Dear friends: The Bible tells us that all are builders. That some are wise and others are foolish. That some are building on the sand, without any protection against the storms and floods, that will surely cause their fall. That some are building with wood, hay or stubble; or with gold, silver and precious stones, without any protection against the day, when the fire will consume these perishable materials. That others, however are building safely and securely, with divinely appointed materials, on the Rock of Ages and the unchanging, impregnable Word of God. That the indwelling Spirit, commonly called the Comforter, is the occupant, strength and life of their temple; and their conscientious observance of the Sabbath, is to them the pledge of Divine favor and the visible sign of their sure protection.

Assistant Builder. All of you no doubt are familiar with the words of the poet, Longfellow:

> "All are architects of fate
>   Building on the walls of time;
> Some with massive deeds and great,
>   Others with the ornaments of rhyme.
> For the structures that we raise
>   God's Word is with materials filled;
> And our todays and yesterdays
>   Reveal the materials with which we build."

> "We have planned today to build
>   A temple—on earth, a heaven;
> A temple on rocks so solid,
>   And with materials divinely given,
> That all who hear the Master's call
>   To service and an endless life,
> May of this be sure, whate'er befall
>   They have builded for time aright."

Life is what we make it out of what God puts within our reach, and every act is a foundation stone for the next one. Walking in the truth, adding to our faith and building a temple all mean advancing one step or stone at a time.

Master Builder. The white stone referred to in Revelation was an emblem of pardon and a badge of friendship.

BUILDING THE TEMPLE 231

The stone ordinarily is an emblem of solidity and enduring strength. In this sense it is an emblem of an eternal truth, or principle. When Peter confessed, "Thou art the Christ," Jesus said in regard to his confession, "Thou art Peter, and on this rock" or fundamental truth, "I am Christ," "I will build my church; and the gates of hell (hades) shall not prevail against it."

David tells us "The Lord set his feet upon a rock." He calls the Lord a rock, a fortress and a high tower; and entreats the Lord to "lead him to the rock that is higher than I." Peter speaks of Jesus as a living stone, and of believers as lively stones that form a spiritual house, an holy priesthood.

We are now ready for the foundation.

"And as we build, let each one pray,
That we may build aright;
That all we do on earth may be
Well pleasing in God's sight."

Chorus. "We're building up the temple,
Building up the temple
Building up the temple of the Lord."

Bearer: We bring the corner stone on which our temple rests.

Master Builder: This stone represents our Lord Jesus, the sure foundation. Let us hear of this stone, the Rock of Ages, what the Bible may tell.

Bearer: "Behold I lay in Zion a chief corner stone, elect, precious; and he that believeth on him shall not be confounded. Unto you therefore which believe, he is precious; but unto them which be disobedient, the stone which the builders rejected, the same is made the head of the corner. Other foundation can no man lay than that is laid, which is Jesus Christ.

He said of himself, I am the light of the world. I am the resurrection and the life: he that believeth in me though he were dead, yet shall he live. And whosoever liveth and believeth in me shall never die. Without me ye can do nothing. My grace is sufficient for thee.

Paul said of him, "We preach Christ crucified, unto the Jews a stumblingblock and unto the Greeks foolishness;

but unto them which are called, both Jews and Greeks, Christ the power of God and the wisdom of God."

Asst. Bearer: Peter said: "Be it known unto you all, and to all the people of Israel,. that by the name of Jesus Christ of Nazareth, whom ye crucified, whom God raised from the dead, even by him doth this man stand before you whole. This is the stone which was set at nought by you builders—the Jews—which is become the head of the corner. Neither is there salvation in any other; for there is none other name under heaven, given among men whereby we must be saved."

Bearer: We bring another stone for the foundation.

M. B. This stone represents the Word of God that endureth forever. Let us hear of this stone what the Bible may tell.

Bearer: "Thou hast known the holy scriptures, which are able to make thee wise unto salvation through faith, which is in Christ Jesus.

All scripture is given by inspiration of God and is profitable for doctrine, for reproof, for correction, for instruction in righteousness: That the man of God may be perfect; thoroughly furnished unto all good works.

The law of the Lord is perfect; converting the soul; the testimony of the Lord is sure, making wise the simple. The statutes of the Lord are right, rejoicing the heart; the commandment of the Lord is pure, enlightening the eyes. The fear of the Lord is clean, enduring forever; the judgments of the Lord are true and righteous altogether."

Asst. Bearer. "Heaven and earth shall pass away, but my words shall not pass away.

"Whosoever shall be ashamed of me and my words, of him shall the Son of Man be ashamed when he shall come in his own glory, and in the glory of the Father and of the holy angels."

"Ye are built upon the foundation of the apostles and prophets, Jesus Christ himself being the chief corner stone; in whom all the building fitly framed together groweth unto a holy temple in the Lord, for a habitation of God through the Spirit." See John 1. 4, 14.

M. B. The two fold foundation of our glorious temple

BUILDING THE TEMPLE

has now been laid. It consists of the Rock of Ages and the Word of God that endureth forever. We are now ready for those good materials for the walls of the temple that are better than wood, hay or stubble, gold, silver or precious stones.

FAITH. Bearer: We bring the stone that represents Faith.

Master Builder: Faith is a goodly stone, and it fits right well. Let us hear of Faith what the Bible may tell.

(Adjust and repeat for the other stones.)

Bearer: By grace are ye saved through Faith; and that not of yourselves; it is the gift of God.

God so loved the world that he gave his only begotten Son, that whosoever believeth in him should not perish, but have everlasting life. He that believeth on the Son hath everlasting life; and he that believeth not the Son shall not see life.

Asst. Bearer: Abraham believed God, and it was accounted to him for righteousness. Know ye therefore that they which are of faith, the same are the children of Abraham. They which be of faith are blessed with faithful Abraham. He that is faithful in that which is least is faithful. Be thou faithful unto death and I will give thee a crown of life. See also Rom. 10:8-10.

VIRTUE—COURAGE. B:Whatsoever things are true, whatsoever things are honest, whatsoever things are just; whatsoever things are pure, whatsoever things are lovely, whatsoever things are of good report; if there be any virtue, and if there be any praise, think on these things.

Thou therefore my son, Timothy, be strong in the grace that is in Christ Jesus and endure hardness, as a good soldier of Jesus Christ.

Asst. B: The Lord said unto Joshua, "Be strong and of a good courage: that thou mayest observe to do according to all the law, which Moses, my servant commanded thee; that thou mayest prosper whithersoever thou goest. This book of the law shall not depart out of thy mouth; but thou shalt meditate therein day and night, that thou mayest observe to do according to all that is written therein; for then thou shalt make thy way prosperous, and then thou shalt have good success." See also Eph. 6:10-17.

KNOWLEDGE. B: The fear of the Lord is the beginning of knowledge. This is life eternal, that they might know thee, the only true God, and Jesus Christ, whom Thou hast sent.

Know ye not that ye are the temple of God and that the spirit of God dwelleth in you? If any man defile the temple of God, him shall God destroy: for the temple of God is holy, which temple ye are. See Prov. 4:7-8; 3: 16-17

TEMPERANCE. Abstain from all appearance of evil. If meat make my brother to offend I will eat no meat while the world standeth. The fruit of the spirit is love, joy, peace, long suffering, gentleness, goodness, faith, meekness, temperance; against such there is no law. And 2 Pet. 1:5-6.

PATIENCE. In your patience possess ye your souls. Let us run with patience the race that is set before us; looking unto Jesus, the author and finisher of our faith; who for the joy that was set before him endured the cross, despising the shame, and is set down at the right hand of the throne of God.

GODLINESS. "Great is the mystery of Godliness: God manifest in the flesh, believed on in the world and received up into glory. Godliness with contentment is great gain. Godliness is profitable unto all things, having promise of the life that now is and of that which is to come. Fear God and keep his commandments: for this is the whole duty of man."

KINDNESS. "Be ye kind one to another, tender hearted, forgiving one another, even as God for Christ's sake hath forgiven you. Love ye your enemies, and do good; lend hoping for nothing again; and your reward shall be great, and ye shall be the children of the Highest: for he is kind unto the unthankful and to the evil."

CHARITY. Though I bestow all my goods to feed the poor, and though I give my body to be burned and have not charity, it profiteth me nothing. Charity suffereth long and is kind. Charity envieth not; beareth all things, believeth all things, endureth all things. And now abideth faith, hope and charity, these three, but the greatest of these is charity." Luke 10:27. I John 3.17.

All repeat 2 Pet. 1:5-8, and review the foundations.

BUILDING THE TEMPLE 235

THE SABBATH. "The Sabbath was made for man and not man for the Sabbath: therefore the Son of Man is Lord also of the Sabbath, and the apostle John calls it the Lord's day."

"From the beginning of the world to the resurrection of Christ, God appointed the seventh day of the week to be the weekly Sabbath; and the first day of the week ever since to continue to the end of the world, which is the Christian Sabbath."

"And the Lord spake unto Moses saying, verily my Sabbaths ye shall keep, for it is a sign between me and you throughout your generations; that ye may know that I am the Lord that doth sanctify you. It is a sign between me and the children of Israel for ever."

Isaiah refers to the Sabbath as a pledge of divine favor. "If thou call the Sabbath a delight, the holy of the Lord and shalt honor it, not doing thine own ways; I will cause thee to ride upon the high places of the earth and feed thee with the heritage of Jacob thy father."

Ezekiel, a prophet of the captivity, older than Daniel and faithful even unto death, refers four times to the pollution of the Sabbath as one of the principal causes of the captivity. "The word of the Lord came unto me, saying, I gave them my Sabbaths to be a sign between me and them, that they might know that I am the Lord that sanctify them. But the house of Israel walked not in my statutes, and my Sabbaths they greatly profaned. Then I said I would greatly pour out my fury upon them to consume them and scatter them among the heathen."

Abraham Lincoln very truly observed, "As we keep or break the Sabbath day, we nobly save or meanly lose the last best hope by which man rises."

Washington and Lincoln, apart from what they did, were great men. The divine element of a God given character belonged to each. Goodness is the basis of greatness, and greatness is character; the ability and willingness to serve.

All unite in repeating the fourth commandment.

THE DESIGN. It can be ornamented with a gilt cross and decorated with evergreen festoons pendant over the ends. Bouquets of the same color can be laid at the corresponding angles.

THE CROSS. "God forbid that I should glory, save in the cross of our Lord Jesus Christ, by whom the world is crucified unto me, and I unto the world." —Paul.

The children bringing bouquets can be supplied with short exercises like the following.

I bring these flowers: Solomon in all his glory was not arrayed like one of these.

These beautiful flowers I bring,
    A grateful offering to my king.

I bring these pretty flowers,
    A fragrant relic of Eden's bowers.

I bring these roses fair
    To Him who hears my evening prayer.

I bring to him this pretty rose,
    Who died and from the dead arose,
To save us all from all our foes.

These flowers I bring to him of whom it was said, "I am the rose of Sharon and the lily of the valleys."

"By their fruits ye shall know them." This is the present test of character; of men, their teachings and institutions.

Fruit, FRUIT, MORE FRUIT.
Every branch that beareth not
FRUIT
He taketh away; every branch that beareth
FRUIT
He purgeth it, that it may bring forth
MORE FRUIT

"In the beauty of the lilies Christ was born across the sea.
With a glory in his bosom that transfigures you and me;
As He died to make men holy, let us die to make men free,
    While God is marching on."

See also Math. 7:30; John 15:5-8, 14, 15.

BUILDING THE TEMPLE

Repeat in unison the call of Jesus for the children: "Suffer little children to come unto me and forbid them not for of such is the kingdom of heaven."

OPPORTUNITY FOR DECISION

Daniel in his youth, purposed in his heart, not to defile himself by eating the king's meat or the wine which he drank. Joshua expressed his decision to all Israel, saying, "As for me and my house, we will serve the Lord."

Choose ye this day whom ye will serve? While the congregation is standing and singing an appropriate, familiar hymn, encourage every undecided person present, to accept Jesus as their savior; and to indicate with the uplifted hand, their decision to live a Christian life.

Provide testaments or bibles for those needing them.

BUILDING DAY BY DAY

"We are building in sorrow and building in joy
   A temple the world cannot see.
But we know it will stand, if we found it on a rock,
   Through the ages of eternity.
Cho. We are building day by day
   As the moments glide away,
   Our temple which the world may not see.
   Every victory won by grace
   Will be sure to find a place
   In our building for eternity.

Every deed forms a part in this building of ours,
   That is done in the name of the Lord;
For the love that we show
   And the kindness we bestow
He has promised us a bright reward.
Then be watchful and wise
   Let the temple we rear
Be one that no tempest can shock;
   For the Master has said
And He taught us in His word
   We must build upon the solid rock."

—H. E. Blair

GROWING UP FOR JESUS

"Growing up for Jesus, we are truly blest,
    In His smile is welcome, in His arms our rest,
In His truth our treasure, in His word our rule,
    Growing up for Jesus, in our Sunday School.
Growing up for Jesus, till in Him complete,
    Growing up for Jesus, oh! His work is sweet;
In His truth our treasure, in His word our rule,
    Growing up for Jesus, in our Sunday School.

Not too young to love Him, little hearts beat true,
    Not too young to serve Him, as the dew drops do.
Not too young to praise Him, singing as we come,
    Not too young to answer, when He calls us home.
Growing up for Jesus, learning day by day,
    How to follow onward in the narrow way;
Seeking holy treasure, finding precious truth,
    Growing up for Jesus in our happy youth."
                —Pres. Board Publication.

OUR HAPPY LAND

A Favorite Children's Chorus.

Land of children, birds and flowers,
    What a happy land is ours!
Here the gladdest bells are rung,
    Here the sweetest songs are sung.
With Thy banner o'er us,
    Join we all in chorus,
Land of children, birds and flowers
    What a happy land is ours.

Let us keep it so we pray,
    Drive the clouds of sin away;
Father by Thy love divine
    Make us, keep us ever Thine.
With Thy banner o'er us, etc.
Keep us Lord from day to day
    In the straight and narrow way.
May it be our chief delight,
    To walk upright in Thy sight;
With Thy banner o'er us, etc.

What a happy land
    What a happy land is ours,
Here the gladdest bells are rung,

BUILDING THE TEMPLE

Here the sweetest songs are sung;
Freedom's banner o'er us,
Join we all in chorus,
Land of children, birds and flowers,
What a happy land is ours.

THE ARCH

The arch, which appears on another page, illustrates in a very striking manner the mutual dependence of all the stones, representing the divinely appointed elements of character, on their crown, the keystone, which represents the Sabbath or fourth commandment, the connecting link between the first and second tables of the law and the visible bond of every man and nation to his Creator.

When the keystone has been placed in position the arch will sustain considerable weight, but if it be removed nearly all of the other stones tumble to the floor in a confused heap. Those who do not remember the Sabbath to keep it holy unto the Lord, may manifest some of these divinely appointed elements of character, but every one who conscientiously observes the Sabbath as a day for public worship, reading and teaching the Word of God, endeavors to develop all of them. The indwelling spirit is dependent on an intelligent knowledge of the Word, and the strengthening influence of the Sabbath is usually according to the good use that is made of it.

EXPLANATORY

A couple of cracker boxes inverted serve for the two foundation stones. The parts of the temple consist of frames made of thin strips, about five inches wide. Each stone is about three inches shorter and one and one-half inches narrower than the one below it, and it rests on supporting strips inserted in the top of the lower one. All can be set aside in the lower one when they are inverted. All are covered with white printing paper and the letters are fastened with little tacks.

The large letters are $2\frac{1}{2} \times 1\frac{1}{4}$ and the small ones $1\frac{1}{2} \times 7\text{-}8$ inches. A bright red color is essential in order to produce the nicest effect.

They can be cut very speedily and uniformly if the cardboard is first ruled with a pen, into squares the size of the letters, and then ruled with a pencil one-fourth of an inch distant from the ink rulings.

The arch is four feet wide at the base. The inner circle is described with a radius of two and the outer one of three feet. The curved edges of each are cut with a scroll saw. Strips of orange boxes or sheets of card board, one foot long, are used to nail on their straight edges. All are covered with cheese cloth or muslin and the letters are placed on a curved line. The arch and temple can both be built on a smaller scale with box board. The lifting of the keystone of the arch, when first inserted is a very interesting performance.

REFERENCES

TEMPLE: 1 Cor. 3:16-17;Math. 7:24-27; Luke 6:47-49; 1 Cor. 3:12-15; James 1:22-24;Rev. 2:17; Ps. 18:2; 31:2-3; 71:35; 40:2; 61:2; 62:2.

JESUS. Isa. 28:16; 1 Peter 2:6; Math. 16:15-18; John 1:1-2-14; Dan. 2:34-35; 1 Cor. 3:11; Math 21:42-44; Acts 4:10-12; 1 Peter 2:4-6.

WORD. 2 Tim. 3:16-17; 1 Peter 1:20-21; Ps. 19:7.10; Heb. 4:12; Ps. 119:105,130; Isa. 40:8; Math. 24:35; Mark 13:31; Luke 9:26; Eph. 2:19-22.

FAITH. John 3:16, 36; Heb. 11:1-3; Eph. 2:4-8; Acts 16:31; Heb. 11:23-26; Mark 11:22-23; Gal. 3:6-9; Luke 16:10.

VIRTUE. Phil. 4:8; Josh. 1:6-9; 2 Tim 2:1-3; 1 John 2:13-14.

KNOWLEDGE. John 17:3; 1 Cor. 3:16-17; Prov. 1:7; Isa. 11:1-2, 33, 6; Prov. 4:7-8; 3:16-17.

TEMPERANCE. Gal. 5:22-24; 1 Cor. 8:13; 2 Peter 1:5-6; Gen. 2:16-17; Dan. 1:8; - Thess. 5:22.

PATIENCE. Luke 21:19; James 5:11; Heb. 10:35-36; 12:1-2.

GODLINESS. 1 Tim. 4:8; 6:6-7; 3:16; Ec. 12:13-14.

KINDNESS. Eph. 4:32; Luke 6:35; Ps. 103:2-4.

CHARITY. 1 Cor. 13:4-8; 13:1-3; 2 Peter 1:5-8.

SABBATH. Ex. 20:8-11; Mark 2:27-28; Ex. 31:13- 17; Isa. 58: 13-14; Ezek. 20:13, 16, 20, 24; Luke 4:16:18; Rev. 1:10.

XXX
MAXIMS AND SUGGESTIONS

RELATING TO THE DEVELOPMENT OF A GOOD CHARACTER AND THE ACHIEVEMENT OF GOOD SUCCESS.—NUGGETS FROM SHORT TALKS TO THE STUDENTS ON FRIDAY EVENINGS.

"Precept upon precept, line upon line, here a little and there a little." Proverbs.

UNSTABLE as water thou shalt not excel. Jacob.

Be gentle in manner, firm in principle, always conciliatory.

Go forward; and if difficulties increase, go forward more earnestly.

In essentials, unity; in non-essentials, liberty; in all things, charity. Augustine.

Find a way or make one, is excellent; but sometimes it needs to read, Find employment or make it.

Whatever cannot be avoided must be endured. Endure hard things bravely.

Patience and Perseverance will perform great wonders.

Early to bed and early to rise will make a man healthy, wealthy and wise. Ben Franklin.

Whoever wins man's highest stature here below must grow, and never cease to grow—for when growth ceases, death begins. Alice Carey.

"There is so much bad in the best of us,
    And so much good in the worst of us;
It is hardly fair for any of us,
    To speak ill of the rest of us."

If thou wouldst know the secret of a happy life, rise in the morn, with armor clasped about thee, for the day's long strife. "Thy duty do."

The very angels then will stoop, when the night brings rest, to cradle thee in heavenly arms because thou didst thy best. Jennings.

Bear and forbear are two good bears to have in every home ,in order to keep peace in the family. Grin and bear it, is another good one. Impatience, scolding and fault-finding are three black bears, that make every one feel badly and look ugly. Don't harbor them.

BIBLE PRECEPTS. Faithful is the Bible word for success.

He that is faithful, is faithful in that which is least.

Owe no man anything. Render to all their dues.

Be not wise in your own conceits. A wise son maketh a glad father; but a foolish son is the heaviness of his mother.

Seek ye first the kingdom of God and all these things shall be added unto you.

Wisdom is the principal thing, therefore get wisdom. Her ways are ways of pleasantness and all her paths are peace.

Honor the Lord with thy substance and with the first-fruits of all thine increase; so shall thy barns be filled with plenty.

So teach us to number our days, that we may apply our hearts unto wisdom. Let the beauty of the Lord our God be upon us, and establish thou the work of our hands. Moses.

The hand of the diligent maketh rich. The hand of the diligent shall bear rule.

Be not slothful in business. A man diligent in his business shall stand before kings; he shall not stand before mean men.

Anger resteth in the bosom of fools. Make no friendship with an angry man, lest thou learn his ways: Let not the sun go down upon thy wrath. Be patient; and not a brawler or striker.

SPIRITUAL POWER. Bring ye all the tithes into the storehouse; that there may be meat in mine house, and prove me now herewith, saith the Lord of hosts, if I will not open the windows of heaven, and pour you out a blessing, that there shall not be room enough to receive it.

HOW SOME MEN ACHIEVED GREATNESS

Abraham believed God and was promptly obedient to His divine call. "The Lord made Abraham rich" and the "Father of the Faithful."

"The Lord was with Joseph," the innocent slave in prison. He led him from the prison to a throne and made him a successful ruler in Egypt.

Daniel the youthful, God-fearing captive at Babylon, "sought the Lord by prayer, supplication and fasting." "The Lord prospered him." gave him favor with princes and made him the greatest statesman of his age.

Job was a "perfect and upright man, one that feared God." Satan said of him, "Doth Job fear God for nought?" Satan then deprived him of his family, property and health. Job still maintained his integrity, saying, "The Lord gave and the Lord hath taken away." The Lord then gave Job twice as much as he had before; so that the latter end of Job was more blessed than his beginning.

When the Lord said to Moses, "Come now, I will send thee unto Pharoah, that thou mayest bring forth my people out of Egypt;" he hesitated, saying, "Who am I?" "They will not believe me;" and "I am not eloquent." But when he obeyed the call and went, the Lord went with him, the people believed, the army of Pharoah was overthrown; and Moses became the first emancipator, a great leader of men and the greatest law-giver in the history of the world.

OAK HILL BE'S

Be Honorable. Never do that which will cause you afterwards to feel ashamed.

Be Honest. Never deceive or take that which belongs to another.

Be True. Stand firmly for the truth and be faithful, though you stand or work alone.

Be Pure. Shun the impure and abhor whatever will corrupt good morals.

Be Polite. Help the weak and never by word or act offend another.

Be Prompt. If you have done badly, hasten with your apology before you are called to account.

Be Thoughtful. Learn how to exercise that forethought that anticipates every future need at the beginning of an undertaking.

Self Control. Self control means self discipline. Self discipline means that I must be willing to:

Be, what I know I ought to be;

Say, what I know I ought to say;

Do, what I know I ought to do;

Go, where I know I ought to go;

Do, with my might what my hands find to do; and be firmly decided, not to do anything I know I ought not to do. It is the ability to control one's thoughts and energies by rule, so as to act prudently, and never impulsively or impatiently.

All make mistakes, some more than others. "To err is human." He succeeds best who makes the fewest mistakes; and most quickly corrects them, when discovered.

"I am not bound to win, but I am bound to be true.

I am not bound to suceed, but I am bound to live up to what light I have.

I must stand with anybody who stands right; stand with him while he is right, and part with him when he goes wrong." Lincoln.

Freedom. True freedom is the freedom to do right, and for it good men contend. The liberty to do what one may wish to do, is not freedom, for that may be wrong.

Tact. Tact is the ability to please rather than offend, by saying or doing the right thing in a pleasant way at the right time, ignoring petty slights and insults and leading disagreeable people to become your friends.

Blessed is the teacher who expects much from his pupils, he is thereby likely to receive it; that has common sense in framing regulations, and backbone to enforce them; whose vocabulary contains more "do's" than "don'ts." Lucy A. Baker.

The little birds, like the busy bees, are cheery and valuable helpers. Encourage their presence and aid, by planting trees for their songs and building little houses for their young.

The domestic animals are our servants and profit-makers, or mortgage lifters. Always treat them kindly. Never permit anyone to strike, or stone them. Even the pig of your neighbor, when he becomes a mischievous intruder in your field, if you give him a friendly chase, will conduct you to a hole in the fence that ought to be closed.

"Kind words can never die,
Cherished and blest;
God knows how deep they lie,
Stored in each breast."

Character. Character is a word derived from another one that means to impress or engrave. It marks our individuality. It is the result of the principles and habits, that have impressed themselves on our nature and the abilities that have been developed. Solomon calls it a good name, which suggests reputation. It is tested and strengthened by overcoming difficulties. A good character is within the reach of all while greatness is possible only to a few.

"When wealth is lost, nothing is lost;
When health is lost, something is lost;
When character is lost, all is lost."

Character. "Character is not what we think, feel or know; but what we are. Character is being; and it is infinitely nobler to be than to have, or know, or do. The rank, value and dignity of character cannot be overestimated. The confidence of the whole world on which trade, empires, homes and real happiness are built is confidence in character. Character is the great end; moral and spiritual education is the greatest means to attain that end."—Martin.

Character is personal power, the poor boy's best capital and the success, that makes him greater than his occupation. The weak wait for opportunities, but the strong sieze them and make even common occasions great.

The world honors success. God honors faithfulness. The world commends worldly achievements, but God rewards character.

Every student should endeavor to build up the community in which he lives commercially, socially and religiously.

Beware of strangers that come to you full of smooth talk and clad in fine clothing. The tree, book, land and other agents sometimes prove helpful. But you will be happier and more prosperous, if you will send for a catalog and get just what you need, and at cost. You will thereby avoid the expensiveness and uncertainty of doing business through a nicely dressed, but irresponsible stranger.

The upright exert a blessed influence long after their departure from the earth. They are remembered in the home, the social circle and the church.

"That man exists, but never lives,
Who much receives but nothing gives;
But he who marks his busy way,
By generous acts from day to day,
Treads the same path his Savior trod,
The path to glory and to God."

Education. Everything from a pin to an engine has its cost and someone must pay the price.

In education the material is human and the product is a new and living worker for the world's work. The material and moral progress of the world has been principally due to the work of educated men and women.

Education has its cost, but the profit of a good christian education is vastly greater than its cost. It pays to educate young people who are christians, that they may become leaders in thought and action.

"A good education enables one to manifest goodness and not badness. Drawing out all the good qualities of head and heart, it magnifies them and suppresses the bad ones. If this seems hard, it should be remembered that all things of value are obtained only by effort."

"For every evil under the sun
There's a remedy, or there's none,
If there is one, try and find it;
If there is none, never mind it."

"A clear and legible handwriting is one of the best means of giving a stranger an impression of force of character, self-control and capacity for skilled work. It wins favor by making the reading of it easy and a source of pleasure. It is one of the crowning attainments of a well cultured life."—Spencer.

MAXIMS AND SUGGESTIONS

"Success follows those who see and know how to take advantage of their opportunity."

The Lord loves to use "the weak things" and "things that are despised." He loves to put the treasure of His grace into the feeble, that the world may be compelled to ask, "whence hath this man power?" Rev. J. H. Jowett.

Self education is accomplished by reading good books, with the aid of a dictionary. Get a Bible dictionary for the Bible, and a Webster or Academic dictionary for other books.

Do all things by rule. A good rule tells the right way to do things. If you do not know the rule ask for it. Never violate a known rule. It never pays to do so; the confidence of someone is sure to be forfeited.

Keep Busy. Keep busy and you will keep happy. Read good books when you cannot work. If you call on a friend and he is busy, do not become an idler or make him one. Either help him or read his best books.

Idleness. Idleness is a sin against God. "Six days shalt thou labor and do all thy work." "In the sweat of thy face shalt thou eat bread." If any man will not work, neither let him eat." It is also a sin against our nature; causing a slow movement, which is a serious disappointment; tardiness, which is like a dead fly in precious ointment; and, that loathsome disease, laziness. Like drunkenness it is an inexcusable shame, that dooms one to poverty and clothes him with rags. Shun idleness as you do the sting of a hornet, or the bite of a rattler.

"We are not here to play, to dream, to drift,
We have our work to do, and loads to lift.
Shun not the struggle; face it. 'Tis God's gift."
"They are slaves who fear to speak,
For the fallen and the weak.
They are slaves who will not choose
Hatred, scoffing and abuse,
Rather than in silence shrink
From the truth they needs must think;
They are slaves, who dare not be
In the right with two or three." Lowell.

Do your best. Put your best efforts in your work, no matter how simple or difficult the task.

"I am passing through this world but once. I will therefore do my best every day, and do all the good to all the people I can."

"I do the very best I know how—the very best I can; and I mean to keep doing so until the end. If the end brings me out all right, what is said against me won't amount to anything. If the end brings me out wrong, ten angels swearing I was right would make no difference." Abraham Lincoln.

Efficiency. Efficiency is the ability to perform work in the shortest and quickest way, by omitting every useless movement.

Faith. Faith rests on facts and realities. It is the basis of home and business. "It swings the rainbow across the dark clouds, makes heroes in life's battles, extracts the poison from Satan's arrows and links us to God and the good in heaven."

Let us have faith that right makes might, and in that faith let us to the end dare to do our duty, as we understand it. With malice toward none, with charity for all, with firmness in the right as God gives us to see the right, let us strive on to finish, the work we are in. Abraham Lincoln at Gettysburg.

Gladness. Gladness is sown for the upright. The joy of the Lord is your strength. Manifest your joy and gladness by wearing the smile of contentment and love. It includes a sparkle in the eye, a little ripple on the cheek and the kind word that "never dies."

"Smile and the world smiles with you,
Laugh and the world will roar,
Growl and the world will leave you,
And never come back any more.
All of us could not be handsome,
Nor all of us wear good clothes,
But a smile is not expensive.
And covers a world of woes."

Energy. Energy is power in action. Stagnant water lacks power, but water in action produces steam, the power that moves the world's machinery and traffic. Knowledge in action means power on the farm, in the home and in the church.

MAXIMS AND SUGGESTIONS

"God bless the man who sows the wheat,
Produces milk and fruit and meat;
His purse be heavy, his heart be light,
His corn and cattle all go right,
God bless the seed his hand lets fall,
The farmer produces the food for all."

Knowledge. Knowledge is power, when it is wisely assorted, assimilated and immediately employed; as is the water of a river, when it is used to produce electric power. The knowledge that leads to sovereign power, includes self-knowledge, self-respect and self-control. The man who does well whatsoever he undertakes, cannot be kept down, except by his own indiscretions.

A good character is essential to the soul winner. It is a false notion that one must meet the world on its own level—drink to win a drinker, smoke to win a smoker, and play the world's games in order to win it to Christ. Richard Hobbs.

Thrift. Thrift consists in increasing the value of our possessions every year, by making good investments of our time and money, and by earning more than is spent for living expenses. "A penny saved is two pence earned."

Our Father in heaven sends no man into this world without a work, and a capacity to perform that work.

"Live for those that love you,
For those you know are true;
For the cause that lacks assistance,
For the wrong that needs resistance;
For the future in the distance;
And the good that you can do."

"A fool with a gun or an axe can destroy in five minutes, what it took nature years to perfect and perpetuate."

A little house well filled,
A little field well tilled,
A good wife well willed, are great riches.

Leaders. Be a leader. A leader does his thinking before hand and endeavors to provide for every need. He must be well informed and know how to arouse interest and stimulate activity. He must discover and adopt only the best methods. The rewards of leadership are a continually increasing power to lead others and the ability to conduct your own life most usefully and happily.

> "A good farmer's tools are under shelter;
> But Pete Tumbledown's lie helter-skelter;
> And when he wants his tools again
> He finds them rusty from the rain."

"Divide and conquer," was Joshua's rule of strategy in the conquest of Canaan. "Separate for the march, unite for the attack," was a maxim of Napoleon. Both are good rules for the people in all our churches, in their constant conflict with vice and iniquity.

The noblest man does not always uphold his rights, but waives them for his own good and the good of others. A keen sense of honor, that condemns dishonorable conduct, is one of the finest results of a good education. Education is expected to do for the mind, what sculpture does to a block of marble.

> "A merry farmer's girl am I,
> My songs are gay and blithe;
> For in my humble country home
> I lead a free, glad life.
> Through fertile fields and gardens mine,
> I love at will to roam,
> And as I wander, gayly sing,
> This is my own, free home,
> My own free home."

Genius. There is no genius like a love for hard work. Hard work develops strength, increases usefulness, and tends to length of days. Six days shalt thou labor and do all thy work. In the sweat of thy face shalt thou eat bread. Labor conquers all things.

> "He lives the best who never does complain,
> Whether the passing days be filled with sun or rain.
> Who patiently toils on though feet be sore,
> Whose home stands by the road with open door;
> Who smiles though down he sits to feast or crust,
> His faith in man sincere, in God his trust."
>
> A. F. Caldwell.

Seek employment by the month or year, rather than by the day; and render unswerving loyalty to those of your

MAXIMS AND SUGGESTIONS

own home, school and church; and those who favor you with employment.

A man's work is the expression of his worth. It should make a man of him, and give him great pleasure and delight. When a man knows his work and does it with the enthusiasm of Nehemiah, it gives him joy and enables him to exert a good influence. "That man is blest who does his best and leaves the rest."

The world owes no man a living, but every man owes the world an honest effort to make at least his own living.

SAVE THE BOY; SAVE THE GIRL!

Save them from bad habits and evil associations. Save them for useful careers, happy homes and a glorious inheritance.

"If a blessing you have known,
'Twas not given for you alone,
Pass it on.
Let it travel down the years,
Let it dry another's tears,
Till in heaven the deed appears,
Pass it on.

Greatness: Goodness is the basis of that service that leads to greatness. The keynote of that service is found in the words: "The Son of man came not to be ministered unto, but to minister, and to give his life for many." The cross is the symbol of a service that is faithful, even unto death.

"So live that every thought and deed may hold within itself the seed of future good and future need."

Undertake great things for God and His glory and expect great things from Him.

"Never trouble trouble
Until trouble troubles you."

Prudent, hopeful and enthusiastic are those who make the "desert to rejoice and blossom as the rose."

Habits: A habit is a cable; we spin a thread of it every day, and at last we cannot break it.

Thoughts leave an ineffaceable trace on the brain or memory.

"Sow a thought and you reap an act,
Sow an act and you reap a habit,
Sow a habit and you reap a character,
Sow a character and you reap a destiny."

A pretty oak tree is a beautiful emblem of the strength, beauty and eminent usefulness of an intelligent and noble man. Train the head, the heart and hand, and thus develop that strength and beauty of character, that fits one for the most eminent usefulness.

A single aim means undivided attention and interest. Concentrate your faculties on the particular work of each day, that later you may be able to give your undivided attention to your chosen employment. All great achievements have been won by those who have had a single aim. "Consider the postage stamp, my son; its usefulness consists in sticking to one thing, until it gets there."—Josh Billings.

Concentrate your energies and be master of your work, The world crowns him who knows one thing and does it better than others.

I will. Always say, "I will" or "I'll try," when work or a duty is proposed, that can and ought to be done. Never say, "I can't" or "I won't", except to resist a temptation to do wrong. While the "I can'ts" fail in everything, and the "I won'ts" oppose everything, the "I will's" do the world's work.

God has a plan for every life. He made you for use and for His own use. He gives power to those whom He uses. Let Him use you. Your happiness depends on the consciousness you are fulfilling your divinely appointed mission; and your success, on your will being in harmony with your work.

Only the tuned violin can make music; and only the life in harmony with God can "please him" or "win souls" to Him. Spiritual power is necessary for spiritual work.

Investments. Invest only where your investment will be under your own personal supervision, or that of a known and trusted friend. Invest only in those kinds of properties, the successful and profitable management of which, you best understand.

Investments in young stock and good real estate in-

MAXIMS AND SUGGESTIONS

crease in value; but investments in rolling stock always decrease in value. Buy low from those who have to sell, and sell to those who want to buy.

Seek counsel only of those who are achieving success, and never trust a stranger.

Home. A home is one of the best investments for every one of moderate means. It provides a shelter for the individual and for the family, no matter what may happen. A regular income must be assured in order to retain a place to sleep in a rented house. The early desire to own a home makes steady employment a source of pleasure.

It is not what we eat, but what we digest, that makes us strong.

It is not what we read, but what we remember, that makes us learned.

It is not what we earn, but what we save, that makes us rich.

Home. A christian home is a precious heritage. It is the divinely appointed educator of mankind. Its seclusion, shelter and culture are invaluable. There the mother whose hand rocks the cradle, moves the world, teaching the lessons of obedience, self-control, faith and trust. Use only a mellow and sweet tone of voice in the home. A kind and gentle voice is a pearl of great price that, like the cheery song of the lark, increases the joy and happiness of the home with passing years.

> "The farmer's trade is one of worth,
> He is partner with the earth and sky;
> He is partner with the sun and rain,
> And no man loses by his gain.
> And men may rise and men may fall;
> The farmer, he must feed them all."

"Man's chief end is to glorify God and enjoy Him forever."

Knowledge. "Other things may be seized by might or purchased with money; but knowledge is to be gained only by study."—Johnson.

"He that studies only men, will get the body of knowledge, without the soul; and he that studies only books, the soul without the body. He that to what he sees adds observation, and to what he reads, reflection, is in the right road to knowledge, provided that in scrutinizing the hearts of others he neglects not his own."—Cotton.

Co-operation. "All real progress of the individual, or of society, comes through the joining of hands and working together in a spirit of helpfulness for the common good."

A brother in need is a brother indeed.

"Whoso hath this world's goods and seeth his brother in need and shutteth up his bowels of compassion from him, how dwelleth the love of God in him?"

Never go security for any one who cannot give you a mortgage or whose word is not as good as his bond. "He that is surety for a stranger, shall smart for it; and he that hateth suretyship is sure."

Eloquence. Eloquence is the expression of a moral conviction. It is overpowering when the moral conviction is tremenduously felt. This was the secret of the eloquence of Lincoln, Beecher and Garrison, when they spoke of the wrong of slavery; and of John B. Gough, Neal Dow and Frances Willard, when they plead for an uprising against the curse of stronk drink.

Marriage. Marriage is a divine ordinance, instituted by our Heavenly Father in the time of man's innocency. It is not a sacrament, but a social institution, intended to promote the comfort and happiness of mankind, through the establishmentofthe family relationship, and a responsible home, where the children may be trained for the service of God and the work of their generation. The gospel hallows all the relations of life and sanctions the innocent enjoyment of all the good gifts of God. It purifies the hearts of those who walk in the way of obedience and induces the peace that passeth understanding.

> "Life is real, life is earnest
> And the grave is not its goal,
> Dust thou art to dust returnest,
>   Was not written of the soul.
> Let us then be up and doing,
>   With a heart for any fate;
> Still achieving still pursuing,
>   Learn to labor and to wait."—Longfellow.

MAXIMS AND SUGGESTIONS 255

Robbers. Idleness, tardiness and "late nights," are three bold bad robbers, that must be strenuously resisted and overcome. Be watchful or they may rob you of the best that is in you.

Spare Moments. It is better to be a busy silent reader in the home or school and learn something useful, than to be an idle, noisy talker, disturbing others and causing the loss or forfeiture of valuable privileges.

Have a book for spare moments in the home. Read only good books, the Bible and catechism first; then those on history, biography, travel, and progress in the arts and sciences, including one on your own occupation. Do not read worthless story books. They will rob you of your time, and the taste for the Bible and other good books. Time wasted in idleness or reading worthless books means bad companions, bad habits, and the loss of opportunity, energy and vitality. Learn to abhor idleness as nature does a vacuum.

Say No. Have the courage to say "no" to every solicitation to violate rule or known duty. "The companion of fools shall be destroyed." "Though hand join in hand the guilty shall not go unpunished." "This is Fabricius, the man whom it is more difficult to turn from his integrity, than the sun from his course."—Pyrrhus.

Writing. Train the hand and inform the mind so you can write the English language,

"Plain to the eye and gracefully combined."

"The pen engraves for every art and indites for every press. It is the preservative of language, the business man's security, the poor boy's patron and the ready servant of mind."—Spencer.

Train: The hand to be graceful, steady, strong;
The Eye to be alert and observing;
The Memory to be accurate and retentive;
The Heart to be tender, true and sympathetic.

Promptness. Promptness takes the drudgery out of an occupation. The decision of a moment often determines the destiny of years. Every moment lost affords an opportunity for misfortune. Punctuality is the soul of business, the mother of confidence and credit. Only those, who keep their time, can be trusted to keep their word. Tardiness is a disappointment and an interruption; a kind of falsehood and theft of time.

Vices. The four great vices of this age are Sabbath-breaking, gambling, intemperance and licentiousness. These must be fought all the time, like the great plagues that attack the body, tuberculosis, leprosy and small pox. The gospel will save any one from all of them; and some day it will sweep them from the earth, as they are now kept from heaven.

> "A Sabbath well spent
> Brings a week of content,
> And strength for the toils of the morrow;
> But a Sabbath profaned,
> Whatso'er may be gained,
> Is a certain forerunner of sorrow."

To be a leader is a praiseworthy ambition. A leader is one who wins the confidence of the people so that they are willing to follow. Our Lord Jesus gave the secret of leadership, when he said: "Whosoever would be first among you, shall be servant of all;" and again, "The Son of Man came not to be ministered unto, but to minister, and to give his life a ransom for many."

America. America is a land of opportunity, where the poor boy secures a home and later may participate in the government. Most of those, who are managing the world's work to day, were poor boys yesterday. If you are in the school of adversity today, do not be discouraged, "thank God and take courage;" for you are merely on the same level with those, who by their energy and thrift, are making sure of success tomorrow. When Lord Beaconsfield became a member of Parliament, and the other members did not care to listen to his youthful speeches, he said to himself, "I am not a slave nor a captive; and by energy I can overcome great obstacles. The time will come when you will hear me."

Books. "The first time I read an excellent book," said Goldsmith, "it is to me as if I had gained a new friend." "Books are the pillars of progress, the inspiration of mankind. They exert a wonderful influence and a mighty power, though silent," says John Knox in Ready Money,"in lifting up humanity and making progress possible." They enable the reader to converse and associate with the noblest and best

FRUITS APPROVED AT OAK HILL IN 1912, FOR THE
HOME ORCHARD IN SOUTHERN OKLAHOMA.

Peaches: 1, Mamie Ross; 2, Waddell; 3, Alton: 4, Capt. Ede; 5, Carman; 6, *Early Elberta*; 7, Illinois; 8, Elberta (Queen); 9, Belle of Georgia; 10, Champion; 11, Late Crawford; 12, Late Elberta.

Apples: 13, Duchess; 14, Maiden Blush; 15, Wilson Red June; 16, Delicious; 17, Jonathan; 18, Wolf River; 19, King David; 20, Stayman Wine Sap; 21, Ben Davis; 22, Mammoth Grimes Golden; 23, Black Ben; 24, Champion; and, Missouri Pippin.

THE FLAMES CONSUMING THE OLD FARM HOUSE, LOOKING NORTHEAST.

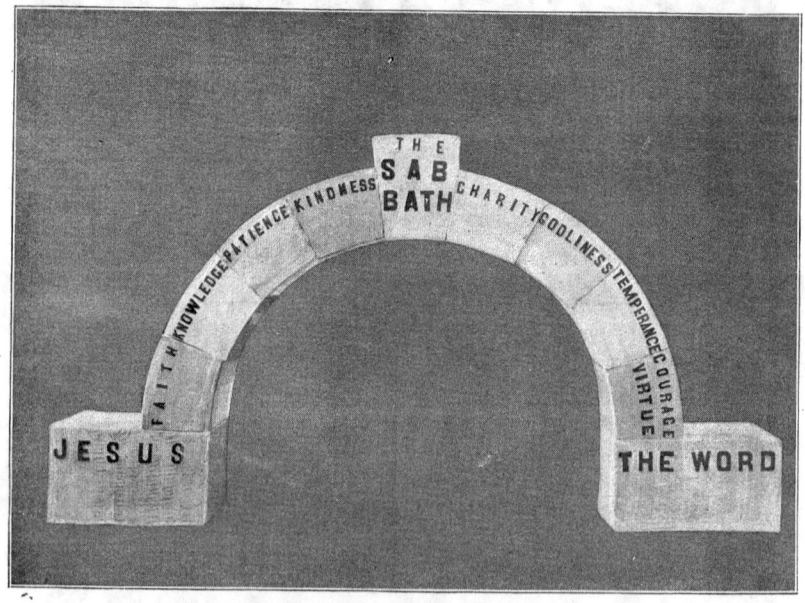

THE BRIDGE OF LIFE.

The Bible elements of a good character; their two-fold foundation, and bond—the Sabbath.

minds. In them we have the thoughts and deeds, the experience and inspiration of all the great ones of earth.

Good books, that breathe the best thoughts and experiences of others, are trusted friends, that bring instruction, entertainment and contentment to the home. As companions and counselors they supply a real want, that makes the home more than merely a place for food and raiment. "Writing makes an exact man, talking makes a ready man, but reading makes him a full man,"—that is a man of intelligence. A man is known by the books he reads and the company he keeps. Let some of the world's best books find an inviting and permanent place in your home.

Books and voices make a glorious combination. No one can tell what good books and good voices may not do. The Word of God and the gospel of our Lord Jesus, have come to us in the form of a book, and we call it by way of pre-eminence, "The Bible," or Scriptures of the Old and New Testaments. Our attention has been directed to them by the living voice. Let your tongues proclaim the glad message of divine truth and redeeming love. The Holy Spirit will record the results in the Lamb's Book of Life.

Read and preserve the books.

WIT AND HUMOR

"Laugh, and grow fat."

"A merry heart doeth good like a medicine."

Aunt Dinah: "How long hab you dis set of dishes?"

Mother Hubbard: "Let me see; I've had 'em—four girls and a half."

Mike: "Do ye believe in the recall of judges, Pat?"

Pat: "That I do not. The last time I was up before his honor he sez: 'I recall that face.—Sixty days.' I'm agin the recall of judges."Life.

Bishop: "Well, Mr. Jones, how do you like your preacher?"

Deacon Jones: "He's de best I eber seed, to take de Bible apart; but he dun' no how to put it to gedder agen."

A Swede, that had not yet had time to learn our language was accused of throwing a stone through a plate glass window. When the lawyers failed to enable him to describe it's size the judge asked:
"Was it as big as my fist?"
"It ben bigger," the Swede replied.
"Was it as big as my two fists,"
"It ben bigger."
"Was it as big as my head?"
"It ben about as long, but not so thick," the Swede replied, amid the laughter of the court.

The German's trouble with the English language.

Visitor: "Those are two fine dogs you have."
Cobbler: "Yes und de funny part of it iss, dat de biggest dog is de leettlest one."
Cobbler's Wife: "You must mine husband egscuse; he shpeaks not very good English. He means de oldest dog is de youngest one."

XXXI

RULES, MOTTOES AND COURSE OF STUDY

WALL MOTTOES

I. OAK HILL MOTTO

Time is precious
Time is money—
Do not stand idle, waiting,
Do not keep others waiting,
Do something useful.
Be a busy, silent worker,
Shun the idle, noisy shirker.

II. RULE OF ORDER

Order is the first law of Heaven, and it is the first rule in every well regulated home, school and church.

IT REQUIRES THAT EVERYONE:

BE in the right place at the right time,
DO the right thing in the right way,
DO the same things the same way,
KEEP everything in the right place; and
COMPLETE whatever has been undertaken.

ENDEAVOR BENEDICTION

"The Lord bless thee and keep thee:

The Lord make his face shine upon thee and be gracious unto thee:

The Lord lift up his countenance upon thee, and give thee peace.

And unto him that loved us, and washed us from our sins in his own blood and hath made us kings and priests unto God and his Father; to him be glory and dominion forever and ever. Amen."

III. ESSENTIALS TO SUCCESS

An unwavering aim,
Unswerving integrity,
Intelligent industry,
Neverfailing promptness,
Indomitable perseverance,
Unbounded enthusiasm,
Willing and strict economy,
In the employment of time,
Talents, money and expenses.

IV. BUSY DAY

THIS is our BUSY DAY.
Do not intrude here to day.
Come some other day.
LOAFERS
Are worse than useless. Their presence here is
STRICTLY FORBIDDEN.

KEY WORDS: The Key words that open or close doors of opportunity, and contrast the characteristics of the good and bad student, are as follows:

GOOD STUDENT

POET: Politeness, Obedience, Economy and Earnestness, Thoughtfulness.

BAD PUPIL

DIED: Disorderly conduct, Idleness, Extravagance, Deceit.

GOOD WORKMAN

STEAM: Steam is a good key word, to enable one to remember how the good workman works efficiently and profitably. He works:
Steadily,
Thoughtfully,
Enthusiastically,
Alone,
Methodically.

RULES AND REGULATIONS
I. STUDENTS

The Superintendent and Teachers wish all the students to be gladdened and strengthened by the joy of successful achievement. To effect this each student must learn to do promptly and thoroughly everything he knows he ought to do, and refrain absolutely from doing anything he knows he ought not to do. "The joy of the Lord is your strength."

Order. Good order must be maintained in all the buildings and premises. It requires that there be a place for everything and everything be kept in its place; that each student know his place and be in it at the right nick of time.

Silence. All are expected to be silent, thoughtful, earnest workers so as to make perfect recitations. The discipline of absolute silence is necessary to the attainment of complete self control, and the achievement of the best results, both as a student and workman. Silence must be observed in the Academy at all times, and only a low tone of voice is appropriate in the other buildings at any time.

Obedience. All are expected to yield a prompt and cheerful obedience to all the Rules and Regulations, and never indulge in any disputes with your teachers.

Students render themselves liable to suspension or expulsion by persistent disobedience, quarreling, disorderly conduct, profane or unchaste language, truancy, or general disregard for the rules of the school.

No student known to be affected with a contagious disease, or coming from a family where such diseases exist, shall be received or continued in the school.

Pupils must procure drinks and make all other necessary preparation for school at playtime, and keep their places after the bell rings.

Pupils shall not ask questions, walk across or leave the room while classes are reciting, nor at any other time without permission.

Pupils must observe the common forms of politeness and at all times treat their teachers and one another with courtesy and respect.

No pupil shall be permitted to leave or be absent from

the school during school hours, except in case of illness without an excuse from the superintendent or parent.

Rooms. The rooms occupied by the students are merely sleeping apartments; and for this purpose the pure cold air in them is conducive to the enjoyment of the most rugged health. They must not be used for study or amusement, especially at night; and drafts of air from the windows must be avoided.

Each student on rising, when no other provision is made is expected to air the bed and room, to empty the slop pail and put it on its shelf in the sun, to make the bed and sweep the room; and after breakfast to report for duty, the boys at the office, and the girls to the matron. They will report in the same way at 2:30 p. m., and the children at 4:00 p. m.

All are expected to refrain from returning to the sleeping rooms during the day, from entering the rooms of others in the evening and from receiving visitors without permission. The doors must be kept closed.

Illness. The first duty of everyone who becomes ill is to report that fact to the superintendent, or matron. He expects everyone to perform every duty assigned in a faithful and responsible manner, until notice of illness has been received.

All are required, even when feeling indisposed and lacking an appetite, to come to the table for warm drinks at the regular meal time.

All requests for meals to be brought to the rooms shall be sent to the matron or superintendent at or before meal time.

Sitting Rooms. The small boys, when needing the comfort of a warm room, must occupy their own sitting room, and the larger boys and girls the rooms provided for them, respectively; each endeavoring to make a good use of their spare moments, while occupying these places, and observe the rule requiring quiet and good order in the buildings.

Chapel Bell. The chapel bell shall be rung at 7:45 and 7:55 a. m.; at 12:45 and 12:55 p. m.; at 2:40 p. m. and at 6:45 and 6:55 p. m. Every student is expected to be in his place and be ready for work on his studies, before the tap bell is heard at 8:00 a. m., 1:00 p. m. and 7:00 p. m.

Farm Bell. The signal for the janitors or fire makers

RULES, MOTTOES AND COURSE OF STUDY

shall be rung at 5:40 a. m., the call to rise, at 6:00 a. m.; for dinner at 11:40 a. m.; supper at 5:40 p. m.; retiring at 8:20 and 8:30 p. m., when all lights in the rooms must be put out.

The dining room bell will ring for breakfast, at 6:20 a. m.; dinner, at 11:55 a. m.; supper, at 6:00 p. m.

All matters for the mail must be delivered at the office before 1:00 p. m.

II. MEETINGS AND CHORES

Genius. All are encouraged to learn how to work hard and constantly, and to use every spare moment for some good purpose. There is no genius like that for hard work. Enthusiastic interest in one's work is essential to success. Idleness is a sin, a waste of life, and cannot be endured at Oak Hill, which is intended to be a hive of industry.

Carefulness. All must learn to use rightly and carefully the books, slates, tools, and furniture entrusted to them. All injuries to books, furniture or buildings must be paid for by those guilty of injuring them.

Services. All, unless specially excused, are required to attend all the religious services on the Sabbath, including the Bible Memory class. The **Endeavor** meeting is the student's special training service; all are expected to participate in it, by at least reading or repeating a verse of Scripture; and in the Bible Memory class by committing an average of one verse a day. All are encouraged to covet the best gifts, especially the power of complete self-control, and the ability to say things forcibly, and do things thoroughly.

Speakers. Those speak with authority, who, instead of telling what they think, or making an apology, tell what the Bible, the law of the Lord, says. All should endeavor to instruct, animate and encourage; none should ever indulge in fault-finding, or allude to any personal grievance.

Leaders. Leaders of meetings are expected to be fully prepared before hand, to stand when they speak; to speak sufficiently loud and distinct as to be easily heard by the most distant listener; to repeat the numbers of the hymns; to request the audience to stand during prayer; to afford an opportunity for volunteer prayers or remarks; and to close the meeting as soon as the interest in it has ended.

Immorality. No one guilty of persistent immoral conduct, will either be admitted, or be permitted to remain at the academy.

Chores. The domestic work in all the buildings, the care of the stock, and the preparation of the fuel, are apportioned among the students, and all are required to do their part.

Janitors. The janitors must see that the kindling has been provided in the evening; rise promptly at the call of the janitor's signal; and have the fires in the sitting rooms and chapel burning in good shape, before the ringing of the rising bell. These fires are to be maintained during the day by those specially appointed to perform that duty. All are expected, to exercise good judgment and practice economy in the use of both the kindling and wood. The ashes from all the stoves must be carried to the heap every morning. Only old vessels may be used for this purpose and these, when emptied, must be returned to their proper places.

Care of Stock. Those assigned the care of the stock are required to be prompt and faithful in caring for it; in the morning, at noon and evening day by day, according to instructions, without having to be prompted. This work must not be left undone or entrusted to others, without first notifying the superintendent.

Other Chores. This rule, requiring faithfulness, applies also to those, who have been assigned the chore work about the buildings, kindling fires, sweeping halls, cleaning lamps, carrying water and wood.

Hall Lamps. The hall lamps, water pails and other fixtures, that are intended to serve all, must never be removed from their places, to render service to an individual.

III. WORK AND THINGS FORBIDDEN

Work Period. All over 13 years of age are expected to render three full hours of faithful and efficient work each day, and on Saturday until 2:30 p. m. Time lost by tardiness, or unnecessary absence during the working period, must be made up before the end of the term.

Object. The aim of your teachers, during these work-periods, is to give you a practical knowledge of the simple arts of life; that you may be intelligent, capable and effi-

RULES, MOTTOES AND COURSE OF STUDY

cient workmen; be enabled to make your own homes more comfortable, and create a demand for your services.

Tool Rules. Each workman, at the close of the work period, must return all tools used to their proper place. If they have been transferred, then the last one using them must return them. None are permitted to use any tools, or touch any musical instrument, until they have been taught the rules relating to them; and have been shown how to use them, and do the work in a skillful and workmanlike manner. Tools must never be taken to any of the rooms to do any repair work.

Non-interference. When students are working under the direction of anyone, they must not be interfered with by others, nor leave the work assigned them, without the knowledge and approval of the one, under whose direction they are working at the time.

Irregularity. Irregularity greatly interferes with a student's progress and the work of his class and teacher. Leave of absence during the term cannot therefore be granted, except for the most urgent reasons. Those, that from any cause, miss one or more lessons, should endeavor to master them when they return.

Caution. All are kindly advised never to be guilty of any word or act, that will be likely to cause you to forfeit the esteem and confidence of the superintendent, or your teachers. A good student endeavors to aid and cheer, but never disobeys or annoys a teacher.

Things Forbidden. Never permit yourself to indulge in any dispute with your teacher in the school room, shop or field.

Don't tease, ridicule or despise others; be polite and courteous to each other.

Don't indulge in the use of profane or obscene language, or in any acts of deceit, falsehood or theft.

Don't use or have in your possession, any intoxicating liquors, tobacco or snuff in any form; gamblers' or obscene cards or pictures; concealed weapons; or soil the floors with spittle or wash water.

Don't indulge in singing, whistling, unnecessary talking or foolish laughter while working with others; or play ball while others are working, or choring.

All communications between boys and girls, and all association or interference on the play grounds are strictly forbidden.

At the close of all meetings, especially those in the evening, the girls are required to go directly and quietly to their hall.

Don't be extravagant or foppish in your dress, or borrow or lend, either clothing or money.

Don't send home for eatables or other unnecessary things. New clothing, especially shoes, should not be sent from home, without having the measure taken. It is better to send the money.

Every article of clothing needing to be washed must have the owner's name.

Don't tamper with the street lamp, or the plugs in the water trough; nor change the pins, tubs or tube at the well; nor roughly jerk the pump handles at the well and cisterns.

Use everything in the way and for the purpose for which it was intended, never otherwise.

Don't leave your seat in the school room, or go out of it during school hours, without permission from your teacher. Never sit on the tops of the desks.

Teachers. Each teacher is expected to keep in an orderly form on the teacher's desk, for use in conducting recitations, a complete set of the Text books used by the classes; and to prepare before hand all lessons or parts thereof that may not be familiar.

The power of suspension or exclusion is vested only in the superintendent. This power must never be exercised by any of his helpers without his previous knowledge and approval.

All matters relating to the repair of the buildings and their equipment should be promptly reported to the superintendent.

The aim of the primary teacher, at the time of recitation, should be to have all the pupils reproduce the entire lesson one or more times in concert and then individually to accomplish this with as few words as possible.

The aim of every teacher should be to make Oak Hill, to all the young people pursuing their studies here, a fountain of inspiration, a sanctuary where fellowship with the Redeemer of the world and a new discovery of the glory of God shall be among the blessings bestowed.

Book Marks. The teachers are required to furnish every new pupil one complete set of approved, folded marginal book marks; one for each text book, and for both the Sunday school and Memory lessons in the Bible. By example and precept, they are expected to require them to keep them in their proper places, and if carelessly lost, to replace them with new ones of their own making. Among the objects to be attained by the enforcement of this rule are the habit of carefulness in little things, to save the books from other injurious methods of marking and to save the time of the teacher, class and pupil.

FIRE PRECAUTIONS

The rooms occupied by the students must be carefully inspected by the matrons or their special monitors every time the students leave them for the school or chapel; to see that the buildings have not been endangered by any acts of carelessness or thoughtlessness.

The ladders must be kept where they may be easily and quickly obtained.

On the first Friday of each term the students shall be organized into a Fire Department, the superintendent serving as chief and the matrons and teachers as his special aids. The fire-fighters shall include the pumpers and a bucket brigade; the life and property savers shall include the ladder squad; and the strenuous work of all shall continue until the building or the last possible piece of property has been saved.

The fire drills shall consist of quick orderly marches, at an unexpected signal, from all the buildings occupied, and the report of each squad for duty to their respective foremen.

TO PARENTS

These suggestions to parents or guardians appear on the monthly report cards.

This report is sent you in the hope it will give you that information you naturally desire to receive in regard to the work and standing of the pupils you have sent to the academy.

In your communications to your children encourage them to be prompt and punctual in meeting every engagement, to remember the Sabbath day, to improve their spare moments by reading the Bible or some good book, to do their best during the hours of study and work each day, and to refrain from association with the idle or worthless.

(1) SALUTE TO THE FLAG

(2) We give our heads (3) and our hearts (4) to our Country. (5) One country, one language (6) one flag.

1. All rise and extend right arm toward the flag. 2 Touch forehead with tips of the fingers. 3. Right palm over the heart. 4. Both hands extended upward. 5. Lean forward, hands at sides. 6. With emphasis, right hand pointing to the flag. Sing America.

"The red is for love that will dare and do
The blue is the sign of the brave and true.
The white with all evil and wrong shall cope,
And the silver stars are the stars of hope."

THE STUDENTS GOODBYE

Good bye, Oak Hill; good bye;
We're off to the fields and the open sky;
But we shall return in the fall, you know,
As glad to return as we are now to go.
Good bye, Oak Hill; Good bye.

THE COURSE OF STUDY

The following is the course of study pursued at the academy, the high school course being added June 1, 1912.

I. PRIMARY DEPARTMENT

First Grade: First Reader, Reading Chart, Primer, Printing, Numbers and Tables. Books of Bible, Memory Work.

Second Grade: Second Reader, Doubs Speller, Printing, Writing, Tables, Primary Arithmetic. Also the Bible, Shorter Catechism and Vocal Music in this and the subsequent grades.

II. INTERMEDIATE DEPARTMENT

Third Grade: Third Reader, Doubs Speller, (Smith's) Primary Arithmetic, Principles of Penmanship, (Spencer or Eaton), Introductory Language Work, Primary Geography.

Fourth Grade: Fourth Reader, Doubs Speller, Primary Arithmetic, Writing, (Thompson's) Principles of Drawing, Primary Geography, (Krohn's) First Book in Physiology.

Leslie's Music Chart and Ideal Class Book; and Thwing's Voice Culture, are used weekly for instruction in the principles, and general drills in gesture, note reading and voice culture.

III. GRAMMAR DEPARTMENT

Fifth Grade: Fifth Reader, U. S. History, Doubs Speller, Primary Arithmetic, Reed & Kellogg's Graded Lessons in English, or Burt's Grammar, Physiology, Writing, Nature Study Chart.

Sixth Grade: Fifth Reader, History of United States or Oklahoma, Doubs Speller, (Smith's) Practical Arithmetic, Writing, Geography, Drawing, Burt's Grammar or Reed & Kellogg's Graded Lessons in English, Agriculture.

Seventh Grade: The Bible, Literary Readings, Doubs Speller, Arithmetic, Grammar, Agriculture, Civics, Writing, Geography Completed.

Eighth Grade: The Bible or Literary Readings, Doubs Speller, Grammar, Composition, (Carson's Handbook), Arithmetic, (Evans & Bunn's) Civics, Constitution of Oklahoma and United States, Writing, Bookkeeping (Stephenson's), Thompson's Drawing for Rural Schools.

Wentworth's Mental Arithmetic is commended for use in the Sixth to Eighth grades.

Frequent reviews of the rules and definitions are essential to the attainment of a thorough knowledge of any textbook and the most rapid advancement in it.

Didactic Electives: Page's Theory and Practice in Teaching; Holbrook on the Teacher's Methods; Wickersham on School Government; Trumbull, the Teacher Teaching; or similar works.

This outline of grades and studies is intended to be suggestive and helpful to the teachers in the Academy in grading and promoting the pupils. The pupils should be arranged in classes according to their several abilities, rather than according to this outline in an arbitrary manner, in order that the classes at the time of recitation may be as large as possible rather than small. Their grade is ascertained by the majority of their studies, and their standing or rank by their percentage in each.

This course has been arranged in harmony with the outline course prepared in 1908 for the public and city schools of Oklahoma, and is intended to prepare pupils for entering the high school course consisting of the Ninth to Twelfth grades, or a normal course consisting of Didactics, Methods in Teaching and School Government.

A suitable certificate is issued to all pupils that complete, in a creditable manner, all the studies in this preparatory course ending with the Eighth grade.

The industrial work and training required of all the boarding pupils is intended to include a practical knowledge of agriculture, animal husbandry, apiculture, poultry raising, carpentry, cobbling, concrete, gardening, domestic science, sewing and laundry work, as the opportunity is afforded and the pupils discover fitness for these arts.

IV. HIGH SCHOOL DEPARTMENT

Ninth Grade: Grammar, Arithmetic, Composition, Civics, Elementary Algebra, Bookkeeping.

Tenth Grade: Algebra, Hill's Etymology, Physical Geography, General History, Rhetoric.

Eleventh Grade: Algebra, Rhetoric, Ancient History, American Literature (Abernathy), Composition, Botany, Plane Geometry.

Twelfth Grade: Solid Geometry, (Hessler & Smith's) Chemistry, Newcomber's English Literature, Political Economy.

Electives: Astronomy, Geology, Zoology, Trigonometry; Surveying, Stenography, Typewriting, Telegraphy.

In January 1908, when P. K. Faison, first superintendent of the public schools of McCurtain county, made his first visit to Oak Hill, he stated that Wheelock and Oak Hill Academies were the only graded schools in McCurtain county at that time.

TEACHING IN SUNDAY SCHOOL

As a help to young Sunday school teachers in the preparation of the lesson and its management before the class Miss Saxe's method of five points of analysis and five points of application are given.

ANALYSIS
1. What is the principal subject?
2. What the leading lessons?
3. Which the best verse?
4. Who are the principal persons?
5. What teaching about Christ?

APPLICATION
1. What example to follow?
2. What to avoid?
3. What duty to perform?
4. What promise to proclaim?
5. What prayer to echo?

XXXII
SAVINGS AND INVESTMENTS

"Gather up the Fragments that nothing be lost."—Jesus.

SAVINGS OR WAGES

IT is a matter of great importance to every one to learn early in life the difference between monthly or yearly savings and wages; and also the difference between personal expenses and profitable investments.

When a boy works on the railroad and has to supply all his daily wants, he knows what his wages are and answers the question quickly, stating what he receives by the day when he makes a full day's work. But when he is asked, "What are your monthly savings?" he is bothered and frankly confesses he cannot tell. Before the end of the second month the wages of his first month have slowly passed through his hands for personal expenses and little or nothing has been saved for profitable investment.

When a boy works for a farmer, who receives him into his home, providing for him a furnished room, fuel, light, boarding and washing, he does not seem to receive more than half what the other boy receives who works for the railroad. When he is asked the same question, "What are your monthly wages and what your monthly savings?" he makes reply by stating the balance in the farmer's hand as his savings, and that is correct; but he cannot tell what his wages are, by way of comparison with the other boy. The first boy at the end of the month has received wages the other boy his savings, save for his clothing. The latter at the end of the year has ordinarily saved more than the former, though all the time he may have imagined he was not receiving sufficient wages, merely because the monthly allowance of the farmer is commonly called "wages," instead of by the right name, "monthly savings."

That which the farmer does for his boy, in providing him a home and helping him to save his earnings, this Industrial Academy is now doing for every boy, that is received into the membership of the Oak Hill Family and makes his home there during the summer season.

At the Academy he not only finds steady employment, but is removed from the places that call for worse than useless daily expenditures; and the monthly allowance, made by the Superintendent, represents not his wages but his monthly savings, in the deposit bank of the institution.

When a parent or boy makes the discovery, that the boys who remain at the Academy during the summer months have more funds to their credit in the Bank of the institution in the fall of the year, than many of those who receive a higher daily wage elsewhere, and that they also make the most rapid progress in their studies, they begin to see the difference between working for savings and working for wages; and how much better off is the boy, who takes the training and grows up under the stimulating and elevating influence of a good educational institution.

INVESTMENTS

A personal expense is an expenditure of money for some article that may indeed be necessary, as a pair of shoes, but it begins to depreciate in value as soon as the expenditure has been made. A profitable investment is an expenditure of money, time or talents, that is expected to increase in value or yield an income. If a lamb is purchased it will grow into a sheep and its value is doubled. If an acre of good land is purchased it is sure to increase in value according to its quality and location.

The ability to avoid personal expenses and to make profitable investments is one of the things that determines our good or ill success in life. The education of a thoughtful, earnest boy or girl is ordinarily a good and profitable investment, for their value or usefulness may be increased many times more than that of the lamb or the acre of land. If they are gratefully responsive to their training no better investment can be made, than that which has for its object the intellectual, moral and religious training of our boys and girls.

A christian educational institution is an investment for producing manhood and character, things that money will not buy. One may invest in bonds or stocks, and make or lose money; but he who aids in the production of christian men and women, trained for service, increases their usefulness and continues to live through their consecrated lives and achievements.

This institution makes its appeal to the friends who have money and who would make a profitable investment; and also to the thoughtful boys and girls, who would greatly increase their value to society, the church and the world, by obtaining a good education in their youth.

GOING TO SCHOOL

THE ORCHESTRA—1912

[274]

YOUTHFUL SWEEPERS
Holding and using the broom aright

OAK HILL—Weimer Photos

XXXIII
SUMMER NORMALS AND CHAUTAUQUA

"Apt to teach, patient."—Paul

THE summer normals were established at the academy in October, 1905, and were continued during the next two years. Their object was to prepare candidates for the ministry, under the care of the Presbytery, to serve also at that time as teachers in the mission, and later in the public schools; and to afford ambitious young people the opportunity to prepare for the same work. They were conducted by the superintendent and Bertha L. Ahrens, the latter serving as instructor in the class room.

At the time they were held, they afforded the only opportunity in the south part of the Choctaw Nation, for the Freedmen to receive this training. When the McCurtain county normal was established at Idabel in 1908, they were no longer needed and were discontinued.

Those that attended the normals were as follows:

In 1905, Mary A. Donaldson of Paris, Texas.

In 1906, Mary A. Donaldson and Lilly B. Simms, Paris, Texas; Mrs. W. H. Carroll and Fidelia Murchison, Garvin, Mary E. Shoals, Grant, and James G. Shoals, Valliant.

In 1907, Zolo O. Lawson, Shawneetown, Mary E. Shoals, Grant; Delia Clark, Lehigh; Virginia Wofford and Solomon H. Buchanan, Valliant.

When the first summer normal was held at the academy in 1905, a request for some lectures or an instructor a part of the time addressed to Hon. J. Blair Shoenfelt, Indian agent, Muskogee, brought the following response from John D. Benedict, superintendent of schools.

"The colored citizens of the Choctaw Nation have not been allowed to participate in the benefit of the school fund of that Nation; hence we have not been able to establish any schools for colored children in the Choctaw and Chickasaw Nations, until this year. We have now a few colored schools in both of these Nations. There has never been any demand for normals or summer institutes for colored teachers in these two Nations. They will enjoy an appropriation of $100,000 for the ensuing year, but there are no funds available for normal schools among them this year." John D. Benedict, Superintendent.

This letter indicates the lapse of provision for the general education of the Choctaw Freedmen and its renewal during the last years of the Territorial government.

LICENTIATES

Those that pursued the course of study, provided during these years, for those that were preparing specially for the ministry, were Noah Alverson, Griffin, and John Richards, Lukfata. Mr. Richards died at 28 in 1908 and Mr. Alverson was ordained in 1910.

CANDIDATES FOR THE MINISTRY

In April 1911, Riley Flournoy, Sylvester S. Bibbs, Fred McFarland and Clarence Peete expressed the desire to become ministers of the gospel and were received under the care of the Presbytery at Eagletown, as candidates. All were members of the Oak Hill church and school.

SUMMER NORMALS AND CHAUTAUQUA

THE FIRST CHAUTAUQUA

In 1907, the last year under territorial government, arrangements were made for a patriotic celebration, in the form of a chautauqua at the Academy. The following account of it is from the columns of the Garvin Graphic:

The Fourth of July meeting by the Freedmen at Oak Hill Academy, near Valliant, was a real patriotic chautauqua, the first meeting of the kind ever held in this part of the Territory, and well worthy of more than a mere passing note. The preparations for the occasion, which included a comfortable seat for everyone, were fully completed before hand. The speakers' stand and the Academy buildings were tastefully decorated with our beautiful national colors, one large flag suspended between two of them, being twelve feet long.

"The exercises included three series of addresses, interspersed with soul-stirring patriotic music by the Oak Hill Glee Club, and the speakers included several of the most eloquent orators in the south part of the territory. The occasion afforded ample opportunity for the free and full discussion of those questions, relating to the administration of our public affairs, that are now engaging the attention of the people; and this fact was greatly appreciated both by the speakers and the people.

"At the forenoon session James R. Crabtree presided with commendable grace and dignity. The Declaration of Independence was read in a very entertaining and impressive manner by Miss Malinda Hall, who has been an efficient helper in the work of the Academy, since its re-opening two years ago. The principal address at this session was delivered by Rev. Wiley Homer, of Grant, a large, well built man with a strong voice, who for many years has been a capable and trusted leader among the Freedmen of this section. Others that participated were Johnson Shoals, of Valliant, who has been pursuing a course of study at the Iowa State Agricultural college, Ames, Iowa, and W. J. Wehunt, one of the prominent business men of Valliant.

"At the afternoon session Isaac Johnson, a natural born orator, presided and, both in his address and happy manner of introducing the speakers, enlivened the occasion with unexpected sallies of natural mother wit and eloquence. Rev.

W. H. Carroll, of Garvin, one of the instructors of the Academy, discussed in an able manner a number of questions relating to the educational and church work among the negroes; and he was followed by Prof. P. A. Parish, of Idabel, the well-known "Kansas negro," but of full-blood African descent, who seemed at his best in the discussion of current and local public questions.

"Rev. Wiley Homer presided at the evening session and the address was delivered by Rev. Chas. C. Weith, of Ardmore. This address, delivered in the cool of the evening, marked the climax of interest. In an eloquent and forceful manner he recalled the events that led to the first declaration of independence, which was for the freedom of the soul by Luther in Germany in 1517; traced the growth of this sentiment in other countries until it found its expression in the Declaration of Independence for the citizen, by our forefathers in 1776; and pressed the urgent need of Godliness on the part of every American citizen, in order to have the highest type of patriot and to insure the permanency of our civil and religious liberty. This address was a rare treat for the people of this section.

"Patriotic solos were rendered by Miss Bertha L. Ahrens, organist, Rev. W. H. Carroll, S. H. Buchanan, Mrs. J. A. Thomas and Miss Hall.

"The barbecue was prepared during the night previous by Charles Bibbs.

"Rev. R. E. Flickinger, the superintendent of the Academy, at the close of the day's sessions, received hearty congratulations for the excellent character of the arrangements for the day and was encouraged to provide for similar patriotic celebrations in the future."

XXXIV
GRACES AND PRAYERS

"In all things, give thanks, pray without ceasing."—Paul.

THE following forms of grace and prayer are intended to be suggestive helps to young people, who have the desire to be ready always to lead in prayer and conduct family worship, with interest and profit to others. Bible reading and private prayer prepare for public prayer; but the latter is rendered much easier, when it is remembered, that it should consist of expressions of thanksgiving, confession, petition and intercession. Those that lead should speak loud enough to be easily heard by everyone, and with an earnestness, that suggests sincerity.

GRACE AT MEALS

BREAKFAST. We thank Thee, our Father, for sweet rest and refreshment in sleep, thy bountiful supply of our wants and the right use of our faculties. Give us wisdom this day in the discharge of duty and in the employment of our time and talents for Jesus' sake. Amen.

DINNER. We thank thee, our Father, that thou dost give to us health and strength to perform our labors and hast surrounded us with the blessings and comforts of life. Feed our souls with the bread of life and enable us to serve thee acceptably for Jesus' sake. Amen.

SUPPER. We thank thee, our Father, that thou hast enabled us to perform the labors of the day and graciously supplied our wants. Establish the work of our hands and forgive our sins for Jesus' sake. Amen.

HELPFUL FORMS OF PRAYER

"Now I lay me down to sleep,
I pray thee, Lord, my soul to keep;
If I should die before I wake,
I pray thee, Lord, my soul to take;
And this I ask for Jesus' sake."

We thank thee, O Lord, for strength of arm to win our daily bread; for enough on which to live and some to give to those that are unfed. We thank thee for shelter from the cold and storm, a place that may be shared with a friend forlorn. We thank thee for thy wonderful love on us bestowed, that we should now be called the children of God.

May thy gracious presence go with us this day. Put good thoughts into our minds and good words into our mouths. Make us strong to do that which is pleasing in thy sight, by making thy word the guide of our lives. Bless our friends that are near and dear unto us. May their lives be found precious in thy sight. Command thy blessing to rest upon our neighbors and all with whom we associate.

May thy richest spiritual blessing rest upon thy servant, our pastor, and all the people to whom be ministers; so that the work of the Lord may prosper in our hands. Bless our children and youth by writing their names in the Book of life and inclining them to walk in thy commands.

Forgive our sins, comfort our hearts, strengthen our faith and enable us to serve Thee acceptably; we ask it for Jesus' sake. Amen.

ANOTHER ONE

We thank thee our Father, for the Bible, thine own blessed word, that teaches us, what we are to believe concerning Thee, and what duties Thou requirest of us. Help us to read it with the understanding heart, that it may prove a lamp to our feet and a light to our path.

We thank Thee for the voice of conscience, prompting us to do right. Enable us by Thy grace to do promptly, that which we know to be right. Help us to remember the Sabbath, to keep it holy unto the Lord. Help us to set our affection on the "house of the Lord;" and when we worship Thee, may the beauty of the Lord our God be upon us. Bless our friends and neighbors; all who seek an interest in our prayers. Forgive our sins and enable us to serve thee acceptably, for Jesus' sake. Amen.

A PRAYER FOR THE AGED

Ever blessed and gracious God, our Father, I humbly pray that thou wilt not cast me off in the time of old age, when my strength faileth. Preserve unto me the right use of my faculties for my soul trusteth in Thee. Comfort and strengthen my soul in the day of weakness that I may attest thy faithfulness in fulfilling all thy gracious promises.

Thou hast taught me to know mine end and the measure of my days, that I might apply my heart unto wisdom; and desire to dwell in Thy presence, where there is fulness of joy; and at thy right hand, where there are pleasures for evermore.

When the time comes for my inexperienced soul to leave its earthly temple, send the blessed angels to carry it to the mansions, thou hast prepared for the redeemed, who put their trust in Thee; and accord unto me an abundant entrance into the Kingdom of our Lord and Savior, Jesus Christ. To whom be praise, dominion and glory, now and forever. Amen.

"How beautiful to be with God!
To lay aside this toil-worn dress,
To wear a crown of righteousness,
And robes of purest white possess;
And sing the sweet redemption song."
—Frances Willard.

XXXV

PRESBYTERIAL MEETINGS AND PICNICS

OAK HILL IN 1905.—NOT A BUCKET.—GOING TO PRESBYTERY. ENTERTAINMENT FOR EVERYBODY.

ON August 31, 1905, the Presbytery of Kiamichi met at Oak Hill, at a time when an attack of malaria at his summer home at Fonda, Iowa, prevented the return of the superintendent. The attendance of visitors was unusually large. It fell to the lot of Miss Eaton, matron, and Miss Ahrens to provide for their entertainment. They were ably assisted by Miss M. A. Hall and Mitchell S. Stewart. They had sixty for dinner on Friday and Saturday and one hundred and twenty-five on Sabbath.

On this occasion three new members were added to the roll, Jack A. Thomas was elected and ordained an elder, and Samuel Harris, a deacon.

The meetings of the Presbytery, which are always evangelistic, have now come to be the most attractive, interesting and profitable meetings held in their respective communities. As the available churches are few in number, the meetings are held in each every two or three years. The coming of the Presbytery is anticipated with a great deal of interest, and a "big crowd" is the delight of the congregation, receiving and entertaining it. This is a fact worthy of special note.

PRESBYTERIAL MEETINGS AND PICNICS

NOT AN OAK HILL BUCKET

In the Territorial days, or, rather previous to the allotment of lands to them individually in 1905, the most attractive meeting, in their various neighborhoods, was the annual old-time picnic, made interesting by the presence of a "merry go round" that relieved them of their nickels, and a platform, where promiscuous dancing was sure to be continued through most of the night, and be accompanied with considerable dissipation and immorality.

When the superintendent discovered the nature of these gatherings, he did not hesitate to declare their dissipating and demoralizing tendency. He also stated the attitude of the institution in regard to them by giving utterance to the following sentiment: "Whilst everything at the academy is available for the betterment of the colored people, there is not an Oak Hill bucket available for use, at a dissipating and demoralizing dance in the timber." This sentiment sounded a little harsh and cruel at first, but it now commands the approval of all the good students and of those, who are doing most to promote the happiness and welfare of the young and rising generation. Since the young people have come to participate, to a greater extent, in the frequent meetings of the Presbytery and in an annual Sunday school convention, the old time "dance in the timber", has become a "thing of the past."

EVERYBODY GOES TO PRESBYTERY

The meetings of the Presbytery are sure to be attended by everyone, living in the vicinity of the meeting, and by as many others as can manage to "get there." It is unusual for any colored minister and his elder to be absent from any meeting, no matter how great may be the difficulties, that have to be overcome in getting there. If the place of meeting can be easily reached, additional delegates are chosen to represent the Sunday school, the aid, Endeavor and Women's Missionary societies.

If these additional delegates get to the meeting, they are duly enrolled and later are accorded all the time they wish in making their oral reports of the work they represent. All seem to enjoy making reports and addresses at Presbytery. Many are animated with the earnest desire to aid in giving their race an uplift, and the address in Presbytery seems to be one of the nicest opportunities to do this. This is especially true of some of those among the older people who cannot read, survivors of the slavery period who inherited good memories and good voices. Several of the most eloquent and deeply impressive appeals, it was the privilege of the author to hear at the academy or Presbytery, were delivered by those, whose condition of slavery in youth and isolated location afterward prevented attendance at school. By frequent participation in religious meetings, where they endeavored to repeat and enforce Bible truths, to which they had given an attentive ear, caused them, like some of the famous philosophers in the days of Socrates and Aristotle, to be held in high esteem as persons of intelligence and influence in their respective communities. Henry Crittenden, Elijah Butler, Mrs. Charles Bashears, and Simon Folsom were all good examples of unlettered, but natural orators, who found their widest sphere of usefulness in the activities of the church.

GOING TO PRESBYTERY

Those, attending the meetings of the Presbytery, often experienced serious disappointments on the way and some little inconveniences, when they got there. Previous to the organization of the church at Garvin in 1905, there

PRESBYTERIAL MEETINGS AND PICNICS

were only two churches, Oak Hill and Beaver Dam at Grant, that were located near the railroad. All the other churches were located in rural neighborhoods, 8 to 20 miles distant from the nearest station. The roads to them were merely winding trails through the timber, that crossed the streams where it was possible to ford them, without any grading of the banks.

That which we witnessed and partially experienced, in making our first trip through the timber to a meeting of the Presbytery at Frogville, about fifteen miles from the station, was characteristic of three other meetings we attended, at a distance from the railroad.

The delegation, that arrived at the station, consisted of nearly two dozen and about half of them were women. We arrived at the place the wagons were to meet us, after walking across the railroad bridge over the Kiamichi river, a short distance west of the station. When we arrived there, we found only one wagon of the three, that were expected. That was a serious but not a stunning disappointment. The luggage was crowded into the bed of that wagon and it carried also a few of the older women. The rest of us set out on a good long walk, indulging the hope other teams would surely meet and relieve us somewhere on the road. As the hour of noon was approaching, we anticipated our needs on the way, by having a box of crackers and a slice of cheese put on the wagon. When we reached a half way place, where there was also a spring of good water, this lunch was greatly enjoyed. We managed to ride the remainder of the distance, and at the end of the journey we heard no one complain the "road am hard to travel."

ENTERTAINMENT FOR EVERYBODY

The problem of entertainment, always seemed beforehand a rather serious one for the few families, living near the church in a rural neighborhood. Their generous hospitality, however, never seemed to be over taxed, but to have an elasticity, that included a cordial welcome to every one, and as much of comfort during the night as it was possible to extend. Many of the younger people on Saturday and Sabbath evenings, when their number would be greatest, would be grateful when they were accorded a pillow and blanket for a bed on the floor, or a bench.

The happy, hopeful spirit, manifested by both hosts and guests, in meeting the responsibilities and unexpected disappointments, that are sometimes experienced while attending meetings of the Presbytery in the rural neighborhoods, reminds one of the happy remark of a little six year old boy, in regard to a sunny visitor, whom he knew had experienced many trials and had just left their home: "Yes, I like her; she goes over the bumps as though her heart had rubber tires."

XXXVI
FARMERS INSTITUTES
1905-1912
FOREST CHURCH.—OAK HILL.—SHORT COURSE IN 1912.—
ISAAC JOHNSON.—EMANCIPATION DAY.

"Agriculture is the most healthful, most useful and most noble employment of man."—George Washington.

THE first meeting, conducted by the Choctaw Freedmen, it was the privilege of the author to attend was their annual Farmers Institute, held in Forest Presbyterian church on Monday, Jan. 1, 1905. Others had been held in other places during previous years but this was the second annual meeting in the Forest church, and it was called the county institute of Fort Towson county. It was their own original method of endeavoring to make a pleasant and profitable observance of Emancipation Day.

On this the first historic occasion the meeting was conducted by Johnson W. Shoals, president, in a very dignified manner. An interesting annual report was read by the secretary, James G. Shoals, Fidelia Murchison read an essay on gardening and Elsie Shoals-Arnold, one on making and marketing butter. The author indulged in a short address and other addresses were delivered by Simon Folsom, Lee V. Bibbs, Charles Bashears and Mitchell Stewart. The principal address however, was by Isaac Johnson, one of their number living along the north bank of Red river, who had learned the teacher's and speaker's art in Texas.

(287)

He seemed to be at his best and discussed good morals, agriculture and the destiny of the Choctaw Freedmen, with so much native wit and humor, we felt well repaid for the long, wearisome journey to the place of meeting.

The meeting consisted of one long session, called a forenoon meeting, and at its close, it fell to our lot to accept an unexpected invitation to enjoy an old-time picnic dinner, which was soon spread on the backless benches in the church. Isaac Johnson was chosen as the new president and he has continued to serve in that capacity.

The meeting the next year was held in this same place and commencing Jan. 1, 1907, they began to he held at Oak Hill Academy.

The meeting held at Oak Hill on Jan. 1, 1907, had some features worthy of special mention. It was the first occasion, when the meeting included the sessions of two days, or any effort was made to have an exhibit of the products of the garden and field. McCurtain county, though not yet organized had been established, and the officers took more pains than usual, to invite the farmers in all parts of the new county to participate in its discussions. It was the first time, that an effort was made to have a special lecturer from the Agricultural college and the young people at Oak Hill, trained to supply the needs of the occasion with vocal and instrumental music. It was very gratifying to note the increased attendance and interest.

For this occasion, Miss Eaton prepared an artistic design, with grains of corn of different colors, for the center of the decoration over the speaker's stand, that attracted the attention and called forth the admiration of all. It consisted of a large tablet having a representation of a large broadly branching oak tree on the summit of a little hill, having a canopy of bright stars over it and the words "Oak Hill" in the form of an arch near its lower branches. Over the tablet was the word "Welcome" and over the ends of it "Happy New Year."

The entire program had been previously arranged, so that all the addresses and discussions might form a part of the course of instruction, in agriculture and animal husbandry to the students. All the proceedings proved interesting and instructive to them. In furnishing the vocal and instrumental music, which formed a very pleasing feature of each session, they were enabled to participate in a way that was very profitable to them, and entertaining to others.

Among those who participated by addresses, on topics previously assigned, were Isaac Johnson, James G. Shoals, Rev. W. H. Carroll of Garvin, Rev. R. E. Flickinger, Adelia Eaton, Malinda A. Hall, Bertha L. Ahrens, who also served as organist, Solomon Buchanan, who also served as pianist, John Richards of Lukfata, Noah Alverson of Lehigh, whose ectures on raising corn and cotton were worthy of special commendation, Rev. Samuel Gladman of Parsons, Martha Folsom of Grant, R. H. Butler of Bokchito and Charles Bibbs,

Illness prevented the attendance of W. S. English, director of the state college.

One of the resolutions adopted was as follows:

"That we note with great pleasure the manifest increase of interest in this session of the Farmer's Institute, on the part of the superintendent, teachers and students of Oak Hill Academy and of the people generally, there being a good local attendance and a larger representation than ever before of interested farmers and speakers from other parts of the surrounding country."

At this meeting it was decided the annual membership fee shall be for men, twenty-five cents; and for women, ten cents.

SECOND OAK HILL INSTITUTE

The closing day of the second observance of Emancipation day by a two-day Farmer's institute at Oak Hill Academy occurred January 1, 1908. Among the new speakers were Rev. Wiley Homer of Grant, Rev. William Butler of Eagletown and Jack A. Thomas. Isaac Johnson and James G. Shoals served as president and secretary and were again re-elected. Prof. C. A. McNabb of Guthrie, Secretary of the State Board of Agriculture, promised two addresses, but failed to arrive. The resolutions included a memorial to congress for the establishment of postal savings banks and a parcels post, both of which were established a few years (1912) later. They also included the following one in regard to the Mexican boll-weevil that during the previous four years had nearly ruined the cotton crop.

"In order that we may do something practical in the way of checking the ravages of the boll-weevil, we encourage every one raising cotton in this section, to plow up and burn as early as possible each fall, all the old cotton stalks, which principally furnish their fall and spring food supply; and as far as possible to avoid planting cotton in the same ground two years in succession."

The record of these two Farmer's institutes at Oak Hill Academy, and of three preceding ones at Forest church, by the Choctaw Freedmen during the period of the Territorial government, is of historic interest, since these annual institutes preceded any similar meetings, by the other folks, in that section of the country. This observation is true also of the three summer normals held at the Academy, during

FARMERS INSTITUTES

the months of October in 1905, 1906 and 1907; and of the first Oak Hill chautauqua, held July 4, 1907.

SHORT COURSE IN 1912

For 1912 the institute was held on the last half day of a three day short course in agriculture and animal husbandry conducted by Prof. E. A. Porter and Mr. R. L. Scott, expert farmers at Hugo; assisted by Prof. J. W. Reynolds of Muskogee, the superintendent and Rev. W. H. Carroll.

In 1913, when the first opportunity was afforded ministers in California to attend a short course in agriculture, lasting one week, at the state university farm, it was attended by five hundred pastors of churches, representing twenty denominations. This fact, as an expression of the trend of public sentiment, is noted with a good deal of interest.

ISAAC JOHNSON

Isaac Johnson, (B. 1859) organizer and president of the Farmer's institute, 1905 to 1912, is a native of Hopkins county, Texas, and in 1865 located near Clarksville. In 1876 he married Anna Wilson of the Choctaw Nation, who died in 1880. He then went to school in Texas and, receiving a certificate in 1889, taught school there four years. In 1893, '94 and '95 he taught successively at Forest, Lukfata and Eagletown, I. T. In 1894 he married Winnie Durant and again located along Red river, south of Valliant, where he is widely known as one of the leading farmers and stock raisers.

The people of the community in which he lives, under his leadership, on January 1, 1897, began to observe Emancipation Day by holding a Farmer's institute, a kind of social meeting, that afforded an opportunity for a number of them to make short addresses, on any topic of public or general interest, and all to participate in the enjoyment of a picnic dinner. He enjoys the distinction of having served as president of this organization a number of years before any similar organization was effected in McCurtain county.

EMANCIPATION DAY

The reasons for the general observance of New Year's day as a legal holiday seem eminently appropriate, for the attention of the people is seldom directed to them. There are several good reasons worthy to be remembered.

It was on January 1, 1863, that President Lincoln issued the memorable proclamation, that emanicipated the slaves in all the states, then at war against the general government. The number of the persons accorded freedom was about four millions.

This event, considered from the standpoint of the number of people affected, was even greater than the Declaration of Independence, for the latter resulted in the freedom of only a part of the people, and their number was one million less than the number set free in 1863. In 1790, when the first census was taken, fourteen years after the Declaration, the entire population was not quite four millions and of that number 697,624 were left in a state of slavery.

That "all men are created free and equal," is a fundamental principle of the Declaration, but, for more than fourscore years, it was regarded as true of only a part of the people. It was not realized by the other part of the people, that was gradually increasing from one to four millions. For them there was but one law and it was, "Servants obey your masters." This was the only rule of conduct for the negro. Under it he became socially "a curiosity." He had no laws or ceremonies regulating marriage; and if such ties were formed, they were liable to be broken at any time,

FARMERS INSTITUTES

by their sale to other and different owners. This rule did not regulate his moral, economic or political life, for he was not recognized as a person or citizen, possessing these faculties and functions. It did not prevent him from worshipping his Creator, but this was done in an ignorant way, that served more for entertainment and amusement, than the development of morality and piety.

After the lapse of a half century, he has not yet been wholly emancipated from these illiterate and low social conditions; but he is approving and pursuing the better way, as he learns from the Bible, "what man is to believe concerning God and what duty God requires of man."

The Emancipation proclamation thus affected the destiny of more persons than the Declaration of Independence, and it marks the beginning of the era of universal freedom; when all the people could unite in saying, America is the "land of the free," as well as the "home of the brave." It also effected national unity, by completely removing the one great cause of previous political dissension. It prepared the way for America to be the home of a happy and united people, knowing no north or south, east or west. In these great facts of national importance there are found good reasons for the annual observance of Emancipation day, as a legal holiday, as well as the anniversary of the Declaration of Independence.

XXXVII
THE APIARY

"Go to the ant, thou sluggard; which gathereth her food in the harvest; consider her ways and be wise."
—Solomon.

THE Oak Hill apiary consists of twenty or more colonies, and their annual yield of comb honey ranges from 300 to 500 pounds. It was started with two colonies in the summer of 1905. These were obtained by the superintendent and H. C. Shoals, from two hollow trees in the timber near Red river, and were what are known as "wild bees." They and their comb were placed in movable comb Langstroth hives, and the native queens were soon afterwards replaced by two pretty yellow Italian queens, obtained by mail from Little Rock. By this means the two colonies of wild bees, in the fall of the year, had become golden Italians.

A DOUBLE SWARM

On a pretty warm day in March, 1910, when the locust trees in the campus were in full bloom, two swarms of bees left their hives about the same time, and both clustered on the low, branching limbs of a small plum tree. After taking a photo of this unusual sight, Miss Weimer and Clarence Peete, who is standing behind the tree, each using a tin cup, gently lifted the bees from the limbs of the tree and placed them in a hive so arranged, that instead of destroying one of the queens, the bees naturally separated into two

THE APIARY
Orchard and Swarm-Sack at left

STANCHIONS FOR CALVES
Ora feeding them with pleasure and profit

THE HEN HOUSE; OPEN FRONT, SEMI-MONITOR ROOF

PIG PEN; MANY CONVENIENCES

THE APIARY

clusters around their respective queens. On the following morning, the swarm intended for Clarence was lifted out by him and put in a separate hive. The operations of hiving and separating the swarms were very successfully performed, without either of them receiving a single sting, and in the fall both colonies had a good supply of surplus honey. As an inducement to the young people to learn to manage bees profitably, a colony was presented to those who undertook the responsibility of caring for them at the Academy.

The first frost in the fall of the year indicates the time to remove the surplus honey from the hives; and to cut a bee-tree merely for its supply of honey and wax. April and May however, are the months to transfer colonies from boxes and hollow trees to movable comb hives, so as to save the "bee."

A MODEL HOG HOUSE

The following description of the hog house is given for the benefit of students and patrons. It was intended to be a model in the arrangement of every part and it is yet unsurpassed in the number of its conveniences. It was built in 1906 and is 24 by 32 feet.

An entry, four feet wide, extends through the length of the building and the pens, with outlots, are arranged on each side. The drip boards of the troughs are arranged along each side of this entry making them easy to fill without wetting the stock or pen. The floors intended for litter are further protected from dampness, by being elevated one inch from the rear to a line parallel with the trough, and about two feet from it. The litter is held on this elevated part of the floor by a guard, 2x4 inches, around its edge. Hanging partitions separate the entry from the pens. Fat hogs are easily and quickly loaded, by merely lifting the partitions and driving them through the entry into the open end of a wagon box, placed at the rear end of the entry.

It has a floor over head for receiving the corn from the field; husking and sorting it. On this loft there is a bin for storing the good corn intended for meal, and mouse-proof boxes for preserving seed corn on the ear until planting time. There are two hatches, one on each side at the rear for passing the husks for litter to the pens below. At the right near the front, there is a shute that conveys the corn for the pigs to a crib at the right in the first apartment below, from which it is taken at feeding time, by raising a self-closing lid near the floor. In the corner of this open apartment there is a large box covered with a hinged lid for ground feed, and a set of steps to the loft. Under the stairs, there is an elevator and purifying pump, that brings up pure and cool water from a brick walled cistern, underneath the floor of the building, and it has never gone dry, when used only for the hogs.

OLD LOG HOUSE

The old log house, which remained until 1910 and in which the school was founded, was for a half century the largest and best building occupied by the Choctaws in the south eastern part of their large reservation. During the period previous to 1860, when it was occupied by Bazeel Leflore, chief of the Choctaw Nation, its halls and spacious porches were the favorite places of meetings for the administration of tribal affairs, social and religious gatherings.

An Indian graveyard was located a few rods from its southeast corner. A neat little marble monument still marks the grave of Narcissa LeFlore, wife of the chief Bazeel. She died at forty in 1854. Small marble tombstones, bearing the names of LeFlore and Wilson, mark a half dozen other graves. One long, unnamed grave is marked by a broad wall of common rock, three feet high, covered with one large flag stone.

Chief LeFlore, about the year 1860, located at Goodland, where he spent the remainder of his days. He left the log house to be occupied by John Wilson his nephew. About twenty years later Wilson left it to his son-in-law, Frank Locke, its last Choctaw occupant. He soon afterwards left it to Robin Clark, the Choctaw Freedman, from whom it was obtained in 1884, for the use of the school.

PAINTING

The pretty and attractive appearance of the premises at Oak Hill was due to a considerable extent to the good work of the boys that learned to use the brush in painting and white washing. The following facts are noted as an aid to them and others.

All the school buildings were painted cream and white. The materials used were white lead and flaxseed oil, mixed in the proportion of 15 to 20 pounds of lead to a gallon of oil. A gallon of the mixture is expected to cover 225 square feet of surface with two coats. The cream tint, a warm color, was obtained by mixing a little chrome yellow (and burnt sienna) with a pint or more of oil and adding as much of this mixture as was needed to produce the desired tint.

The red paint, used on the farm buildings and large gates, consisted of Venetian red, a dry paint, and oil, five to eight pounds of paint to the gallon of oil. A white trimmer was used on the face boards of the roof, doors and windows.

The white wash used on the board and pale fences consisted of quick lime slacked under water and gently stirred during this process. It should be allowed to stand a day or two before it is used. A pound of salt to the gallon of quicklime, the salt being first dissolved in water, improves its wearing quality. A little boiled rice flour improves its adhesiveness for indoor use.

Skimmed sweet milk, used the day it is mixed, is an inexpensive substitute for oil in applying venetian red to old gates. One coat will make them look right well for one or more seasons. Milk however should never be used except to brighten up some old work for one or two years, and each gallon should contain three pounds of Portland cement, frequently stirred.

SEED CORN IMPROVED

Large yields of corn are secured only by planting seed that has vitality sufficient to produce a good ear as well as a stock. Careful and successful farmers raise and endeavor to improve their seed from year to year. This may be done on a small scale as follows:

Select ten good sized, straight rowed, deep-grained ears. Remove the tips and butts. Shell each ear separately and plant in separate rows, marked and numbered from one to ten. As soon as the corn in these rows begins to tassel go through them every few days and remove the tassel from every stalk that is not forming an ear; so that the pollen or tassel dust of the barren stalk may not fall on the silks of the corn-bearing stalks.

At husking time husk and weigh the yield from each row or ear of seed separately. Missing hills and barren stocks indicate a low vitality in the seed-ear and also in the crop. Select the seed for the next year from the rows that yield the largest crop.

The yield of the cotton crop can be increased two fold by gathering the seed at picking time from only the best fruited stocks.

HEALTH HINTS. Health means a sound mind in a sound body.

"Know thyself", and remember, that "self-preservation is the first law of nature."

An open window, day and night, is better than an open grave.

"Warm sleeping rooms have killed more people, than ever froze to death."

"A good iron pump, over a well protected well, costs less than a case of typhoid."

"Wire screens in the windows may keep crape from the door."

"A fly in the milk often means a member of the family in the grave."

Work when you work and rest outstretched, when you rest.

Avoid all sins of the flesh. Overeating and eating in-

OAK HILL, 1902; LOOKING NORTHWEST

OAK HILL, 1903; LOOKING NORTH
M. S. Stewart at left, Mary Scott at right of Supt.

DOUBLE SWARM OF BEES
(1910)

PLANTING SWEET POTATOES
Carriers, Droppers and Trowelers

READY FOR A PULL

jurious foods or drinks are responsible for many ills of body and mind.

He who said, "I am the bread of life," said also, "He that eateth me shall live by me."

Cherish a cheerful, hopeful spirit by reading at least one promise from the Bible, for meditation, every day. Learn how to look pleasant, even when you may be feeling otherwise.

Fix the mind on the virtue to be cultivated rather than on the vice to be overcome.

If the heart action is sometimes weak, avoid all acts of over-exertion and sleep on the right side. Avoid snoring, by breathing through the nose.

Sleep is "nature's sweet restorer." Pure air, pure water and proper exercise are nature's healthful invigorators. Use them freely.

HEADACHE. Headaches are due to three causes, namely, eye-strain, indigestion, and exposures to dampness and cold.

To avoid eye-strain, bathe the eyes frequently with cool water, and avoid using them intently too long, when the light is not good, especially in the twilight after sun set. To avoid the sick headache eat slowly and temperately; and drink water frequently both at and between meals. The ache in the back of the head, caused by exposure to drafts of air, cold and dampness to the feet, may be relieved by the application of hot damp cloths to the parts affected, and warming the feet and limbs until the perspiration is started. Never use dopes or preparations for headache, pure sparkling water is always much better.

Hot water, sipped frequently, tends to relieve a cough, difficult breathing and a weak heart action. Pure air, inhaled by frequent daily deep breathings, and out-door exercise do more for weak lungs than medicines.

CHILLS. A chill is the protest of the liver or lungs after an exposure one or more days previous, that was not followed by a proper warming of the feet, especially in the evening. Sulphate of quinine, a tonic for the stomach, is a standard remedy for malarial troubles but its use should always be preceded or accompanied with a tonic for the liver.

SMALLPOX. A mixture consisting of one ounce of cream of tartar, and two ounces of sulphur flour, should be in every home, to be taken a little occasionally as an antidote, and kept as an approved remedy for smallpox.

XXXVIII
THE OAK HILL AID SOCIETY
AND OTHER CONTRIBUTING SOCIETIES AND INDIVIDUALS.
THE OAK HILL AID SOCIETY

On Oct. 30, 1904, during the period of vacancy, ten persons interested in its continuance met in the Academy and organized an aid society, to aid the Freedmen's Board in maintaining it. Solomon Buchanan and Samuel Harris took the lead in calling the meeting. James R. Crabtree served as chairman and Bertha L. Ahrens as secretary. The others present were Mitchell S. Stewart, Wilson Clark, S. S. Bibbs, Charles B. Harris and Mrs. J. A. Thomas. The organization was effected by the election of M. S. Stewart, president; J. A. Thomas, (absent) secretary; B. L. Ahrens, treasurer; and Samuel Harris, field secretary:

May 28, 1905, George Shoals was elected president and S. S. Bibbs, secretary. On June 25th, 1905 a constitution was adopted, in which its object was stated as follows:

"The aims and object of this society shall be: To help the Presbyterian Board of Missions for Freedmen; to raise the funds required to pay for the land on which the buildings are located; to devise ways and means by which the academy may be directly aided with supplies of food, live stock and other things, when money cannot be given; and, to do what we can, to enlarge its course of study and provide new departments of industry.

THE OAK HILL AID SOCIETY 301

"It is understood, that all money raised shall be sent to the aforesaid Mission Board and be applied by it to the general needs of this institution, when no specific object has been named by this society. It is also understood, that this society shall not hinder the aforesaid Board, in its absolute control of the academy and farm."

The annual membership fee is twenty-five cents, other offerings being entirely voluntary, each giving, "as the Lord hath prospered him." The first week in October was designated, as the time for an annual public meeting, to give emphasis to the work of the society and solicit free-will offerings from everybody. Other congregations were requested to form similar organizations, to create a visible bond of union in the support of the academy.

The first visible result of this lowly organization, founded as a forlorn hope, appeared on the 15th of April 1905, when at the close of the eloquent appeal of Samuel Harris, its field secretary, before the Presbytery at Grant, Rev. F. W. Hawley, the Synodical Missionary of Indian Territory, challenged all present to unite with him in making a pledge of support toward the purchase of the land. Heading the list with a pledge of $10.00, all were surprised to find it increased, in a few minutes, to $210.00. Two weeks later Mr. Harris made a similar appeal at Oak Hill, and $45.00 more were pledged. He visited Forest church and received pledges to the amount of $45.00. George Shoals visited Bethany church at Parsons, and $15.00 more were pledged, making the amount pledged, $315.00.

Sam Harris, in the fall of 1905, voluntarily went to Atoka and had forty-five acres of land allotted to his wife and four of his children, in order that they might later be added to the Oak Hill farm; and the education of his children be provided for, at that institution. His death occurred the next year, and in 1912, the last of these lands were added to the Oak Hill farm. His children are now enjoying the privileges of the institution.

He belonged to a generation that could neither read nor write, and that which he accomplished for Oak Hill and his needy children during the short period of his co-operation with the superintendent, is but another beautiful illustration of what may be done for a needy and worthy cause, by one, however unlearned, whose sincere and burning interest leads him to lend a helping hand and to use the power of his voice in its behalf.

He had come to appreciate and, before the Presbytery, emphasized the importance of these three vital facts:

1. The need of a good christian education for all the members of his own rapidly growing family.

2. The great value of the educational and religious privileges, and the facilities for industrial training, afforded the young people of the colored race at Oak Hill Academy, located in the very midst of them.

3. The great meaning of the changes, that were taking place in the country around them since the building of the railroad, the transition to statehood, the allotment of the lands to them individually, and the incoming of large numbers of white folks from Arkansas, Texas and other sections; who were founding and building towns, leasing and occupying the farm lands, gaining control of the business interests of the community; and thus making it ten fold more necessary for the young people of the colored race to have sufficient intelligence to enable them to do their own thinking and manage successfully their own business interests, in

order to avoid the impending doom, of being soon crowded out of their present homes and possessions.

His burning desire as he often expressed it, was to bring it to pass, that their children and the generations to come might rise up and be able to say, "Our Fathers, in grateful acknowledgement of the inestimable value of the educational, moral and religious privileges, that the Presbyterian Board of Missions had established and so long maintained, for the benefit of the colored people of that section, had contributed the funds, paid for and donated the lands occupied by the buildings of Oak Hill Industrial Academy."

The members of his family, in whose names the allotments for Oak Hill were secured, were Catherine, his wife; Roland (died Nov. 24, 1911), John, Margie and Ellen.

LAND FUNDS CONTRIBUTED

The following is a brief summary of the funds contributed for the purchase of the land at Oak Hill.

Rev. F. W. Hawley, Sam Harris, Bertha L. Ahrens, Adelia M. Eaton, Wiley Homer, William Butler, R. D. Colbert, Malinda A. Hall, Noah S. Alverson, R. E. Flickinger and Jo Lu Wolcott, each $10.00; Samuel Gladman, W. J. Starks, S. H. Buchanan, John Richards and Finley Union Sunday school, Lehigh, per Isabella Monroe, each $5.00; Virginia Williams, and Matt Brown, each $3.00; Simon Folsom and Alonza Lewis, $2.50; specials from churches in Oklahoma, as follows: Anadarko, Bartlesville, Perry and Vinita, each $2.00; Chelsea, $2.50; Muskogee and Wagoner, each $3.00; Oklahoma First, $5.00; Oak Hill $10.00; and Alva $50.00.

The Oak Hill Aid Society in 1906 gave $39.00; in 1907 $46.00; in 1908, $16.00 and in 1910 to 1912, $19.00; making for it $120.00, and altogether $335.00.

This amount covers the cost of the forty acre allotment of Samuel A. Folsom, on which the Academy and Boy's Hall are located. This was the first tract purchased, and it was obtained August 30, 1908, a few days after the Choctaw Freedmen were legally authorized to execute warranty deeds.

These facts are worthy of note, since to that extent they indicate the achievement of that object, for which Sam Harris plead so earnestly and effectively at Presbytery.

A lady at San Jose, California, gave $200 in 1909, for an annuity bond to cover tract No. 5, on the Oak Hill plat, containing twenty acres and allotted to Caroline Prince. Bertha L. Ahrens in 1908 purchased the three fourths inheritance of three of the heirs of William Shoals, in tract No. 8, containing thirty acres, that in course of time, it might be included; and in 1909 and 1913, R. E. Flickinger donated tract number 4, containing twenty acres north of the buildings. These three specials include and cover the 70 acres on section 20, north of the public road, north of the buildings.

The Oak Hill Women's Missionary society was organized in October 1906, and at the end of its first year contributed to Home Missions, Gunnison, Utah, $5.00; and to the Board of Freedmen, $15.00.

LOCALITY OF DONORS

The following exhibit shows the location of the generous contributors, who united in furnishing the general expense funds for the support of the students and furnishing the Temporary Boy's Hall, as it appeared in the report for July 1, 1909.

	Expense Fund	Furnishing Boy's Hall	Total
California	$444.20	$13.41	$457.61
Illinois	55.00		55.00
Iowa	96.75	5.00	101.75
Kansas	19.23	12.25	31.48
Ohio	105.00		105.00
Oklahoma	117.00	80.49	197.49
New York		5.00	5.00
Pennsylvania	329.00	5.00	334.00
Total	$1166.18	$121.15	$1287.33

DONORS TO THE GENERAL SUPPORT

A record has already been made of those who contributed toward the purchase of the farm in response to the appeal through the Oak Hill Aid society. A grateful men-

THE OAK HILL AID SOCIETY

tion of the Women's and Young People's societies and individual donors, who contributed to the support and extension of the general work of the institution, seems eminently appropriate. They include the following list:

ALABAMA: The Negro in Business by Booker T. Washington, Tuskeegee.

CALIFORNIA: Alhambra, Dinuba, Rev. H. J. Frothingham, Elsinore; Eureka, Lampoc, Long Beach, Mrs. O. L. Mason; Los Gatos, Los Angeles, First; Mrs. Margaret Daniels, Mrs. Archibald; Central, Mrs. Hiram Leithead; Highland Park, Mrs. Kate C. Moody M. D.; Third, Mary A. Clark, Boyle Heights, Hollywood, Immanuel, Spanish Mission, Carrie E. Crowe, Westminster; Nordhoff, Margaret Daniels; North Ontario, New Monterey, Monte Cito, Oakland, Mattie Hunter; Orange, Red Bluff, San Diego First, Mrs. A. W. Crawford; San Jose First and Second, Mrs. Frances Palmer, Mrs. G. H. Start, Mrs. Mary Langdon; Lebanon of San Francisco, San Martin, Santa Barbara, Santa Clara, Santa Cruz, Santa Paula, San Louis Obispo; Upland Ventura, Watsonville.

COLORADO: Fort Morgan, Gunnison, Timnath.

CONNECTICUT: Miss A. C. Benedict, Waterbury.

ILLINOIS: Cairo; Chicago, Bethany, J. H. Jones, Leslie Music Company; Fairbury, Mrs. J. J. Pence; Mason City, Springfield Second.

INDIANA: William Elliot, Lafayette $5,000 for Elliott Hall; Greensburg, Winona Lake.

IOWA: Alta, Lucy M. Haywood; Boone, Burlington First, Clarinda, Corning, Corning Presbytery, Crawfordsville, Creston, Des Moines Central, Fonda, M. E. Church, Mrs. A. S. Wood, Adele Curkeet, Adelia M. Eaton, Mrs. R. E. Flickinger, Geo. Sanborn, Mrs. J. B. Weaver, Mrs. John E. Jordan, Clark Perry; Fort Dodge, Gilmore City, Mrs. Bert C. McGinnis, Clarence M. Patterson; Grimes, Hamburg, Knoxville, Lenox, Malvern, Manchester, Nodaway, Princeton, Red Oak, Rockwell City, Ella T. Smith, Elmer E. Johnson, John H. Mattison; Sanborn, Sigourney, Shenandoah, State Center, Storm Lake, Washington, Bethel, Winfield, Walnut.

KANSAS: Auburn, Burlington, Clay Center, Derby, Edgerton, Herrington, Halstead, Highland, Humboldt, Junction City, Kansas City, First, Grand View Park, Western

Highland; Lincoln Center, Lawrence, Lyons, Manhattan, Morganville, Mulberry Creek, Neodesha, Oakland, Osawatomie, Oswego, Phillipsburg, Roxbury, Stanley, Sterling, Syracuse, Topeka, First, Second, Third and Westminster, M. B. True; Waverly, Wichita, First.

MASSACHUSETTS: Marblehead, Mrs. J. J. Gregory.

MICHIGAN: Coldwater, Harrington.

MISSOURI: Kansas City, Montgomery Ward & Co., Maryville, Prof, J. C. Speckerman; St. Louis, Majestic Range Co.

NEBRASKA: Beatrice.

NEW YORK: Mexico, Mrs. Mary O. Becker, Mrs. Mamie G. Richardson; Plattsburg, Mrs. M. D. Edwards; Honoye, Anna M. Bowerman; New York, Am. Bible Society, Oliver Swet Marden.

OHIO: Bellefontaine, Mrs. D. O. Spade; Columbiana, Mrs. Mattie C. Flickinger; Dayton Lorenz Music Co.; Denison, College Hill, Miss H. M. Wilson; East Liverpool First, Mansfield, Springfield First, Wellsville First.

OKLAHOMA: Alva, Mrs. H. E. Mason, Anadarko, Atoka, Annie Osborne, Ardmore, Rev. Charles C. Weith, Bartlesville, Blackwell; Mrs. Emma F. McBride, Coalgate; Cement, Central, Cimmaron Presbyterial; Chickasha, Edmond, Elk City, El Reno, Mrs. F. R. Farrand, Enid, Eagletown, Kiamichi Presbyterial; Garvin, Rev. and Mrs. W. H. and Emma A. Carroll; Hobart, Mrs. Geo. D. Willingham; Frederick, Griffin, Charity Glover; Granite, Grant, Susan Seats, Kaw, Kingfisher, MacAlester, Millerton, Rance Cherry, Joseph Garner; Muskogee First, Mulhall, Norman, Prof. Geo. N. Gould; Oklahoma First, Phil C. Baird D. D., Mrs. W. A. Knott; Okmulgee, Perry, Ponca, Shawnee, Stroud, Tulsa, Tonkawa, Oak Hill, Valliant, Solomon H. Buchanan, Dining Table and Chairs, Samuel Folsom, Front Door of Elliot Hall, Lucretia C. Brown Communion Service, Bertha L. Ahrens, Adelia M. Eaton, John Claypool, Malinda A. Hall, R. E. and Mary A. Flickinger; Vinita, Wagoner, Watonga.

NORTH DAKOTA: Fillmore, Mary I. Weimer.

PENNSYLVANIA: Armagh, Bakerstown, Black Lick, Blairsville First, Blairsville Presbyterial, Braddock, First and Calvary; Buelah, Coatesville, E. Lilley; Cresson, Congruity, Derry, Doe Run, Easton, College Hill, Brainard and

THE OAK HILL AID SOCIETY

South Side; East Liberty, Ebensburg, Greensburg, First and Westminster; Anna B. Hazleton, Irwin, Jeanette, Latrobe, Ligonier, Johnstown, First, Second and Laurel Avenue; Lewistown, Manor, McGinnis, Murraysville, Philadelphia, Lena D. Fieber and Prof, H. W. Flickinger; Pittsburg, First and Second, Ellen M. Watson, Mary R. Scott; Port Royal, Parnassus, Pleasant Grove, Poke Run, Plum Creek, New Alexandria, New Kensington, South Danville, Mrs. W. A. Reagel; Turtle Creek, Westmont Chapel, Wilkinsburg, Martha Graham, Mrs. J. J. Campbell, Williamsburg, Windber and Windsor.

SOUTH DAKOTA: Volga, Hartford, Mrs. M. E. Crowe.

TEXAS: Bushy Creek, Mary A. Pierson, Crockett, Mrs. John B. Smith.

XXXVI X

TRIBUTES TO THE WORKERS

AHRENS. — EATON. — CLAYPOOL. — WEIMER. — WOLCOTT. —HALL. — DONALDSON. — BUCHANAN.

"Our lives are songs, God writes the words,
And we set them to music at pleasure;
And the song grows glad, sweet, or sad
As we choose to fashion the measure."

MARY A. FLICKINGER

MRS. Flickinger is gratefully remembered for five years of untiring service as assistant superintendent.

The sphere of her observation and suggestion included all the women's work in the buildings, occupied by the students, and the special care of the garden and Boy's Hall. In connection with this daily oversight, there was always manifested a feeling of personal responsibility, to carry to completion at the end of the day, any unfinished work, that would otherwise prevent some of the larger girls from enjoying the privileges of the school, during the evening study hour.

Trained in her youth to execute speedily all the kinds of work, usually required on a well arranged farm, and also as a sewer and nurse, she proved a very valuable helper. She became the home physician, administering the medicines and caring for the sick. Her method of treatment included the prevention of some of the milder, but common forms of disease, by the regular administration of some inexpensive antidotes. These two principles were frequently expressed: "Self-preservation is the first law of nature," and "Prevention is better than cure." The young people were also encouraged to learn, how to keep and intelligently use, a few simple remedies in the home.

She and her husband are both natives of Port Royal, Juniata county, Pa., and their marriage occurred there, June 20,1878. They have filled pastorates at Doe Run, Pa., Walnut, and Fonda, Iowa. They raised the funds and secured the erection of churches at Marne, Fonda, Pomeroy and Varina, Iowa; and a commodious parsonage at Fonda. He has served as a trustee of Corning Academy, Buena Vista college and of the Presbytery of Fort Dodge; stated clerk and treasurer of the latter twelve and a half years, and as Moderator of the Synod of Iowa, at Washington in 1901; and by special request, as author of the Pioneer History of Pocahontas county, Iowa, in 1904. Mrs. Flickinger in her youth became a teacher in the Sunday school, and during all the years that have followed, has been an efficient and aggressive solicitor and teacher of the children, in that important department of the work of the church.

She has ever manifested an unusual degree of energy, always preferring to do all her own home work, rather than have it done by others. One who enjoyed the privilege of witnessing her unflagging energy and enthusiastic devotion to her work, rising early and working late, at a time when she was supposed to be unable to do more than take care of herself, paid to her this friendly compliment: "You work with the untiring industry of a bee, the patient perseverance of a beaver, the overcoming strength of a lion, and the double quickness of a deer."

Her liberal responses to the calls of the needy have been limited only by her ability to work, save and give.

BERTHA LOUISE AHRENS

"I'll praise my Maker with my breath;
And when my voice is lost in death,
Praise shall employ my nobler powers."
—The Psalmist.

Bertha Louise Ahrens (B. Feb. 26, 1857), missionary teacher among the Choctaw Freedmen of Indian Territory since 1885, and principal teacher at Oak Hill Academy,, 1905-1911, is a native of Berlin, Prussia. Her parents, Otto and Augusta Ahrens, in 1865, when she was 8, and a brother Otto 5, came to America and located on a farm near Sigourney, Iowa, after one year at Bellville, Ill.; and four, at Harper, Iowa. The schools and churches first attended used the German language. Her first studies in English were in the graded schools at Sigourney and here at seventeen, she became a member of the Presbyterian church under the pastorate of Rev. S. G. Hair. He loaned her some missionary literature to read and it awakened a desire on her part to become a missionary. This desire was expressed to the Women's Missionary society of the church and she was encouraged to attend the Western Female Seminary, now college, at Oxford, Ohio. After a course of study at this institution she enjoyed a year's training in the Bible school connected with Moody's Chicago Avenue church, Chicago.

During the next year, after hearing in her home town an appeal in behalf of a Negro school in the south, she was led to offer her services to the Presbyterian Board of Missions for Freedmen. In December 1885, she received a commission with request to locate among the Choctaw

TRIBUTES TO THE WORKERS 311

Freedmen at Lukfata, in the southeast part of Indian Territory. The route at that early date was quite circuitous. Going south through Kansas City over the M. K. T. Ry., to Denison, Texas, she passed eastward by rail to Bells, through Paris to Clarksville, Texas; and thence northward forty miles to Wheelock and Lukfata. Clarksville, south of Red river continued to be the nearest town and station during the next ten years.

She has now completed twenty-eight years of continuous and faithful service as a missionary teacher among the Freedmen. During these years she has served the following communities and churches.

Lukfata, Mount Gilead	11 years	1885-1896.
Fowlerville, Forest	3 years	1896-1899.
Goodland, Hebron	1 year	1899-1900.
Grant, Beaver Dam	4 years	1900-1904.
Valliant, Oak Hill Academy	6½ years	1904-1911.
Beaver Dam	1 year	1911-1912.
Wynnewood, Bethesda Mission	2 years	1912-1914.

She is now serving as principal teacher in the Bethesda Home and School, located three miles northeast of Wynnewood in the Chickasaw Nation. This school was opened Nov. 1, 1899. It was founded by Carrie and Clara Boles and others; and its obect is to provide a home and christian education to the orphan and homeless youth of the colored people.

Miss Ahrens has been a life long and conscientious Christian worker, among the Freedmen of the Choctaw Nation. Her name is a household word to all of them. She found it necessary from the first to locate as a lonely teacher among them in territorial days, and share with them the unusual privations, incident to a life of such seclusion and unselfish devotion. During the first fifteen years, she had to live alone in little, rudely constructed huts in a sparsely settled timber country, where quarrels and murders, among both the Indians and colored people, were events of common and almost annual occurrence; yet she never thought of leaving her work or forsaking her mission on account of personal danger.

The following is an accurate description of the little hut she occupied three years while at Forest church. It was built of saplings, eight feet square and chinked with mud. It had a fire place, an opening eighteen inches square for light, and another one for entrance, that was about three inches lower than her height. The chimney was built of mud, so small and crooked that only a part of the smoke could be induced to go up it, on a windy day. The blind for closing the window opening was so open, it merely broke the force of the wind, it could not keep it out, nor the lamp from blowing out. The little door left similar openings above and below it. On windy days the smoke found its way out through these and other openings overhead. These conditions after a while were relieved, by the insertion of a window in the opening, and covering the walls of the room with sheets.

The floor space was fully occupied, when it was supplied with a bed, trunk, sewing machine, book case, table and one chair. It lacked room for the organ, which had to be kept in the chapel.

There was no porch, and into this little room the children on Sabbath afternoons would crowd to sing, standing until they grew weary, and then sitting on the floor. This rude and lonely hut was located about one fourth of a mile from the church. Near it was another and larger one-room

TRIBUTES TO THE WORKERS 313

cabin, having a porch, that was occupied by a good elder of the church, his wife and a family of six children.

The school rooms, that she had to occupy, in order to fulfil her mission, though the best the colored people could afford, were also of the rudest sort. It was a difficult task, to make them look within like tidy temples of knowledge.

Her work was also very elementary. As the pupils would advance and their work become interesting, they would drop out of school. Yet it never occurred to her the work was wearisome, because it was monotonous and often disappointing. If experiences were disappointing, or the day, gloomy, there remained to her the Bible, with its precious and unchanging promises; and the organ, responsive as ever to the touch of her hand. These were home comforts, that enabled her to forget the trials and burdens of each day, before its close.

Her work as a teacher has been increasingly attractive. The secret of this unflagging and ever increasing interest, is found in the large place, given the Bible in all her teaching work. It has been a daily text book in the school room. On the Sabbath, her opportunity to read and explain it to all the people of the community, as superintendent of the Sunday school, has been even greater than that of some of the ministers in charge, when the latter was only a monthly visitor, while she served faithfully every Sabbath.

The world is needing the light of Bible truth. It is life giving. "Go teach," is as urgent as the commission, "Go preach." The opportunity to supply the world's great need, with the life giving Word of God, is an inspiration to the consecrated christian teacher.

She has felt this inspiration, and has become a very capable interpreter and practical expositor of the Bible. She has been well equipped to lead the people in song, and has received many evidences of the highest appreciation of her work, as a Bible instructor.

Though not possessing what might be termed a rugged constitution, she has never lost a week, at any one time, from the school room on account of illness. She has been free to express the desire to continue to labor, as a faithful and efficient teacher, among the Freedmen as long as her strength will permit. Ruth expressed her sentiments, when she said to Naomi:

"Entreat me not to leave thee; where thou lodgest I will lodge; Thy people shall be my people and thy God my God."

She has been a true missionary hero. She has been willing to work in one of the most solitary places, for the lowliest of people, without the ordinary comforts of home and friends. Whilst her Bible work has been continued through the entire years, with but two exceptions, her income—a mere pittance—has been limited to the terms of school. This has made necessary very close economy in personal expenses, but has not prevented liberal offerings to promote the work of the church. Her seclusion, privations and dangers, during the first fifteen years, were as great as of many of those, who have gone to the remote parts of the earth. The heroic spirit of Martin Luther, translator of the German Bible she learned to read in youth, has always proved a source of great inspiration, to be faithful and courageous. When he was warned of the danger of martyrdom at Worms, where he had been summoned for trial for declaring the plain words of the Bible, he bravely

TRIBUTES TO THE WORKERS

said, "Were they to make a fire that would extend from Worms to Wittemberg, and reach even to the sky, I would walk across it, in the name of the Lord, I would appear before them and confess the Lord Jesus Christ." And a little later, "Were there as many devils (cardinals) in Worms, as there are tiles upon the roofs, I would enter," for the Elector had promised him a safe conduct. When he arrived at Worms and stood before his accusers, he finally said: "Here I am, I neither can, nor will retract anything. I cannot do otherwise; God help me." These noble and courageous words of Luther are well adapted, to prove an inspiration to every one that reads them.

Her courage has led and kept her in the place of privilege and duty. Her faithfulness and devotion have enabled her to win the confidence and esteem of all who have come within the sphere of her acquaintance and friendship. She continues to pursue her chosen and loved employment, of serving as a missionary teacher among the Freedmen of Indian Territory, now Oklahoma, in the spirit of the Psalmist.

"My days of praise shall ne'er be past,
While life, and thought, and being last,
Or immortality endures."

ADELIA M. EATON

The superintendent, teachers, students and friends of Oak Hill were called upon to sustain a great loss and experience a deep sorrow, as the sun was setting, on June 5, 1908, when Adelia M. Eaton, our highly esteemed matron, after three and one half years of unusually efficient service, and a brief illness of one week after the end of the term, peacefully and trustfully passed from the scene of her faithful missionary labors, to the enjoyment of her eternal reward. Her illness, which terminated with heartfailure, seemed to be the outcome of a weariness that ensued after rendering some voluntary but needed services for the comfort of others.

She was the second daughter of Harvey Eaton, one of the hardy, prosperous pioneer farmers of Pocahontas county, Iowa, She grew to womanhood on the farm, where she learned to be industrious and earnest.

She early became identified with the work in the Presbyterian church and Sunday school at Fonda where she received her first training in christian work. After enjoying a four years' course at Buena Vista college, Storm Lake, associated with her elder sister, she spent four years in mercantile pursuits in Sioux City and Fonda. All of these previous employments and experiences seemed to be parts of a varied training, to fit her most fully, for the position she filled as a missionary teacher at the Academy. In the management of the affairs of this institution, her responsibilities and duties made her the executive helper of the superintendent. Here she found responsiblities and opportunities, that called forth all her noblest powers, and enabled her to make it the most highly useful and crowning period of her life.

She naturally possessed an attractive personality. She was tall, slender and erect in form, very prompt, dignified and graceful in movement. Her countenance indicated intelligence, energy and culture. She had a good voice for public address, possessed rare executive ability and was so gentle in manner that obedience to her commands was accorded with pleasure and delight. Though never unmindful of her resources, she never manifested any pride, save that which every truly noble soul manifests in the quality of its work,

TRIBUTES TO THE WORKERS 317

by putting forth a constant effort to perform every duty in the most thorough and efficient manner.

She was a happy, willing worker. The key note of her work as a teacher seemed to be the one expressed in the words: "My meat is to do the will of Him that sent me and to finish his work." John 4, 34. Although she had many other important duties on that day, she was always present at the services on the Sabbath. The memory of the living will not soon forget the personal interest she manifested in the spiritual welfare of every member of her large class of older students in the Sunday school, her tender and affectionate appeals to the young people at the Endeavor meetings, her interesting and instructive addresses at institutes and conventions, and how she voluntarily lingered to extend friendly greetings at the close of the church services.

The call, to engage in this educational work among the Freedmen in Indian Territory, came to her at an unexpected, but opportune time. When the need for her services and desire for her co-operation were stated, she immediately gave her assent to make a trial of the work for a term of three months. As the work progressed her interest in it increased, and she became more firmly attached to it. Her affections, interest and ambitions seemed to be transferred to the people and work at the Academy. Her attachment and devotion to this work was as remarkable as it was unexpected. This was the secret of the unusual merit of the service rendered. In this new sphere of usefulness, she found a field of opportunity that afforded full scope for the exercise of all her intellectual, moral and spiritual powers, and, engaging in this work with all the enthusiasm of her noble nature, she rendered a continuous service so faithful and efficient, as to call forth heartfelt appreciation and words of highest commendation.

MRS. JOHN CLAYPOOL

Mrs. John Claypool, matron 1908-9, the successor of Adelia Eaton, came from membership in the class of Mrs. A. W. Crawford of the First Presbyterian church of San Diego, California. Her work is gratefully remembered for its uniform faithfulness and efficiency, and the sweet beneficent influence exerted by the noble womanhood and manhood of herself and husband, previously employed in a bank, who also came and remained with her at the institution. Through the aid of the latter, the profit on the poultry was greater that year, than in any other. The garden that year was greatly enlarged and surrounded with a new fence. He nailed the pales on the panels and they remain as a memento of his interest and handiwork. The fact that she represented one of the churches giving most loyal and liberal support to the Academy, and was thus a living link connecting the work of the institution with the many friends, supporting it on the Pacific Coast, gave to her work an additional charm that was greatly appreciated. They are now living in Texas.

MARY I. WEIMER

Mary I. Weimer, who served as matron 1909 to 1911, a native of Port Royal, Pa., came to Oak Hill from Knox, in the Devils Lake Region of North Dakota; where, after a course of preparation at the state teachers college at Fargo, she achieved an unusual degree of success, both as a teacher and manager of affairs on the farm. These interests prevented her from coming the previous year when first solicited.

At the Academy she rendered a service so efficient and faithful as to merit the gratitude of all. After the loss of the Girls' Hall, which occurred during her first year, when all of its occupants were deprived of comfortable quarters, the fear was entertained she would want to be excused from further service. Instead of pursuing this course she became one of our best counselors and helpers in the effort to provide for the comfort of herself and the girls, and keep the latter from returning home at that critical period.

The superintendent will never cease to be grateful for her favorable decision at this trying hour, and the self-denial she voluntarily proposed to undergo, in order to make it possible, to continue the work of the institution. It was the period when Mrs. Flickinger was a helpless invalid at Fonda, patiently awaiting the return of her husband, with daily anxiety. He could not leave, however, until the cellar excavation and concrete walls of the building had been completed. This done, Samuel Folsom was ready to serve as foreman of the carpenters, in the erection of the new building, and it fell to the lot of Miss Weimer, to serve as general manager, in the absence of the superintendent. The situation was one, that required unusual courage, as well as prudence and self-control. Her heroism was equal to the call to duty. Loyalty and faithfulness were her constant watchwords.

At the end of the next term in 1911, she found it necessary to give her personal attention anew to the interests of her own home and farm. She enjoys the distinction of having served as matron, the last year in the Girls' Hall and the first one in Elliott Hall. She is gratefully remembered by all, who became the subjects of her daily care and domestic training.

MISS JO LU WOLCOTT

Miss Jo Lu Wolcott, matron, February to June, 1912, was a daughter of the late Dr. Wolcott of Chandler, Okla. She has had considerable experience as a teacher in the public schools of Kansas and Oklahoma, and in the government school for the Indians at Navaho Falls, Colorado. She is now serving as a teacher in an Indian school in South Dakota.

MALINDA A. HALL

Malinda A. Hall rendered six years of faithful and efficient service as assistant matron, and teacher. Having completed the grammar course at Oak Hill in 1900, and then a four years course at Ingleside Seminary in Virginia, she was well prepared for the work at the Academy, and proved a very reliable and valuable helper. She was capable and always willing, when requested, to supply any vacancy occurring among the other helpers. She enjoyed good health, and never lost a day from illness. Her strength and energy enabled her to execute promptly and efficiently, every work entrusted to her. Her work throughout was characterized by a never failing promptness, faithfulness and energy. She was familiar with the needs and traits of her people, was thoroughly devoted to the promotion of their best interests, and her suggestions were always gratefully received. The ability and enthusiasm of her work, as the teacher of a large class in the Sunday school and leader of the young people in their Endeavor meetings, will never be forgotten by those, who came within the sphere of her voice and influence.

Since her marriage in 1911 to William Stewart she has been devoting her time and attention to the improvement of their home on the farm near Valliant. She is need-

TRIBUTES TO THE WORKERS 321

ed on the farm, but the thought lingers, that there continues to be a great need for her services in the educational work among her people.

Miss Hall's exploits, as a sharpshooter with her own gun, during her first year as a teacher at Oak Hill, indicate her responsiveness to the spirit of chivalry, that prevailed among the people during the period of her youth.

One day in the spring of the year, while hunting eggs in the second story of the old log house, she discovered a large snake on one of the rafters over her head. Hastening quietly to her own room for a gun, she brought the snake to the floor with the first shot. It measured over four feet in length, was dark in color and was of the kind, that eats eggs and chicks, commonly called a chicken snake. She also, at the request of Mrs. Flickinger, stunned a small beef, that they together butchered, at a time the superintendent was absent.

MARY A DONALDSON

When Carrie E. Crowe was called away in January 1906, the place was rather reluctantly assumed but very acceptably filled by Mrs. Sarah L. Wallace of Fairhope, Alabama. After two months she also was called away. The place was then filled by Mary A. Donaldson of Paris, Texas. She had been an attendant at the first Oak Hill Normal, in 1905, and then became a missionary teacher at Grant. Attendance at the Normal led to her recognition, both at Grant and Oak Hill. After teaching several years she pursued another course of training at New Orleans and has become a professional nurse.

SOLOMON H. BUCHANAN

"He that is faithful in that which is least, is faithful." Solomon H. Buchanan is a native of Glen Rose, Somervell Co., Texas. At the age of eight he was bereft of both of his parents, and those, into whose care he drifted, were not willing he should learn a letter. By some means he attracted the favorable notice of Miss Mary A. Pearson, a missionary of our Home Mission Board. Furnishing him the funds for the trip, she sent him at the age of 18 in 1903, to Oak Hill Academy with request to become an earnest Christian teacher. At the Academy Mrs. Mary R. Scott of Pittsburgh became his teacher. She taught him his letters and first lessons in spelling and reading, giving him considerable time and attention, while the other boys were playing. Perceiving his special fondness for music, she taught him the chords on the piano, and thus gave him a start on that noble instrument, which has ever since been his favorite.

He has always found the study of books a rather difficult task, owing to the lack of early training in them; but he has proved a good student and a very valuable helper at the Academy. The longing desire to become a capable and successful teacher, has kept him there, amid all the changes that have occurred since his arrival in 1903. He has now acquired an unusual degree of skill as a performer on the piano and his enthusiastic accompaniments on that noble instrument contributed greatly to the pleasure and delight of the work at the Academy. He has become an earnest worker in the Sunday school and endeavor meetings. He has a strong voice for song or public address, and has become an excellent leader of religious meetings. He served one year as an assistant teacher at the Academy. He has

TRIBUTES TO THE WORKERS 323

proved himself a very efficient and valuable helper at the Academy, always looking after the entertainment of visitors.

In 1912 he was ordained an elder of the Oak Hill church and in May of that year was sent as one of the commissioners of the Presbytery of Kiamichi, to the general assembly at Louisville, Ky. Through the courtesy of Rev. E. G. Haymaker, he spent the summer of 1903 at Winona Lake, Ind. He is now serving, as superintendent of the farm work and musical instructor, at the Bethesda Home and school at Wynnewood, Okla.

The boy who wins is,

"Not the one who says, 'I can't';
Nor the one who says, 'Don't care;'
Not the boy who shirks his work,
Nor the one who plays unfair.
But the one who says, 'I can',
And the one who says, 'I will;'
He shall be the noble man,
He the place of trust will fill."

STUDENT WORKERS

These tributes to worthy workers seem incomplete, without some reference to the faithful co-operation of some of the young people, who, making rapid progress in their studies and industrial training, during the later years of this period, and serving efficiently as workers, foremen and occasional teachers, made possible the large amount of improvement work necessary to overcome the losses sustained. The memory recalls the names of the following students, whose responsible and efficient co-operation was thus worthy of grateful mention.

Occasional Teachers and Leaders: Paul Thornton, Vina Jones, Delia Clark*, Isabella Monroe, Ruby Moore*,

*Deceased.

Virginia Wofford, Sarah Milton, Celestine Seats, Solomon Buchanan, Riley Flournoy, Clarence and Herbert Peete.

Carpenters and Cement Workers: David Folsom*, Solomon Burris, Louis and Alvin Pitchlin, Isaiah Nelson, Clarence Peete, Noah Alverson, Riley Flournoy, Fred and Percy McFarland, Thomas Wilson, George Hollingsworth, Frank Dickson, Ashley and Alonza McLellan and Brown Gaffony.*

Painters: Solomon Buchanan, Frank Dickson, John Black, Eugene Perry, Wesley Lewis, Herbert Peete and Cornell Smith.

Farmers and Trustworthy Teamsters: James Stewart, James Burris, James Richards, Dee McFarland, Robert Johnson, Robert Maxie, S. S. Bibbs, and Everett Richards.

---

*Deceased.

XL

CLOSING DAY, 1912

ELLIOTT HALL DEDICATED. — CONCERT. — RESOLUTIONS.—
STUDENTS AFFECTION. — FAREWELL NOTE.

THE following account, of the closing day of our last term of school, is taken from the last issue of the Oak Hill Freedman's Friend, a news-letter, intended to promote the interests of the Academy, and sent to its patrons and friends as a quarterly at first, but later as an annual, from February 1905, to September 1912.

CLOSING DAY, 1912

June 13, 1912, was a day of unusual interest. It was the last day of the last term of school, under the management of the superintendent, and the contemplation of this fact frequently suggested a thought of sadness, since it meant the last meeting with many friends and co-workers.

It was also the second day set for the dedication of Elliott Hall, and the third day announced for a visit and address by Rev. Phil C. Baird, D. D.,pastor of the First Presbyterian church of Oklahoma City. His leading and unusually happy participation in the events of the day, made his visit and services on this occasion thrice welcome and valuable.

At 2:00 p. m. Dr. Baird delivered the principal address to a large and very appreciative audience in the Academy. He chose for his theme, The Essentials of Success; and emphasized these three, namely "Labor, purpose and perseverance."

ELLIOTT HALL DEDICATED

At the close of the address of Dr. Baird, the meeting was transferred to the cozy and spacious front porch of Elliott Hall.

The story of the Hall as a grateful and permanently useful memorial of the late Alice Lee Elliott, and the generous gift of $5,000.00 on the part of her surviving husband, David Elliott of Lafayette, Indiana, now at Minneapolis, Minn., was briefly related by the superintendent. Rev. W. H. Carroll reported that voluntary offerings to the amount of $29.48 had that day been donated toward the expense of furnishing the two bath rooms. The prayer of dedication was offered by Rev. Wiley Homer of Grant, who has been a faithful annual visitor and constant guardian of the good name and welfare of the institution ever since it was founded in 1886. The benediction was pronounced by Rev. P. S. Meadows of Shawneetown, moderator of the Presbytery of Kiamichi.

CLOSING CONCERT

The program provided for the evening consisted of a vocal and instrumental concert by the students, such as had been given, with one exception, at the close of each term. Several of the selections, rendered as full choruses, were from Leslie's Ideal Class, the music book most frequently used by the superintendent in the training work of note reading and vocal culture. They included the anthems, "Break forth into Joy," "I was Glad," by I. B. Woodbury, "Before Jehovah's Throne," and patriotic Glees, "Hail to the Flag," "Now a Mighty Nation," and "Unfurl the Sail."

When the time arrived to announce the closing chorus, the superintendent, after expressing appreciation of the fact there were present so many ministers of the Presbytery, patrons and friends; and gratitude for their constant cooperation, then made known to them, for the first time, the fact that several months previous he had tendered his resignation to the Board of Missions for Freedmen, and that in due season, Rev. W. H. Carroll, the principal, would be promoted to fill the vacancy, when it occurred.

After hearing these announcements, every minister present manifested a desire to participate in the meeting, by bearing voluntary testimony to the good work that had been done at the Academy under the leadership of the superintendent. Rev. Dr. Baird was the first speaker, and he acted as a leader or chairman during this temporary interruption of the program. He bore testimony to his previous knowledge of the faithfulness and administrative ability of the superintendent, and his pleasant surprise at the results achieved at this institution. Grateful tributes to the efficiency of his work, as superintendent of the Academy, were then expressed by Rev. Wiley Homer of Grant, Rev. T. K. Bridges of Lukfata, Rev. P. S. Meadows and Rev. W. H. Carroll.

Rev. W. J. Starks of Frogville read and presented for adoption the appreciative resolutions that follow:

Their unanimous adoption by a rising vote was immediately followed by a general waving of handkerchiefs, a touching expression of good wishes and parting cheer.

RESOLUTIONS

Whereas the Rev. R. E. Flickinger, our beloved superintendent and friend, has announced his resignation as superintendent of Oak Hill Industrial Academy, now Alice Lee Elliott School; and whereas such resignation has come to us at a very unexpected time; We, citizens of the neighborhood, patrons, students and teachers of the Academy, and members present of the Presbytery of Kiamichi, do hereby unite in adopting the following resolutions:

First. That the announcement of his resignation brings to us profound grief and disappointment, as it takes from among us a friend and brother bound to us by many unusual and lasting ties.

Second. That we lose in Rev. R. E. Flickinger, the founder of the new and the real Oak Hill Industrial Institution, through the accomplishment of the following achievements, during his administration:

When he re-opened the doors of this academy seven and a half years ago, it had been closed for the year, and for months there seemed to be but little prospect it would be opened again. The evidences of neglect, decay and desertion were manifest on every hand. Under his magic hand the school was re-opened, only a few students were enrolled the first term, but the piles of rubbish in every corner, and underbrush began to disappear, and one of the buildings was neatly painted by the boys. At this time the Board did not own the land on which the buildings were located. After the removal of the restrictions in 1908, the title to one small tract was promptly secured by purchase. A dozen other adjoining little tracts have since been added to this first one, as their purchase became possible and at their virgin price; so that now there belongs to this school, as a means of promoting its local support, the magnificent domain of 270 acres of beautiful and valuable tillable lands of which about one-third is now cleared, enclosed and under cultivation.

"Enlargement and Permanent Improvement," became the watchwords of progress, when the title to the second tract was secured. Upon this stable material basis there has been systematically organized and developed an important Industrial institution, where boys and girls are trained not only in the great fundamentals of the best intellectual and moral culture, but also in the essential industrial arts of life.

The accomplishment of these results has cost the superintendent an indescribable amount of toil and labor. His great staying powers and ingenuity were taxed to their utmost, when, in quick succession, the two largest buildings were suddenly destroyed by unexpected fires, that left nothing but ashes and discouraged friends. The testimony that he has proved himself capable of overcoming these staggering losses appears in the temporary Boys Hall, an addition to the Academy building after the first fire in 1908, and in the large and commodious new building, bearing the name "Elliott Hall" of which he enjoys the honor of having been its architect and builder, through the labors of the students and the teachers of the academy; and, in this creditable student body of well trained young people.

Third. In grateful recognition of his unusual patience and perseverance, his unceasing toil and never failing interest, his self denying generosity and for his noble, manly exemplary christian life, we tender to him our heartfelt lasting gratitude; and, enrolling his name among the worthy founders of Oak Hill Industrial Academy, shall enshrine it as one to be given to children's children, as the educator and organizer, who infused new life into this institution and greatly enlarged the scope of its work.

Fourth. That a copy of these resolutions be sent to the Board of Freedmen, to the Interior, The Valliant Tribune and the Times, Fonda, Iowa.

PHIL. C. BAIRD,
Chairman of Meeting.

A TOKEN OF AFFECTION AND REGARD FROM THE STUDENTS

Dear Superintendent:

I have been requested by the boys of this institution, to offer you a slight token of our affection and regard. I cannot tell you how delighted I am to be the means of conveying to you this expression of our united love. What we offer you is a poor symbol of our feelings, but we know you will receive it kindly as a simple indication of the attachment, which each one of us cherishes for you in our hearts.

You have made our days and months pleasant to us. We know that we have often tried your patience and forbearance, but you have dealt gently with us in all our waywardness; teaching us by example as well as precept, the advantages of magnanimity and self control.

We will never forget you. We shall look back to this institution in after life; and, whenever memory recalls our school days, our hearts will warm toward you as they do today.

I have been requested by my school mates, not to address you formally, but as a beloved and respected friend. In that light, Dear Superintendent, we will regard you.

Please accept our good wishes. May you always be as

happy as you have endeavored to make your pupils; and may they—nothing better could be wished them—be always as faithful to their duties to others, as you have been in your duties to them.

Very truly yours,
W. RILEY FLOURNOY.

In behalf of the boys of Oak Hill Academy.

An expression of gratitude from Simon Folsom, an elder of the Forest church, who gave us very cordial co-operation, and whose voice, ringing with pleading eloquence and words of glad encouragement to the students, was frequently heard at the Endeavor meetings or morning services, by the young people during term time:

Dear Sir: I want to thank you for your interest, help and work among my people. I feel that you have done us a great service here. It is my prayer that God will reward you in time for all your services in labor, thought and interest. This is the plea of one whom you have been serving.

July 21, 1912.   A Friend,
SIMON FOLSOM.

FRUIT BULLETIN

The superintendent continued to have charge of the improvement and other work of the Academy and farm, until the first of October; publishing in the mean time the last issue of the Freedman's Friend in September; and, remaining during the month of October, prepared and published a bulletin entitled, "Approved Fruits for Southern Oklahoma."

The aim of the author, in preparing and publishing this fruit bulletin, was to furnish a short and reliable text book on horticulture, for use in the Academy; and to supply the patrons of the institution, the information they were needing, to enable them to secure, when making their first investments, profitable early, medium and late, fruit-bearing varieties of trees for a small home orchard on their respective allotments.

FAREWELL

The farewell words of the superintendent, briefly summarized, appeared as follows in the last issue of the Freedman's Friend:

With the sending forth of this issue of the Oak Hill Freedman's Friend, Rev. R. E. Flickinger lays aside the mantle of service, as superintendent of the Academy and Farm, and cordially commends Rev. W. H. Carroll, his successor, to the confidence and esteem of all the patrons and friends of the institution.

The opportunity afforded here during the last eight years, to engage in the educational work among the colored people of our beloved land, has been the realization of an earnest desire awakened in the early part of our ministry, but not expressed until the opening occurred at this place. The silent but deeply impressive cry of need, the golden opportunity to lay the foundation for the organization and development of an important Industrial Educational Institution in this new section of country, and the cordial co-operation of local ministers, teachers, patrons and friends, have combined to make this work throughout, intensely interesting.

It has enlisted our noblest and best powers of mind, heart and hand. The constant probability that our term of service would at best be brief, and the desire to accomplish the greatest possible results, have proved an incentive to incessant industry. When difficulties increased, they served as a signal to go forward more earnestly.

We have done what we could to add our mite, most effectively, to the great educational work needed in this south land. That which has been done, has been due to the constant and cordial co-operation of our Board of Missions for Freedmen, and of the immediate patrons and friends of the institution. It remains, that we express to you all our lasting gratitude, for your cordial co-operation, and for the present, say, Farewell!

"God bless you, till we meet again."
    Very truly,
      R. E. FLICKINGER.

PART III

HISTORY

...OF THE...

PRESBYTERY OF KIAMICHI

...AND THE...

SYNOD OF CANADIAN

"My church is the place, where the Word of God is preached, the power of God is felt, the Spirit of God is manifested and the unity of God is perceived.

"There, I am to meet my Saviour, to meditate on his redemption, to listen to his commands, to bow in reverence before him, to pray for his guidance, to sing his praise, to ask for his help, and to sit quietly in his house.

"It is the home of my soul, the altar of my devotion, the hearth of my faith, the center of my affections and the foretaste of heaven.

"I have united with it in solemn covenant, pledging myself to attend its services, to pray for its members, to give to its support, to obey its laws, to protect its name, to reverence its building, to honor its officers and to maintain its permanence.

"It claims the principal place in my activities, and its unity, peace and progress, concern my life in this world and that which is to come."—F. Hyatt Smith.

XLI
THE PRESBYTERY OF KIAMICHI

CONSTITUTED IN 1896.—ORGANIZED AT GRANT.—BOUNDARY ENLARGED IN 1907.—REPORT IN 1913.—GROWTH, 1868 TO 1913.—DEARTH OF MINISTERS.—FAVORITE SONS.—NEW ERA.

"Neglect not the gift which was given thee, with the laying on of the hands of the Presbytery."—Paul.

THE ministers and group of churches, that first formed the Presbytery of Kiamichi, belonged originally to the Presbytery of Choctaw; which included the territory allotted in 1832 to the Choctaw Nation, comprising the southeast one-fourth of Indian Territory, after the establishment of Oklahoma Territory in 1890.

CONSTITUTED BY SYNOD

The Synod of Indian Territory, at the meeting held at South McAlester, Oct. 22-25, 1896, in response to an overture for division from the Presbytery of Choctaw, established the new Presbytery by the adoption of the following resolutions:

1st. That the Choctaw Presbytery be divided into two Presbyteries, according to the following geographical boundaries: First, beginning at Durant on the M. K. & T. Railroad, east on the 34th parallel to the Arkansas line, thence South to the Texas line, thence west with the Texas line (Red river) to the M. K. & T. Railroad, thence north with the M. K. & T. Railroad to Durant, the starting point; this Presbytery to be known as the Presbytery of Tuskaloosa, and to embrace the following churches now within its bounds: St. Paul, Oak Hill, Bethany, Forest, Beaver Dam, Hebron, Sandy Branch, New Hope, Oak Grove and Mt. Gilead

—10; and to embrace the following ministers, now members of the Presbytery of Choctaw: Rev. E. G. Haymaker, (white) Rev. E. B. Evans, (white) Rev. Wiley Homer, Rev. J. H. Sleeper, and Rev. Samuel Gladman—5.

2nd. That the Presbytery of Tuskaloosa meet at Beaver Dam (Grant) on the Saturday before the third Sabbath in November, 1896, at 11 o'clock a. m. and be opened with a sermon by Rev. E. G. Haymaker, or in his absence, by the oldest minister present, who shall preside until a new Moderator is elected."

ORGANIZED AT GRANT

The first meeting of this new Presbytery was held at Grant, in the Beaver Dam church of which Rev. Wiley Homer was pastor, Nov. 14-16, 1896, seven months after the death of Parson Stewart, who had organized and developed all these churches. The meeting was opened with a sermon by Rev. Edward G. Haymaker, superintendent of Oak Hill Academy, Clear Creek; and he was chosen to serve as the first stated clerk. The first annual report, April 1, 1897, showed an enrollment of 5 ministers, 11 churches and 292 communicant members. The name of the Choctaw church at Wheelock, Garvin, P. O. was included in this report, and Richard D. Colbert was enrolled as a licentiate and appointed stated supply of New Hope and Sandy Branch churches.

The name given this new Presbytery, which was the name of a county and county seat town in Alabama, was not entirely satisfactory to those, who were included in it; and in making their first report to synod in the fall of 1897, they requested the name be changed to Mountain Fork, the name of a branch of Little river, that flows from the east end of Kiamichi mountain. While this matter was under discussion at synod the name of the principal river flowing through the bounds of the Presbytery, "Kiamichi," (Ki a mish ee) signifying "Where you going," was suggested by Rev. Wiley

THE PRESBYTERY OF KIAMICHI 337

Homer; and it was approved both by the Synod and Presbytery.

The roll of the Presbytery, at the time of its first report in the spring of 1897, included two Choctaw churches, namely, Oak Grove at Grant, and Wheelock, having 5 and 70 members respectively. During this year Oak Grove was disbanded and dropped; and Wheelock, becoming vacant, was transferred to the Presbytery of Choctaw; Rev. Evan B. Evans, its last pastor, having gone to Mulhall, in the Presbytery of Oklahoma. Bethany, a colored church previously reported as having 9 members was also dropped. These changes reduced the Presbytery to one consisting entirely of colored churches and of colored ministers, with the single exception of Rev. E. G. Haymaker, superintendent of Oak Hill Academy, who was engaged in the educational work among them.

The annual report for 1898, the first one under the new name, "Kiamichi" that included only colored churches, shows that the Presbytery then consisted of 4 ministers, E. G. Haymaker, Wiley Homer, John H. Sleeper and Samuel Gladman; 2 licentiates, William Butler and R. D. Colbert; and 8 churches, Oak Hill, 40; Mount Gilead, 25; Saint Paul, 14; Beaver Dam, 34; Hebron, 13; New Hope, 25; Sandy Branch, 16; and Forest, 20; having 187 members and 248 Sunday school members.

BOUNDARY ENLARGED

In May 1907, when the General Assembly at Columbus, Ohio, united and rearranged the synods and Presbyteries of the Presbyterian and Cumberland churches, after the union of their Assemblies at Des Moines the previous year, the boundary of the Presbytery of Kiamichi was defined as follows:

CHOCTAW FREEDMEN

"The Presbytery of Kiamichi shall consist of all ministers and churches of the Negro race in that part of the synod of Oklahoma, lying south of the south Canadian river, and south of the Arkansas river, below the point of confluence of these two rivers." Min. G. A. 1907, 214.

The north half of Oklahoma was included in the Presbytery of Rendall, then established and two men Rev. Burr Williams and Rev. David J. Wallace, who had been members of Kiamichi, since 1899 were transferred to it.

In 1910 the colored Presbyterian ministers and churches in east Texas were added to the Presbytery of Kiamichi. These included Rev. J. A. Loving, M. D., and the Mount Zion church, at Jacksonville, Texas; and Rev. J. M. McKellar and the Mount Olivet church at Rusk, Texas.

ANNUAL REPORT IN 1913

In 1913, the Presbytery included 14 ministers and 16 churches as follows:

Minister	Address	Church	Elders	Members	S. S. Members	Missionary Offerings	Self Support
Wiley Homer, H. R.	Grant, Okla.						
Robert E. Flickinger, H. R.	Rockwell City, Iowa						
x Samuel Gladman, Ev.	Eufaula, Okla.						
Thomas K. Bridges	Lukfata, Okla.	Mt. Gilead	2	26	25	$ 13	$ 25
William Butler	Eagletown, Okla.	St. Paul	4	27	38	8	98
	Millerton, Okla.	Forest	3	13	17	3	25
	Lukfata, Okla.	Pleasant Valley	2	27	37	8	15
Richard D. Colbert	Grant, Okla.	Hebron	2	19	15	8	12
William J. Starks	Garvin, Okla.	Garvin	3	30	57	11	190
William H. Carroll	Valliant, Okla.	Oak Hill	3	69	85	55	78
Noah S. Alverson	Griffin, Okla.	Ebenezer	1	12	13	4	
Plant S. Meadows	Shawneetown, Okla.	Mt. Pleasant	2	8	10	3	
	Millerton, Okla.	Bethany	3	23	30	10	10
Samuel J. Onque	Grant, Okla.	Beaver Dam	4	41	55	10	53
Julius W. Mallard	Frogville, Okla.	New Hope	3	26	59	11	24
	Frogville, Okla.	Sandy Branch	2	29	37	6	30
		Pleasant Hill, v		4			
J. A. Loving	Jacksonville, Texas	Mt. Zion	3	28	45	14	
J. M. McKeller —14	Rusk, Texas	Mt. Olivet —16	1	18	60	6	
			38	400	583	$170	$560

x Died, Eufaula, January 8, 1913, at 65.

THE PRESBYTERY OF KIAMICHI 339

These churches now represent 38 elders; 400 members, and 583 Sunday school members. They contributed $180.00 to our Missionary Boards and $560.00, towards self-support.

At the next meeting of the synod in the fall of 1913, the two ministers and churches in Texas were transferred to the Presbytery of White River, Arkansas.

Other ministers and churches, that have been enrolled as members or a part of this Presbytery, and their names have not yet been mentioned, were as follows:

Rev. Thomas C. Ogburn, who in 1890 and 1891 served Beaver Dam, New Hope and Hebron.

Rev. William G. Ogburn, who in 1890, served Saint Paul and Mount Gilead.

Rev. Burr Williams, who from 1899 to 1902 served Conwell chapel at Springvale, and from 1902 to 1903, served Mount Zion at Monger, O. T.

Rev. David J. Wallace, Langston, in 1899, and in 1906 at Okmulgee, Ok. Ter.

Rev. Hugh L. Harry, New Hope at Frogville in 1904 and 1905.

SUCCESSION OF STATED CLERKS

Edward G. Haymaker. Clear Creek, Nov. 14, 1896-1903.
John H. Sleeper, Frogville, 1903-1904.
Thompson K. Bridges, Lukfata, 1904-1906.
Samuel Gladman, Millerton 1906-1910.
William J. Starks, Garvin, 1910-1914.

EXHIBIT OF GROWTH, 1868 TO 1913

The following exhibit shows the comparative growth of the work among the colored people of the Choctaw nation in Indian Territory, the summaries commencing with the results of the work as left by Parson Charles W. Stewart, when he was honorably retired from further active service among the churches, on account of the infirmities of age, in 1890, from Beaver Dam, New Hope, Hebron, St. Paul, and Mount Gilead, and in 1893, from Oak Hill and Forest. The report for 1898 is the first one of the new Presbytery of Kiamichi to include only colored churches.

Church	Address	Stewart began services	Date of organization	Members in 1890	1893	1898	1913
Beaver Dam	Grant	1874	1881	15		34	41
Hebron	Messer	1868	1872	12		13	19
New Hope	Frogville	1869	1872	38		25	26
St. Paul	Eagletown	1877	1878	18		14	27
Mt. Gilead	Lukfata	1883	1885	25		25	26
Oak Hill	Valliant	1868	1869		30	40	69
Forest	Millerton	1885	1887		7	20	13
Sandy Branch	Sawyer		1895			16	29
Ebenezer	Griffin		1903				12
Bethany	Millerton		1904				23
Garvin	Garvin		1905				30
Pleasant Valley	Lukfata		1906				27
Mount Pleasant	Shawneetown		1906				8
Pleasant Hill							4
Total in Oklahoma				108	(145) 37	187	354
Mount Zion	Jacksonville, Texas						28
Mount Olivet	Rusk, Texas						18
Total in Presbytery							400

DEARTH OF MINISTERS

This exhibit shows that the membership of the 7 churches, when relinquished by Parson Stewart in 1890 and 1893, numbered 145, and in 1898, when the Presbytery under the name "Kiamichi" made its first report, including only colored churches, the number was 187; suggesting a gain of 42 members by his successors in 8 years. If, however, the 16 members at Sandy Branch be taken from the 1898 column, it shows the 7 churches served by Stewart, gained only 26 members during all those eight years.

THE PRESBYTERY OF KIAMICHI 341

This lack of growth, during this important period, was in great measure due to the fact most of the churches were left vacant, during a considerable part of that period. Thirty years had passed since the people had been accorded their freedom, but so great had been the lack of educational facilities, a sufficient number of acceptable men, that could read and expound the scriptures profitably to others, could not be found. Other communities throughout the south were experiencing the same need, and had no young men to spare for these needy fields.

FAVORITE SONS BECOME MINISTERS

It devolved upon each community to solve this problem, relating to the supply of ministers, by encouraging their own brightest and best boys to train for the ministry. That was the way this problem had to be solved by the Choctaw Freedmen in the south part of Indian Territory.

While the native young men were under training, and the churches were vacant, the services had to be maintained by the elders and most capable women; and they deserve great credit for their faithfulness and efficiency in maintaining them from year to year.

The church, that during this period made the greatest gain—13 members—was Beaver Dam, the one that was first to furnish from its own membership, an acceptable and capable minister for its own pulpit, by commending Wiley Homer for licensure in 1894, when he was appointed the stated supply for that church and Hebron.

In 1897 the same church presented Richard D. Colbert, another of its sons for licensure that he might take charge of the church at Frogville and Sandy Branch.

Eagletown presented William Butler, as their favorite

son, for licensure; and beginning then, he is still serving that church and Forest.

In 1905, Ebenezer church at Griffin presented Noah S. Alverson for licensure, and beginning then, he is still faithfully serving that field.

In 1905, Mount Gilead church at Lukfata presented for licensure John Richards, a youth of considerable promise, who died at 25, in June 1907, while pursuing his studies under the superintendent of Oak Hill Academy.

Under the ministry of these native youth, aided by several others who have joined them, the membership of the Presbytery was increased from 187 to 350; or, nearly doubled, during the period from 1898 to 1913, and five new churches have been organized.

Parson Stewart, serving all his seven churches life-long periods, and these favorite sons, following loyally and faithfully in his footsteps, have greatly honored the permanent pastorate, though none of them have ever been installed. In this matter of long pastorates, these ministers and people have made a record, worthy of the emulation of the church at large; especially those congregations that seem to take pride in having "itching ears" and the consequent doom of standing vacant and idle half the time, and those perambulating ministers, who remind one of the proverb of the "rolling stone that gathers no moss."

NEW ERA REQUIRES THAT PREACHERS BE TEACHERS

On the other hand it is proper to note, that, commencing with Parson Stewart all of these worthy men were licensed and ordained to the full work of the gospel ministry, after taking a very "short course" of educational training. This was due to the fact they were needed to meet

THE PRESBYTERY OF KIAMICHI 343

an emergency, an unexpected and unusual condition, that called for immediate action. The extraordinary call, these men were encouraged to accept, came to them during the Territorial days, when there was no adequate provision for public education. They were then abreast of their times, and the very best their several communities could furnish.

Now the times are different. The change came with the allotment of lands in 1904 and 1905, followed by statehood in 1907 and the establishment of a public school system immediately afterwards. Public schools are now found in every community, where there are a sufficient number of pupils to justify the employment of a teacher. The demand for good teachers is now greater than the supply, and with passing years the call will be for better ones. There are many reasons now, why every candidate for licensure should first prove himself to be an acceptable and successful teacher, as well as a good speaker. Teaching is now, and for many years will continue to be, the secondary employment of the colored minister in the rural districts. Recognizing that fact, every future candidate for the ministry should be animated with the noble ambition, to stand at the front in the teacher's profession, in order that there may be a constant demand for his services as a teacher, in the community he serves as a preacher.

More ministers are needed, and promising young men, in every community, should be encouraged to train for that sacred office. The church is standing ready to co-operate with them, in their effort to secure a good and thorough education, as a fitting preparation for their future work. "Go and teach" is a divine call to a noble work, but "Go and preach," is recognized as a divine call to a still nobler and greater work, as the Bible and its mission are greater than that of any other book. A greater work suggests the need of greater preparation. The extraordinary incidents of the past were not intended to be regarded as precedents, or as a rule for the future. The time is now at hand when all, who present themselves to the Presbytery, before they have graduated from the Grammar department, or 8th grade of a well accredited school, should be enrolled and held merely as "candidates for the ministry," until they have completed their studies to that extent, before "licensure to preach" is accorded to them. Ordination should ordinarily be deferred, until the licentiate has completed the theological course prescribed for all in the standards of the church. Young men are frequently impatient to enter upon their ministerial life work. They do not always know, that expert or thorough training in youth, doubles their value in the activities of life; and that this is especially true of the teacher and preacher.

XLII
HISTORIES OF CHURCHES

" I was glad when they said unto me, let us go into the House of the Lord."—David.

"There's a church in the valley by the wild-wood
No lovelier spot in the dale;
No place is so dear to my childhood,
As the little brown church in the vale."

BEAVER DAM CHURCH

THE early history of the Beaver Dam Presbyterian church at Grant carries us back to the year 1873, when Wiley Homer, one of the enterprising young men of the community, built an arbor in the timber, and held the first religious meetings among the colored people of that neighborhood.

Parson C. W. Stewart, of Doaksville, the next year held occasional services in the arbor, and in 1875 secured the erection of the first house of worship. It was built of saplings, and at the place previously occupied by the arbor. Wiley Homer continued to serve as leader of the regular Sabbath meetings, when the parson was not present.

In 1881 the church was organized with the following persons as original members:

Wiley Homer, Laney Homer, his wife, Louisa Roebuck, Martha Folsom, Amy Walton, Adaline Shoals, Rhoda Larkins.—7.

Wiley Homer was the only elder ordained at that time. A year or two later, Richard Roebuck, and in 1888 Richard D. Colbert and Wellington Bolden (died 1892) were ordained. Wiley Homer and Richard D. Colbert continued to serve as elders until they were ordained to the full work of the gospel ministry in 1895 and 1903, respectively.

The elders in 1913 are as follows:

William Goff, ordained	1892
Aaron Green, ordained	1894
Wiley Brown, ordained	1912
Walter McCulloch, ordained	1912

Others that served as elders were:

Nick Colbert,	1891 to 1894
Peter Nolan	1893 to 1896
Moses Folsom	1904 till death, 1912

The succession of pastors has been as follows:

Parson C. W. Stewart, Doaksville	1874 to 1890, 16 years
Thomas C. Ogburn, Goodland	1890 to 1892 2 years
Wiley Homer, Grant	1892 to 1912 20 years
Samuel J. Onque, Grant	1912 to date 1914

The comfortable and spacious chapel, now occupied by the congregation, was built in 1904 during the pastorate of Wiley Homer, the God-fearing cowboy, who 30 years before had built the arbor in the timber.

NEW HOPE CHURCH AT FROGVILLE

The New Hope Presbyterian church at Frogville, Choctaw county, was organized about 1872 by Parson Charles W. Stewart, who had conducted occasional services in this neighborhood for some time previous.

The first elders were Elias Radford, who died in 1908 after 36 years of faithful service, and James Pratt, who, after 40 years of faithful official service, is still living (1914) in his own cozy cottage home near the church. In the interest of the church, which is located in the Oak forest, along Red

HISTORIES OF CHURCHES 347

river southeast of Hugo, and still fifteen miles from railway, he has from the first been the principal host, to receive and entertain the Frogville circuit-riders, as in the days of Stewart and Homer; and provided rooms in his own home for the resident ministers as in the days of Sleeper, Harry and Starks. When the Presbytery meets at Frogville, he generously plans to entertain about one half the people that are present from a distance. The good he has already accomplished, by his faithful, life-long service in the church and Sunday school, make him worthy to be long and gratefully remembered, as one of the noblest and most generous benefactors in the community in which he lives.

Others that have been ordained and are still serving as ruling elders in this church are Willis Buffington, ordained Sept. 7, 1902; and Garfield Pratt, son of James, April 9, 1911.

The succession of pastors of the New Hope church has been as follows:

Charles W. Stewart, Doaksville	1872—1889.
Thomas C. Ogburn, Goodland	1889—1891.
Wiley Homer, Grant	1891—1892.
Samuel Gladman, Atoka	1897—1899.
Richard D. Colbert, Grant	1899—1900.
John H. Sleeper, Frogville	1900—1904.
Hugh L. Harry, Frogville	1904—1905.
William J. Starks, Frogville	1905—1912.
Julius W. Mallard, Frogville	since Jan. 4, 1913.

Wiley Homer, an elder and catechist in the Beaver Dam church at Grant, as an aid to Parson Stewart conducted most of the services during his last two years, 1887 to 1889.

This church in 1913 reports 26 members and 59 in the Sunday school. In all probability it was the second church organized by Parson Stewart.

ST. PAUL CHURCH, EAGLETOWN

In 1877, Parson Charles W. Stewart of Doaksville began to hold occasional religious services in the colored settlement at Eagletown, and Saint Paul Presbyterian church was organized in 1878.

Rev. Charles Copling, a missionary to the Choctaws also conducted an occasional service among the colored people, during the year preceding the organization of the church.

The elders ordained at the time of organization were Elijah Butler, Primas Richards and Solomon Pitchlyn. In 1885 William Butler was ordained to supply the vacancy, occasioned by the removal of Elijah Butler, and Primas Richards to Lukfata, where they became that year two of the first elders of the Mount Gilead church. William Butler continued to serve as an elder until 1897, when, as a licentiate of the Presbytery, he became the stated supply of St. Paul and Forest Presbyterian churches. Shepherd Riley served a number of years as an elder of this church. Those serving as elders in 1913 are Calvin Burris, Monroe Lewis, George Burris and Adam Lewis.

The ministers serving Saint Paul have been:

Parson Charles W. Stewart	1877 to 1889.
William G. Ogburn	1890 to 1891.
John H. Sleeper	1894 to 1897.
William Butler	1897 to date, 1914.

William Butler, a favorite son and elder of this church, continuing to serve it acceptably in the pastorate ever since he was made a licentiate in connection with Forest has made a very noble record. He is a pastor who has acquired the art of emphasizing in a very pleasant way the word "come."

"Oh, come to the church in the wildwood,
To the trees where the wild flowers bloom;

HISTORIES OF CHURCHES

Where the parting hymn will be chanted,
We will weep by the side of the tomb.
"From the church in the valley by the wildwood,
When day fades away into night;
I would fain from this spot of my childhood,
Wing my way to the mansions of light.
"Come to the church in the wildwood,
Oh, come to the church in the vale,
No spot is so dear to my childhood
As the little brown church in the vale."

MOUNT GILEAD CHURCH, LUKFATA

The Mount Gilead church at Lukfata was organized July 26, 1885, by a committee of the Presbytery of Choctaw, consisting of Rev. John Edwards, superintendent of Wheelock Academy, and Elder Charley Morris, a Choctaw. The members enrolled on this date were:

Elijah Butler and Amanda Butler, his wife; Elisha Butler and Vina Butler, his wife; Easter Butler, Francis Butler, Jane Butler, Francis Burris, Daniel Burris, Kate Burris, Primas Richards, Rhoda Butler, Nelson Butler and Adaline Butler.—14.

Elijah Butler and Elisha Butler, his son, and Primas Richards were elected and ordained as the first elders. On Jan. 29, 1896, Matthew Richards was ordained an elder.

This church was called "Mount Gilead," the home of the prophet Elijah, in honor of Elijah Butler, one of the first elders, who, having served a few years as one of the first elders of Saint Paul church, conducted the first religious meetings among the colored people, that led to the organization of this Presbyterian church at Lukfata.

Parson Charles W. Stewart held occasional services in the neighborhood of Lukfata, two or three years before the church was organized in 1885, and then continued to be its monthly supply during the next five years.

In 1890 it was grouped with St. Paul church at Eagletown and supplied by Rev. William G. Ogburn from that place. From 1895 to 1899 it was supplied by Rev. John H. Sleeper, who then moved to Frogville. From 1901 to 1903 it was served by Rev. Samuel Gladman, who then took charge of Bethany near Wheelock.

Rev. Thompson K. Bridges, after serving and organizing Ebenezer church at Lehigh the previous year, located at Lukfata in the fall of 1903, and has been the local teacher and regular supply of the church, since that date, a period of eleven years.

XLIII
PARSON CHARLES W. STEWART
DOAKSVILLE, 1823-1896.

"A soldier of the cross,
A follower of the Lamb,
Who did not fear to own his cause,
Or blush to speak His name."

THIS pioneer circuit rider of the Choctaw Freedmen came forth from a period of slavery, to the Choctaw Indians in the wilds of Indian Territory, that covered the first 42 years of his life. His home was afterwards located near the Kiamichi river, seven miles west of Doaksville. He grew to manhood and always lived in an unimproved, sparsely settled timber country in an obscure and inaccessible corner of the world.

Taking John the Baptist, as his ideal of a good christian worker, he became the leading herald of the gospel message to his people, first in the valley of the Kiamichi, and then going forth in every direction in the larger valley of Red river, he established a monthly circuit of preaching stations, that included the most thickly settled neighborhoods of the colored people in the territory, now included in Choctaw and McCurtain counties. Like John, he seems never to have sat before a camera long enough to leave the world his portrait, and, though serving faithfully as a minister more than 25 years he never enjoyed the privilege and pleasure of attending a meeting of the General Assembly.

Judging him, however, by the results of his work, the circle of churches established and acceptably served for an unusually long period of years, and the number of talented young men, whom he discovered, in the communities visited, and enthused with the longing desire and ambition to become leaders of their race especially useful and efficient teachers and preachers of the gospel, he proved himself worthy to be rated as one of the most aggressive and successful of the early leaders of his race.

> "A man he was to all the country dear,
> Remote from towns he ran his godly race,
> Nor ever changed, nor wished to change his place."

PERIOD OF SLAVERY, 1823-1866

Charles W. Stewart was a native of Alabama, and, at the age of ten in 1833, was transported with the Choctaws, to whom as a slave he belonged, to the southeastern part of Indian Territory. John Homer was then his master, and he located about three miles northeast of the present town of Grant. His first marriage occurred, while he was serving Homer. The wedding of one of Homer's daughters occurred a few years later, and his wife was assigned to serve in the home of the newly married daughter. She located in a distant part of the reservation, and he was thus deprived of his first wife, Charlotte Homer.

Charles Stewart, a white man, keeping store at Doaksville, soon afterwards became his owner, and his previous name, "Homer" was then changed to "Stewart", after the name of his new master. About the year 1860, Samson Folsom, a Choctaw who lived eight miles southeast of old Goodland, became his new and last owner.

THE PRESBYTERY OF KIAMICHI, GARVIN, OKLA., APRIL, 1914.

WILEY HOMER, HIS PEOPLE AND CHAPEL AT GRANT, 1904.

Rev. T. K. Bridges.

Rev. W. J. Starks.

W. R. Flournoy.

Doll Beatty.

Rev. P. S. Meadows.

James R. Crabtree.

PARSON CHARLES W. STEWART

PERIOD OF FREEDOM, 1866-1896

He began to hold religious meetings as early as 1856, when he belonged to Stewart, and lived at Doaksville. Mrs. Stewart, who had been a missionary teacher, encouraged him to learn to read and furnished him with books for that purpose. Rev. Cyrus Kingsbury, pastor of the Choctaw church, gave him the instruction in the Bible, that fitted him for the work of the ministry, and accorded to him the privilege of holding meetings in the church, for his people, on occasional Sabbath afternoons.

He was accorded ordination by the Presbytery of Indian (southern) in the fall of 1870, and was then officially assigned the pastoral care of the congregations he had previously developed at Doaksville and its vicinity, and at Wheelock, or Oak Hill. He greatly appreciated the recognitions accorded to him by the Presbytery, which had previously given him a license to preach; and he endeavored to magnify his office, as an evangelist, by going to the "regions beyond," as fast as the door of opportunity opened for him. During the early sixties he gathered new congregations for worship at his home on the Folsom farm and in the Horse Prairie neighborhood. The Oak Hill appointment was established soon after he was accorded his freedom.

During the year 1883, the evangelistic work among the Freedmen in Indian Territory, was voluntarily transferred by the Southern to the Northern Presbyterian church, with the conviction the latter was better prepared to successfully prosecute it. At the time of this transfer Charles W. Stewart was enrolled as an ordained minister and designated as the Stated Supply of the following organized churches: Beaver Dam, Hebron, New Hope, Oak Hill and St. Paul. During the next two years three more of his appointments, Mt. Gilead, Forest and Horse Prairie were enrolled, as the fruit of his labors, and added to his circuit. At this early date he had also a preaching station at Caddo near Durant, and the distance across his circuit of appointments, from Caddo eastward to St. Paul at Eagletown, was 118 miles.

In 1886 when the Synod of Indian Territory was formed by the union of three Presbyteries having 24 ministers, his circuit included 8 of the 43 churches that were then enrolled. He continued to serve all of these churches four more years.

Previous to this latter date, 1890, he was the first and only Presbyterian minister that preached the gospel to the colored people of Indian Territory. During that period, he laid the foundation for most of the churches, that are now enrolled in the Presbytery of Kiamichi and give employment to a half dozen ministers. He was now advanced in years and beginning to feel the infirmities of age. He relinquished, in favor of two new men from a distance, all of his circuit of churches, except Oak Hill and Forest, which he continued to serve three more years, or until 1893. He was then at the age of 70 honorably retired by the Presbytery, after a long and remarkably successful career in the gospel ministry.

CIRCUIT OF CHURCHES

The following exhibit of the churches he established and served is as nearly correct as it is possible at this date to make it.

PARSON CHARLES W. STEWART

Post office	Church	Services began	Church organized	Work dropped by Stewart	Members	Years of service
Doaksville		1856				
Pine Ridge		1858				
Caddo		1860				
Horse Prairie		1863	1870 ?	1890		27
Wheelock	Oak Hill	1868	1869	1893	30	25
Goodland	Hebron	1868	1872	1890	12	22
Frogville	New Hope	1869 ?	1872 ?	1890	38	21 ?
Grant	Beaver Dam	1874	1881	1890	15	16
Eagletown	St. Paul	1877	1878	1890	18	13
Lukfata	Mt. Gilead	1883	1885	1890	25	7
Wheelock	Forest	1885	1887	1893	7	8
					145	

About 1890, he moved to a home near Forest church, and died there at 73, April 8, 1896; after an aggressive ministry of more than twenty-five years after his licensure, which had been preceded by nearly ten years of earnest volunteer service for the betterment of his people. He was buried in the Crittenden grave yard.

He left three children, the offspring of his marriage to Catherine Perry, namely, Thomas, Betty married to Benjamin Roebuck, and Harriet, married to Rev. Pugh A. Edwards.

In 1886, after the death of Catherine, he married the widow of Jeffers Perkins, and she died at 65 in 1905, survived by seven of twelve children by her first marriage, namely, Charles and Louis Perkins, Mrs. R. D. Arnold, Fredonia Allen, Virginia Willians (d. 1913), Fidelia Murchison and Jane Parrish.

CHARACTERISTICS AS A PREACHER

Charles W. Stewart was a man of medium height and rather stout build. The rugged features of his face suggested a man, possessing strong and sturdy elements of character. He grew to manhood under circumstances and changes that made an early education impossible. His education, which was very limited was acquired by the private study of a primer, catechism, Bible and other books, furnished him by Mrs. Stewart, his real owner, and, Rev. Cyrus Kingsbury (d. 1870).

Parson Stewart was a faithful christian worker, who did not become weary in well doing. He made his long journeys on horseback. He endeavored to arrive at his monthly appointments the previous day so as to have time for the discipline or re-instatement of wayward members, or hold an evangelistic meeting. He manifested so much of hopeful enthusiasm in his work that he seemed unmindful of the loneliness and wearisomeness of the long journeys in the wilderness and regarded it merely as a passing incident, when he had to spend a day or even a night in the timber, waiting for the overflow of flooded streams to subside, so he could safely ford them.

He was an aggressive christian worker. He strived to preach the gospel, "not where Christ was named, lest he should build upon another man's foundation," but, as it is written, "To whom he was not spoken of they shall see, and they that have not heard shall understand." He was on the alert to hear the cry of Macedonia, "Come over and help us," and he was always ready to enter and hold a new field while his strength lasted. When he was licensed, all the land of the Choctaw Nation seemed to be spread out before him, as his field of effort, as the land of Canaan was before Joshua, when the Lord encouraged him to be "strong, very courageous and possess it," for his people. He knew he had the "book of the law," that his people needed and his whole nature seemed to be enthused with the promise, "Every place that the sole of your foot shall tread upon, that have I given unto you." His ambition, to carry the message of gospel light and liberty into new settlements of his people, was limited by the necessity laid upon him, to continue to serve those he had already acquired.

He was an enthusiastic Presbyterian. He frequently delighted, as well as instructed the people, by explaining to them the Bible, by repeating familiar portions of the shorter Catechism and Confession of Faith. These were his most familiar and best commentaries on the Bible. He encouraged the elders, to become leaders of meetings, and teachers of the people, by maintaining regular Sabbath services, for the study of the Bible and Catechism, to promote their spiritual welfare.

He was a forceful and acceptable preacher. In his later years he was sometimes slow in finding the hymn, Scripture lesson and text. But when he found the hymn, it was always one the people could sing, and in leading them with his own powerful voice, he needed neither tuning fork or organ accompaniment. He read the Scripture with such a variety of emphasis, as to awaken the desire to catch every word. In the delivery of his message he manifested so much sincerity and earnestness, that every one felt he was speaking to them "direct from the shoulder."

He grew in favor with the people. He held, to the end of his lifelong ministry, the love and affection of the people, whom he served. He saw their need of teachers and preachers, and encouraged the young people in every neighborhood, to prepare themselves to supply that need. As a direct result of his personal influence and encouragement, Wiley Homer, Richard D. Colbert, William Butler, Elisha Butler, Simon Folsom and others came to be recognized, as efficient Bible teachers and religious leaders, in their respective settlements. Acceptable and permanent preachers could not be found, for the group of churches from which Stewart retired in 1890, until Homer, Colbert and Butler were licensed, and two churches assigned to each of them.

The worthy veteran lived long enough to see Wiley Homer licensed in 1893 and become his successor at Beaver Dam and Hebron. The other two were licensed in 1897, the year after he "entered into the joy of his Lord." It was not until this year, when, John H. Sleeper continuing to serve Mt. Gilead, William Butler became his successor at St. Paul and Forest, and R. D. Colbert was assigned New Hope and Sandy Branch, that all of the churches in the circuit of Stewart had regular supplies.

He was a real pioneer "circuit rider," who has left the good impression of his personal work, upon the colored people of a large section of country, and of him it may well be said:

> "This man never preached for money,
> If he did he never got it;
> He had some faults, but more virtues:
> He was conscientious and devoted,
> Persevering and determined;
> Long his name will be remembered."

"He was a faithful circuit rider—though a slave in his youth;

His artless earnest sermons were the simple tale of truth,

How the Son of God who loved us, left a scepter, crown and throne,

All the joys of highest heaven, to go, seek and save his own."

> "Soldier of Christ, well done!
> Praise be your new employ,
> And while eternal ages run
> Rest in the Saviour's joy."

The opportunity to prepare the foregoing tribute to the memory of Charles W. Stewart, and give it an historic setting in this volume, has been greatly appreciated by the author. Rising above the limitations of his condition as a slave, during the first half of his natural life, he consecrated himself to the betterment of his race and thus, under the most unfavorable circumstances, prepared himself for the wider field and greater opportunities, that came to him with the dawn of freedom.

This story of noble achievement by one of their own number, is well worthy of long and careful preservation; that it may thrill to noble endeavor, the present and future generations of the Choctaw Freedmen.

"Let us labor for the Master,
From the dawn till setting sun;
Let us talk of all his wondrous love and care,
Then, when all of life is over,
And our work on earth is done,
And the roll is called up yonder, we'll be there."

XLIV
REV. WILEY HOMER

"Patience and Perseverance will perform great wonders."

IT has been said, "some men are born great, some have greatness thrust upon them, while others achieve greatness." Many, however, who have inherited a great name, wealth or power have failed to meet the expectation of their parents and friends. When, therefore, any one, reared in the home of poverty and educated in the school of "hard knocks," rises above the unfavorable limitations of his surroundings and achieves a noble career of eminent usefulness in church or state, he merits commendation.

The subject of this sketch is a good illustration of the self-made man. He inherited good lungs, a strong voice and a splendid physique. He is really a physical giant, his stalwart frame towering upward six feet, and tipping the beam at 265 pounds. His erect and dignified movements have made him a commanding figure among his people. His constant endeavor to promote their best interests has made him a popular leader among them. A slave by birth and denied the privilege of books and papers, lest he should learn to read, his eager desire for knowledge led him to devise ways and means of self-education, to enable him to rise above the fetters that bound him in youth. His successful career as a minister of the gospel, serving the same people amongst whom he was born and raised during the entire

REV. WILEY HOMER

period of his active ministerial life, was as unusual and worthy of special commendation, as it was long and useful. Wiley Homer was born March 1, 1851, in the south part of the Choctaw Nation, known as the Red river valley. His parents were Isam McCoy and Adaline Shoals, who lived about three miles northeast of the present town of Grant. As his parents were called after the family name of their masters, in accordance with the usual custom in slavery times, he was called "Homer" after the name of his master, John Homer, a full-blood Choctaw.

LEARNING THE ALPHABET

His self-education began, when at fourteen, he was employed as a cowboy, to herd cattle on the little prairies and hunt them, when scattered through the timber. The timber was a general pasture for the cattle of everybody, and their ownership was told by the brand which consisted of the initial letters of the owner's names, burned on the hip, or back of each. It became necessary for him, to learn how to distinguish these brands, one from another, for he was sometimes asked to hunt the cattle of other people. To do this he began by drawing the outline of familiar brands in the dust or sand, where the ground was smooth, and then on slips of paper. In a short time, the list on the paper slips included the brand of every owner in the settlement, and nearly all the letters of the alphabet.

A man once called on his employer, Samson Loring, to see if he could hunt his cattle. When asked if he could identify the new brand, "A. B.", he took a stick and, stooping down before them, drew the outline of these letters, in the loose sand of the road. On seeing this performance one remarked to the other, "That boy will make a smart nigger." That remark was a source of considerable encouragement to him, and awakened the desire, to take advantage of every opportunity to gain knowledge.

LEARNING TO READ

When, at 16 in 1867, he was accorded his freedom he obtained a primer and first reader, and undertook to master these by private study. About four years later, a testament and shorter Catechism were given him. He now had what was regarded as a good library for a young man and he applied himself to the reading and study of these books, in the evenings and other periods of spare time. The testament was frequently taken to the field when plowing, in order that he might learn to read a verse or two, while the team was resting, or get a neighbor, passing on the road, to read it for him. The reading of the testament soon awakened a desire to be a teacher and preacher, and this greatly increased his interest in the study of that book.

He learned to sing from his mother, who greatly enjoyed whiling away spare hours on the Sabbath, singing the songs they used to sing in slavery times. The only help of a teacher, that he enjoyed was a period of three months, to enable him to read the Bible aloud correctly. This instruction was given only on Sabbath afternoons, and for it he had to cut and split for the teacher 250 oak rails.

THE MAN WHO BUILT THE ARBOR

The story of the incidents, that prepared the way and providentially led him into the ministry, is as novel and interesting as the one relating to his method of learning the alphabet.

When he had learned to read portions of the Testament and Catechism there were no meetings held in his neighborhood on the Sabbath, for the religious instruction of the colored people. He had a good voice and loved to sing. He had experienced as much joy and delight in learning to read the Bible, as many do, when they learn to play a musical instrument. He longed for an opportunity to read the Bible for others.

This yearning first took the form of a prayer, that God would provide for them a church or place for meeting. When this prayer had been offered a few times, at the foot of an oak tree in the timber he told others of his earnest desire for a church; and proposed to some friends, that they unite with him in building an arbor in the timber for a meeting place. This proposal was not taken very seriously, and yet none of his friends cared to oppose it. A day was finally appointed and all, who were interested, were requested to meet at the place selected for the arbor, and help to build it.

On the morning of that day, he went alone to the appointed place, which was near the oak tree at the foot of which he had before knelt in prayer, and by noon he had cut and erected the frame. Another friend arrived in the afternoon and assisted to cover it with branches of trees and supply it with seats.

On the day following, which was the Sabbath, the colored people of the neighborhood assembled to see the new arbor and enjoy a meeting. Now it happened that no one present had ever led a meeting, and the first question to be settled was, "who should lead the meeting?" Every one, that was asked to lead it, insisted, "the man who built the arbor" must serve as leader of the meeting.

Young Homer accepted the situation and led the meeting in the best manner possible. The exercises consisted of a prayer, the reading of a familiar passage from the Bible, some remarks by the leader and others, and the singing from memory of a few plantation melodies, such as "Kentucky Home," Swanee River", and "The Angels Are Coming to Carry Me Home."

At the second meeting, which was held on the following Sabbath, the people were formed into a class for instruction in the Bible and catechism, and Homer was chosen to be the leader. This was the organization of the Sunday school for that neighborhood.

At this meeting Homer offered prayer the first time in the presence of others; and it happened in this way. When he called on the friend, who led in prayer at the first meeting to do so again, he politely declined, saying: "Homer you lead in prayer, yourself."

A TEACHER, ELDER AND PREACHER

This arbor, which was the tiny beginning of the Beaver Dam church, was built in 1873, the year after he became of age. The next year this place was visited by Rev. Charles W. Stewart, and it then became one of his regular monthly appointments. Homer was again appointed Bible teacher and leader of the meetings, on the other Sabbaths.

In 1875 a church house or meeting place was built of saplings, near the old arbor, that continued to be used for many years.

In 1881 he was elected as the first elder of the church, and in 1887 was appointed a Catechist. Encouraged by these recognitions and duties he secured a good library of religious books including a Bible dictionary and a Webster. He read many of them with great profit, and was soon recognized as an intelligent and valuable instructor of the people. The Bible and the shorter Catechism, the one containing all of Bible truth and the other, a brief compend of Bible doctrine, were the two books that were studied most and proved most helpful.

REV. WILEY HOMER

In 1893 he was licensed to preach by the Presbytery of Choctaw and assigned the pastoral care of Beaver Dam and Hebron churches. On Sept. 28, 1895, by the same Presbytery, meeting at Oak Hill Academy, now known as the Alice Lee Memorial, he was ordained to the full work of the gospel ministry. He continued to serve Beaver Dam, his old home church, until Oct. 1, 1912, when, after a pastorate of twenty years, he was honorably retired from the active work of the gospel ministry. In 1904 he secured the erection of a commodious chapel at Grant that, during the next five years, served also as the most convenient place for holding the neighborhood school. After serving Hebron about ten years on alternate Sabbaths, in connection with Beaver Dam, he relinquished that field and served Sandy Branch and Horse Prairie, each a short period.

When the Presbytery of Kiamichi met in the new chapel at Grant, in April 1905, he conducted the Bible lesson for the entire Sunday school, as had been his custom ever since the early days. The writer was pleasantly surprised and profoundly impressed, by his scholarly and highly instructive management of it, and the many useful, practical lessons he endeavored to impress.

THE POWER OF THE BIBLE

Wiley Homer is a good practical illustration of what the Bible is intended to do for all men. If he were asked, what book, in the process of his self-education, had proved most valuable to him, he would unhesitatingly reply, "the Bible." His prayer in regard to it has been that of David in the 119th Psalm, "Let my heart be sound in thy statutes," and his testimony, that of David in the 19th Psalm, "The law of the Lord is perfect, converting the soul; the testimony of the Lord is sure making wise the simple. The statutes of the Lord are right, rejoicing the heart, the commandment of the Lord is pure, enlightening the eyes."

If he were to name the next most helpful book, it would be, The Shorter Catechism, with the statement on its first page, that, "The chief end of man is to glorify God, and to enjoy him forever."

The private study of the Bible and Catechism prepared him for lifelong usefulness as a teacher, discovered to him and his people his divine call to the ministry and enabled him to do the most important work of his life. He has been a faithful and efficient teacher of these two books, but of these only, to all the people and, as a result, he has become recognized as their spiritual leader.

The habit of private study, formed while learning to read the Bible, fitted him to search for knowledge in other fields of literature, and he has thus become one of the most intelligent, highly respected and successful citizens of the community in which he lives.

He has been an ardent friend and promoter of education among his people. When in 1889, it was decided to make the school at Oak Hill an industrial institution, he donated two head of cattle to start the herd. He has ever since taken a personal interest in the welfare of that institution. During recent years, he has made one or two visits each year, for the purpose of delivering special lectures and sermons to the young people gathered there. He thus brought to them the encouragement of his own word and example, in solving the problems of their education and lifework.

A COMMISSIONER TO THE GENERAL ASSEMBLY, SIX TIMES

He has enjoyed the unusual distinction of having been chosen a commissioner and to have represented his Presbytery in the General Assembly, five times during the last fourteen years as a minister, and once before as a ruling elder, making six times in 24 years. The times and places of these meetings were as follows: In 1889, New York; in 1899, Minneapolis; in 1901, Philadelphia; in 1903, Los Angeles; in 1905, Winona Lake, Ind.; in 1913, Atlanta, Georgia. In attending these great meetings he has passed over the entire length and breadth of this land. To appreciate the unusual character of this privilege and honor it is merely necessary to state the fact, that the eminent man, who was chosen Moderator of the Assembly at Atlanta in 1913, Rev. John Timothy Stone, D. D. of Chicago, was attending the Assembly on that occasion, the first time as a commissioner; and Rev. Charles W. Stewart, the worthy founder of Presbyterianism among the Choctaw Freedmen, never so much as got there once.

These frequent voluntary recognitions, on the part of his brethren in the Presbytery, suggest the power of leadership he has modestly, but always exercised among them. His brethren have found him a wise and prudent counselor, and an unselfish helper; and he has always been held in the highest esteem by them.

A LIFE-LONG LEADER OF THE CHURCH HE FOUNDED

He has been a man of strong and positive convictions and a persevering worker for the moral and spiritual uplift of his people. He learned from his own early experience as a slave, the trials and urgent needs of his people and, as the way became clear before him, he consecrated himself unreservedly to the promotion of their welfare.

As a preacher he has emphasized the necessity of repentance and forgiveness of sins, willing obedience to all the commands of Christ, and the joyous rewards of faithful service. As he surveys the progress of recent years, he sees the fulfilment of Isaiah's prediction, "The people, that walked in darkness, have seen a great light, they that dwelt in the land of the shadow of death, upon them hath the light shined."

Thirty years have now passed, since he began to hold the ever memorable meetings, in the little arbor in the timber. Ever since that date he has been the faithful Bible instructor of all the people, during the lesson hour of the Sunday school, and the resident pastor of the Presbyterian church for twenty years. The cozy chapel, and the good congregation of happy christian people, that regularly meet there for worship and Bible study, are visible reminders of his consecrated genius and unselfish devotion to the best interests of his people.

"Dare to do right, dare to be true,
You have a work that no other can do."
"Since God is God and right is right,
Right the day shall win;
To doubt would be disloyalty,
To falter would be sin."

Wiley Homer and Laney Colbert were married in 1867 and their family consisted of ten children, of whom five died in childhood and youth. Those that are living are Susan, Mary Shoals, Hattie Lewis, Sarah Williams and Lincoln.

In 1890, after the death of Laney, he married Rhody Tutt; and in 1906, after her decease, Lizzie Homer.

REV. WILEY HOMER 369

In October 1912, he was granted by the Presbytery, an honorable retirement from the performance of the public duties required of the active ministry. As the sunset of life approaches, and the shadows lengthen toward the closing day, he enjoys the consciousness of a well spent life, as a source of comfort and consolation to sustain and strengthen, until the recording angel shall proclaim, the gracious benediction, "Well done good and faithful servant, enter thou into the joy of thy Lord."

HAYSTACK MEETING

The use of the shadow of the oak tree, and later of the arbor near it, as a place for prayer and worship, reminds one of the historic prayer meeting that was held near Williamstown, in 1806, when Samuel J. Mills, and four other students of Williams college, Newell, Nott, Hall and Judson, met in the shadow of a haystack and united in prayer, that God would fit them and prepare the way for them to carry the gospel into heathen lands.

After making two tours to the southwest as far as New Orleans, distributing and selling Bibles and organizing Bible societies, Mills made the suggestion, that led to the organization of the American Bible society in New York, May 11, 1816; and to the Synod of New York, the plan of educating negroes to carry the gospel to Africa. In 1817 he was sent as a missionary to Western Africa, including Sierra Leone. He died on the homeward voyage and like his friend Adoniram Judson, who went to farther India and translated the Bible for the Burmese, was buried in the sea.

XLV

TRIBUTES TO OTHER MINISTERS AND ELDERS

BUTLER. — COLBERT. — GLADMAN. — BRIDGES.—STARKS.— MEADOWS. — AND ELDERS CRITTENDEN. —SHOALS. — FOLSOM. — BUTLER.

"Walk about Zion and go round about her; tell the towers thereof. Mark ye well her bulwarks, consider her palaces; that ye may tell it to the generation following."
—David.

REV. WILLIAM BUTLER

"The kindly word, how far it goes along life's way!
The kindly smile, how it lights up a sad, gray day;
The kindly deed, how it repays the doer."
—Mary D. Brine.

REV. William Butler (B. 1859), pastor of St. Paul Presbyterian church at Eagletown, and of Forest church near Red River south of Millerton, is a native of the community in which he still lives. His parents, Abraham and Nellie Butler, were the slaves of Pitchlyn and Howell, Choctaws; and William was about seven, when freedom was accorded the family in 1866. His home and work as a minister until recently have been in localities remote from the railway and good schools. The short period of one and a half months was all the time he ever went to school. He learned to read by a regular attendance at Sabbath school, and by private study at the fireside. The Bible and the

WILLIAM BUTLER

Shorter Catechism were the books that occupied his spare time and attention. As a natural result, he became a christian and united with the church at an early age.

In 1885, at the age of twenty-six, he was ordained an elder in the St. Paul Presbyterian church. He then began to read the Bible to the congregation and to hold religious meetings. While preparing himself for the work then in hand, he was led to see the great need of more teachers and preachers for the colored people, and, believing he could render efficient service as a minister, he undertook a special course of reading and instruction under Rev. John Sleeper, his pastor, and later of Rev. E. G. Haymaker, superintendent of Oak Hill Academy, instructors who lived 12 and 35 miles distant, respectively.

In 1894 he was enrolled as a candidate for the ministry under the Presbytery of Choctaw. Three years later he was licensed by the Presbytery of Kiamichi and appointed the stated supply of St. Paul and Forest churches. He has continued to serve these two congregations, faithfully and acceptably ever since that date, a period now of sixteen years. His ordination occurred in 1902. Other fields, that he developed and served for short periods are, Bethany, two years; Mount Gilead, one year; and Mount Pleasant, one year.

A WINNER OF SOULS

Mr. Butler is a man, who experienced a hard struggle in early life, in the effort to train himself for his life's work, as a minister and farmer. He has overcome many of these difficulties in a manner, that is very praiseworthy and commendable.

He is a man, who carries with him a happy, hopeful spirit, and a countenance full of good cheer. Seeing the need of a religious leader among the people of his home community, he decided to fit himself to supply that need, and has done so hitherto in an efficient and admirable manner. To win souls to Christ and instruct them aright from the word of God, have been his aims during his ministry. He has been to the people an example in righteousness, and has labored with faith and zeal in the vineyard of the Lord.

His annual visits to Oak Hill Academy during term time, were always anticipated with considerable interest. They were made the occasion for special evangelistic services, followed with an opportunity for decisions; and many times his heart was gladdened at the close of the sermon, by seeing more than a dozen of the young people manifest their decision to live a Christian life.

The people, whom he serves regularly, have shown their appreciation of his efficient and long continued work among them, by according to him a loyal and constant support. He has always lived in the wilderness far removed from the railway, notwithstanding the fact the Frisco railway in 1902 passed through the country, lying between Eagletown on the north and Forest church on the south. He has always had a pony circuit, of two or more rural churches, widely separated. The faithful and acceptable service rendered these widely distant churches, makes him a good representative of the itinerant work of Parson Stewart, his pioneer predecessor.

The following lines by Hastings, are an appropriate prayer for all, who like Bro. Butler faithfully and patiently minister to those, who dwell in the wilderness.

"O thou, who in the wilderness
The sheep, without a shepherd, didst bless,
Oh, bless thy servants, who proclaim
In every place thy wondrous name.

May voices in the wilderness,
Still with glad news the nations bless;
And, as of old, in deserts cry,
'Repent', God's kingdom draweth nigh."

REV. RICHARD D. COLBERT

Rev. Richard D. Colbert of Grant, is one of the young men, enlisted in the work of the church, by Parson Stewart. He attended Biddle University from October 1884 to June 1887, three years, when he returned home, on account of impaired health. Regaining his health after a few months, he became a teacher and taught school eleven years during the territorial period.

In the spring of 1897, he became a licentiate of the Presbytery of Kiamichi, and two years later was assigned the pastoral oversight of New Hope and Sandy Branch churches. He was ordained in 1903. Most of his ministerial labors have been devoted to Sandy Branch and Hebron churches, serving the latter until 1913. As a result of accidents that happened in making the journey to the Hebron church in 1911 he experienced the loss of an eye and other injuries that resulted in total blindness in 1913. He endeavored to make a good record as a teacher and preacher, and has served his generation faithfully.

REV. SAMUEL GLADMAN

Rev. Samuel Gladman, who died Jan. 11, 1913, at Eufaula, Okla, was a native of Westchester, Chester county, Pa. During the early seventies he went to western Texas and engaged in teaching. Sometime afterwards he was licensed and ordained to the work of the gospel ministry.

In 1896, when the Presbytery of Kiamichi was organized, he was enrolled as one of its charter members. He was then living at Atoka. During the next year he served New

Hope and Sandy Branch churches, but continued to reside in Atoka until 1900, when he located at Lukfata. Three years later he took charge of Bethany, near Wheelock, and in 1905, effected the organization of the church in the new town of Garvin. In 1910, he voluntarily resigned the work at Bethany and the office of stated clerk of the Presbytery, and located at Eufaula.

As a minister and lifelong teacher, he rendered a very helpful service to the various communities, in which he lived and labored.

REV. THOMPSON K. BRIDGES

Rev. Thompson K. Bridges, (B. Dec. 6, 1856), Lukfata, is a native of Ellisville, Jones county, Miss. He grew to manhood and received his early education at Claiborne, Jasper county. Later he attended the city school at Meridian, and then took a course in theology at Biddle university. He began to teach public school at the age of 21 in 1877, and taught fourteen years in Mississippi. In 1891, he located in Indian Territory, and has now taught sixteen years in Oklahoma. In 1899 he was licensed to preach by the Presbytery of Catawba and in April 1902 was ordained by the same Presbytery. His first ministerial labors were at Griffin, Indian Territory, where in 1903 he effected the organization of the Ebenezer church. The next year he continued to serve Ebenezer, but located at Lukfata, where he has since continued to serve as the stated supply of the Mount Gilead church, and teacher of the local school. He served two years, 1904 and 1905, as stated clerk of the Presbytery of Kiamichi.

Mr. Bridges has been a progressive teacher and minister. In his youth, he formed the habit of having a good book or paper always at hand to occupy his attention prof-

TRIBUTES TO OTHER MINISTERS 375

itably, whenever he had a spare moment. That habit of private study in spare moments has enabled him to keep abreast of the times, and the changes that have taken place in recent years, by the addition of new branches of study to the public school course. Ever since he began to render service to his people as a teacher, he has made a highly creditable record for efficiency and faithfulness. As he looks forward to the future it is full of hope and bright prospects.

He has never ceased to be grateful, for the benevolent aid, generously furnished him by the Presbyterian church and Sunday school at Purcell, Okla., while he was pursuing his theological studies at Biddle university. The persons, whose names are most associated with these grateful memories, are those of the pastor, Rev. S. G. Fisher, and two of the elders, Mr. Lotting and Will Blanchard. This generous aid, which made possible an education for the gospel ministry, has led the recipient ever since to feel, that he is under a special but very delightful obligation, to render to the church a faithful and efficient service, as long as he lives.

REV. WILLIAM J. STARKS

The Lord Jesus, who brought to the world the glad tidings of the gospel often finds his messengers in strange or unexpected places; and leads them, in remarkable ways to the accomplishment of his purposes. No one can tell, what is going on in the mind of a young man, brought under the influence of the divine Spirit; nor how deep the impressions, that may have been made upon the heart of those, who naturally seem most unlikely to become heralds of the gospel.

William J. Starks (born March 14, 1876), Garvin, is a native of Chambersburg, Pennsylvania. After completing the grammar course in the public school of that place, he prepared for college under special teachers.

The Falling Spring Presbyterian church of that city, maintained a mission, that was attended by white and black. Mr. J. M. McDowell, a white lawyer, was the superintendent of this mission. His special interest was awakened in young Starks, by the fact he committed the entire list of 107 questions and answers in the shorter catechism, in one week after a copy was placed in his hands. The superintendent proposed, he undertake special studies under him as his teacher. In 1897, he entered the college at Lincoln university and graduated from it in 1901, and from the Theological department in 1904.

After one year spent in mission work at Mercersburg, Pa., he became in 1905 the stated supply of the New Hope church at Frogville, and in 1908, also of Sandy Branch. On November 1, 1912, he became the successor of Rev. W. H. Carroll at Garvin.

During his residence of seven years at Frogville, he maintained a six months term of school every year in the chapel, serving the first five years as a mission teacher under our Freedmen's Board, and the last two as a teacher of public school. In September, 1910, he was elected stated clerk of the Presbytery of Kiamichi, and is still serving in that capacity. In October, 1910, he served as moderator of the synod of Canadian at Little Rock, Ark.

REV. PLANT SENIOR MEADOWS

Plant Senior Meadows, (Born Feb. 15, 1841) Shawneetown, is a native of Lewis county, Mo. At 17 in 1859, he was sold by the administrator of the Cecil Home, and a sugar planter at St. Mary's Parish, La., became his master. Here he was employed at various kinds of mechanical work, until

TRIBUTES TO ELDERS 377

he was accorded his freedom, at 26 in 1865. Mrs. Cecil taught him to read, and during this early period, he made the best possible use of his spare moments, by reading all the good books that were available. As soon as he was free, he became a teacher and in connection with ministerial duties taught twenty-two years in Texas, and since 1908, in Shawneetown, Okla.

On Nov. 10, 1867, he was licensed and in 1869, ordained to the full work of the gospel ministry, by the A. M. E. church of Texas. After 41 years of faithful service in that church, which included a term as presiding elder, in 1908 he located within the Presbytery of Kiamichi, Okla., and, becoming a member of it, was placed in charge of the Presbyterian church at Shawneetown. Bethany and Pleasant Hill have since been added to his field. He has made a good record and is still doing splendid work at 73.

OAK HILL PIONEERS

Henry Crittenden,	1830-1894.
Teena Crittenden	1831-1898.
John Ross Shoals	1849-1885.
Hattie Crittenden Shoals,	1850-1909.

Henry Crittenden and Teena Crittenden his wife, John Ross Shoals, his son-in-law and Hattie C. Shoals, his wife, all of whom were buried in the Crittenden Burying Ground near the old Crittenden pioneer home east of Valiant, were four of the six original members of the Oak Hill church in 1869.

During the last years of the slavery period, they lived in the neighborhood of Doaksville, and there enjoyed the occasional privilege of attending Sabbath afternoon meetings for the colored people, in the Choctaw Presbyterian church. These meetings were at first conducted, by Rev.

Cyrus Kingsbury and Mrs. Charles Stewart, wife of the storekeeper, and later by Parson Stewart. The instruction, given by the parson, consisted principally in reading selections from the Bible and shorter catechism. The rest of the time was spent in singing familiar hymns and giving testimonies. They became Presbyterians and formed a part of Parson Stewart's first congregation at that place.

When they were accorded their freedom about the year 1865, they chose their permanent location in the Oak Hill neighborhood, about fifteen miles eastward. Parson Stewart followed them, and began to hold occasional services at the home of Henry Crittenden. He became the first elder of the Oak Hill church, when it was organized in 1869, and during the remaining 25 years of his life rendered a zealous and faithful service.

Henry Crittenden enjoyed the reputation of being a "master mechanic." During the slavery period, he was trained as a blacksmith, tinsmith and carpenter, and later acquired the art of repairing jewelry. Soon after he located on the Crittenden land, he built a shop. His intelligence and skill as a workman enabled him to attract customers from long distances. He was industrious and economical, and accumulated savings more rapidly than any of his neighbors.

He was a firm believer in the Bible and a regular attendant at church. He encouraged the establishment of the Oak Hill Sunday school, of which J. Ross Shoals, his son-in-law in 1875, became the first teacher. He furnished most of the materials for the first frame school house in the Oak Hill district in 1878, and in 1887, when it was used in the erection of a larger building near the "Old Log House" and since known as Oak Hill Academy, he covered the deficit on the building estimated at $100.00.

MATT AND MRS. BROWN

THE TEACHERS, 1899
Photo by Mattie Hunter

HENRY CRITTENDEN

SIMON FOLSOM

ELIJAH BUTLER

MRS. PERKINS STEWART

REV. C. L. PERKINS

MRS. R. D. ARNOLI

JOHNSON W. SHOALS

JAMES G. SHOALS

ISAAC JOHNSON

He and Parson Stewart were the most influential of the Choctaw Freedmen, in securing the establishment of Oak Hill Academy, as a training school for teachers. He manifested his joy, not only on the day of its lowly establishment by Miss Hartford in February 1886, but at every successive enlargement of its work, while he lived. He knew better, than many of his fellow Freedmen, the value of youthful training, and was enthusiastic in his zeal, to have every family far and near take advantage of its open door. An early teacher, who frequently heard him, writes: "He was a dear, good old man, a remarkable man in many ways. His ability to read was quite limited, but his voice was splendid for service in meetings."

Teena Crittenden, his amiable wife, was as industrious and frugal in the home, as her husband, in the shop and on the farm. She was a devout christian, one that loved the Bible and enjoyed the privilege of having a place at the meeting for prayer. She died at 67 in 1898, having outlived her husband four years.

John Ross Shoals, in addition to the Sabbath afternoon meetings at Doaksville, took some additional night work, that fitted him to become the first Sunday school teacher in the Oak Hill neighborhood in 1875, and an efficient elder in the church. He died at 36 in 1885, leaving to Hattie, his wife, the responsibility of raising and educating a family of nine children.

Hattie Crittenden Shoals inherited the industrious and religious traits of her parents, in or near whose home she always lived. She surpassed many of her people, in the intelligent forethought she manifested in all her plans, and in the ability to exercise a correct judgment of men and conditions.

"I mean to have my children begin life, at a higher step than I did." This was an ambition oft expressed in the presence of her children. She succeeded in giving all of them a good education, by sending them first to Oak Hill and then to other institutions, including Biddle university, Scotia Seminary, Tuskeegee and the Iowa State Agricultural college.

SIMON FOLSOM

Simon Folsom, one of the first elders of the Forest Presbyterian church is now one of the oldest living representatives of the slavery period. Nancy Brashears, his third and present wife, enjoys the distinction of having been the most influential of the early leaders in effecting the organization of that church. He became an elder in 1887. After twenty-six years of faithful service under very unfavorable circumstances, he is still trying "to hold up for the faith."

In 1901 he enjoyed the privilege of being one of the commissioners of the Presbytery of Kiamichi, and attended the meeting of the General Assembly in Philadelphia. Many of the good things heard and fine impressions received on that occasion, have never been forgotten, and they have furnished him interesting themes, for many subsequent addresses. Though unable to read, he quotes the Bible as one very familiar with that sacred book. He inherited a good memory, that serves him well in public address, and he is always happy and ready when it comes his turn to "speak in meeting." His messages are always notes of joy and gladness, and the ebb and flow of his voice in prayer often seem like the chanting of a sacred melody.

He was an ardent supporter of the Oak Hill school and two of his sons, Samuel and David, both now deceased, were among the brightest and most promising, that have attended that institution. He has been for many years the coffin maker, for the people of his community, and both of these boys became skilled carpenters. Samuel, after completing the grammar course at Oak Hill, spent two years 1903-5 at Biddle University and served one year as a teacher at Oak Hill. His skill as a workman and ability to serve as a foreman of the carpenters, made it possible for the superintendent in 1910, to erect Elliott Hall by the labor of the students and patrons of the Academy. Both worked faithfully on this building and died soon after its completion, during the early months of 1912. Both were members and Samuel an elder of the Oak Hill church.*

ELIJAH BUTLER

Elijah Butler, Lukfata, was an uncle of Rev. William Butler. He was one of the early leaders in christian work in what is now the northeast part of McCurtain county. In 1878, when St. Paul church was organized at Eagletown, he was ordained as one of its first elders, and became an active christian worker. A few years later he moved to Lukfata, and when the Presbyterian church of that locality was organized, July 26, 1885, he and his son, Elisha Butler, were chosen as two of the first elders of that church.

Elijah Butler, like Apollos of old, was a man, "fervent in spirit," and was teaching others of the people, what he knew of God and the Bible, when Parson Stewart first visited the Lukfata neighborhood. His zeal and faithfulness, in magnifying the call of God to him to be a christian leader among his people, suggested to them the propriety of naming their church, at the time of its organization "Mount Gilead," the home of the prophet, Elijah, in his honor. As an elder and christian worker, he "kept the faith" and "finished his course with joy."

---

*Simon died May 17, 1914,

XLVI
THE SYNOD OF CANADIAN

FIRST MEETING AT OKLAHOMA.—SECOND AT OAK HILL.—AT GARVIN IN 1912.—AN UNINTENTIONAL INJUSTICE.—GRATEFUL RECOGNITION.—WOMEN'S SYNODICAL MISSIONARY SOCIETY.—DEPENDENT CONDITION OF THE CHURCHES. — UNSYMPATHETIC ISOLATION. — EDUCATIONAL INSTITUTIONS.—POPULAR MEETINGS.

"Christ loved the church and gave himself for it; that he might sanctify and cleanse it with the washing of water by the word. That he might present it unto himself a glorious church."—Paul.

CONSTITUTED IN 1907

THE following is the enabling act of the General Assembly at Columbus, Ohio, May 24, 1907, establishing the synod of Canadian, to consist of the colored Presbyterian ministers and churches in the states of Arkansas and Oklahoma.

IT IS HEREBY ENACTED BY THE GENERAL ASSEMBLY

"That the Synod of Canadian is hereby erected and constituted, to consist of the Presbyteries of White River, Kiamichi and Rendall; and the synod of Canadian, as thus constituted, shall meet in the meeting place of the First Colored Presbyterian congregation in Oklahoma City, on Tuesday, the 8th day of October, 1907, at 7:30 o'clock p. m.; that the Rev. W. L. Bethel shall preside until the election of a Moderator, that the Rev. W. D. Feaster preach the opening sermon and that elder J. H. A. Brazleton act as temporary clerk, until the election of a stated and permanent clerk."

THE SYNOD OF CANADIAN 383

The assembly at this time enlarged the boundary of the Presbytery of Kiamichi so as to include the south half of the state of Oklahoma and established the Presbytery of Rendall to include the north half of it, the Canadian river, and below its mouth the Arkansas river, forming the boundary line between them. It also enlarged the boundary of White River Presbytery to include all the colored Presbyterian ministers and churches in the synod, or state, of Arkansas.

FIRST MEETING AT OKLAHOMA

The first meeting of the synod of Canadian, was held in the colored Methodist church of Oklahoma City. The Presbytery of Kiamichi was represented by 3 ministers and one elder, namely, Rev. R. E. Flickinger, and Elder Jack A. Thomas, representing Oak Hill church at Valliant, Rev. W. H. Carroll, Garvin, and Rev. T. K. Bridges, Lukfata.

The Presbytery of Rendall was represented by Rev. W. L. Bethel of Oklahoma, who served as moderator, John S. May of Watonga; William T. Wilson, Reevesville; Oscar A. Williams, M. D. Okmulgee; Samuel J. Grier, Guthrie; and elder J. H. A. Brazleton of Oklahoma, who served as temporary clerk.

The Presbytery of White River was not represented by any ministers or elders.

The Oak Hill church was also represented by Miss Malinda A. Hall, representing the Women's Missionary and Christian Endeavor societies, and by Solomon H. Buchanan, representing the Sunday school and Oak Hill Aid society.

At the first meeting, held on Tuesday evening, Oct. 8th, a special address was delivered by Rev. William A. Provine, D. D., representing the Board of Publication of the Cumberland Presbyterian church at Nashville, Tennessee. Another visitor, who was present with him at this first meeting, also delivered a short address in behalf of the cause he represented.

Inasmuch as White River Presbytery was not represented by a minister or elder, the sentiment prevailed, that those present did not form a quorum, and nothing further was done save to adjourn until the next morning.

At the meetings held on Wednesday morning and afternoon considerable indisposition to organize was manifested by most of those participating in the discussions, because the colored people had not been previously consulted as to their wishes, before the Synod of Canadian was established by the General Assembly. As nothing further was accomplished the meeting was adjourned a third time.

On Wednesday evening Oct. 9th, after a sermon by Rev. R. E. Flickinger, the Synod of Canadian was organized. Rev. William L. Bethel was elected Moderator and elder J. H. A. Brazleton, clerk. The principal business transacted was the enrollment of delegates, the arrangement of the standing committees and the appointment of a special committee, to prepare a set of standing rules to be submitted at the next meeting.

SECOND MEETING AT OAK HILL

The second meeting of the Synod of Canadian was held at Oak Hill Academy Oct. 1-4, 1908. The Presbytery of Rendall was represented by Rev. W. L. Bethel, who delivered the opening sermon, and elder J. H. A. Brazleton of Oklahoma. The Presbytery of White River was represented only by Rev. W. A. Byrd, Ph. D., of Cotton Plant, Ark., and he was elected Moderator. Rev. William H. Carroll of Garvin was elected stated clerk, after the adoption of the standing rules presented by Rev. R. E. Flickinger. The meetings,

THE SYNOD OF CANADIAN 385

which included one in behalf of the Women's work, were continued over Sabbath.

In 1909 the Synod met at Okmulgee, Oklahoma. In 1910 it met at Little Rock, Arkansas, and Rev. W. J. Starks of Frogville served as moderator. At this meeting a resolution was adopted establishing a Synodical Women's Missionary society by the appointment of Mrs. C. S. Mebane of Hot Springs, president, and Miss Cassie Hollingsworth of Little Rock,, Ark., secretary. The next meeting of synod was held at Hot Springs, Ark., Oct. 6, 1911, and the foregoing resolution was re-approved.

AT GARVIN IN 1912

On Oct. 3, 1912, the Synod of Canadian met in the new Presbyterian church at Garvin, Okla., and the opening sermon was delivered by Rev. C. S. Mebane, D. D., of Hot Springs, in the absence of the moderator, Rev. A. M. Caldwell. Rev. Virgil McPherson of Camden, Ark., was elected moderator and Rev. M. L. Bethel of Oklahoma, temporary clerk.

The representation and attendance at this meeting, the sixth one, was greater than at any previous one. It consisted of 15 ministers and 5 elders as follows:

C. S. Mebane, A. E. Rankin and Virgil McPherson from the Presbytery of White River.

Martin L. Bethel, the Synodical Sunday school missionary, and J. S. May from the Presbytery of Rendall.

Wiley Homer, T. K. Bridges, R. E. Flickinger, William Butler, R. D. Colbert, W. J. Starks, W. H. Carroll, the stated clerk, N. S. Alverson, P. S. Meadows, J. A. Loving, and elders, Calvin Burris, St. Paul, Solomon H. Buchanan, Oak Hill; Lee V. Bibbs, Forest; T. H. Murchison, Garvin, and William Harris, Hebron; from the Presbytery of Kiamichi.

13

At this meeting Rev. R. E. Flickinger presented his fifth and last report on the work of the Board of Missions for Freedmen. He had performed a leading part in effecting the organization of the Synod, at a time when it lacked a legal quorum, because of the previous order of the General Assembly establishing it. The General Assembly at its next meeting approved the organization and made it effective.

GRATEFUL RECOGNITION

The following words of grateful recognition have been taken from the minutes of the synod of 1912, the first year they have been printed.

Rev. R. E. Flickinger, superintendent of Alice Lee Elliott School, in a lengthy and very pathetic address, made known to synod his intention of giving up his charge and returning to his home in Iowa.

The period of eight years which he spent in our midst was ended with many deep regrets on the part of all with and for whom he labored.

"His work as superintendent of Oak Hill Academy, now called Alice Lee Elliott school, will be long remembered, for he secured and permanently established the Oak Hill Farm, and developed industrial features in the school far beyond what was even expected. We cherish for him the feelings of gratitude and appreciation, that belong to the unselfish worker he was."

WOMEN'S SYNODICAL MISSIONARY SOCIETY

The Women's Missionary meeting at synod in Garvin in 1912 was the first one at which a complete organization was effected. It is therefore of historic interest.

The meeting was opened by Mrs. C. S. Mebane of Hot Springs, convener, and she was later elected president. Mrs.

W. H. Carroll was elected secretary, Mrs. W. J. Stark, treasurer, Mrs. Emma P. White president of the Young People's Work, and Miss Bertha L. Ahrens, corresponding secretary. Others who were present and enrolled as members were Mrs. M. L. Bethel, Mrs. Martha Folsom, Mrs. L. Walker, Mrs. Nellie Milton, Sarah Milton, Ledocia Milton, Mrs. Fidelia Murchison, Mrs. Garfield Lewis, Mrs. Ed. Thomas, Mrs. Violet Shelton, Emma Beams, and Emma L. Carroll.

The address at their popular meeting in the evening was delivered by Rev. A. E. Rankin of Crockett, Texas; and a paper from Mrs. D. J. Wallace of Okmulgee was read by Mrs. M. L. Bethel. Muskogee was chosen as the place for the synodical meeting in 1913.

DEPENDENT CONDITION OF THE CHURCHES

The synod in 1913 the sixth year after its organization, represents three Presbyteries, that include all our colored ministers and churches in the states of Arkansas and Oklahoma, and, since 1910, those also that are in the east half of Texas. Its roll includes 42 ministers and 46 churches, whose membership of 1269 contributed to all local purposes, such as maintenance of buildings and pastoral support, the sum of $3,212.00. This is an average of less than $70.00 for each church in the synod and less than $48.00 each, for the churches in Oklahomo and east Texas. This statement indicates, that the ministers serving these churches are almost wholly dependent for their income, on what they receive from other sources, than the dependent congregations they serve, and, that only by the practice of the most rigid economy, in personal expenses, is it possible for them to make ends meet and maintain a good name in their respective communities.

POPULAR EVENING MEETINGS

The evening meetings of synod and a part of the afternoon sessions may be made very profitable to the local congregation, by arranging before hand for special addresses on the part of representatives of the Boards, or members of the synod. There are some causes, such as education, evangelism, the Freedmen and Women's work that are of popular interest, and a stirring address on these subjects is always appreciated. Such addresses are a means of instruction and serve to awaken popular enthusiasm.

Some synods have adopted the plan of holding an annual Sunday school convention during the evening and day preceding the meeting of the synod. These endeavor to bring before the young Sunday school workers, the very best speakers available, on the subjects to be discussed.

The arrangements for the popular addresses should be made several weeks in advance, so the speakers may be prepared and the people be duly notified.

BENEDICTION

"May the God of peace that brought again from the dead our Lord Jesus, the great shepherd of the sheep, through the blood of the everlasting covenant, make you perfect in every good work to do his will, working in you, that which is well pleasing in his sight through Jesus Christ; to whom be dominion and glory for ever and ever. Amen.

REV. R. D. COLBERT

REV. M. L. BETHEL

THE SWEET POTATO FIELD, 1911
Looking north from the Frisco railway; the boys' temporary hall at the right.

TWO SETS OF PORTABLE ROOFS FOR SWEET POTATO PITS

1. A set of roofs set aside on their edges for the summer.
2. A set as they appear when set over a pit The ends are closed during Winter. Looking northeast toward the rear of Elliott Hall.

PART IV

THE BIBLE IN THE PUBLIC SCHOOL AND NATION

The two following chapters, relating to the supreme importance of reading the Bible daily in every public school of the land, are a supplement to the brief discussion of this subject, that appears in the introductory part of this volume.

"Truth crushed to earth shall rise again,—
The eternal years of God are hers;
But Error, wounded, writhes in pain,
And dies among his worshippers."

"Truth forever on the scaffold;
Wrong forever on the throne;
Yet that scaffold sways the future;
And behind the dim unknown,
Standeth God, within the shadow,
Keeping watch above his own."

Queen Victoria said to the King of Siam: "England owes her greatness to this book—The Open Bible."

The Bible, and the public school to make known to all the children its moral principles and religious truths, have brought liberty, greatness and enlargement to the United States of America and Great Britain.

These two instrumentalities—the open Bible and public school—will bring the needed blessings of intelligence, happiness and prosperity to the people of the United States of Mexico, of Central and South America, when they are accorded a fair chance.

XLVII
THE PUBLIC SCHOOL

AN OUTGROWTH OF THE REFORMATION.—PORTO RICO.—MISSION SCHOOLS.—COLONIAL SCHOOLS.—MASSACHUSETTS AND CONNECTICUT.—NEW YORK AND PENNSYLVANIA.—THE BIBLE, THE STANDARD OF MORALITY.—RISE AND FALL OF INTOLERANCE.—DANIEL WEBSTER.—THE BIBLE, THE FREEDMAN'S BEST BOOK.—THE CHURCH, SUNDAY SCHOOL, PUBLIC SCHOOL.—ENCOURAGING MOVEMENTS.

"Education is the cheap defense of a Nation."—Garfield.

"Wisdom is the principal thing, therefore get wisdom. The fear of the Lord is the beginning of wisdom."—Solomon.

THE public school is the general and permanent agency for the education and uplift of the colored people. Religious and independent schools may do a splendid work in their several localities, but the public school is intended to be state-wide. It alone reaches the masses of colored children, and it should receive its due share of the public funds. The fact that they have not received anything like a fair share of the public funds, for their equipment and support, has already been stated. This, to a great extent, is an act of injustice. Conditions however are gradually improving. They are made better as a good use is made of present educational facilities, and earnest appeal is made for more and better ones. A vast amount of self-sacrificing work, on the part of teachers and parents, is needed to bring the schools of the Freedmen up to their proper standard, and to secure them, where they are still needed both in city and rural district.

The Freedman alone cannot do all that is needed, to provide adequate educational facilities for all his people; but there is so much that may be done, in the way of awakening local interest, supplying local deficiencies, and appealing for more and better equipment, as to enlist the united and persistent co-operation of all intelligent, public spirited Freedmen.

AN OUTGROWTH OF THE REFORMATION

The public school system, in the United States, is an outgrowth, or by-product of the Protestant Reformation of the sixteenth century in Europe. Harvard college was established at Cambridge, near Boston, in 1639, less than twenty years after the first arrival of the Pilgrim Fathers. Its object was to provide a supply of trained ministers and christian teachers, to meet the rapidly growing needs of the colony.

The Society for the Propagation of the Gospel in Foreign parts, organized in London, England, in 1701, aided the colonists in the establishment of free schools, by sending them donations and supplies of bibles and testaments. Christian teachers were employed in these free schools and two of the text books used were the Bible and the New England primer. This primer was illustrated with Bible pictures and contained the shorter catechism.

These colonial free schools of New England were gradually extended to the other colonies, but not without calling forth some opposition in some of them, especially where there was opposition to the use of the Bible. This fact has been rendered quite memorable, by the rather unenviable

THE PUBLIC SCHOOL 393

remark of Governor Berkeley of Virginia in 1670, to the effect, "I thank God, there are no free schools in Virginia." The scattered condition of the population rendered difficult and greatly retarded the progress of free schools in the south. Planters were often widely separated, and many of them preferred to send their children away to school, or employ a private tutor for them. They did not care to provide schools for the Negroes.

When, by the adoption of the Constitution the colonies became states, the protection of religion and encouragement of education were left as they had been, as matters to be considered by the legislatures of the several states. As one state after another has been admitted to the Union, extending it over a vast extent of country, a system of public education has been adopted in each, ranging from the rural school to the state university. The system in every state is quite complete and more or less efficient to accomplish its objects. The entire system is due to the presence of the Bible in our land, and especially during the formative period of our government. The states have deemed it necessary to train the young and rising generation in the interest of good government and progress.

As the church of the Reformation in Europe, and of our forefathers in New England, found it necessary to establish academies, colleges and theological seminaries, in order to train a constantly increasing supply of christian teachers, statesmen and ministers, the states have realized that it is their duty to maintain public and high schools, in order to have an intelligent and prosperous citizenship; and to maintain normal schools and universities, in order to provide a sufficient number of professional teachers, legislators, jurists and efficient captains of industry.

The system of public education in all the states is one, of which every citizen of the land may well be proud, and endeavor to take every possible advantage of it as teachers, patrons and pupils.

PORTO RICO 1898-1913

A splendid illustration of its inestimable value has just been received from Porto Rico. In 1898 when the United States received the transfer of Porto Rico from Spain, it had been for centuries under the control of Romanism. There was then only one building on the island, specially erected for school purposes, and more than eighty per cent of the population could neither read nor write; and only 26,000 children had been enrolled as attending school. So rapid has been the progress toward enlightenment and a better civilization under Protestant American rule, that at the end of fifteen years there are 40 school buildings and 162,000 children are enrolled as attending school; and the number of the illiterate has been reduced from 80 to 14 per cent.

THE BIBLE AND CHRISTIAN TEACHERS

One is now ready to inquire, "Wherein does our splendid system of public education differ from that provided by the various Protestant denominations, in their mission schools, academies, colleges and universities?

Both are essential to the well-being of the state. They are two strong pillars that, supplementing and standing near each other, support the power and promote the material prosperity of the state. Their mutual relation is aptly expressed, by the sentiment of the two brothers on the shield of Kentucky, "United we stand, divided we fall." They look so nearly alike in buildings and equipment, the passing observer sees little or no difference in their outward appearance.

Nevertheless there is often a difference in their objects and products, which has already been noted, and in the means employed to accomplish these objects. This difference is fundamental. It is found in the law of their establishment.

In the admirable system of public education in the state of Iowa, which is second to none in the land for the goodness and greatness of its beneficent results, there is found the following statute, and it is a fair illustration of similar statutes in other states.

"The Bible shall not be excluded from any public school or institution in this state, nor shall any pupil be required to read it contrary to the wishes of his parents or guardian." Sec. 1764.

This statute takes it for granted the Bible is in the schools, and that is excellent; it has also a concession and the latter often prevails. Many Jews read only the old Testament, and many Catholics out of regard for the pope, a foreign potentate, think they ought not to read any part of the Bible. The state is a secular power and the result, of this concession to religious freedom, is, that the Bible and the Christian teacher, in many localities, are not regarded as essential features of its educational work.

This leaves the moral character and relative value of our public schools, to a considerable extent, to the caprice of those who are in the majority or authority, as directors and teachers in any particular community. In christian communities they are invariably found exerting a christian influence.

The Bible and the christian teacher are essential for the accomplishment of the greatest good. These are seldom separated, and when they are found together in the public school, it becomes a fountain of elevating christian influences. This privilige is enjoyed by many of our communities, where the supply of christian teachers is equal to the demand.

This discussion of the public school has been included here, for the general knowledge of christian families among the colored people. Since the enactment of laws, limiting the teachers in the public schools of the colored people, to those of the "colored persuasion," there is now, and will continue to be, an ever increasing demand for capable christian teachers. Christian teachers come from christian homes and christian schools.

COLONIAL SCHOOLS

The historic facts, showing that the open Bible has been the corner-stone of the American public school system, have been so interesting and suggestive to the author, as to lead him to take the initiative, in effecting and maintaining a local Bible society in Fonda, and to make the distribution of the Scriptures among the people, a special feature of his ministry there, and later at Oak Hill Academy. The hope is indulged, that the following facts, relating to the place accorded the Bible in the schools of the colonies, will prove of interest to every reader, especially among the Freedmen.

Our fore fathers and the stalwart statesmen of their day, were not led astray by the "higher" or more properly called destructive criticism and infidelity, that is now permeating much of the literature of our day to the great injury of all who are influenced by it. Indebted to the Scriptures for their ideas of "life, liberty and the pursuit of happiness," and, prizing them as the foundation of their civil and ecclesiastical privileges, they manifested both their sense of obligation to them and dependence upon them, by mak-

THE PUBLIC SCHOOL 397

ing them the corner stone of every institution they established. The word of God in their hand, like a pillar of cloud by day and of fire by night, led them to locate in this land, awakened in them the spirit of heroism amid all their privations and sufferings, and served as their common guide and comforter, in all their struggles and progress.

If there are any who have the right to judge and to have their judgment respected, as to the nature of the education needed in this republic, surely those men of sagacity, patriotism, piety and comprehensive statesmanship, who founded both the system of education and the Republic, are among the number.

During the Colonial period the towns were little republics, with the Bible for their foundation, and their schools were established for general instruction in that book. The exclusion of the Bible from those early schools would have been repugnant to their founders. They regarded the Bible not merely as an authoritative book in all matters of conscience, but as the charter of their liberty and their guide to the independent ownership of land.

MASSACHUSETTS

The Colony of Massachusetts Bay, as early as 1647, less than twenty years from the date of their first charter, made provision by law, for the support of schools at the public expense; for instruction in reading and writing in every town containing fifty families, and grammar schools in those containing one hundred families. This noble foundation suggests the religious foresight that laid it. The preamble to this school law contained the following motives: "It being one chief object of Satan to keep men from the knowledge of the Scriptures, as in former times keeping them in unknown tongues, therefore, that learning may not be buried in the graves of our fore fathers, the Lord assisting our endeavors, it is ordered," etc.

Horace Mann, secretary of the Massachusetts Board of Education, has left on record this noble testimony for all the teachers of our country. "As educators, as friends and sustainers of the common school system, our great duty is to impart to the children of the commonwealth the greatest practicable amount of useful knowledge; to cultivate in them a sacred regard for truth, to keep them unspotted from the world; to train them to love God and also their fellow men; to make the perfect example of Jesus Christ lovely in their eyes; to give to all so much religious instruction, as is compatible with the rights of others and the gains of our government, so that, when they arrive at the years of maturity, they may intelligently enjoy the inviolable prerogatives of private judgment and self-direction, the acknowledged birthright of every human being."

Rufus Choate, the eminent statesman and jurist in one of his orations very emphatically exclaimed: "Banish the Bible from our public schools? Never! So long as a piece of Plymouth Rock remains big enough to make a gun-flint." This is an expression of true patriotism on the part of one, who knew well the history and cost of American freedom. "He is the freeman, whom the truth makes free."

CONNECTICUT

In the Colony of Connecticut as early as 1656, explicit laws were added to the general law by which the schools were first established, and constables were required to take care ,"That all their children and apprentices, as they grow capable, may through God's blessing attain at least so much as to be able to read the Scriptures, and other good books in the English tongue."

THE PUBLIC SCHOOL 399

"The schools of this state" says the state school Journal, "were founded and supported chiefly for the purpose of perpetuating civil and religious knowledge and liberty, as the early laws of the colony explicitly declare. Those laws, published in the first number of this Journal declare, that the chief means to be used to attain these objects, was the reading of the Holy Scriptures."

This enlightened policy of the Puritans, in regard to the establishment of free schools, for the general dissemination of a knowledge of the Bible and the development of a pure morality among the young, was a great step in advance of all the countries in the old world. The results have wonderfully justified their wisdom and forethought. The schools they established, having the Bible as a universal text book and basis of moral instruction, became nurseries of piety and knowledge. The very thought of excluding the Bible from schools, they had established with great sacrifice for its special study, would have been received with a shudder of horror.

"The interests of education," says Chancellor Kent, chief justice of New York, "had engaged the attention of the New England colonists, from the earliest settlement of the country, and the system of common and grammar schools, and of academical and collegiate instruction, was interwoven with the primitive views of the Puritans. Everything in their genius and disposition was favorable to the growth of freedom and learning. They were a grave, thinking people, having a lofty and determined purpose. The first emigrants had studied the oracles of truth as a text book, and they were profoundly affected by the plain commands, awful sanctions, sublime views, hopes and consolations, that accompanied the revelation of life and immortality. The avowed object, of their emigration to New England, was to enjoy and propagate the Reformed faith, in the purity of its discipline and worship. They intended to found republics on the basis of Christianity, and to secure religious liberty, under the auspices of a commonwealth. With this primary view, they were early led to make strict provision for common school education, and the religious instruction of the people. The Word of God was at that time almost the sole object of their solicitude and studies, and the principal design, in emigrating to the banks of the Connecticut, was to preserve the liberty and purity of the gospel. We meet with the system of common schools, in the earliest of the Colonial records. Provision was made for the support of schools in each town, and a grammar school in each county. This system of free schools, sustained by law, has been attended with momentous results; and it has communicated to the people, the blessings of order and security, to an extent never before surpassed in the annals of mankind."

STATE OF NEW YORK

George Clinton, the first governor, in presenting the matter of public education to the first legislature of New York, used the following language: "Neglect of the education of youth is one of the evils consequent upon the evils of war. There is scarcely anything more worthy your attention, than the revival and encouragement of seminaries of learning; and nothing by which we can more satisfactorily express our gratitude to the Supreme Being for his past favors, since piety and virtue are generally the offspring of an enlightened understanding."

Later, when the phrase "Common schools" had come into use, he emphasized morals and religion as their foremost objects. "The advantage to morals, religion, liberty and good government, arising from the general diffusion of knowledge, being universally admitted, permit me to recommend this subject to your deliberate attention."

In 1804, his successor, Governor Lewis, emphasized the necessity of establishing common schools in the following words: "In a government resting on public opinion, and deriving its chief support from the affections of the people, religion and morality cannot be too sedulously inculcated. Common schools, under the guidance of respectable teachers, should be established in every village and the poor be educated at the public expense."

In 1810, his successor, Governor Tompkins, brought the matter anew to the attention of the legislature. "I cannot omit inviting your attention to the means of instruction for the rising generation. To enable them to perceive and duly estimate their rights, to inculcate correct principles, and habits of morality and religion, and to render them useful citizens, a competent provision for their education is all essential."

In 1811, in response to these successive appeals, the legislature of New York appointed five commissioners, to report a system for the organization and establishment of common schools to carry forward the educational work, that had been previously maintained by the voluntary contributions of christian people in their various communities.

These commissioners, in their report, recommending the establishment of common schools for the state of New York, expressed their own sentiments and those of the people they represented, as follows:

"The people must possess both intelligence and virtue; intelligence to perceive what is right, and virtue to do what is right. Our republic may justly be said to be founded on the intelligence and virtue of the people, and to maintain it, 'the whole force of education is required.' The establishment of common schools appears to be the best plan, that can be devised, to disseminate religion, morality and learning, throughout a whole country."

In referring to the branches to be taught there is added in this report, as follows: "Reading, writing, arithmetic and the principles of morality (Bible) are essential to every person, however humble, his situation in life. Morality and religion are the foundation of all that is truly great and good and are consequently of primary importance."

After calling attention to the "absolute necessity of suitable qualifications on the part of the master," the report continues in regard to the Bible, as one of the books to be used:

"Connected with the introduction of suitable books, the commissioners take the liberty of suggesting that some observations and advice, touching the reading of the Bible in the schools, might be salutary. In order to render the sacred volume productive of the greatest advantage, it should be held in a very different light, from that of a common school book. It should be regarded, not merely as a book for literary improvement, but as inculcating great and indispensable moral truths. With these impressions, the commissioners are induced to recommend the practice, introduced into the New York Free School, of having select chapters read at the opening of the school in the morning and the like at the close in the afternoon. This is deemed the best mode of preserving the religious regard, which is due to the sacred writings."

This admirable report closes with these significant

THE PUBLIC SCHOOL 403

words: "The American empire is founded, on the virtue and intelligence of the people. The commissioners cannot but hope that that Being, who rules the universe in justice and mercy, who rewards virtue and punishes vice, will graciously deign to smile benignly, on the humble efforts of a people in a cause purely his own; and that he will manifest this pleasure, in the lasting prosperity of our country."

The public school system of New York, with the Bible as its corner stone, was established the next year, 1812. Ten years later, Governor DeWitt Clinton, encouraging their liberal support, said, "The first duty of a state is to render its citizens virtuous, by intellectual instruction and moral discipline, by enlightening their minds, purifying their hearts and teaching them their rights and obligations."

STATE OF PENNSYLVANIA

The status of the Bible, in the early schools of Pennsylvania, may be gathered from the following extract from a report, approved by the National Convention of the friends of public education, that met in Philadelphia in 1850.

"In the common schools, which are open for the instruction of the children of all denominations there are many whose religious education is neglected by their parents, and who will grow up in vice and irreligion, unless they receive it from the common school teacher. It seems to us to be the duty of the state, to provide for the education of all the children, morally as well as intellectually; and to require all teachers of youth, to train the children in the knowledge and practice of the principles of virtue and piety.

"The Bible should be introduced and read in all the schools in our land. It should be read as a devotional exercise, and be regarded by teachers and scholars, as the text book of morals and religion. The children should early be impressed with the conviction, that it was written by inspiration of God, and that their lives should be regulated by its precepts. They should be taught to regard it, as their manual of piety, justice, veracity, chastity, temperance, benevolence and of all excellent virtues. They should look upon this book, as the highest tribunal to which we can appeal, for the decision of moral questions; and its plain declarations, as the end of all debate."

It was about the year 1840, that the Catholics in Pennsylvania began to manifest opposition to the reading of the Bible, in the schools of that state. In view of this opposition the board of directors, for the Fourth section in Philadelphia, adopted the following resolutions:

(1) "That we will ever insist on the reading of the Bible, without note or comment in our public schools; because we believe it to be the Word of God, and know that such is the will, of the vast majority of the commonwealth.

(2) "That we look on the effort of sectarians to divide the school fund, as an insidious attempt to lay the axe at the root of our noble public school system, the benefits of which are every day manifested in the training of our youth.

(3) "That we will use every means proper for christians and citizens to employ to maintain our present school system, and to insure the continuance of the reading of God's holy word in all our schools."

BOARD OF NATIONAL EDUCATION

The constitution of the Board of National Popular Education contains in its sixth article, the following pledge, as one required of teachers, as well as the board. "The daily use of the Bible in their several schools, as the basis of that sound christian education, to the support and extension of which, the board is solemnly pledged."

In its fifth annual report, which is for the year 1852, the necessity of a free and open Bible in our common schools was emphasized as the only possible way, in which our nation can continue to be self-governed. The Bible, for the masses, is God's great instrument for governing men and nations. "There is but one alternative," said Mr. Sawtell, "God will have men and nations governed; and they must be governed by one of the two instruments, an open Bible with its hallowed influences, or a standing army with bristling bayonets. One is the product of God's wisdom; the other, of man's folly; and that nation that discards or will not yield to the moral power of the one, must submit to the brute force of the other. The open Bible, in our schools, is the secret of our ability to govern ourselves. Take from us the open Bible and, like Samson shorn of his locks, we would become as weak as any other people. Take away the Bible, and like Italy, Austria and Russia, we would need a despot on a throne, and a standing army of a half-million to keep the populace in subjection."

JESUS, THE GREAT TEACHER

It was our Lord Jesus himself, who said, "Suffer little children to come unto me, and forbid them not." He did not suggest, that they be sent for moral instruction to the schools of the Pharisees, or the unbelieving Sadducees, but that they should come to him, and receive his word and blessing. He saw no sectarianism in the message of love, life and forgiveness, he brought from the Father; for he described it, as, "living water," "living bread which came down from heaven," "the light of the world," and its object, "that they might have life more abundantly." He knew, it was a matter of utmost importance to every individual, to receive that message in childhood and youth.

THE BIBLE, THE STANDARD OF MORALITY

The Word of God is supreme in all matters of conscience or morality. The man, whose conscience is in harmony with the Word of God, must be recognized as on the side of God and right. Elijah on Mount Carmel, having only the Word of God, prevails over four hundred misguided prophets of Baal. When those, who were prejudiced against the gospel in the days of Peter, imprisoned and undertook to silence him and others, he gave the right answer, when he said, "We ought to obey God rather than men." Peter and Elijah, teaching the Word of God, were progressive upbuilders of the Kingdom of God, while their suppressors were merely blind opposers and destructionists. The enlightened consciences of Peter and Elijah were of more value and more to be respected, than those of the hosts of souls, in the darkness of unbelief, arrayed against them. Whilst the work of Peter and the apostles tended to make the world better, and better men of all their opposers, the work of the latter, tended to put a real check, on the cause of human progress. Those, who opppose the reading of the Scriptures in the public schools of this, or any other land, commit the very same folly.

The Bible is the Word of God to all mankind. It is his provision for our intellectual, moral and spiritual natures, as the light, air, water and food have been provided for our physical natures. It was originally written in the language of the people to whom it was given, the Old Testament in Hebrew to the Hebrews; and the New Testament in Greek to the Greek speaking Jews, in the time of Christ.

Our English version was made from the original lang-

HOME OF THE LATE CAROLINE PRINCE.

NEW HOME, MRS. SAM HARRIS.
Representative Homes of Choctaw Freedmen, near Oak Hill.

A Virgin Prairie, Improved by Mr. and Mrs. Flickinger, 1884-1914.

At the left: Grove of maples and walnuts, orchard, grapes, garden, oat-bin, double corn-crib, house, front yard, chick-yard, bees, barn, implement shed, hen-house, pig-pen, calf and pig pastures. Two and a half miles of tile drains.

uages in the time of King James, and it is an error in judgment to call it, either a Protestant or Sectarian Bible. There is, indeed, a sectarian version of the Bible in use in this country. It is printed in the latin language, the language of pagan Rome, which the common people no longer use or understand.

It seems a queer freak of our human nature, that those who use the Bible in a dead, foreign language, unsuited for use in our public schools, should call our English version of the scriptures a sectarian book, and then oppose its use in our public schools.

Our English version of the Scriptures is no more a sectarian book, than are the ordinary books on astronomy, geology, botany, and natural history. Nevertheless when Romanists oppose its use, others of all sorts in the community, who like them need its gracious message of light, life and love, but instead profess not to regard it as a message from God, are liable to unite with them in their unfortunate opposition.

No one has an inherent right, to exclude the Bible from the public schools of America. As the one authoritative book of God, it ought to be there. As the charter of American liberty, and the corner stone of our system of public education and jurisprudence, it ought to be there. No one has any more right to exclude the Bible from the public schools of America, than he has to exclude the sun, for both are God's own provision of light. It is intended of God to be the one unchanging standard of morality and purity, for old and young; and to be as free for all, as the common air that we breathe. Its use, at an early age, tends to develop the conservative principles of virtue and knowledge, which serve as the world's best protectors against ignorance, barbarism and vice.

RISE AND FALL OF INTOLERANCE

Excluding the Bible, from the public schools of America, is an old world innovation. In some countries of Europe, books on science, literature or philosophy have not been permitted to be published, without the previous approval of the government. "The Bible itself, the common inheritance, not merely of Christendom, but of the world, has been put exclusively under the control of government, and has not been allowed to be seen, heard, or read, except in a language unknown to the common inhabitants of the country. To publish a translation in the language of the people, has been in former times a flagrant offense." (Story on the Constitution, page 263.)

The popes, as early as the eighth century, condemned the circulation and reading of all writings unfriendly to the papacy. In 1515, after the art of printing had been invented, the papal decree was issued, "That no book should be printed without previous examination by the proper ecclesiastical authority, the Inquisition. The books prohibited by it included the bible in the English and German languages, and all the books published by Luther, Calvin, Zwingli and other Reformers. While the Reformers were called, heresiarchs, they proved themselves to be the world's greatest benefactors, by giving the people the Bible.

When Roman Catholicism was the state religion of Italy, France, Spain and Britain, it was intolerant, and by massacres and persecutions endeavored to suppress the reading of the Bible and also its publication in the language of the people.

In 1531, when the bishops were almost universally statesmen, lawyers or diplomats. Henry, the King of England, by an act of parliament, which consisted of a convocation of the clergy, became the recognized head of the church in England, instead of the pope at Rome. The principle now begins to prevail, that "Truth possesses the power to defend itself." As a result Wiclif, Tyndale, Sir Thomas More, Thomas Cromwell, Archbishop Cranmer, Miles Coverdale and others, with the approval of the king successively, encourage the translation, publication and circulation of the Scriptures among the clergy and people. It was at this time and in this way, that the principle of toleration in matters of religion had its beginning, and the first check was put upon the cruel intolerance of the church of Rome in England. The church of England, episcopal in form then became the established, or state church; and it is so still, but the king is no longer the head of it and the parliament no longer consists of the clergy, as in the days of King James. It was in 1566 that the Puritans, followers of Calvin and other foreign reformers, withdrew from the established church of England, because they did not approve all the forms and ceremonies, then required in the public worship of the established church.

The official act of religious toleration in England was passed during the reign of William III, 1689-1702, (and Mary), who, as the prince of Orange and founder of the Dutch republic in 1680, had previously distinguished himself as the friend of liberty.

Roger Williams, founder of the Colony of Rhode Island 1636 to 1647, established there the first government in America, upon the principle of universal toleration. William Penn, founder and proprietor of Pennsylvania, in 1684 incorporated the same principle in the government of that colony; and, as the expression of his own views and sentiments, respecting religion and civil government. These men exercised government, by instilling into the minds of the people the principles of religion, morality, forbearance and friendship. Americans do well to cherish the memory of these men, who wrought so nobly a century before the American Revolution.

NOBLE DEFENSE BY DANIEL WEBSTER

Our American public school system represents the accumulated wisdom of many generations of Bible readers, and in promoting it we preserve for future generations the foundations so wisely laid in the earlier years of our history.

Daniel Webster, one of the advocates of the system and early defenders of the Bible in it, stated its fundamental principle when he said, "In all cases there is nothing, that we look for with more certainty, than this general principle, that christianity is part of the law of this land." He explained its object and motive in the following passage, which is worthy to be repeated in every generation.

"We seek to educate the people. We seek to improve men's moral and religious condition. In short, we seek to work upon mind as well as upon matter; and this tends to enlarge the intellect and heart of man. We know that when we work upon materials, immortal and imperishable, that they will bear the impress which we place upon them, through endless ages to come. If we work upon marble, it will perish; if we work upon brass, time will efface it. If we rear temples, they will crumble to the dust. But, if we work on men's immortal minds—if we imbue them with high principles, with the just fear of God, and of their fellow men,—we engrave on those tablets, something which no time can efface, but which will brighten and brighten to all eternity."

The exclusion of the Bible from the public schools in

New York state had its rise in 1838 and concerning this movement, Mr. Webster said, "This is a question which in its decision is to influence the happiness, the temporal and the eternal welfare of one hundred millions of human beings, alive and to be born in this land. Its decision will give a hue to the character of our institutions. There can be no charity in that system of instruction from which the Bible, the basis of christianity, is excluded."

The public school, with daily instruction to the young in the Bible, is an American system of education. It had its origin in the belief of its founders, that general instruction in the Bible was essential to the permanency of that freedom, civil and religious, and that independent ownership of land, they came to America to enjoy. If the early Pilgrims, more particularly those of Massachusetts and Connecticut, had not struggled and toiled for this great object, and if they had not been immediately succeeded by men, who imbibed a large portion of the same spirit, the free school system of New England would never have been extended to all parts of our land. We have inherited the public school through the Bible, and the feeling prevails, that only by maintaining a general knowledge of the Bible, among the young and rising generation through it can the countless blessings, that flow from it, be conserved for future generations.

THE FREEDMAN'S BEST BOOK

These historic facts, relating to the original establishment of free schools among the colonies, during the period of the early settlement of this country, and the place accorded the Bible in them by their faithful founders, are well suited to be suggestive, and to prove an inspiration to every friend of freedom, to promote the good cause of maintaining the daily reading of the Bible, in all of our public schools at the present time.

Christian parents among the Freedmen, having children that are bright and studious, are encouraged by these facts, to train one or more of them to be teachers and helpers, in promoting the educational and moral uplift of the race. All are encouraged to co-operate with your teachers, in making the public school of your neighborhood, an attractive and inviting place for your own and your neighbor's chlidren.

Send the children regularly to school during the term, for the terms are short. Do all you can, as long as you live, to supply your public schools with bibles and christian teachers, in order that they may attain the highest degree of efficiency, and bring the greatest amount of public good, to you and your children. Remember, that the Bible is the mother of the public school and that it awakens a desire for more knowledge, drives back the darkness of ignorance and inspires the courage to do right.

Many have been led astray by reading bad books and papers, but none from reading the Bible. Its blessings of comfort and guidance to individuals, and of civil and religious liberty to nations, have come to us like the dew of Hermon, that made "the wilderness and solitary place to be glad, and the desert to rejoice and blossom as the rose."

In view of these important historic facts, it is certainly strange that any parents, who permit their children to read all sorts of trashy and worthless books, without protest, should pretend they do not want them to read the Bible, the one infallible and incomparable book, that does not become old and out-of-date like the best of other books, but is as fresh and life giving to day as twenty centuries ago.

THE PUBLIC SCHOOL 413

The number of those, who have opposed the reading of the Bible in the public schools have comprised but a small part of the entire population of our land, and they have always represented that part of it, that have most needed its enlightening and uplifting influence.

One million immigrants from other lands are now coming to our shores every year, that they may enjoy the civil and religious privileges, that have here been secured, through the influence of the Bible. One of their greatest needs, immediately on their arrival, is faithful instruction in the living and eternal truths of God's Holy Word, that they may know and understand the genius or spirit of our American, civil and religious institutions.

There is urgent need to day for more of that holy compulsion that Jesus exercised, when, surrounded by a lot of hungry people, he required the disciples to "Make the men sit down," and then added, "Give ye them to eat."

THE CHURCH AND SUNDAY SCHOOL

When Jesus said, "The son of man came not to be ministered unto but to minister," he gave to the world one of its clearest visions of the Kingdom of God, and his own, the highest ideal of life, the one that produces the noblest type of manhood.

It is the great business of the church to bring all its children and youth to this true conception of life, and it aims to do this through the christian home, the Sunday school, young peoples' meetings and church services. But these alone are not adequate, to reach all the children and youth of the land, including those of the one million immigrants, arriving annually from other lands.

Margaret Slattery in the Charm of the Impossible has very truly remarked:

"Men of all creeds and of none agree, that religious instruction ought to be given, to all the children and youth of the land, but the task of attempting it is a tremendous one, and the best manner of doing it is not clear to all. Some say religious instruction should be given in the home. This is usually done, in the intelligent christian home; but there are many homes, where it is impossible, and others indisposed. The fact that the church has seen, as if with a new vision, the method of Jesus, the Great Teacher of all men, reveals itself more clearly in the Sunday school, than in any other department of its work. There it attempts the task of religious education by instruction from the Bible, and endeavors to inspire the child, youth and man with the purest and greatest motives for action."

MAKE THE PUBLIC, A BIBLE SCHOOL

There is, however, no instrumentality in our country, so convenient and favorable for giving all the children and youth of our land a general knowledge of the Bible, as the public school. The Bible is the embodiment of all lofty ideals, and when it is daily read in all of our schools, there is in them a uniform standard of morals. Schools, that neglect or suppress the daily reading of the Bible, do not keep the vision of those attending them on the christian ideal, or develop the christian motive in them, during the most impressionable period of their lives.

'The Bible is the light of the intellect, the fore runner of civilization, the charter of true liberty and secret of national greatness. The Bible is the one, all-important book for the Freedmen and their children. Its weekly use, in the church and Sunday school, is to be appreciated and promoted; but the home and the public school are the golden places, where its daily use should be required, and the opportunity be magnified.

American patriotism relies on the public school, conducted with moral and social aims, as the one preeminent, assimilating agency to bind together the older and newer elements of our population, in a common devotion to our common country. It has been "America's greatest civil glory and chief civil hope." The enthusiasm, that led to its establishment, was well nigh sacred. It needs to day the support of a public spirit, that will insist on the restoration of the daily reading of the Bible, as the basis of moral instruction in it.

Concerning its educational value President Woodrow Wilson has recently very truthfully said, "The educational value of the Bible is, that it both awakens the spirit to its finest and only true action, and acquaints the student with the noblest body of literature in existence; a body of literature, having in it more mental and imaginative stimulus, than any other body of writings. A man has deprived himself of the best there is in the world, who has deprived himself of the Bible."

How true to day is Paul's description of the people that were living without the Bible in his day. He describes them as "filled with all unrighteousness, fornication, wickedness, covetousness, maliciousness; full of envy, murder, deceit, haters of God, despiteful, proud, boasters, inventors of evil things, disobedient to parents, without understanding, unmerciful."*

Our own and every heathen land furnishes abundant proofs, that whenever the gracious promises of the Bible are gratefully received, the proud become humble, the dis-

*Rom. 1. 27.

obedient dutiful, the drunkard sober, the dishonest, honorable; the profligate, prudent; and the miserable become happy. Nothing else has ever done this, but the gospel of Christ always does it, when gratefully received.

ENCOURAGING MOVEMENTS

The legislature of Pennsylvania, in 1913, restored the use of the Bible in the public schools of that state, by a statute requiring the daily reading of at least ten verses of the Bible, in the hearing of all the pupils under every teacher, and making a neglect of this duty a proper cause, for the suspension of the teacher.

The National Reform Association at its last meeting in Portland, Oregon, in 1913, resolved to raise $25,000, for the purpose of undertaking to place a copy of the Bible, in every public school in the land, from which it may have been excluded; and to aid in keeping it, where it is now adopted, as the standard of moral instruction.

Commissioner Claxton, in welcoming the members of the council of church Boards of Education, representing fourteen denominations, at their third meeting in Washington, D. C., in January 1914, very correctly stated the leadership of the church in the educational work of our country, and the importance of its continued relation to it, in the following language:

"The church has been the leader in educational development, at a time when the state was unable and unwilling to pay the large cost for education. Honor should be given the church for its splendid, formative work in education, during the time the state was occupied in building up its political relations. It is indeed a happy thing, that the church is so deeply interested in education, as to maintain national agencies, known as boards."

In regard to the secondary schools he prophetically added, "The day will come, when the Bible will be read in the public schools, just as any other book. There is no good reason, why the Bible should not have its rightful place, in our public school curriculum."

The Gideons, an organization among traveling salesmen, are endeavoring to place a copy of the Bible in every bedroom of all the public hotels in the United States. At the end of 1913 they had supplied bibles for 220,000 rooms, and had reached all but three states, Utah, Nevada and Washington.

These are movements in the right direction and suggest the proper attitude of every christian parent, teacher and legislator. Do not hesitate to advocate the daily reading of the Bible, and the employment of christian teachers, in all the public schools, provided for the Freedman and his children.

"There's a dear and precious book,
Though it's worn and faded now,
Which recalls those happy days of long ago;
When I stood at mother's knee
With her hand upon my brow,
And I heard her voice in gentle tones and low.
Blessed book, precious book
On thy dear old tear-stained leaves I love to look;
Thou art sweeter day by day,
As I walk the narrow way,
That leads at last, to that bright home above."
—M. B. Williams.

XLVIII
A HALF-CENTURY OF BIBLE SUPPRESSION IN A NATION, OR FRANCE, DURING THE PERIOD, 1572 TO 1795.

THEISM, DEISM, PHILOSOPHISM.—APPEAL FOR BREAD.—MORAL AND FINANCIAL BANKRUPTCY.—FIRST POPULAR ASSEMBLY.—REPUBLIC OF FRANCE.—REIGN OF TERROR.—PEOPLE UNPREPARED FOR FREEDOM.—INSURRECTION OF WOMEN.—RESULTS.—LAND OF JOHN CALVIN.—LAFAYETTE.—ROMANISM, BEHIND THE TIMES.—HUMAN REASON, BLIND.—LIGHT, LIFE AND LIBERTY.

"The entrance of thy word giveth light, it giveth understanding to the simple. Open thou mine eyes, that I may behold wondrous things out of thy law."—David.

AN American citizen does not need to go to far-off India or Africa to learn how people live without the Bible. Every heathen nation, living in ignorance and degradation furnishes a practical illustration. This illustration may be found by visiting the countries on the other side of the southern boundary line of the United States, where for several centuries under dominant catholic influence the Bible has been a forbidden book in the few public educational institutions of the country. The result may now be seen in the general prevalence of ignorance, poverty and oppression; the ownership of land limited to a comparatively few persons, corruption and rapacity on the part of public officials, general improvement checked and the country impoverished by frequent insurrections and revolu-

HALF-CENTURY OF BIBLE SUPPRESSION 419

tions, that indicate incapacity for stable and prosperous self-government.

France, however, once made the actual experiment of suppressing the Bible and Bible readers for two centuries, during the period from 1572 to 1795, while the Reformation of the 16th century was progressing in Germany, Switzerland, Britain and other countries.

Thomas Carlyle, in his history of the French Revolution, that occurred 1788 to 1795, has very dramatically portrayed scenes and incidents, which become pregnant with new and thrilling interest, when briefly summarized to illustrate the folly and sad consequences of suppressing the Bible and Bible readers in that nation. The historic value of these incidents should make this story interesting and instructive to every student and teacher.

ATHEISM, DEISM, PHILOSOPHISM

Louis XV, king of France, at the end of a reign of fifty-nine years, dies unwept and unmourned in 1774. Affirming there is no God or heaven, at the beginning of his long reign, and not permitting any of his courtiers to mention the word "death" in his presence, he abandons himself to a life of forbidden pleasure, humiliates and scandalizes the people of France instead of enlightening and elevating them. He inherits and maintains the tyrannous and oppressive feudal system, that prevents the common people from acquiring ownership of land. His career has been described, "as an hideous abortion and mistake of nature, the use and meaning of which is not yet known." The persecution of Bible readers, or Protestants, is begun with a general massacre at Paris, on the anniversary of Saint Bartholomew in 1572. Those who escape the bloody horrors of that occasion, are commanded to emigrate from France, on pain of death. The following events occur, during the latter part of the last half century, preceding the French Revolution.

The leaders in thought are the shameless and selfish infidels and deists, Voltaire, Rosseau, Robespierre and others like them. Paris admires her deistical authors and makes them the objects of hero-worship. They are called "Philosophs," and Bible readers must not stand in their way. Philosophism sits joyful in glittering saloons, is the pride of nobles and promises a coming millennium Crushing and scattering the last elements of the Protestant Reformation, they blindly and falsely talk of a Reformed France. The people applaud, instead of suppressing these false teachers. The highest dignitaries of the church waltz with quack-prophets, pick pockets and public women. The invisible world of Satan is displayed and the smoke of its torment goes up continually. No provision is made for the general education of the common people and yet the government is fast becoming bankrupt.

In 1774 Louis XVI succeeds his father, as the last King of France. He is youthful, uneducated, imbecile. He is wedded to a giddy superficial queen. Both are infidels and incapable of any intelligent acts of government. With imbecility and credulity on the throne, corruption continues to prevail among high and low. Instead of individual thrift and general prosperity, poverty and famine prevail throughout the land.

APPEAL FOR BREAD

In 1775, impelled by a scarcity of bread, a vast multitude from the surrounding country gather around the royal palace at Versailles, their great number, sallow faces and squalid appearance indicating widespread wretchedness and want. Their appeal for royal assistance is plainly

HALF-CENTURY OF BIBLE SUPPRESSION

written, in "legible hieroglyphics in their winged raggedness." The young king appears on the balcony and they are permitted to see his face. If he does not read their written appeal, he sees it in their pitiable condition. The response of the king is an order, that two of them be hanged. The rest are sent back to their miserable hovels with a warning not to give the king any more trouble.

Mirabeau, a French writer, describes a similar scene that occurs later that same year. "The savages descending in torrents from the mountains our people are ordered not to go out. The bagpipes begin to play, but the dance in a quarter of an hour is interrupted by a battle. The cries of children and infirm persons incite them, as the rabble does when dogs fight. The men, like frightful wild animals, are clad in coarse woollen jackets with large girdles of leather studded with copper nails. Their gigantic stature is heightened by high wooden clogs. Their faces are haggard and covered with long greasy hair. The upper part of their visage waxes pale, while the lower distorts itself into a cruel laugh, or the appearance of a ferocious impatience."

These proceedings are a protest of the common people, of whom there are twenty millions, against government by blind-man's-buff. These people, paying their taxes, are protesting against corrupt officials depriving them of their salt and sugar, in order to maintain royal and official extravagance. Stumbling too far prepares the way for a general overturn.

MORAL AND FINANCIAL BANKRUPTCY

There is no visible government. Its principal representative is the Chancellor of the Exchequer, or king's treasurer; and "Deficit of revenue" is his constant announcement, to the feudal lords, who exercise local government.

In 1787 Cardinal Lomenie becomes the king's new treasurer. His predecessor has been ousted because the treasury was bankrupt, but his unscrupulous methods continue to be adopted because no better ones can be devised. As late as the next year the cardinal demands the infliction of the death penalty on all Protestant preachers.

The period has become one of spiritual and moral bankruptcy. The Bible has been suppressed and blind human reason has been exalted. There is no bond of morality to hold the people together. Men become slaves of their lusts and appetites, and society, a mass of sensuality, rascality and falsehood. Infidelity, despotism and general bankruptcy prevail every where. There is no royal authority and the palace of justice at Versailles is closed.

The poverty and misery, experienced by the peasants in their comfortless hovels, awakens a feeling of discontent and protest. This feeling of protest, among the poor and illiterate, permeates upward and becomes more intense as it proceeds. In this unorganized protest the hand of one is arrayed against his fellow man. The common people are arrayed against the nobles; the nobles, against each other, and both nobles and people are bitter against the government. Townships are arrayed against townships and towns against towns. Gibbets are erected everywhere and a dozen wretched bodies may be seen hanging in a row. The mayor of Vaison is buried alive; the mayor of Etampes, defending a supply of food, is trampled to death by a mob exasperated with hunger, and the mayor of Saint Denis is hung at Lanterne. The ripening grain is left ungathered in the fields, and the fruit of the vineyards is trodden under foot. The bloody cruelty of universal madness prevails everywhere.

A frightful hail storm, that destroys the grain and

fruits of the year at the beginning of harvest, is followed by a severe drought in 1788. Foulon, an official grown gray in treachery and iniquity, when asked,
"What will the people do?" makes response,
"The people may eat grass."

The royal government is now described, as existing only for its own benefit; without right, except possession; and now also without might. "It foresees nothing, and has no purpose, except to maintain its own existence. It is wholly a vortex in which vain counsels, falsehoods, intrigues and imbecilities whirl like withered rubbish in the meeting of the winds."

Commerce of all kinds, as far as possible, has come to a dead pause, and the hand of the industrious is idle. Many of the people subsist on meal-husks and boiled grass. Armed Brigands begin to make their appearance and a "reign of terror," is ushered in.

FIRST POPULAR ASSEMBLY

On May 4, 1789, the first popular assembly meets at Versailles, more churches than other buildings having been used as polling places, at this first election in France. The assembly is composed of nobles, clergy and commoners, the last representing the people.

Six "parlements," consisting only of nobles, have previously been convened by the king's treasurer, and as often have been dismissed by the king, because they were not willing to tax themselves more, to increase the revenues of the king. In this assembly, there are six hundred commoners, who, when the king dismissed the assembly, under the leadership of Mirabeau refused to be dismissed, and bind themselves by an oath, to remain in session, until they have framed and adopted a constitution.

This act of the commoners is the beginning of the French Revolution. This Revolution has been defined, as "An open, violent rebellion and victory of unimprisoned anarchy, against corrupt worn-out authority; breaking prison, raging uncontrollable and enveloping a world in fever frenzy, until the mad forces are made to work toward their object, as sane and regulated ones."

These commoners are shut out of their hall and their signatures are attached to their oath in a tennis court. They are later joined by Lafayette, the friend of Washington, and by other nobles and 149 Roman clergy. They are treated offensively, but cannot be offended. They are animated with a desire to prepare a constitution, that will regenerate France, abolish the old order and usher in a new one.

Paris, always very demonstrative under excitement, grows wild with enthusiasm for the commoners, and others, who compose their first National Assembly. They go simmering and dancing, thinking they are shaking off something old and advancing to something new. They have hope in their hearts, the hope of an unutterable universal golden age, and nothing but freedom, equality and brotherhood on their lips. Their hopes, however, are based on nothing but the "vapory vagaries of unenlightened human reason," instead of the unchanging truths and principles of Divine Revelation. They experience an indescribable terror, of the unnumbered hordes of Europe rallying against them, in addition to the constant dread of their own cruel, armed brigands and inhuman official executioners.

Unfortunately the commoners had not been previously trained in the art of statesmanship, and after a long session, that lasted until September 14, 1791, the constitution then proposed was still incomplete, and had to be submitted

HALF-CENTURY OF BIBLE SUPPRESSION 425

to another assembly to be completed. They however accomplish some things worthy of note. In 1789 they abolish feudalism, root and branch; and the payment of tithes. The latter meant the separation of church and state, in matters of support and government; and this event seemed to the deists, like a time of Pentecost.

REPUBLIC OF FRANCE

On Sept. 22, 1792 the Republic of France is declared. On Jan. 1, 1793, King Louis XVI, who had become a runaway king, and on October 16th following, Marie Antoinette, the queen, are executed. These events are followed by another reign of terror, the plundering of churches and a war with Spain.

The Republic of France, when first established, proves to be one of a mob, robbing and murdering those, who had property. The people become despotic as soon as they have disposed of their useless king, and queen. There were only nine prisoners in the bastile, when it was destroyed, but now in two days and under the name of liberty, eight thousand innocent persons are massacred in prison. Walter Scott in his Life of Napoleon adds: "Three hundred thousand other persons, one third of whom are women, are ruthlessly committed to prison," the executioners usurping the place of the judges and, without trial, pronouncing sentence against them". Their watchwords, while the Revolution continues, are, "Unity, Brotherhood or Death." These principles are enforced by edicts of exile, imprisonment, or death by the guillotine.

REIGN OF TERROR

This reign of terror continues until July 28, 1794, when the cruel hearted Robespierre and his consorts are condemned to death on the guillotine, a cunningly devised beheading machine, on which he had been practicing with innocent and helpless victims, for twenty-two years.

In 1795 a new constitution is adopted, and after the suppression of a number of bloody riots and insurrections that year, by the young Napoleon with his batteries of artillery, public order is restored and the Revolution is regarded as ended.

PEOPLE UNPREPARED FOR FREEDOM

These are but a few of the many riotous and disorderly events that occurred in France just at the close of the American Revolution, in which Lafayette co-operated with so much honor to himself and his country. These suffice to show how unprepared the people were for any great or concerted movement, and how destitute the nation was of men, fit to serve as leaders in thought and action, until the rise of Napoleon with his genuis for military affairs. Mirabeau, their first trusted leader, dies before the end of their first assembly. Lafayette, a prominent member of the first assembly, when made military commander at Paris, finds the rabble will not listen to his counsels, and he resigns. In 1782 he makes another attempt to re-instate authority in Paris, and the attempt proving a failure he retires from further participation in public affairs.

No one is able to anticipate the next movement of the populace, or win and hold their confidence, any length of time. One event follows another "explosively." Men, fearing to remain longer in their huts or homes, fugitively rush with wives and children, they know not whither. Under the the leadership of the infidels, Rosseau and Robespierre, they experience terrors such as had not fallen on any nation, since the fall of Jerusalem.

HALF-CENTURY OF BIBLE SUPPRESSION 427

INSURRECTION OF WOMEN

An insurrection of women is suddenly started in Paris, in October 1789, at the call of a young woman who seizes a drum and cries aloud, "Descend O Mothers; Descend ye Judiths to food and revenge!" Ten thousand women, quickly responding to this call, press through the military guard to the armory in Hotel de Ville, and when supplied with arms march on foot to Versailles, and, taking the king and his family captives, bring them and the National Assembly to Paris the next day, October 5th, followed by a good natured crowd, estimated at 200,000. Now that the king occupies the palace of the Tuileries at Paris, the people hungry, but hopeful, shake hands in the happiest mood, and assure one another "the New Era has been born."

RESULTS

The principal results of the French Revolution may be briefly summarized as follows:

Good riddance of a half century line, of worse than useless, atheistic kings and queens; the suppression of the tyrannous feudal system, that prevented the common people from acquiring ownership of land, the suppression of the bastile, a feudal prison and robber den, and of the guillotine; the suppression of religious persecution, and the separation of church and state in matters of government and support; and the adoption of a constitution, that provides for the people to have a voice, in the management of the affairs of the government.

LAND OF CALVIN AND LAFAYETTE

France is the land that gave birth and education to John Calvin, the pioneer advocate of civil and religious liberty, and in his day the good work of the Reformers had gained an encouraging foot hold in his native land, but after the lapse of a century of cruel extermination, one looks in vain to see the expected fruits of his great work. A century, of Bible suppression and persecution of Bible readers, has left the people in ignorance of the Word of God, which is the Light and Life of the World, and in its place catholicism and infidelity, like hoar frosts or destructive black clouds, have spread over the land. Oppressed with a feeling of need and seeking something not clearly defined, the people grope in darkness and stumble on events, as if playing blind-man's-buff. The one hundred and forty-nine Roman clergy in the first assembly are so lacking in intelligence and patriotism, they exert no special influence worthy of note.

Very different were the scenes that Lafayette witnessed, during the period he co-operated with the colonies of America, in their struggles for liberty and independence. Here he met many of the descendants of the very people, whom the bitter persecutions in France had driven to this country. Many of them, as early settlers in New York, Pennsylvania, Delaware and Virginia, exerted a considerable influence, in moulding the character of the American people. He found all the people engaging intelligently in the cause of freedom. Their leaders knew what they were endeavoring to achieve, and every movement was characterized by good order, patriotism and superior wisdom.

ROMANISM BEHIND THE TIMES

This historic contrast of the good fruits of the open Bible among the people in America, with the sad and deplorable results of Romanism and infidelity in France, previous to the great revolutions, that occurred in both countries in the days of Lafayette, is certainly very interesting and instructive.

Other countries in which Romanism has been dominant and the Bible suppressed, as Ireland, Spain, Mexico, the Philippine Islands and the states of Central and South America, show a similar unfavorable contrast. In South America, where Romanism has suppressed the Bible for centuries, only two percent of all the college students in 1913, according to Bishop Kensolving of the Episcopal church in Brazil, "affirm their allegiance to any religious faith."

In Spain, according to a recent issue of the Herald of Madrid, there are 30,000 towns and rural villages, that are yet without schools of any kind. There are thousands of the people whose homes can be reached only by bridle-paths. They lack schools, roads and railroads. Seventy-six per cent of the children and youth are unable to read and write. In Spain, Mexico and South America, Romanism has proven itself to be, but little more than a pious form af paganism, an oppressive and wide-spread relic of ancient, pagan Rome.

During the two hundred years preceding the Revolution in France no one was ever persecuted for being an atheist, deist, infidel or Roman catholic, but all of these united in suppressing the general use of the Bible and the presence of Bible readers, to the great injury of the public welfare. If that country had not foolishly and wickedly exterminated the people, that were fast becoming Bible readers at the time of the Reformation, it would no doubt have been saved from many of the blind and bloody scenes of the period of the Revolution.

Romanism, by suppressing the Bible, encourages ignorance, superstition and bigotry. It also tends to break down the sanctity of the Sabbath as the Lord's day; winks at the liquor traffic, and by its confessional strikes at the very foundation of free manhood, freedom of thought and liberty of conscience.

This contrast, shows clearly that Romanism, whatever good it may have done, is now many centuries behind the times. This is a very serious defect. It has the Bible, a latin version called the Vulgate which it claims as its own. It has the New Testament and for that reason it is classed as a christian religion. It has however, opposed and suppressed the reading of the Bible by the people, lest the spread of intelligence, through a personal knowledge of its contents, would lessen the respect and obedience of the people to the false claims of the pope, clerical orders and priesthood.

Several generations of slave holders in this country gave this same reason, as a good one for not providing educational facilities for their slaves, fearing that intelligence, which greatly increases the value of the workman, would tend to lessen their authority over them. It serves to illustrate the old worn-out adage, that "might makes right," instead of the newer and better one, "God is with the right."

The ability to rule, in both cases, is based on the ignorance, instead of the intelligence of the subject. When thus expressed in plain words, it certainly does not sound very creditable, or as if it were the best policy. It is not uncharitable to say, that as a policy, it is "out of date." Our Lord Jesus was a teacher as well as Saviour. He went from place to place, teaching and encouraging the people to "search the scriptures," that they might know, what to believe concerning Him, in order to inherit eternal life and "have life more abundantly."

This is one of the good features of Protestantism. It is based on a personal knowledge of the Bible and the general intelligence of the people. Its motto is "Let the Light Shine." Truth is mighty and in the end will prevail, for "justice and judgment are the habitation of God's throne."

HUMAN REASON BLIND

When the Bible was suppressed in France and human reason exalted, all the infernal elements of a depraved human nature held high carnival. Enthusiasm and fanaticism, the allies of ignorance and superstition, caused the people to think and act wildly. If in his heart there is no devout faith, to develop the sense of personal responsibility and duty, man becomes ready for any evil under the sun. Sin, however, has been and always will be the parent of misery. "The wages of sin is death." This one terrific experiment, of a half-century in France without the Bible, should be enough for a thousand worlds, through countless years."

LIGHT, LIFE AND LIBERTY

The life-giving word of Divine Truth is the salt, that preserves learning and a sense of personal obligation to do that which is right, amid the changing scenes of time and life. Learning is knowledge based on fact, and not on fiction or unbelief. Duty as a practical matter has regard for that "righteousness, that exalteth a nation." as well as the salvation that saves the individual.

"Ye shall know the truth and the truth shall make you free." A knowledge of the truth tends to produce that self-restraint, that is essential to freedom; and that sense of duty and right, that results in faithful public service. Genuine liberty has never been realized, where there has not been also an intelligent self-restraint.

The fundamental principle of the Reformation was expressed by Luther as follows: "The Word of God, the whole Word of God, and nothing but the Word of God."

This was based on the following passage from Augustine in the fourth century: "I have learned to pay to the canonical books alone, the honor of believing very firmly, that none of them has erred; as to others, I believe not what they say, for the simple reason, that it is they who say it;" and the previous saying of Paul, "Should we, or an angel from heaven, preach any other gospel unto you, than that which we have preached unto you, let him be accursed, for it is written, the just shall live by faith."

This principle of the Reformation appears in our common form of attestation, "The truth, the whole truth and nothing but the truth;" and in the patriotic motto of Pennsylvania, "Virtue, Liberty and Independence."

Think on these things. Search the scriptures. Know that the Bible is the Word of God to all people, that it is the sword of the Spirit, and the Truth that makes you free. The Master hath need and calleth for thee. Be of good courage. Be loyal to the truth and let it shine through you.

THE END

INDEX

Ahrens, Bertha L. 127, 154, 289, 300, 310
Aid Society 300
Allen, Fredonia 149
Allotment of lands 3, 154
Alverson, Noah S. 289, 342
Apiary 294
Arch of Character 257
Arnold, Olivia, Mrs. R. D. 378
Baird, Phil C. D. D. 226, 325
Bartholomew St. Massacre 77
Bashears, Charles 287
Beatty, Doll 353
Bees, Double Swarm 299
Becker, Mary O. 141
Benediction, Endeavor 259
Bethel, M. L. 226, 353
Bethesda Mission 70
Bibbs, Samuel S. 151; Lee, Charles 287-9
Bible, first book, 71; Cause of Reformation, 76; in Public School, 35,391; Memorized, 173; Uplifting Power, 181; Only Standard of Morality 406
Biddle University 70
Boggs, V. P. Mrs. 90, 158
Boll Weevil 218, 290
Books, Value of 256
Book Marks 267
Boys' Hall 135, 204, 217
Brasco, Livingston 192
Brackeen, Rosetta 275
Brown, Lucretia C. 151, 224; Matt 379

(433)

INDEX

Buds of Promise 146
Buchanan, Solomon 160, 224, 300, 322
Building the Temple 227
Burrows, Emma 137
Butler, William Rev. 148, 183, 226, 290, 370; Elijah
.... 378, 381
Calvin, John 72, 427
Campbell, Anna E. 108, 112, 119
Candidates for Ministry 276, 342
Carroll, William H. Rev. 159, 224, 289, 327
Character, Formed 33, 157, 227, 241
Chautauqua, First 277
Cherokees 7, 19
Chickasaws 7
Choctaws 7, 14
Claypool, John Mrs. 159, 318
Clear Creek 11
Churches: Beaver Dam, Oak Hill (101), New Hope, St.
  Paul, Mt. Gilead 345
Colbert, Richard D. Rev. 146, 353, 373
Concert, Closing 326
Constitutional Amendments 49
Cowan, Edward L. Rev. 91
Craig, Carrie 137
Crabtree, James R. 277, 353
Crawford, Dan 40
Creek Indians 8
Crittenden, Henry 101, 109, 377
Crusaders 67
Crowe, Carrie, Mrs. M. E. 116, 137, 142
Daly, Sam.. 200
Decision Days 183, 192
Doaksville 29

INDEX

Domestic Training 198
Donaldson, Mary A. 160, 321
Donors, Oak Hill 305
Early, Lou K. 137, 193
Eaton, Adelia M. 155, 159, 288, 315
Education 62, 93
Edwards, John Rev. 15, 22, 105
Elliott, Alice Lee, David .... IV, 212
Elliot Hall .... II, 205, 208, 210, 326
Emancipation Day 42, 292
Farewell 331
Farmer's Institutes 287
Fields, Rilla 137
Fisher, Jessie 137
Flag, Salute 268
Flickinger, R. E. and Mrs. 155, 160, 308
Flournoy, William R. 329, 353
Folsom, Iserina, Martha, 137, 149; Samuel, 150, 160, 224; Simon 330, 378
Forest Church 125, 130
Fort Towson 28
France, Bible Suppressed 418
France, Republic of 425
Freedmen, Homeless, 42; Choctaw 65
Fruits, Bulletin 256, 330
Gaston, John Rev. 91
Gideons 417
Girls Hall, Weimer Photo 109, 132, 210
Gladman, Samuel Rev. 373
Going to School 274
Gordon, Mary, Lela, Inez 137, 275
Gossard, Verne 137
Graces at Meals 279

INDEX

Grandfather Clause 51
Green, Fannie 137
Hall, Malinda A. 149, 224, 277, 289, 320
Harris, Nannie, Sam, 149, 300, 379; New Home of Catherine 406
Hartford, Eliza 107, 115, 121
Haymaker, Edward G. and Mrs. 108, 134, 339, 379
Haymaker, Priscilla G. 108, 111, 118
Hawley, Rev. F. W. 301
Headache 299
Health Hints 298
Hen House 295
Highland Park College 199
Hodges, Celestine 147, 149
Homer, Wiley Rev. 148, 226, 277, 352, 360
Homer, Hattie, Mary, Susan 147
Homes, Representative 406
Huguenots of France 75
Hunter, Anna, Mattie 116, 137
Huss, John 70
Idleness 247
Improvements 166, 202
Independent Ownership of Land 78, 193, 197
Indian Schools and Churches 15
Indian Territory, Slavery 7, 19, 106
Inquisition, The 76
Intolerance, Rise and Fall 408
Investments 272
Johnson, Isaac 277, 291, 378
Jones, Edward T. 149; Josie, 137, 379; Fannie, Marie Martha 147, 149
Key Words 260
Kingsbury,, Cyrus, Rev. 28, 65, 105

INDEX

Knox, John 75
Lafayette, Land of 427
Land Funds 303
Lee, Lilly E. 137
Liberty, Civil, Religious 81, 431
Licentiates 276
Lincoln, Abraham 172
Lincoln University 71, 88
Log House, Old 109, 257
Luther, Martin 72, 431
Massacres of Bible Readers 77
Maxims, Character, Success 241
McBride, James F. and Mrs. 131, 136
McGuire, James 117
McNiell, Sudie B. 224
Meadows, Plant S., Rev. 326, 353
Memory Trained 175
Methodism, Rise of 80
Ministers, Dearth of, Teachers 340, 342
Moore, Ruby 160
Mottoes, Wall 259
Murchison, Fidelia 148, 287
Mexico 418
Negro, American, Voices 39, 59, 96
Newspapers, First 82
Normals, Summer 275
Oak Hill, Church, School, 12, 101, 103; Groups in 1902 and 1903 299
Orchestra, Buchanan, Flournoy, Dixon, Ashley and Alonza McLellan, Clarence and Herbert Peete, Harris, Smith 274
Painting 297
Park College 194

Perkins, Charles, Fidelia 149, 355, 378
Perry, Ora Maxie 160, 294
Picnics 282
Pig Pen 203, 295
Pledges, Endeavor, Self-help 169
Porto Rico 394
Prayers, Forms of 280
Presbyterian Church, Board 84, 90
Presbytery, Indian, Meetings 17, 282
Presbytery, Kiamichi; at right, Homer, Onque, Bibbs, Alverson, Bridges, Starks, Crabtree, Frazier, Harris, Richard; 3d row, Elisha Butler, Mills, Wm. Butler, Edmunds, Lewis 335, 352
Prince, Caroline, Henry 406
Pulling Stumps, Percy, Ashley, Alonza, Dee, Mark, Herbert, Thomas 207, 298
Reformation, the 72, 392
Reid, Alexander, Rev. 15, 23, 105, 146
Richard, Everett 224
Romanism, Behind Times 428
Rules, Mottoes 259
Rutherford, Matthew 121
Sands, Rev. Marie Jones 148
Schools, Colonial 395
Scott, Mary 137, 299
Seats, Celestine 275
Seed Corn, Cotton, Improved 298
Self-control, Education 174, 244, 247
Self-help, Support 163, 185
Shaw, Sadie 137
Shoals, John Ross, Johnson 149, 277, 287, 378
Shoals, Virginia Wofford, Perry 148, 160
Study, Course 268

INDEX 439

Success, What, How Attained 260
Sunday Schools 80, 271, 413
Sweepers, Rosetta, Mary, Helen, Beatrice Emma Evelina,
    Ellen 274
Synod of Canadian 382
Spain 429
Teachers, Christian, Aim of 36. 266, 270
Teachers in 1899, Mr. and Mrs. Haymaker, Anna Hunter
    (sitting), Mrs. M. E. Crowe, Visitor, Josie Jones; photo
    by Mattie Hunter 379
Uncle Wallace 25
Uplifting Influences, Inventions 65. 82
Vacation Workers 188
Valliant 12
Voice Culture 157
Wallace, Sarah L. 160
Waldo, Waldenses 69
Washington, Booker T. 199
Watt, Lizzie 150
Webster, Daniel 410
Weimer, Mary I. 159, 193, 275, 318
Weith, Rev. Charles C. 278
Westminister Assembly 79
Wiclif, John 70
Williams, Henry, Virginia 147, 149
Wit, Humor 257
Wheelock Academy 21
Wolcott, Jo Lu 159, 320
Working by Rule 162, 208, 264
Women's Miss. Soc. Oak Hill, 304; Synod 386

CORRECTIONS

Page 203, Line 22, read "pigpen," instead of "loghouse."
Page 403, Line 9, read "1812," instead of "1892."

INDEX

----, Elizabeth 114-115
ADAMS, John 81 Samuel 81
AHRENS, Augusta 310 B L 300
   Bertha L 127 154-155 159 275
   278 289 300 303-304 306 387
   Bertha Louise 310 Miss 282 311
   Otto 310
ALFRED, The Great 69
ALLEN, Dr 116 Fredonia 355 Mrs
   R H 142
ALVA, Duke of 77
ALVERSON, Mr 276 N S 385 Noah
   276 289 324 Noah S 303 338
   342
ARCHIBALD, Mrs 305
ARNOLD, R D 355
BAIRD, Dr 325-326 Phil C 226 306
   325 329 Rev Dr 327
BANKS, Gen 43
BARBER, D J 142
BASHEARS, Charles 130 287 Mrs
   Charles 284
BEAMS, Emma 387
BEATTY, Charles C 121 Dr 121
BECKER, Mary O 141 306 Mrs 141
BEECHER, Henry Ward 47
BENEDICT, A C 305 John D 276
BERKELEY, Gov 393
BERTHLETT, 29
BETHEL, M L 226 385 Martin L
   385 Mrs 387 W L 382-384
   William L 384
BIBBS, Charles 130 278 289 Fannie
   151 Lee 104 130 Lee V 287 385
   S S 151 300 324 Samuel S 151
   Sylvester S 276

BISMARK, 171
BLACK, John 324
BLAIR, H E 237 John 119
BLANCHARD, Will 375
BOBBET, Betsy 117
BOGGS, Mrs V P 158 V P 159
BOLDEN, Wellington 346
BOLES, Carrie 311 Clara 311
BOWERMAN, Anna M 306
BOWLES, J R 206
BRASCO, Livingston 184
BRASHEARS, Nancy 380
BRAZLETON, J H A 382-384
BRIDGES, Mr 374 T K 184 226
   327 383 385 Thomas K 338
   Thompson K 339 350 374
BRINE, Mary D 370
BROUGHAM, Lord 171
BROWN, Albert 147 Ara 151
   Lucretia C 151 160 306 Matt
   102 303 Wiley 346
BRUCE, Blanche K 50
BUCHANAN, Mr 156 S H 278 303
   Soloman 154 Solomon 155 206
   289 324 Solomon H 102 160
   275 306 322 383 385
BUFFINGTON, Willis 347
BURRIS, Calvin 348 385 Daniel
   349 Francis 349 George 348
   James 324 Kate 349 Solomon
   324
BURROWS, Emma 137
BUTLER, 358 Abraham 370
   Adaline 349 Amanda 349 Easter
   349 Elijah 284 348-349 381
   Elisha 349 357 381 Francis 349

BUTLER (continued)
  Jane 349 Mr 184 371 Nellie 370
  Nelson 349 R H 289 Rhoda 349
  Vina 349 William 124 183 226
  290 303 337-338 341 348 357-
  358 370 381 385
BYRD, W A 384
CAIRNES, Earl 171
CALDWELL, A M 385
CALL, Gen 9
CALVIN, 74-75 408-409 John 72
  427
CAMPBEL, L miss 117
CAMPBELL, Anna E 112 119 140
  Annie 140 Frank 140 Miss 112-
  113 119-120 Mrs J J 307
  Rebecca S 140
CARLYLE, Thomas 419
CARROLL, Emma A 306 Emma L
  387 Mrs 159-160 275 387 W H
  159-160 278 289 291 306 326-
  327 331 376 383 385 William H
  102 338 384
CARSON, Sadia L 142
CARY, 33
CECIL, Mrs 377
CHARLES V, King of France 70
CHARLES IX, King of France 77
CHERRY, Rance 306
CHOATE, Rufus 398
CLARK, Delia 275 323 Mary A 305
  Reindeer 101 Robin 104 132
  153 297 Wilson 300
CLAXTON, Commissioner 416
CLAYPOOL, John 306 Mrs 318
  Mrs John 159
CLINCH, Gen 9
CLINTON, Dewitt 403 George 400
COFFLAND, Mary 132
COLBERT, 358 Hattie 148 Laney
  368 Nick 148 346 R D 303 337
  358 385 Richard D 146 336 338

COLBERT (continued)
  341 346-347 357 373
COLIGNY, Adm 75 77
COLUMBUS, 72
COPLING, Charles 348
COVERDALE, Miles 409
COWAN, E P 92
CRABTREE, James R 102 277 300
CRAIG, Carrie 137
CRANMER, Archbishop 74 409
CRAWFORD, Dan 40 Mrs A W
  305 318
CRITTENDEN, Elder 117 Hattie
  379 Henry 65 101-102 108-109
  111 284 377-378 Teena 101 377
  379
CROMWELL, Thos 409
CROWE, Carrie E 137 142 150 160
  305 321 James B 138 M E 138
  139 141 150 Mrs 139 141-142
  Mrs M E 137 307
CURKEET, Adele 305
CUSHING, Emiline 97
DALLAS, George M 103
DALY, Sam 200-201
DANIELS, Margaret 305
DICKEY, John M 88
DICKSON, Frank 324
DONALDSON, Mary A 160 275
  321
DOUGLASS, Frederic 47
DURANT, Winnie 291
EARLY, Lou K 137
EATON, Adelia 289 318 Adelia M
  1 155 159 216 303 305-306 315
  Harvey 316 John 43 Miss 282
  288
EDWARD VI, King of England 74
EDWARDS, 107 Harriet 148 355
  John 18 22 24 105 108 111 118
  349 Mr 108 Mrs M D 306 Pugh
  A 148 355

ELDER, Miss 108
ELLIOT, William 305
ELLIOTT, Alice Lee 212-213 326
    David 212 214 326 Mr 213-215
    Mrs 214
EMERSON, 37
ENGLISH, W S 289
EVANS, E B 336 Evan B 23 337
FARRAND, Mrs F R 306
FARREL, 72
FEASTER, W D 382
FENELON, 75
FIEBER, Lena D 307
FIELDS, Rilla 133 137
FISHER, Anna Marie 98 Jessie 137
    S G 375
FLICKINGER, H W 307 Mary A
    159 306 308 Mattie C 306 Mrs
    155 216 308-309 319 321 Mrs R
    E 305 R E 102 159 221 278 289
    303-304 327-328 331 383-386
    Rev 155 Robert E 338
FLOURNOY, Riley 276 324 W
    Riley 330
FOLSOM, 353 David 206 324 380
    Iserina 143 150 Martha 137 150
    289 345 387 Moses 150 346
    Nancy 380 Samson 352 Samuel
    306 319 380-381 Samuel A 102
    150 160 206 303 Simon 130 284
    287 303 330 357 380
FOULON, 423
FRANKLIN, Benjamin 81-82
FRIARSON, Henry 104
FROTHINGHAM, H J 305
GAFFONY, Brown 324
GAINES, Gen 9
GARLAND, Col 28 Mary 151
GARNER, Joseph 306
GARRISON, William Lloyd 47
GASTON, John M 45

GLADMAN, Samuel 184 289 303
    336-339 347 350 373
GLADSTONE, 33 171
GLOVER, Charity 306
GOFF, William 346
GORDON, Mary 137
GORE, T P 226
GOSSARD, Verne 137
GOULD, Geo N 306
GRAHAM, Alexander J 24 Martha
    307
GRANT, 57 Gen 43 Ulyses S 28
GREELEY, Horace 47
GREEN, Aaron 346 Fannie 137
GREGORY, Mrs J J 306
GREGORY IX, Pope 76
GRIER, Redonia 151 Samuel J 383
GRUNDY, Mary 131
HAIR, S G 310
HALL, 369 M A 282 Malinda 149
    277 Malinda A 149 155 160 221
    289 303 306 320 383 Miss 211
    278 321 Robert 102
HAND, Daniel 96
HARRIS, Catherine 303 Charles B
    149 300 Ellen 303 Emily 101
    John 303 Margie 303 Mr 301
    Nannie 149 Roland 303 Sam
    301 303 Samuel 282 300-301
    304 William 385
HARRISON, Benjamin 88 William
    Henry 172
HARRY, Hugh L 339 347
HARTFORD, Eliza 1 117-118 121
    212 Miss 108-112 116 119-122
    146-147 379
HASTINGS, 372
HAWLEY, F W 301 303
HAYMAKER, E G 119 135 323
    336-337 371 Edward G 102 336
    339 Edward Graham 134

HAYMAKER (continued)
George R 119 Miss 111-112
116-120 Mr 137 154 Mrs 135
Mrs Edward G 149 Priscilla 119
Priscilla G 111 118 132
HAYWOOD, Lucy M 305
HAZLETON, Anna B 307
HENRY, King of England 408
Patrick 81
HENRY VIII, King of England 74
HILL, James J 37
HODGES, Celestine 131 147
Charlotte 147 Samuel 147
HOLLINGSWORTH, Cassie 385
Edward 160 206 George 324
HOLMES, Mary 144
HOMER, 347 358 363-364
Charlotte 352 Hattie 148 368
John 352 361 Laney 345 368
Lincoln 368 Lizzie 368 Mary
148 368 Rhody 368 Sarah 368
Susan 147 368 Wiley 147-148
184 204 226 277-278 290 303
326-327 336-338 341 345-347
357-358 360-361 365 368 385
HOOKER, Thomas 79
HOWELL, 370
HUNTER, Anna 139 Anna F 137
Mattie 137-139 305
HUNTINGTON, Lady 80
HUSS, John 70-71
HUTCHINSON, 26
HUTNER, Anna T 137
HUXLEY, Prof 86
INDIAN, Chief Bazeel 296 Osceola 9
INGLIS, John 181
INNOCENT III, Pope 70
JACKSON, Andrew 29 Gen 8
JAMES, King 409
JEANES, Anna T 97
JEFFERSON, Thomas 7 81

JOHN, King of England 70
JOHNSON, A B 184 Anna 291
Elmer E 305 H A 94 Isaac 277
287-290 Robert 324 Winnie 291
JONES, Edward D 149 Fannie 147 J
H 305 Josie 137 Marie 147
Martha 149 Vina 323
JORDAN, Mrs 305
JUDSON, 33 369 Adoniram 369
JULIUS II, Pope 77
KENSOLVING, Bishop 429
KENT, Chancellor 399
KINGSBURY, Cyrus 28 65 105 353 356 378
KNOTT, Mrs W A 306
KNOUFF, John 189
KNOX, John 75
LAFAYETTE, 424 426 428
LAFON, Tommy 97
LANGDON, Mary 305
LARKINS, Rhoda 345
LATIMER, Bishop 75
LAWSON, Wilfred 171 Zolo O 275
LEE, Lilly E 137
LEFLORE, 297 Bazeel 296 Chief 297 Narcissa 296
LEITHEAD, Mrs Hiram 305
LEWIS, Adam 348 Alonza 303 Bud 148 Gov 400 Hattie 148 368 Monroe 348 Mrs 387 Wesley 324
LILLEY, E 306
LINCOLN, 33 Abraham 47 82 172 Pres 42 292
LIVINGSTONE, 33 40
LOCKE, Frank 297
LOMENIE, Cardinal 422
LONG, Jefferson 50
LONGWELL, O F 199
LORING, Samson 361
LOTTING, Mr 375
LOUIS XV, King of France 419

LOUIS XVI, King of France 420 425
LOVING, J A 338 385
LOYOLA, Ignatius 76
LUTHER, 71 74 278 408 Martin 72 314
MAGELLAN, 72
MALLARD, Julius W 338 347
MANN, Horace 398
MARDEN, Oliver Swet 306
MARIE ANTOINETTE, Queen of France 425
MARY, of Orange 409
MASON, Mrs H E 306 Mrs O L 305
MATTISON, John H 305 Nathan 103
MAXIE, Robert 324
MAY, J S 385 John S 383
MCAFEE, John A 194-195 Josephine 137
MCBRIDE, Anna 133 Emma F 148 306 Howard 137 James F 1 131 Mr 132 136 147 Mrs 131 133 136 138 Mrs J F 133
MCCLUSKY, James H 120
MCCOY, Isam 361
MCCULLOCH, Walter 346
MCDOWELL, J M 376
MCELVENE, Fannie 151
MCFARLAND, Dee 324 Fred 276 324 Percy 324
MCGINNIS, Mrs 305
MCKEE, John 98
MCKELLAR, J M 338
MCKELLER, J M 338
MCLELLAN, Alonza 324 Ashley 324
MCNABB, C A 290
MCNAIR, Mr 147
MCPHERSON, Virgil 385
MCRUER, Duncan 226

MEADOWS, P S 326-327 385 Plant S 338 Plant Senior 376
MEBANE, C S 385 Mrs C S 385-386
MELANCTHON, 72
MICHAEL, David 184
MILLER, Samuel 227
MILLS, Samuel J 369
MILTON, Ledocia 387 Nellie 387 Sarah 324 387
MIRABEAU, 421 423 426
MOFFAT, 33
MONROE, Isabella 303 323
MOODY, Kate C 305
MOOR, Mr 119
MOORE, Ruby 160 323
MORE, Thomas 409
MORRIS, Charley 349
MURCHISON, Fidelia 148 275 287 355 387 T H 385 Thomas H 148
MURRAY, George W 50
NAPOLEON, 425-426
NELSON, Isaiah 324
NEWELL, 369
NOLAN, Peter 346
NOTT, 369
O'BANNON, 226
OGBURN, Thomas C 339 346-347 William G 339 348 350
ONQUE, Samuel J 338 346
OSBORNE, Annie 306
PALMER, Frances 305 Mrs 140 Mrs F D 139
PARISH, P A 278
PARK, George S 195
PARRISH, Jane 355
PATTERSON, Clarence M 305
PAYNE, Henry N 143
PEABODY, George 96
PEARSON, Mary A 322
PECK, Carrie 131

PEETE, Clarence 276 294 324
    Herbert 324 Ruby 160
PENCE, Mrs J J 305
PENN, William 409
PERKINS, Charles 355 Fidelia 148
    355 Fredonia 355 Jane 355
    Jeffers 355 Louis 355 Virginia
    355
PERRY, Catherine 355 Clark 305
    Eugene 324 Ora 160 Virginia
    148
PIERSON, Mary A 307
PITCHLIN, Alvin 324 Louis 324
PITCHLYN, 370 Solomon 348
PORTER, E A 291
PRATT, Garfield 347 James 346-347
PRINCE, Caroline 147 149 Henry
    221 Henry D 151
PROVINE, William A 383
RADFORD, Elias 346
RAIKES, Robert 80
RAINEY, Joseph H 50
RANKIN, A E 385 387
REAGEL, Mrs W A 307
REID, 24 107 Alexander 23 25 105
    146 153 Alexander M 121 John
    G 25 Mr 25
REVELS, Hiram R 50
REYNOLDS, J W 291
RICHARDS, Everett 151 324 James
    324 John 276 289 303 342
    Lucretia C 151 Matthew 349 Mr
    276 Primas 348-349
RICHARDSON, Mamie G 306
RIDLEY, Bishop 75
RILEY, Shepherd 348
RITCHEY, Alice Lee 214 John 214
    Maria 214
ROBERTS, W H 88
ROBESPIERRE, 420 425-426
ROCKEFELLER, John D 97
ROEBUCK, Benjamin 355 Betty
    355 Louisa 345 Richard 346
ROGERS, John 75
ROOSEVELT, Ex-pres 58 Pres 10
ROSSEAU, 420 426
ROUNDS, Mary 104
RUSKIN, 35
RUTHERFORD, 122 Matthew 121
SANBORN, Geo 305
SANDS, Mr 147
SAWTELL, Mr 405
SCHERMERHORN, Harvey R 27
SCOTT, Mary 137 Mary R 307 322
    R L 291 Walter 425 Winfield 9
SEATS, Celestine 324 Susan 306
SHAW, Mary E 98 Sadie 137
SHELTON, Violet 387
SHOALS, Adaline 345 361 George
    151 300-301 H C 294 Harriet
    147 Hattie 149 379 Hattie
    Crittenden 377 Henry C 155
    Hettie 101 J Ross 101-103 147
    149 378 James 101 James G 275
    287 289-290 John Ross 377 379
    Johnson 101 149 277 Johnson
    W 287 Martin 148 Mary 148
    368 Mary E 275 Redonia 151
    Virginia 147-148 William 184
    304
SHOALS-ARNOLD, Elsie 287
SHOENFELT, J Blair 276
SIMMS, Lilly B 275
SLATER, John F 96
SLATTERY, Margaret 413
SLAVE, Aunt Minerva 25 Uncle
    Wallace 25
SLEEPER, J H 336 John 371 John
    H 337 339 347-348 350 358
SMITH, Cornell 324 Ella T 305 F
    Hyatt 334 Mrs 307
SPADE, Mrs 151 Mrs D O 306 Mrs
    O D 151

SPECKERMAN, J C 306
STARK, Mr 27 Mrs W J 387 Oliver P 27
STARKS, 376 Oliver P 17 W J 226 303 327 385 William J 338-339 347 375
START, Mrs G H 305
STEED, Rose 18
STEWARD, Malinda A 149
STEWART, 340 347 353 358 Ara 151 Bettie 133 Betty 355 C W 345-346 Catherine 355 Charles 352 Charles W 2 19 102 105 339 346-349 351-353 359 364 367 George 151 206 Harriet 148 355 James 151 324 M S 300 Malinda A 320 Mary 151 Mitchell 287 Mitchell S 102 282 300 Mrs 353 356 Mrs Charles 378 Parson 19 65 124 137 148 336 342 347 356 373 378-379 381 Thomas 355 William 149 320
STOKES, Caroline Phelps 97
STONE, John Timothy 367
STOWE, Harriet Beecher 47
SUMMER, Charles 47
TAYLOR, Zachary 29
TEIS, E B 226
THOMAS, J A 300 Jack A 102 282 290 383 Mrs 387 Mrs J A 278 300
THORNTON, Paul 323
TOMPKINS, Gov 400
TRUE, M B 306
TUTT, Rhody 368
TYNDALE, 75 409 William 74
VERNER, A W 61
VICTORIA, Queen 26 33 171
VOLTAIRE, 420
WALDO, Peter 69-70
WALKER, Mrs L 387

WALLACE, David J 338-339 Mrs D J 387 Sarah L 160 321
WALTON, Amy 345
WARD, Amos 150 Iserina 150
WASHINGTON, 33 57 424 Booker T 43 97 199 305 George 81
WATSON, Ellen M 307
WATT, Lizzie 143 150
WEAVER, Mrs J B 305
WEBSTER, Daniel 410 Mr 410
WEHUNT, W J 277
WEIMER, Mary 184 Mary I 159 306 318 Miss 211-212 294 319
WEITH, Charles C 306 Chas C 278
WESLEY, Charles 80 John 80
WHITE, Emma P 387 George H 50 Mr 26 Prof 25
WHITEFIELD, George 80
WHITFIELD, A J 226
WICLIF, 71 409 John 70
WILLARD, Frances 33 281
WILLIAM, Prince of Orange 74
WILLIAM III, Prince of Orange 409
WILLIAMS, Burr 338-339 Henry 104 147 M B 416 Oscar A 383 Roger 79 409 Sarah 368 Virginia 303
WILLIANS, Virginia 355
WILLINGHAM, Mrs 306
WILLIS, Mr 184 W J 23 184
WILSON, 297 Anna 291 H M 306 John 297 Thomas 324 William T 383 Woodrow 58 415
WITHERSPOON, John 81
WOFFORD, Virginia 160 275 324
WOLCOTT, Dr 320 Jo Lu 159 303 320
WOLFINGER, Leslie 13
WOOD, Mrs A S 305
WOODBURY, I B 326
WORDEN, James A 227

WRIGHT, Alfred 16 18 21-23
ZWINGLI, 72 408

www.ingramcontent.com/pod-product-compliance
Lightning Source LLC
Chambersburg PA
CBHW051334230426
43668CB00010B/1256